THEORIZING THE LOCAL

Theorizing the Local

Music, Practice, and Experience in South Asia and Beyond

EDITED BY

Richard K. Wolf

OXFORD
UNIVERSITY PRESS

2009

OXFORD
UNIVERSITY PRESS

Oxford University Press, Inc., publishes works that further
Oxford University's objective of excellence
in research, scholarship, and education.

Oxford New York
Auckland Cape Town Dar es Salaam Hong Kong Karachi
Kuala Lumpur Madrid Melbourne Mexico City Nairobi
New Delhi Shanghai Taipei Toronto

With offices in
Argentina Austria Brazil Chile Czech Republic France Greece
Guatemala Hungary Italy Japan Poland Portugal Singapore
South Korea Switzerland Thailand Turkey Ukraine Vietnam

Published by Oxford University Press, Inc.
198 Madison Avenue, New York, New York 10016

www.oup.com

Library of Congress Cataloging-in-Publication Data
Theorizing the local : music, practice, and experience in South Asia
and beyond / [edited by] Richard K. Wolf.
p. cm.
Includes bibliographical references and index.
ISBN 978-0-19-533137-0; 978-0-19-533138-7 (pbk.)
1. Music—South Asia—History and criticism. I. Wolf, Richard K., 1962–
ML330.T44 2009
780.954—dc22 2008041052

Recorded audio and video tracks (marked in text with 🔊)
are available online at www.oup.com/us/theorizingthelocal
Access with username Music2 and password Book4416
Usernames and passwords are case-sensitive.

Printed in the United States of America
on acid-free paper

ACKNOWLEDGMENTS

In 2002, thinking about how to engage scholars in discussions about the music of South Asia in a broad, interdisciplinary context led me to propose and then organize a five-day-long International Council for Traditional Music Colloquium entitled "Local Theory, Local Practice: Musical Culture in South Asia and Beyond." The program committee members—Anthony Seeger, Shubha Chaudhuri, Martin Clayton, Michael Herzfeld, and myself—all participated in the seminar, shared substantive organizational ideas, suggested the names of other participants, and aided in the formulation of grant proposals. The authors maintained an unflagging collaborative spirit throughout the seminar and the period of manuscript preparation that followed. The independent writer/dramaturge Rustom Bharucha, the late musicologist Harold S. Powers, and several others who also participated in the original seminar provided comparative and cross-disciplinary reflections that are lodged in ways not always traceable in many of the papers and in the introduction. The authors and I are all deeply grateful to the many local performers and other consultants in South Asia and Iran, too many to enumerate here, who have made it possible for us to write widely on the local musical traditions of this large region.

Several institutions provided financial and administrative support. The Radcliffe Institute for Advanced Study funded and administered the major part of this event, which was held over four days as a Radcliffe Advanced Seminar. The then dean of Radcliffe (and as of this writing, president of Harvard), Drew Gilpin Faust, was critically supportive at a time in which the "Advanced Seminar" as a Radcliffe program was still in the process of establishing an identity. Radcliffe's Phyllis Strimling and Anna Chesson were cheerful and efficient in their nuts-and-bolts administration of the seminar. Generous support was provided by the American Institute of Pakistan Studies, the Harvard University Asia Center, the Office for the Arts at Harvard, and the Harvard Department of Music. The seminar and colloquium would not have been successful without the practical assistance of Harvard's ethnomusicology graduate students Kiri Miller, Aaron Berkowitz, and Sarah Morelli. Kiri Miller in particular devoted careful attention to planning the event and corresponding with the authors afterward. Gitanjali Surendran, a graduate student in the Department of History, provided careful editorial assistance at the final stages of manuscript preparation.

C. Scott Walker, digital cartography specialist at the Harvard Map Collection, devoted considerable care and attention to creating maps for each chapter. Widener Library at Harvard University provided the book (C. E. Yate, *Khurasan and Sistan*, Edinburgh: William Blackwood and Sons, 1900) from which the map used as a background on the cover was obtained. The bagpiper and other musicians on the cover participated in the Nanda Devi festival, Almora, in the state now known as Uttarakhand (August 29, 1998), are members of Bhuvan Ram and Party (a music and dance group from Jageswar). Although this book does not discuss Indian bagpipe music, and although Uttarakhand is not part of Khorasan or Sistan, the images are meant to stimulate the reader's imagination about what the "local" means over time. Bagpipes, like several other instruments, have become indigenized, while continuing to index past relations between South Asia and Europe. The domains of social and linguistic groups frequently transcend the boundaries of states and provinces; the boundaries themselves are also indices of interventions, often by colonial agencies.

At Oxford University Press, I owe a debt of gratitude for Suzanne Ryan, who saw the value of this project the first time I mentioned it to her.

NOTE ON TRANSLITERATION

In this volume, names of cities and countries generally appear in their common, English-language spellings. Diacritics for well-known place names are not used except when they appear in titles of published works or quotations. Because local pronunciations vary, as do the scripts from which authors transliterate, words that are the same or closely related in different languages sometimes appear with different spellings. The glossary takes account of some of these variations. Very common terms associated with South Asian music, such as raga, tala, guru, and tabla, have entered the English lexicon and so appear without diacritics or italics in the body of the text. Transliterations, variations, and definitions of some of these terms are provided in the glossary. Pluralization is indicated using an "s" at the end of the word unless otherwise noted. The *ALA-LC Romanization Tables: Transliteration Schemes for Non-Roman Scripts* (1997 edition) are used for transliterating most of the South Asian language terms represented in the volume. The Kota language, which is not included in these tables and does not have a script, is transliterated in a manner consistent with these schemes; it is a modification of the system used by T. Burrow and M. B. Emeneau in *A Dravidian Etymological Dictionary* (1984 [2nd edition]), whereby bullets are replaced by macrons to represent vowel length. David Henderson uses, for Nepali, *A Comparative and Etymological Dictionary of the Nepali Language* (1994); for Newari, *Newari-English Dictionary* (1986); for words shared with Hindi, *The Oxford Hindi-English Dictionary* (1993). Stephen Blum uses a simplified version of well-known transliteration conventions for Persian. The "i"s and "u"s for Persian words in his chapter are long with the exception of the initial "i" in 'ilm. Otherwise, short versions of these vowels are indicated by "e" and “o,” respectively. The macron over the “i” in radīf and zahīrok is maintained so that these terms are spelled consistently throughout the volume. Azerbaijani and Khorasani Turkish are written in the Latin alphabet of Azerbaijan. The glossary indicates the languages in which key terms appear and provides additional details on transliteration.

CONTENTS

Contributors ix
Note on Transliteration xi
List of Maps xiii

1. Introduction 5
Richard K. Wolf

PART I. BODIES AND INSTRUMENTS

2. Women and Kandyan Dance: Negotiating Gender and Tradition in Sri Lanka 29
Susan A. Reed

3. Listening to the Violin in South Indian Classical Music 49
Amanda Weidman

4. Local Practice, Global Network: The Guitar in India as a Case Study 65
Martin Clayton

PART II. SPACES AND ITINERARIES

5. Constructing the Local: Migration and Cultural Geography in the Indian Brass Band Trade 81
Gregory D. Booth

6. The Princess of the Musicians: Rāni Bhaṭiyāṇi and the Māngaṇiārs of Western Rajasthan 97
Shubha Chaudhuri

7. Music in Urban Space: Newar Buddhist Processional Music in the Kathmandu Valley 113
Gert-Matthias Wegner

PART III. **Learning and Transmission**

8. Disciple and Preceptor/Performer in Kerala 143
Rolf Groesbeck

9. *Sīna ba Sīna* or "From Father to Son": Writing the Culture of Discipleship 165
Regula Burckhardt Qureshi

10. Handmade in Nepal 185
David Henderson

PART IV. **Theorizing Social Action**

11. Modes of Theorizing in Iranian Khorasan 207
Stephen Blum

12. *Zahīrok*: The Musical Base of Baloch Minstrelsy 225
Sabir Badalkhan

13. *Varṇams* and Vocalizations: The Special Status of Some Musical Beginnings 239
Richard K. Wolf

Glossary 265
Notes 277
Bibliography 299
Name Index 315
Subject Index 319

CONTRIBUTORS

Folklorist Sabir Badalkhan is pro-vice chancellor and professor at the University of Balochistan, Quetta, Pakistan. He has also taught in the United States and Italy.

Stephen Blum teaches at the City University of New York Graduate Center. He is consulting editor for music of the *Encyclopaedia* Iranica.

Gregory D. Booth is an associate professor of ethnomusicology at the University of Auckland. He has published widely on South Asian brass bands and Hindi film song.

Shubha Chaudhuri, director of the Archives and Research Centre for Ethnomusicology of the American Institute of Indian Studies, focuses on audio-visual archiving in ethnomusicology.

Martin Clayton is professor of ethnomusicology at the Open University. His publications include *Time in Indian Music* and *Music and Orientalism in the British Empire.*

Rolf Groesbeck, associate professor of music history/ethnomusicology and director of the Indian Percussion Ensemble at the University of Arkansas at Little Rock, publishes on the music of Kerala.

David Henderson, associate professor in music, film studies, and Asian studies at St. Lawrence University, has written primarily on song in the Kathmandu Valley.

Regula Burckhardt Qureshi, professor emerita at the University of Alberta, is academic director of the FolkwaysAlive! project and director of the Canadian Centre for Ethnomusicology.

Susan A. Reed, cultural anthropologist and director of the Center for the Study of Race, Ethnicity and Gender at Bucknell University, is the author of *Dance and the Nation: Performance, Ritual, and Politics in Sri Lanka.*

Gert-Matthias Wegner teaches ethnomusicology at the Free University Berlin and at Kathmandu University. His interests include drumming, music, and ritual.

Amanda Weidman teaches in the anthropology department at Bryn Mawr College. She is also a violinist in the Western classical and Karnatak traditions.

Richard K. Wolf, professor of music at Harvard University, writes on classical, folk, and tribal music in south India and on music in Islamic contexts. He also plays the *vīṇā*.

MAPS

1. South Asia and beyond 2
2. Sri Lanka 28
3. Tamil Nadu and Kerala 48
4. Metropolitan centers in India 64
5. The Delhi network of migrant bandsmen 88
6. The Mumbai network of migrant bandsmen 89
7. Western Rajasthan 96
8. Bhaktapur, Nepal 112
9. Daily processions of the three oilpresser groups of Bhaktapur 123
10. Places (1–4) which Bhaktapur's *gūlābājā* groups visit during *gūlā* (other castes visit Silu [Gosainkuṇḍa] during full moon) 124
11. *Gūlābājā* processions of Sākvalā oilpressers (1–17: musical offerings for gods on the way) 126
12. Standard procession of the Inācva Sākya *gūlābājā* 128
13. Inācva Sākya *gūlābājā* visiting the Aṣṭamātṛka and Sūrya Bināyak Gaṇeś 129
14. *Cibhāpūjā:* Bhaktapur Buddhists offering lamp wicks and mustard oil to all stone *caityas* in town. *Gūlābājā* leads the procession, playing processional music throughout and invocations at every monument 132
15. Processional route of the five Dīpaṅkara Buddhas 133
16. Kerala 142
17. North India 164
18. Nepal 184
19. Khorasan and Balochistan 204
20. Tamil Nadu 238

THEORIZING THE LOCAL

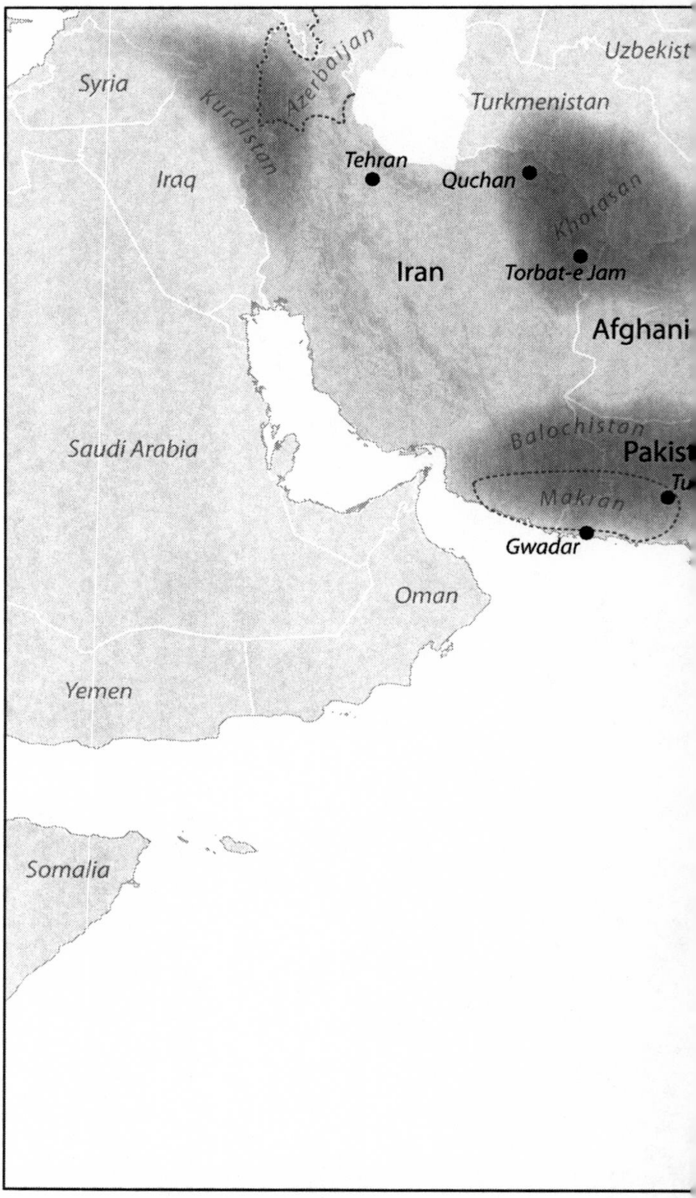
Uzbekist
Syria
Azerbaijan
Kurdistan
Turkmenistan
Tehran
Iraq
Quchan
Khorasan
Iran
Torbat-e Jam
Afghani
Balochistan
Saudi Arabia
Pakist
Makran
Gwadar
Oman
Yemen
Somalia

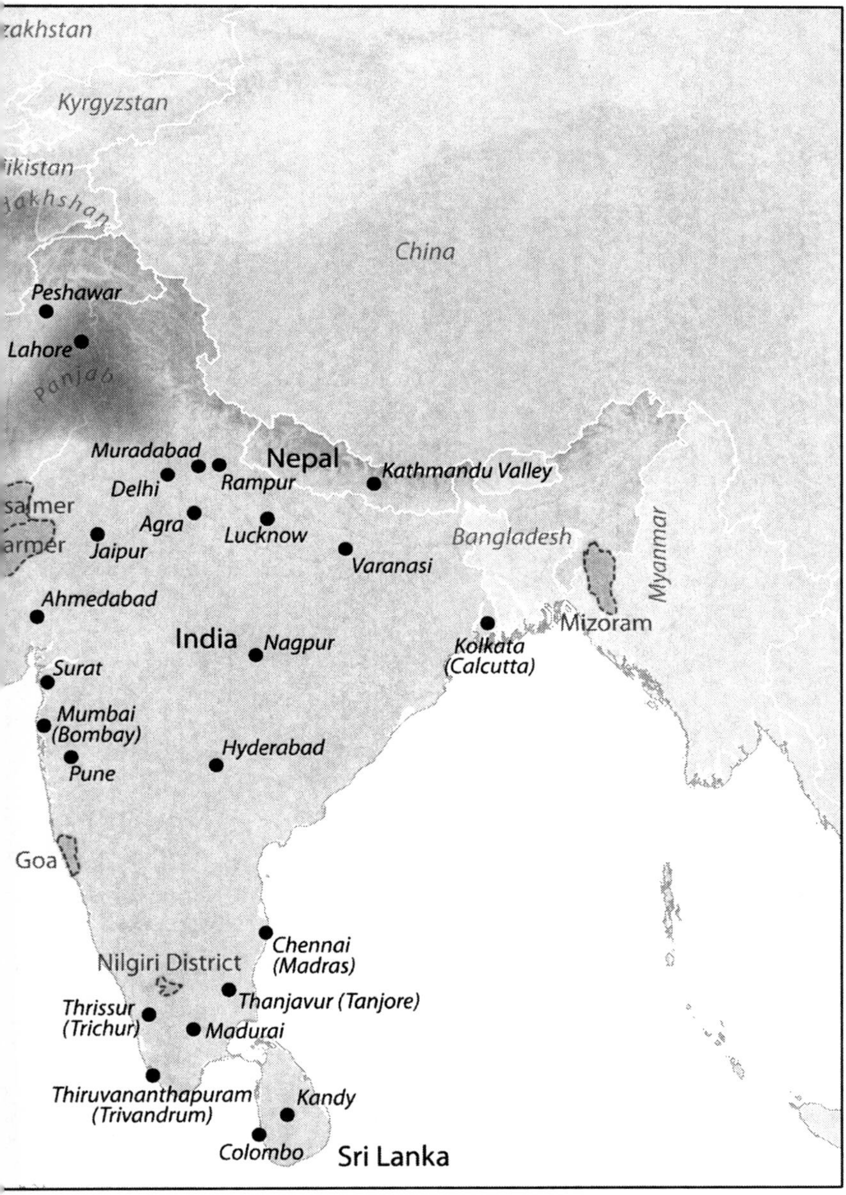
zakhstan
Kyrgyzstan
ikistan
akhshan
China
Peshawar
Lahore
Panjab
Muradabad
Nepal
Kathmandu Valley
Delhi
Rampur
salmer
Agra
Lucknow
Bangladesh
armer
Jaipur
Varanasi
Myanmar
Ahmedabad
Mizoram
India
Nagpur
Kolkata
(Calcutta)
Surat
Mumbai
(Bombay)
Hyderabad
Pune
Goa
Chennai
(Madras)
Nilgiri District
Thanjavur (Tanjore)
Thrissur
(Trichur)
Madurai
Thiruvananthapuram
(Trivandrum)
Kandy
Colombo
Sri Lanka

CHAPTER I
Introduction

RICHARD K. WOLF

In the "global hierarchy of value" only the best stuff, from an international market perspective, comes to represent a country like India or Ireland, or a vast region like Africa.[1] Sitar music, with its combination of virtuosic melody lines and thick droning, stands so closely for India that it has become cliché in advertisements and incidental music. Riverdance has brought Irish step dancing to the world stage and inspired many to learn Irish traditional music. African drumming groups, their complex polyrhythms led by master drummers and accompanying brightly dressed dancers, stand in a similarly synecdochical relationship with Africa itself. Films like *The Lion King* present their own kinds of stereotypes of African music and dance, colorful composites that have little to do with any particular place but everything to do with the idea of Africa.

From some perspectives, music that transcends locality is more interesting and lucrative than the so-called traditional music of a particular place. Colorful and engaging Māngaṇiār singers of Rajasthan combine the "rawness of the folk and the complexness of classical music" (Abel 2008). They capture the imagination of cosmopolitan Indians and other international consumers who see in them the animating spirit of the European Roma and the fire of flamenco. Their music taps into the musical sensibilities of a vast cross-cultural population. It is easy to forget—or never to learn—about the local social order in which the Māngaṇiārs operate, or the story that implicates them in a local system of patronage and the growth of a shrine complex (Chaudhuri, this volume).

Some music combines language, images, and musical techniques for the explicit purpose of embracing a wide listening public. Take the versatile *qawwālī* singer,

Nusrat Fateh Ali Khan: right arm up, head cocked to the side, eyes shut, lips curving and twisting as he enunciates the embellishments of an ecstatic melody. This image offers an unusual example of a musical style that touches the hearts of listeners beyond the Pakistani homeland, and in so doing, projects possibilities for larger human accord and Sufistic peace. Many "world music" consumers attend mainly to such spectacular aspects of cultural circulation. Indeed, the assumption that music is to be shared—and its corollary, that music is to bring people together—is so widely held in the modern, industrialized world that it seems hardly worth mentioning.

But much is left out in this world of extraordinary visibility, this world of an assumed, shared aesthetic. Many kinds of South Asian participatory circle dances and songs accompanying them, for instance, "circulate" in the sense of finding a place in local South Asian contexts and on stage shows organized by diaspora communities. Yet a group of ordinary villagers singing such songs and dancing such dances are unlikely to solicit enough interest to attract international sponsorship—unlike their more spectacular, sometimes clichéd, counterparts. As Steven Caton has observed for Arabic oral poetry, "it is virtually impossible for us [Americans, Europeans] to imagine an aesthetic that is sensitive to the specific context of its production, and if we can nonetheless imagine it, we may still have trouble appreciating its value as art" (Caton 1990, 106). This is perhaps why, when, in 1994, I approached an American recording company with a proposal to publish field recordings of folk music from south India, I received a letter back expressing interest only in music that "transcends context." The response I never delivered was that the music they sought did not transcend context, but could rather assimilate to that of the consumer without soliciting further thought or examination.

Contemporary academia invests transcendence of place with its own kind of capital—for reasons different from those of the international music market. Do the increasing humanistic and social scientific emphases on the so-called forces of globalization, like the market's search for music that transcends context, disguise and undermine the ongoing relevance of local music and local senses of music in the world?[2] While it is inevitable that ethnomusicological research on South Asia will engage increasingly with issues of globalization, many of us do not view the globalization literature as offering the only pertinent framework or point of departure for ethnomusicological studies of South Asia. We use "theorizing the local" to signal the continued value of comparative microstudies that are not concerned primarily with the flow of capital and neoliberal politics, but which take forms of interconnection, within and beyond South Asia, very seriously.[3]

This group of essays is probably the first major attempt to broaden the discourse among South Asian music scholars across other fields of scholarship and across genres in South Asian music since Bonnie Wade's (1983) edited volume *Performing Arts in India*. That volume contained essays on classical dance and music, organology, *qawwālī*, and a useful and succinct introduction pointing out their interrelationships.[4] Just a few years before that, Daniel Neuman's landmark work (1980) on the social organization of classical musicians in north India (mainly Delhi) opened up pathways for anthropologists to study aspects of a tradition that had hitherto been primarily the domain of musicologists. Perhaps the first significant "theorizing the local" in the present context was the early work of Milton Singer, who helped bridge the anthropological study of small-scale or village-based societies with the study of complex, literate civilizations. His focus on what he called "cultural performances" as "the most concrete observable units of Indian culture" allowed him to navigate through some of the complexities of urban life in Madras via "a ladder of abstractions" leading from these concrete units (Singer 1958, 351). Since that time, many scholars have refined our tools for thinking about the performing arts of India, broadly speaking. They have produced detailed genre studies; studies of schools or styles of north and south Indian classical music; analyses of patronage; insights into melodic and rhythmic improvisation and relationships between music and dance; understandings of music in Christian, Muslim, and Hindu contexts; studies of instruments and individual performers; ethnographic studies with major musical components that focus on minority populations; and a variety of other topics, some of which are represented in the present book.

In presenting our studies, some of which concern South Asian classical music, we do not presume the reader has already acquired a vast store of insider knowledge of names and styles, terms and concepts. The technical vocabularies of many other historically robust and less well-known traditions on the subcontinent are complex, as well. Our attempt has been to represent these systems in somewhat equitable terms and to take as little as possible for granted in opening up these musical worlds to those who are not already South Asianists.

Our turn to what we call the "local" is not a departure on all fronts from what our enterprising colleagues have produced before. Rather it is an attempt to think through where we stand in our studies of music in South Asia; to consider how focusing on particular kinds of "local" can offer us ways of thinking beyond the borders of South Asia, and beyond some of the epitomizations of South Asian music (e.g., as a place of ragas and talas) that people from many parts of the world take for granted. What, then, is meant by "local"?

Locals and Theories, Scales and Margins

For many of us, the local signals attention to small-scale, microlevel, musical and bodily processes; sites of interaction and transmission; attention to the familiar in unfamiliar ways. It often involves what Tim Ingold calls a "dwelling perspective," which focuses on peoples' learning and understanding of the world through pragmatic engagement with their surroundings (Ingold 2000). The notion of the local draws attention to the "scale" (Tsing 2000a) at which a scholar or practitioner of music envisions theorization to take place. As any given set of actors make sense of their musical activities as regional, they engage notions of what is distant and temporally removed; they create "horizons of meaning" (Munn 1990) that ought to figure in a consideration of local theorizing.

The local, then, can refer to a concrete locale where musicians make and think about music, such as a venue for performance or instruction. It also implicates the metaphorical site of theorization—for example, a musical phrase that serves as a basis for discussion or comment—regardless of where the musical tradition is located geographically or how far it extends. Musical events or objects (such as a violin), while discretely located at a given moment, are often experienced as connected with sounds, objects, and activities located elsewhere and situated differently in time. Distal traditions within South Asia and elsewhere in the world, including "the West," may be coimplicated in the musical experiences of South Asian performers and listeners. "South Asia and beyond" as a frame of musical reference for this volume, then, urges us to ask how any geographically local tradition fits into the larger regions in which it is embedded. Answering such a question engages perspectives of the practitioners themselves as well as of observers of many kinds (including scholars) who formulate views based on implicit or explicit comparisons—synthesizing close and distant vantage points.

Theorizing, like the notion of local, can be understood in more than one way: for some, all knowledge is acquired through some sort of theorizing; others restrict theorizing to self-conscious, verbal attempts at systematic explanation. For several contributors, theorizing the local means paying attention to forms of knowledge implicit in performing and experiencing music; for some, the "local" turn entails questioning the processes that have led to the creation of grand intellectual and institutional schemes. For most of the writers, theorizing is not simply the creation of theories, or building on a knowledge base with a series of hypothesis-driven inquiries, but rather a kind of contemplation of what constitutes a local musical universe. To me, it also signals a procedure of thinking through ethnographic materials, a principle of induction not unlike Singer's ladder of abstractions.

Regardless of their positions regarding "theorizing," ethnomusicologists have been drawn with others into an array of discourses that pit the specificity of the local with the generality of the global, but many remain uncomfortable with the dichotomy. Perhaps ethnographers fear that they will slip back into a naive localism, one unaware of or complicit in colonial or missionary encounters that gave rise to and supported the study of others in earlier times. One of the negative artifacts of this dialectical orientation is what Anna Tsing calls "a singular anthropological globalism." The problematic implication is that today's "local" differs from that of yesterday because it is defined (by the range of scholars in Tsing's critique) against globalism per se, rather than in relation to many kinds of global or translocal processes (Tsing 2000b, 342). This creates a hierarchy of locals, whereby some ethnographic examples are more important (because they forward au courant globalism discussions) than others (that do not). This is not the place to review the vast literatures that engage with more subtle local-global relationships, but Tsing's observation on the reification of discursive categories should make it fairly obvious that a restrictive notion of "theorizing the local" in this work would not be a helpful intervention.

Tsing suggests that focusing on "regionalisms and histories of place making within an appreciation of interconnection" can be productive to the extent that it avoids the implication of a single globalism. She has advocated interrogating "scale making projects," ways in which actors bring into being (successfully or not) their ways of viewing the world in spatial dimensions. These include various "scapes" (Appadurai 1997), visions of the global, commitments to regionalism, and a multiplicity of cosmopolitanisms (Tsing 2000a, 120). These would also include what Slobin identifies as the capacity of musicians to manipulate their "visibility" (Slobin 1992, 10 and passim); the representation of music as an "ocean" that can fit into "the little cup that is in your brain" (Qureshi, this volume); the claim that "tār-knowledge [i.e., knowledge associated with the dotār] is an infinite [realm of] knowledge" (Blum, this volume); and the metonymic idea that the comportment of Sri Lankan women has implications for the whole nation of Sri Lanka (Reed, this volume).

Focusing on how encompassing units such as the nation act to constrain and culturally exclude populations, to make them marginal, is another productive approach (see Tsing 1994). Those who occupy positions of marginality creatively rework their positions, play with the representations of cultural borders, to reconfigure themselves in relation to others (see also Herzfeld 2004). Marginality has figured largely in Indian national, academic, and regional discussions concerning the so-called tribal populations of India. Musically speaking, Carol Babiracki (1991a) has shown how Mundas of Chota Nagpur constructed their seasonal *karam* repertoire from regional sources outside the tribe, thereby taking ownership of a larger local and changing, musically, the terms by which Mundas can be categorically other.[5] The Kota people of south India also use broader resources to construct statements of connections with and difference from others in musical, religious, and spatial terms. They have not only incorporated pan-local Hindu deities in their local pantheon, for example, but they have also imported (they say) a particular rhythmic pattern from Telugu-speaking, Scheduled Caste ("untouchable") drummers to use for those deities (Wolf 2000/2001a). Mundas turn the categories around completely, because they view themselves as human beings and everyone else as foreigners. Kotas play on the national construction of tribals as sons of the soil to assert their essential rootedness in the nation of India; yet they are as exclusive as the most conservative Brahmans when it comes to their village temple rituals.[6]

The complexity and systematicity of South Asia's classical musics, which has been an asset in establishing them in largely Eurocentric music departments, have had the effect of limiting the accessibility of scholarship, at a deeper level, to nonspecialists. There is no question that classical music, in a very different way from tribal music, is marginal to the lives of most music listeners in South Asia. Karnatak and Hindustani music scholarship is heavily technical and largely focused on questions internal to these classical worlds. Our attention to local theorizing in the classical realm means bringing the fine-grained activities of musicians, musicologists, their patrons, and their audiences to bear on larger questions; it means understanding how the visions and ideas of a few do or do not have an effect beyond the quintessentially local acts of writing, teaching, and communicating by example.

Scale, marginality, and the creation of meaning horizons whereby spatiotemporal distance is brought into immediate experience are themes that, implicitly or explicitly, run throughout this book. Recently, anthropologists have suggested that spatial, geographic-oriented metaphors are limited because they fail to capture the "temporalities that inhere in cultural traffic," whether those are temporalities of simultaneity (the subjectivity of being in two places at once),[7] speed (rates at which movements, flows, operate), and interruptions of velocity (Mascia-Lees and Himpele 2006, 9, 11). We may usefully join space and time to view vectors of movement—for example, how quickly spectacles of musical attention might exert influence in one direction (on Indian guitarists, for instance) and not in another (back toward the creators of genres prominent in America or Europe). In Martin Clayton's chapter, Indian guitarists draw influence and inspiration from what they view as the "West."[8] Many belong (or have historically belonged) to marginalized communities of Anglo-Indian or other Christians and self-identify personally and musically as quasi Western, and yet "Westerners," as Clayton puts it, remain "largely uninterested" in them. The vectors of musical attention move toward Anglo-Indians from Western genres of rock and jazz and have done so for some time; the return influence and interest in the Western musical world is more diffuse, largely mediated by Indian films, and, perhaps, slower. These are the spatiotemporal horizons of meaning (cf. Munn 1990, 5) that accrue to the guitar for some performers in India.

Background and Organization

The contributors, a majority of whom participated in a five-day seminar entitled "Local Theory/Local Practice: Musical Culture in South Asia and Beyond," have contemplated their positions regarding local theorizing for about five years now. They acquired knowledge of their "locals" in different ways: Blum, through repeated field visits to Khorasan over about forty years; Wegner, through prolonged residence in Bhaktapur, Nepal, and apprenticeship to a drummer; Badalkhan, through growing up in Baluchistan and, later in life, entering the field of folklore and traveling extensively through his home territory; and Chaudhuri, through processing archival records of many South Asian musical traditions, organizing performances and workshops, and conducting her own fieldwork. The writers have drawn on their diversity of experience and background and interpreted the themes of "local," "theory," and "practice" as they saw fit.

Their writings here span a range of musical and other performance traditions: Kandyan national dance in Sri Lanka, Kota tribal music in south India, drumming for rituals in Nepal and dance dramas in south India, narrative songs of Baluchistan (Pakistan and Iran), brass band and guitar music, bardic traditions of northeast Iran, and aspects of classical music training and colonial history. These are challengingly different in scope and codified in different degrees and ways. The availability of their written histories varies and the cosmopolitanisms of their practitioners range in depth. The authors, practitioners, and consumers of these traditions differ in their degree of emphasis on artistic products. The representation of all these traditions in one volume invites rich comparisons within and beyond South Asia.

The present organization of chapters embodies the "ground-up" orientation of our project as a whole. We begin with the materiality of dancing bodies, musical instruments, and the relationship of instruments to the body. From there we set these bodies and instruments in motion, moving from the networks Clayton specifies in his study of the Indian guitar to several other kinds of networks and configurations of musicians. These musicians create spaces and itineraries, in variously local or extensive landscapes, through ritual, story, and economic necessity. The third section moves from the rather physical treatment of bodies and instruments creating space through movement to the more mental or intellectual ways in which musicians and reciters acquire knowledge. This distinction between physical and mental should not be overdrawn, for one of South Asia's most persistent themes in the transmission of so-called traditional knowledge is its very physicality, its involvement in skills. Ways in which people know are intimately bound up in the disciplines through which they learn to move their bodies or repeat iterations (chapters by Groesbeck, Henderson, and Qureshi). The trajectory of this section toward knowledge and intellection continues in our final section, titled appropriately, "Theorizing."

Throughout the volume, contributors sustain a tension between discussion of microlevel workings in a particular South or West Asian context, that is, on kinds of local theorizing, and questioning what it means for something to be local—defining locality in different ways and in that sense potentially theorizing the local. Our attention to local theorizing is not radically different from the general sensitivity toward local knowledge that marks most good work in ethnomusicology, anthropology, and folklore; but focusing on different kinds of theorizing does constitute a subtle difference in emphasis. Another difference is a reluctance to allow topics that are marked today as important—the movement of capital, rapid exchanges through media and travel, responses to inequalities that have been attendant on globalism (in its many forms), and some others[9]—to divert attention from other ways in which local forms of knowledge might be connected in a larger region, or transcend the boundaries of a recognized geographical area.

In this book, the chapter groupings provide one framework for comparison in and beyond South Asia, but many themes transcend these groupings. None of them denies or ignores the larger workings of the modern world system; indeed, few would disagree that globality must be understood, at least in part, via the consideration of specific instances in which it is embedded.

The idea that the authors have free rein in their implicit or explicit uses of the local needs to be tempered with the recognition that the study of local knowledge, however one wishes to define it, has its own history and institutional form. In the case of the ethnomusicology of South Asia, issues of the local are more significantly inflected from the perspective of South Asian studies than of the field of ethnomusicology as a whole. Concepts of classical music in relation to individual styles or schools, or in relation to other genres of music, have their parallels in the ways scholars have tried to conceptualize Hinduism in relation to the diversity of practices, authorities, and beliefs on the ground. The need to localize the local in this study is signaled by such key terms as "great tradition" and "cultural performance," which find their way (usually loosely) into academic writing about cultural processes in many parts of the world, but were most famously used in relation to India. I shall first turn to this issue of localizing the local in South Asia, then consider each chapter in order of appearance. I close with a short discussion of how the essays challenge one another and a longer treatment of themes that draw the entire volume together: gender, induction, and "the beyond." Gender considerations are given particular care as they draw attention to sensitive interpersonal dynamics everywhere; in that sense, gender localizes all interpersonal interactions, including those involving music and dance.

Localizing the Local

Any attempt to localize what the "local" means in the history of scholarship on South Asia would be incomplete without reference to Milton Singer and Robert Redfield's discussion of "great" and "little" traditions (Redfield and Singer 1954). Great traditions are what "professional literati" based in "orthogenic" cities and towns built up from "local folk cultures" or "little traditions." A different group of intellectual elites (urban, modern), "intelligentsia," transformed these great traditions as orthogenic towns underwent "secondary urbanization"—expansion through extensive contact with "alien" peoples, goods, and ideas (Singer 1958, 347). Singer saw in Madras an ideal place to study the transformation of great traditions (he recognized that there were more than one) under extensive secondary urbanization. He famously contributed not only the specifically South Asian version of the great tradition concept to anthropology (and ethnomusicology), but also the aforementioned concept of cultural performance, the observable unit in which versions of the great tradition might be found.[10]

Ethnomusicologists have continued to use the terms "great" and "little" even as they fell out of common use in anthropology, perhaps because they seem to parallel indigenous terminological distinctions like *mārga* and *deśī*. Sheldon Pollock, speaking of Sanskrit literary traditions, glossed the distinction between these as the "cultural practices of the great 'way' and those of 'place'" (Pollock 2002, 21). Perhaps these terms seem to fit music because treatises, commentaries, and hereditary specialists fortify the art musical traditions much as they did the religious world Singer described in his early Madras studies. The problem that remains with the formulation, for ethnomusicology, is its implication of a mapping between great and little. It implies that the little is a local variant, a version of what is found in the great tradition; and we cannot assume such relationships of part to whole. Many musical traditions of South Asia cannot be placed in these boxes.[11] Mapping the great tradition onto the classical also functions to further isolate and perpetuate categories of musical distinction that do not adequately capture the diversity of the ways music is either performed or conceptualized on the ground.[12]

It is not necessary to resort to clumsy categories of great and little, and their implied historical trajectories, to recognize the many tantalizing continuities of process, idea, and experience that run through different South and West Asian places, many of which are not easily traced to one another. A brief glance at world-system theory of a few decades ago, the current and ongoing research on religion, art, and society along the Silk Road (e.g., Liu 1996), and recent literature on cosmopolitanism (with its recognition of differential engagement between locals and others) all demonstrate that interconnectedness between people and places in many parts of the world has ebbed and flowed historically. Sheldon Pollock's monumental project of comparing Latin and Sanskrit cosmopolitanisms over time, for instance, shows the vastly different results of literary and documentary spread of dominant languages up through the end of the first millennium. Early in the second, writers consciously decided to "reshape the boundaries of their cultural universe by renouncing the world for the smaller place, and they did so in full awareness of the significance of their decision" (Pollock 2002, 16; see also Pollock 2006). Just as interconnections have ebbed and flowed historically among people of different nations, so have they remained various and diverse even within the rough confines of India, Pakistan, Nepal, Sri Lanka, and Iran.

Many of us are interested in rethinking the horizons of "South Asian music." There is often good reason to view local musical practices as variants of a classical tradition or as products of grand historical forces that have affected whole nations or states. But such views can also be limiting because they presume and predetermine the terms by which interconnection can be discussed. Recently, like Amanda Weidman in her thoughtful considerations of the politics of voice in south Indian music (2003; 2006; and this volume), Lakshmi Subramanian (2004; 2006) and Janaki Bakhle (2005), among others, have emphasized the modernity of musical classicism in South Asia. Music now seen as classical, their arguments run, was constituted as such in the nineteenth and twentieth centuries in the colonial encounter and through nationalist projects.

The turn to historicizing the construction of classicism is a salutary advancement, but it may have the unintended effect of reifying the very mapping of musical system onto nation (India in this case) that it seeks to critique.[13] Moreover, it has the potential to limit how we think of "classical" in relation to the valorization of other kinds of theoretical formulations. Blum lists six possible areas in which one might identify what he calls "incentives for theoretical formulations." These would encompass the needs that arose in the nineteenth and twentieth centuries for rulers and musical elites to foster an art music that might compete with that of Europe, for example. But they would allow us to understand these historical developments in relation to other, perhaps more regional, incentives to theorize, such as needs of religious specialists, "professional networks and lineages in competition with others," and bards and storytellers, who are no less important to our understanding of how music operates on the ground (Blum, this volume).

Qureshi makes the point that the act of writing about the principle of oral transmission contained in the phrase *sīna ba sīna* (lit., "chest to chest," "heart to heart," etc.) has the effect of "converting the oral and particular" into the "literate and universal"—the so-called "great" or "classical." This, she argues, belittles the significance of what actually takes place between masters and disciples in the intimacy of their individual encounters; her solution is to make way for the voices of the hereditary musicians, to let them tell their own stories.

The hiddenness of hereditary musicians' voices is not peculiar to the twentieth and twenty-first centuries, and neither is the establishment of art-musical authority. Under various names, traditions of cultivated, theorized, musical traditions date back several thousand years on the subcontinent. As theorists over the centuries described what they saw around them and tried to take account of what came before, they began to take up terms of geographical and temporal encompassment, *mārga* and *deśī*.[14] Indian music theorists long ago recognized continuities and disjunctures between *mārga* music that operated according to established schemes and new *deśī* material that challenged them to adjust their representations of contemporary musical practice accordingly. Theorizing the local in that sense has a long history on the subcontinent. But just as the *mārga* music before 500 C.E. is not the same as "classical" music today, neither is the "local" of our study merely a modern projection of the *deśī*.

Bodies and Instruments

Bodies and instruments are sites where actors create microlevel theories, express their motivations, and react to what they perceive as encompassing discourses. As sites of the local, bodies and instruments are ideal points of departure for the authors of articles in part I to contemplate performing artists and their arts in relation to broader prevailing discourses of gender, nation, modernization, and the West.

Susan Reed's chapter is, in part, a story of how a male ritual dance in Sri Lanka developed from the 1940s into a classical dance, an important part of the Kandyan national dance of today. Notions of feminine respectability and modernity in Sri Lanka have both influenced and been shaped by ways in which women articulated themselves through dance as individuals, as women, and as artists. Expectations of how women should project a respectable feminine image have varied across Kandyan dance genres of the folk and the classical and in relation to dancers' ideas about sexuality and modernity. As the male ritual tradition did not prescribe or codify roles for women dancers, they have considerable scope in choreographing and interpreting dances in ways they deem properly feminine.

The female Sri Lankan dancers in Reed's discussion stretch the possibilities of the stereotypically feminine, or *lāsya,* style. Depending on the particular dance and teacher, dancers may be overtly feminine in the sense of being submissive, graceful, and responsive, or they may convey "an image of strength, agility, and composed confidence." Reed's treatment of Kandyan dance at different scales—views of an individual practitioner and widely held stereotypes—shows how individual practices serve as guides to inchoate theory or as challenging counterpoints to prevailing explanatory discourses among participants in a tradition. This is an example of the kinds of tension between local theory and practice that many contributors bring to the foreground. Different artists, even within a single performance tradition, may operate according to more than one "implicit theory" (Blum, this volume).

In Sri Lanka, introducing female dancers into the incipient Kandyan national form instigated change and ambiguity in the role of both men and women in the dance. In south India, introducing the violin into Karnatak music stimulated a transformation of aesthetics that feeds into versions of the modern south Indian voice. In localizing the study of Karnatak music to the violin, Weidman unearths surprising instrumental foundations to a music south Indians consistently assert to be essentially vocal. Styles of playing Karnatak music on the violin have blossomed and faded in popularity in accordance with changing conceptions of the voice. How could an instrument that ostensibly accompanies be so influential? How could this (what Weidman terms) "colonial" instrument, introduced from the West and often used by south Indians as a sign of the West, become naturalized as part of an authentic Indian sound? The violin and the voice in south Indian classical music engaged in "a series of displacements," one standing for and influencing the other. This process moved from the making of metonymic chains to the expansion of scale because, in the late twentieth century, south Indian classical musicians and listeners articulated a desire to create an "Indian" sound distinct from anything Western.

A different set of stories describes the lives of guitarists in India. Martin Clayton's chapter discusses the ways the guitar—particularly as employed for such

"Western" genres as rock and jazz—is theorized by Indian musicians. Extensive quotations from interviews with Indian guitarists describe origins of the instrument, its associations with regional, religious, and other identities, and implications of the guitar in national and international systems. While musicians have found ways to include guitars in many genres of Indian music, including classical, guitarists in India have by and large belonged to Anglo-Indian and other Christian communities. Their understandings of themselves in relation to dominant notions of what is truly Indian differ in important ways from those of their south Indian violinist counterparts. Moreover, some of these guitarists are less interested in creating a purely Indian sound than in accurately reproducing musical styles associated with the guitar in Europe and America. They would like to participate actively in and affect the transnational musical world of which they see themselves a part. Clayton uses the guitar case study to argue that more studies of local theory are necessary even—perhaps especially—where mass-mediated global styles such as rock and jazz are involved.

Perhaps more than in any other section of this book, the chapters here negotiate across a range of encompassing scales of vision: bodily sites of music-making, groups of consumers and organizers, networks of media and performance locations, and other representations of gender, social group, region, nation, and the wider world.

Spaces and Itineraries

Next in our journey, we move from the body dancing and playing to aspects of the local in processions, professional networks, and the geography of shrines. "Spaces and itineraries" emphasizes how individual places of music making are connected to other places through itineraries of moving musicians. Itineraries, paths, and mental processes trace out larger geographic areas, "spaces" that depend on human acts of connection for their existence.[15] Theorizing the local entails understanding these spaces, figuring out the configurations of human relationships across neighborhoods and regions of different sizes. Theorizing these forms of local also involves understanding the systems of support and patronage that make changes in geographic scale, expansions or contractions of space, possible.[16]

Gregory Booth outlines ways in which socio-professional organization in the commercial brass band tradition in India has been mapped onto geographic space. Brass bandsmen organize themselves into networks that cover major South Asian regions. The networks' social bases are communities of low-caste musicians who live in what Booth calls "source nodes." Musicians travel seasonally from these small towns and villages, where living costs are low, to perform in the major labor markets, located in larger cities and towns. The social and geographical boundaries of each network in which musicians operate make it possible for band leaders to ascertain the likely musical abilities of a bandsman searching for employment. A bandsman's social identity and the familiarity of his home town similarly help the bandsman get gigs with a band. The implicit theory that undergirds the movements of bandsmen is a form of mapping not unlike the instrument-community mapping Clayton describes. Both represent practical states of affairs that musicians can imagine to be otherwise; some choose to act on these possibilities.[17] Booth's contribution to the study of local theory is in explicating bandsmen's understandings of the "rules" that govern movement within and between these networks.

Māngaṇiār musicians in western Rajasthan state operate in different kinds of networks, some of which involve the relationship of musicians to shrines devoted to their patron deity, Rāni Bhaṭiyāṇi. Shubha Chaudhuri recounts local stories that continue to support the hereditary right of Māngaṇiārs to earn their living playing for this goddess. Variations of the story serve as ongoing iterations of local theory with respect to musical-social interactions. Earlier versions of the origin story focused on princess Rāni Bhaṭiyāṇi's act of self-immolation (*satī*) for her deceased brother-in-law. Current descendants of the in-laws' clan, who belong to a prominent Rajput Hindu community, have attempted to eradicate implications of sexual impropriety by circulating their own versions of the story. Through these reworkings of local theory, they distance themselves from the Māngaṇiārs and other hereditary musicians as they transform some of the older shrines into larger, more mainstream Hindu ones. Rajput clans also reap financial benefits by forbidding hereditary musicians from performing in the main shrines and thereby denying them a share of donations. But beliefs in the deified princess's powers, local notions of musicians' efficacy in helping devotees get possessed by her spirit, and the narratives themselves have led several communities to build their own shrines. This popularity has created new sources of patronage and has increased the density of performance venues in the vicinity of Jasol, where Rāni Bhaṭiyāṇi was first cremated.

The processional routes described by Gert-Matthias Wegner cover an even more dense series of performance venues: religious monuments in the Newar town of Bhaktapur in Nepal. Castes of Buddhist priests, goldsmiths, and oilpressers drum pieces from the *gūlābājā* genre to draw on the divine power of these sites. Wegner likens the drum patterns to phone numbers: each deity or power in a place has one. Such indexical links between places on the procession route and pieces performed by the various ensemble dominate local understandings of the music.

The significant sites in the procession are metonymic of the town of Bhaktapur in much the same way as processions, often with music, create scales of town or neighborhood in other South Asian traditions. At a larger level, Wegner claims, the processional design is a *maṇḍala* (a design representing the cosmos); activities of the processioners make the *maṇḍala* come alive and thereby renew connections between inhabitants of the town and the gods. Indeed, musicians make grand claims in their conceptions of both the whole world and the massive span of world time cycles; but the "meaning horizons" (Munn 1990) they create through ritual do not involve real or imaginary transactions with others across national or cultural borders. Drummers may hold global aspirations for the magnitude of their musical influence, but that does not indicate their willingness to engage with "unfamiliar cultures and places" (Werbner 2006, 7).

The three chapters implicate space and time through travel in different ways: ongoing adjustments to economic routes of musicians from season to season; historical dimensions of change in the relationships of performers and patrons to potential performance venues; repetitive, small-scale acts of moving from place to place in relation to abstract representations and philosophies that persist historically and across regions. The persons involved in these accounts are often the ones who envision their professional lives in terms of their scale of geographical potential. Some of them recognize their marginality in the musical worlds to which they are nevertheless connected.

Learning and Transmission

As we progress from playing bodies to moving bodies, we pause a moment to consider a site of theorization that, in the life of any individual, is prior to both playing and moving: transmission of knowledge. In South Asia, performers and listeners continually rearticulate a tension, common to many performance traditions, between faithfulness to received versions of the past and aspirations to create something recognizably new. We commonly speak of the transmission of musical knowledge, but this must be obtained by the development, in each generation of performers, of new skills; and this presupposes an environment in which skills can be incrementally developed, by individuals, reacting to their teachers, their codisciples, and adapting to schedules, local tastes, and economies specific to their situations (see Ingold 2000, 291 and passim). Individuals assert their traditional roots, the foundation of their arts in faithful reproduction of techniques, ways of building melodic and rhythmic interest, and utterances of texts. Performers disagree about what innovations are superficial or substantial, but they all strive to keep their arts alive, keep them new. In some ways performers perpetuate a model of absolute, master-to-disciple hierarchy that demands perfect reproduction of sounds; and yet, in their search for creativity, they may undermine it.

Two forums for training serve as points of departure for Rolf Groesbeck's examination of how actual practice challenges commonplace assumptions about the master-disciple relationship in South Asia. Drumming for Kathakali dance drama is one of many arts taught at the Kerala Kalamandalam, the premier educational institute for performing arts in the south Indian state of Kerala. In one forum, the open-air pedagogical arena, students learn to reproduce percussion patterns more or less exactly. In the other, more advanced drumming students join with singers and actors to rehearse as a group. Training in the open-air arena does not fully prepare drummers for improvisation and accompaniment in the group rehearsal. Drummers must find their way by watching the dancers and drawing from lifelong intuitions about drum accompaniment that have not been taught directly. The significant insights students gain from "peer-group immersion" show that a significant horizontal dimension of learning accompanies the vertical (master-disciple) structure of transmission in Kathakali. The particularities of this art form and the institutional form and history of the Kerala Kalamandalam account for some of the distinction between horizontal and vertical forms. However, one suspects that the discourse of vertical hierarchy in many South Asian musical traditions that feature gurus or ustāds may mask important forms of horizontal learning.

In the milieu of hereditary sārangī players, Regula Qureshi directs our attention to processes of musical enculturation and socialization that form part of the broader, family-based, teaching of Hindustani music. The phrase *sīna ba sīna*, meaning to give something valuable and creative from the heart of one, as we might say in English, to the heart of another, refers specifically to the passing of a tradition in the male line. This is marked by acts establishing and affirming discipleship, not unlike rituals associated with discipleship in Sufism (the focus is mainly vertical here). Some such acts form the ritual of *shāgirdī*, which Qureshi describes as part of a musical conversation in which both the content of the student's playing and aspects of the relationship of teacher to student are subjects of commentary. The ustād shows how one musical idea can give birth to fifty more ideas. Musicians must apply elaborate and flexible procedures to their store of musical knowledge to generate interesting musical structures in performance. This notion of "expansion" (*baṛhāt*) is superficially similar to the idea, in Indonesia, that performers keep "pieces in their memories in compressed form, along with information about how to decompress them during performance" (Spiller 2004, 76). One of the differences is the lack of emphasis on composed pieces in the Hindustani tradition, and the great emphasis on the physical process of practicing (*riyāẓ*), which itself, as if by magic, transforms rote repetition into real music.

Getting knowledge into the body and feeling that knowledge as self-evident and self-contained involve more than one kind of theorizing. David Henderson brings experiences of studying both the classical tabla and the Newari drums prominent in Bhaktapur processions into dialogue with neurological, phenomenological, and anthropological perspectives on bodily knowledge. Drummers in Nepal face challenges not unlike those of Kathakali drummers when they move from the security of learning fixed compositions to the unpredictability of accompanying and responding to dancers. Learners not only mimic the actions of their teachers until they can feel the proper motions of performance in their hands but they also engage in multiple layers of communication with their bodies and through language. Knowing entails being able to feel proper ways of striking an instrument or combining recognizable passages. Feeling here is a measure of value that counterposes forms of value Henderson's teachers express in their verbal assessments of modern Nepali taste. The experience of drumming properly is localized value, seemingly impervious to regional or global hierarchies.

All three chapters show how issues of knowing in South Asian musical performance are tied up in specific kinds of repetitive bodily experiences. They show the multiple agents and techniques that help guide bodily mimesis and transform the practice, the doing, of music into knowledge, into being able to think and do independently. Yet they also show how complex and important are interactions with others in the learning process: watching, conversing, gesturing, and otherwise responding. "Transmission" as a key concept in our collective theorizing subsumes, in some ways, those of body/instrument and movement in parts I and II.

Theorizing Social Action

Theorizing the local and explicating what purport to be native theories of music obviously implicate spheres of social action that extend beyond the performance of music and dance. Musicians sometimes represent scale in terms of musical knowledge: music is often compared to a vast ocean in South and West Asia; but an individual's understanding may be rather shallow. Musicians and other listeners evaluate and otherwise respond to a musical performance in part by comparing what they hear with other possibilities made available through a larger body of knowledge. People may attempt to access such possibilities through introspection, dialogue with others, study and discussion of texts, deepening engagement in performance genres and rituals, and so forth.

These dynamics of understanding performances form part of Stephen Blum's consideration of modes of theorizing in the Khorasan province of northeast Iran. Using statements of bards in Khorasan and neighboring regions and formulations offered by South Asian musicians and those who have written about them, Blum provides a useful model for thinking more generally about the relationship between what a performer knows and the forms of access others have to that knowledge: performances and pedagogical presentations. The model suggests that the dynamics of interaction between musicians' performances and their pedagogical presentations remain uncertain. This draws attention to the limits to which musicians can control and communicate relevant portions of their knowledge.

Theorizing, in Blum's formulation, takes in many sorts of "episodes of generalizing" and begins whenever an agent draws together a body of perceptions and ideas and acts on them, as against remembered or imagined alternatives. Theoretical statements made by a local body of practitioners may themselves take conventional formats, a list of which reveals the principle categories and names that act as building blocks of local theorizing.

The *zahīrok* is a particularly rich example of such a category and name. The *zahīrok* song genre and set of melody types is found mainly along the Makran coastal area in southern Baluchistan (Pakistan and Iran). Sabir Badalkhan describes the texts and contexts of these songs of longing, which were once commonly sung by camel drivers and are now sung by people of many social backgrounds. Some Baloch represent the *zahīrok* to be the structural basis upon which all Baloch music is built. The names assigned to *zahīroks* by Baloch performers enable them to theorize about appropriate sequences of melody-types in performances that may last from dusk until dawn. *Zahīroks* are of comparative interest as they resemble other genres in South and West Asia that straddle the borders of song, melody, and melody-type. When professionals sing *zahīroks* in narrative songs, they must know which melodies are appropriate to the mood and message of each section. They must also know how to insert a free-rhythmic section called *čīhāl* at crucial scene shifts. This section, which begins in an upper vocal register, serves to excite the audience and draw their attention to the song section that follows. *Čīhāls* always precede *zahīroks* in the narrative genre; they are also seen as part of the *zahīrok* and in that sense serve as signs of what will follow musically.

In south India several kinds of musical gesture, song section, and genre serve as signs to what follows and are points of departure for local theorizing. One analog of the *zahīrok* is the *varṇam*, which is both an exercise and a kind of composition performed at the beginning of a Karnatak music concert. Although south Indians would not claim that the *varṇam* (like the *zahīrok* for the Baloch) is the basis of their musical culture, they commonly represent the *varṇam* as a corpus of essential information about particular ragas and rhythmic permutations in a tala. In my own essay, I consider the *varṇam* not merely as a kind of beginning or encapsulation of accepted truths about a raga but also as a site in which influential musicians and musicologists can make their marks as artists and theorists. Beginnings in other genres of south Indian music have other implications. Sequences of vocables in several Tamil folk genres, for instance, are an informative kind of beginning in that they provide the *cantam,* the rough metrical outline of verse and flow of melody, that continues throughout a song. Some beginnings provide minimal information. Members of the Kota tribe in the Nilgiri Hills use minute differences in the standard warm-up melody fragment on their shawms to articulate their primary categories of ritual, social, and moral action connected with divinity and death. Although these warm-up fragments provide little melodic information about what is to come, their very difference is of great importance and, like similar differences in other areas of Kota ritual performance, is reflected upon verbally.

* * *

Each of the studies in this volume has the potential to challenge the others. The critical histories presented by Weidman and Reed challenge us to look more closely at the movements and sounds that local agents (listeners or performers) present as natural. Clayton and Booth examine the flip side of Weidman's "colonial" violin, in which imported instruments become central to local networks and musical worlds, but remain largely ignored by consumers in the Euro-American cultures to which those instruments and the music played upon them have historical relationships.[18] Henderson's discussion of how knowledge of drumming entered into his hands might make us wonder whether theorization too can feel as though it is a process of the body, detached from our consciousnesses. Sabir Badalkhan's study of how Baloch construe *zahīrok* songs and melody types as the core of their Baluchi musical being raises questions about which peoples and cultures in a nation have the power to raise their canonical repertoires and theories to the status of national emblems.

Gender

The hierarchies associated with tensions between theories and practices have long implicated the roles of men and women in South Asia as holders and transmitters of knowledge. These hierarchies also pertain to gender associations of particular artistic activities and instruments, which may or may not be tied to the gender of the performer.[19] The degree to which a tradition is represented as belonging to or extending beyond a geographic area is often linked to the reputation of male musicians or writers; the degree to which musicians can or wish to be in the public eye depends in some degree on whether they are male or female; and the idea of protected musical knowledge in the Hindustani classical tradition seems to be linked with the idea of male lineages. Gender, tied to creations of scale in all these ways and more, is highly significant to theorizations of the local in and beyond South Asia.

Female musicianship is, in some traditions, associated with domesticity; in that realm, women are more "local" in the limited sense of less in the public eye, less geographically expansive in their influence, and so forth. Some of these contrasts are captured in the ancient Tamil poetic categories of *akam* (domestic, interior, female, etc) and *puṟam* (public sphere, exterior, male, etc); for this reason, a number of writers on south India have found these to be useful "native" categories, even for the analysis of modern social life.

If some of these statements seem sweepingly general, maybe that is because in South Asia, as in many diverse regions, the value of gender is expressed in more than one way at the same time. The idea that musical transmission from "heart to heart" (Qureshi, this volume) implies the passing of a tradition specifically in the male line persists in a South Asian musical world in which female vocalists have been recognized for the superiority of their voices, a world in which women have made significant marks in popular and classical realms, in the media and in concert halls, both nationally and internationally. Historically, *dēvadāsi*s, *tawā'if*s, and other women of artistic communities have been especially active in developing singing and dancing. Their agency has been represented as more extensive—with dance steps like "thunder" and voices like "lightning" (Lakshmi 2000, xix)—than the domestic stereotype might suggest.

Yet the social environments for some kinds of music making are ill-suited to women in the vast majority of South Asian communities. The peripatetic life of brass bandsmen and the perceived immodesty of participating in processional music militate against women's participation and help to gender the activities themselves as male.[20] In Booth's book-length treatment of brass band culture in South Asia, he recounts a fruitless search for an alleged "Ladies Band." The excitement generated over this ill-founded rumor is an index of the degree to which women are out of place in this tradition (Booth 2005, 105–7).

In the case of guitarists, Clayton shows a historical dominance of Catholic, Anglo-Indian men. If a Hindu male musician such as Dilip Nayak had to fight against prejudice to make his way, it would be hard to imagine what a woman would have had to sustain to survive in the public world of film music or Western bands. But we are reminded that the status quo can be disrupted when we read Wegner's description of the rise of "girls" playing the Newar farmer's processional drum (*dhimay*); even if this was instigated by Wegner's own act of teaching a girl to play, the presence of Westerners and erstwhile outsiders of many kinds is part of a modern reality that cannot be conveniently ignored.

In much of South Asia, it is commonplace for women to be associated with a kind of primordial power, often related to sexuality and potential for emotionality. Whether it is the rage of a woman who has been mistreated, or the sustaining presence of a woman who has immolated herself to preserve family honor, the reconfigured agency of woman-as-spirit animates many tales of origin, including those associated with music. In Chaudhuri's chapter Rāni Bhaṭiyāṇi's story lies at the heart of a cult and a set of relationships among Māngaṇiār musicians and their patrons.

In Reed's study, some consultants emphasized the naturalness of gender in the different ways men and women danced. For women, some of this lay in their ability to be more flexible in dancing, and thus more convincing in inhabiting the character of males. Badalkhan explains in his chapter that emotions of longing and separation motivate singers of *zahīrok* in Baluchistan. In South Asia, as in many parts of the world, such emotions are gendered as female.[21] While one theory posits that *zahīrok* songs were originally composed by women whose husbands were absent for extended periods, another finds stylistic origins in the gait of camels: male camel-drivers rode as they sang the prototypical forms of *zahīrok*. In looking at articulations of *zahīrok* theory via an analysis of *zahīrok* names, the types associated with women are marked as such, and are thus, now, subsumed in a hierarchy that is managed by male performers. A professional male performer (*pahlawān*) may draw upon a range of types in a public performance, including those named for women's activities (certain kinds of work) or social-emotional states (widowhood). Women, who presently sing only the specific types of *zahīrok* associated with their status and activities, do not have the opportunity to create a performance by piecing together *zahīroks* that include men's repertoire.

If gender was conspicuous by its absence in several studies because of a seemingly natural misfit between women and social context, in other studies, what South Asians represent as "natural" to men and women often serve as the basis of local theory.

Induction

Induction in this volume might be likened to an epistemological journey in Peircian semiotic terms (Peirce 1955). The essays in part I hold together, in part, because of their attention to what Charles S. Peirce called "firsts"—relationships of likeness, similitude, mimesis, embodiment. These are firsts because an observer perceives the relationship of a sign to its object as being unmediated, inherent, and hence somehow basic. Many interesting problems come along with recognizing resemblance, with striving to resemble or distance oneself from others, and the ideologies of dominant and weaker populations which guide and resist such intersubjective identifications.

Essays in part II focus on phenomena related to Peircian "seconds"—relations of physical connection, indexicality. Processions and routes of travel are often in relations of seconds with their associated musical forms: certain pieces or styles are played at particular locales, at particular moments (e.g., starting or stopping), and in conjunction with ritual activities along route. When Māngaṇiārs in Rajasthan sing, they call to mind the story of Rāni Bhaṭiyāṇi and the geography of her influence in the musical world of Rajasthan.

A semiotically interesting aspect of part III in the South Asian context concerns the ways in which firsts become "thirds," that is to say, the ways in which imitations (rote learning) give rise to system-level knowledge. Peircian "thirds" are defined, depending on their placement in one of three "trichotomies," as "laws," "symbols," or "arguments"—all of which I am suggesting concern system-level knowledge.[22] Our fourth part focuses on what such knowledge might mean in concrete practices and discussions of music. Here, our theorizing of the local is not so much concerned with obvious sets of rules codified as music theory, but rather with how individual practitioners deal with the problems of knowing and doing and stimulating themselves or others to know and do appropriately. All human activities involve a complex mixture of firsts, seconds, and thirds, and so too do the discussions in each section. In stressing the movement from firsts to thirds here, my intention is to draw out aspects of induction in the volume as a whole.

Beyond

These studies cohere around themes that extend beyond South Asia to many other performing traditions, particularly in other parts of Asia. Several focus on how bodies figure in the directionality, control, and interpretation of mimesis—in teaching, practicing, and performing: the problematic mimesis of the dancer's body with respect to culturally recognized types; mimesis between "India" and the "West";[23] the partial mimesis between the Karnatak violin and the voice, the *suroz* and the melody of the bard, and Persian instrumental "responses" (*javāb*) to singers. Singers' realizations of phrases in a common improvisational vocabulary are not always "models" that instrumentalists are "obliged to emulate" with exactitude (Blum, this volume). So too, the examples of one's teachers and the directives of patrons and organizers serve as stimuli for possible creativity, reflection, or manipulation, and not merely reproduction.

The studies also point outward to processes of general significance in the South and West Asian spheres. Sabir Badalkhan's discussion of *zahīroks* as both songs and types of melody may recall such borderline raga entities as *ḍhāḷ* in Gujarat (Thompson 1995) and *varṇameṭṭu* in Karnatak music (Allen 1998). Wegner's mention of musical pieces associated with places along a processional route, and the mixed Buddhist and Hindu associations of the rituals themselves, calls to mind many similar uses of melodic and rhythmic compositions in rituals of Hindus, Muslims and others, such as tribals, who may not identify with either of these categories. The tension between learning by rote from a masterful authority and learning by experimenting and picking up is one that appears in a range of traditions in South Asia, modulated perhaps by the strength of the authority (role of guru or ustād) and the range of ways in which musical learning is institutionalized.

How are we to view some of the apparently commonplace local peoples and places in these studies in light of contemporary discussions that deemphasize names and the boundaries of maps? And how do we contextualize them in light of arguments that disrupt the internal integrity of peoples and places to focus on connectedness across categories, which is elemental to many globalist discourses?[24] One way is to remember that many ethnographic subjects continue to be concerned with the discreteness of their corporate identities, and continue to map their knowledge, their subjectivities, and their music, onto places (Daniel 1984; Diehl 2002; Werbner 2003; Wolf 2006). Even in the implicitly mixed and hybrid world of Indian guitarists described in Martin Clayton's work (this volume and 2001), participants continue to associate musical styles with discrete communities. Some displaced persons, such as Tibetan refugees in Dharamsala, India, are preoccupied with "place"—the Tibet to which they hope to return (Diehl 2002, 11).[25] In their new Indian surroundings, Tibetans borrow to enhance what one Tibetan scholar refers to as the "sacred" (Diehl 2002, 65) in a way that is roughly analogous to how

Mundas and Kotas demarcate themselves using musical materials common to the environment in which they interact with others.

* * *

The "beyond" in our title suggests many possibilities of scale extension, not least of which includes the disciplinary and regional expertise of the contributors. The horizons of "music," here, logically extend into movement and dance, poetry and religious recitation, religious rituals, and commerce. To study everything is to study nothing, so we have limited our geographic "beyond" to the western extensions of South Asia, as Pakistani Baluchistan meets Iran, and into the Khorasan region of Iran itself. But even to study the music of these places, we are forced to confront the histories of interaction that brought such instruments as guitars and violins to India, and the ways in which the users of such instruments position themselves in relation to India and the West, as they view them.

The case studies presented here offer a subtle range of ways to think about how societies both systematize their musical practices and choose to represent aspects of their musical practices as systematic. The selection of genres and geographic breadth of the examples hopefully broaden our view of what regionally grounded case studies have to offer ethnomusicology and related fields; in each case, this is accomplished by narrowing the range of study to microsituations that do not easily fit the scholarly, national, or regional commonplaces used to epitomize the musical practices of the regions. Nevertheless, claims of what particular instruments, pieces, and genres can do resonate with very similar claims in the wide region of South Asia as it expands into West and Central Asia.

The very diversity of contributions to this volume is the source of its strength. We hope to challenge readers, as we ourselves have been challenged, to reflect upon what may be significant for a larger South Asian understanding of music, practice, and experience, and what really transcends the various political, linguistic, religious, cultural, and music-systemic ways of viewing South Asia as a single region.

PART I

BODIES AND INSTRUMENTS

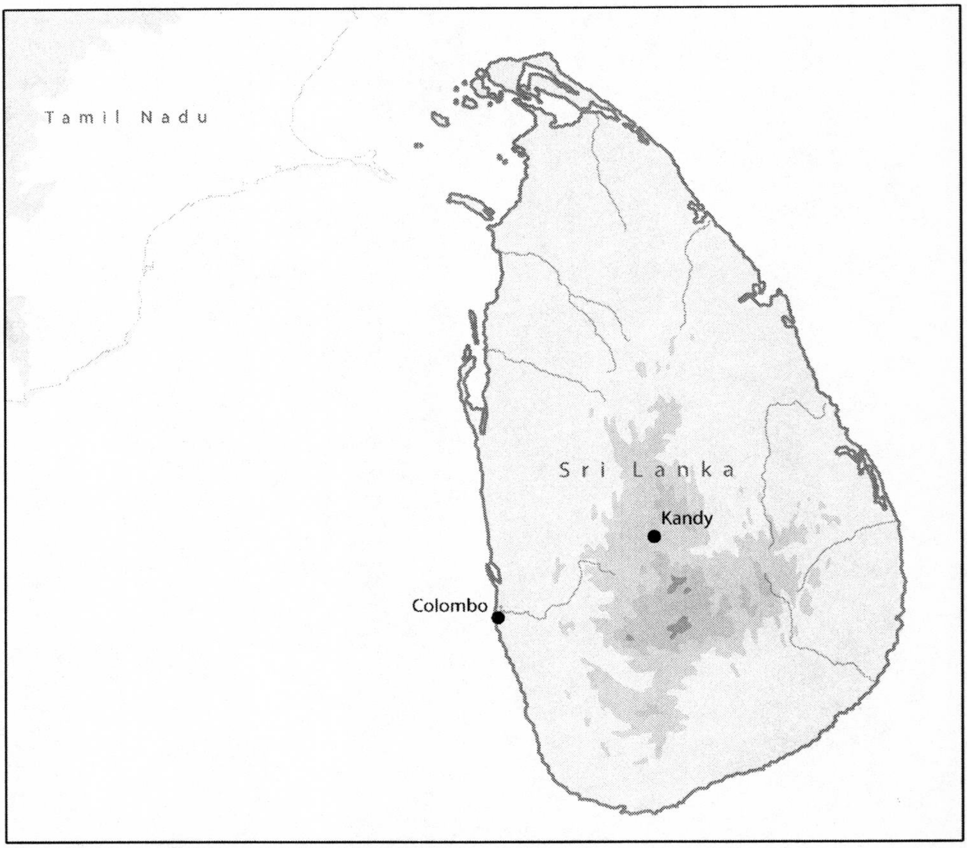
Tamil Nadu
Sri Lanka
Kandy
Colombo

CHAPTER 2

Women and Kandyan Dance

Negotiating Gender and Tradition in Sri Lanka

SUSAN A. REED

Women and girl dancers are ubiquitous in contemporary Sri Lanka, performing in sites ranging from school concerts, private dance classes, and aesthetic teacher training institutes to government ceremonials, religious processions, weddings, and Buddhist temples. As in many societies, women in Sri Lanka are viewed as the embodiment of the nation and protector of its traditions, and thus their public performances are often potent sites of debate.[1] Despite the prominence and popularity of women dancers in contemporary Sri Lanka, their position is fraught with ambivalence and contradiction.[2] The public display of their bodies and the confidence and assertiveness they show on stage clash with Sinhala ideals of demure and modest womanhood.

Kandyan dance, for women, simultaneously sustains, challenges, and expands notions of respectability and of Sinhala Buddhist womanhood. In this chapter, I explore how aesthetic theory and ideals of the feminine have shaped the Kandyan dance, analyzing how these are construed by dancers and choreographers.[3] I ask: What images of femininity are expressed in women's dance? How does women's dance reinforce or challenge stereotypical gender roles? And finally, how do women's dance practices create the potential for both objectification and agency? Answering these questions requires a detailed examination of local conceptions of dance, gender, and body and comparison with aesthetic theory and transmission practices from elsewhere in South Asia.

Women's dance practices have expanded greatly since the 1940s, when they first began performing Kandyan dance, promoted by the state as Sri Lanka's national dance. Prior to the Sinhala nationalist revival of the 1940s and '50s, women's dancing was associated with sexual impropriety and, with few exceptions, Sinhala Buddhist women did not dance.[4] Now, women vastly outnumber male dancers in almost all spheres of performance.[5] At the university-level Institute for Aesthetic Studies, for example, more than 90 percent of the students are women. While men hold many of the high-level state positions in dance, there are a number of respected women teachers who have achieved considerable prominence. Women see themselves as the future of dance in Sri Lanka, and many consider themselves superior to men as preservers of the dance tradition. As they expand their spheres of influence, however, women must constantly negotiate their practice in relation to dominant, Sinhala Buddhist ideas of respectability.

Male nationalists of the late nineteenth and early twentieth centuries sought to "[transform] women into symbols of national greatness" by "instilling the virtues of Victorian femininity, domesticity, discipline and restraint" (Hewamanne 2003, 74). The work of these nationalists has left its mark on ideals of Sinhala Buddhist womanhood today. Sinhala Buddhist women are expected to be moral exemplars, embodying the virtues of "piety, purity, submissiveness and domesticity" (Silva 2002, 121). In Sri Lanka, the " 'respectability' of the ideal, ethnically pure, middle-class woman is the counterpoint of the 'crude' and 'licentious' behavior of the 'other'—the prostitute, the working-class woman, or in the case of Sri Lanka, the woman of mixed ancestry" (Silva 2002, 121).

Virginity is highly valued, and unmarried women who live alone, or away from their families, arouse intense anxiety. Neloufer de Mel notes that the idealization of the "de-sexualized" virtuous woman in contemporary Sri Lanka is supported both by Sinhala Buddhist morality and, as suggested by Jayadeva Uyangoda, "the moralistic discourse of the radical left" in which woman is conceived of as *sahōdari* (sister) (De Mel 1996, 185). Any threat to women's morality is considered a threat to the nation's "cultural purity and survival" (Hewamanne 2003, 75). In Sri Lanka the state, which is the major employer of dancers, stresses conformity to these ideals of womanhood by frequently sending communiqués to its female employees that emphasize the necessity of behaving and dressing modestly (De Alwis 1999, 105).

Although Kandyan dance has been characterized as conservative, reproducing "stereotypical gender images" (Hewamanne 2003, 87) of respectable womanhood, the perspectives of influential members of the dance community provide challenges to this view. The highly respected Kandyan dance teacher, Mrs. Esmee Jayasinghe, for instance, emphasized that "if a girl becomes a dancer, she has to break the accepted traditions (*sampradāya*) of our country" (Jayasinghe, pers. comm., 1992). Dancers apparently do, for as another well-known teacher, Srimathi Jothiratne, commented when I inquired about how female dancers are seen in society: "Villagers are shocked by the way we dance on stage, because our behavior on stage is totally different than how we behave in the village. Some people say dancing is not good for girls because of their behavior. . . . If the dancer acts in society the same way she acts on the stage, people would say the dancing is not good and she behaves badly" (S. Jothiratne, pers. comm., 1992).

Kandyan Dance

Kandyan dance is identified with Sri Lanka's majority Sinhala Buddhist ethnic community. Derived from the village ritual of the *kohoṃba kankāriya,* a ceremony propitiating the local gods of the Kandyan region, the dance was traditionally performed by males of the Berava (drummer) caste. Since the 1940s and '50s the Sinhala-dominated state has promoted the dance as an ethnic and national symbol, primarily by including it in the school curriculum. Today, the state employs the majority of dance professionals as teachers, and Kandyan dance is taught in almost every school in the Sinhala-speaking regions of the island. The state also provides financial support for private dance schools (*kalāyatanayas*).

In its traditional form, Kandyan dance is a *nṛtta* or "pure dance" form devoid of overt emotional expression or dramatic and mimetic gestures. The character of the dance is majestic, regal, and heroic. The elaborate costume worn by male ritual dancers, referred to as the *ves* costume, is said to be composed of half of the ornaments of the healer-king Malaya, a central figure in the *kankāriya*'s origin myth. The male performer's identity as heir to the healing powers of King Malaya is critical to the aesthetic qualities of nobility and dignity valued in dancing, whether in ritual or on stage.

The most important and sacred element of the *ves* costume is the *ves taṭṭuva,* a spectacular silver headdress adorned with shimmering bo leaves. Traditionally, ritual dancers kept the headdress wrapped in cloth in a special woven box in a deity shrine or Buddhist temple. The *ves taṭṭuva* was conferred on dancers only after years of training, in the initiation ceremony of *ves bǎndīma,* the tying of the *ves*. At the ceremony, the initiate's teacher dressed him in the ritual regalia of King Malaya, tying the silver *ves* headdress on his head. Though today few male dancers perform in the *kohoṃba kankāriya,* the *ves* is worn in stage performances and in ritual processions (*perahǎras*) and still retains some significance as a sacred object.

Due to ideas of women's impurity, women were traditionally prohibited from touching the *ves* headdress or even watching the *ves* initiation ceremony. In 1941, defying these traditional taboos, a very young woman dancer named Chandralekha performed on stage wearing the full *ves* costume. Shortly after one of her performances, Chandralekha died. Many of the traditional dancers attributed her death to her wearing of the *ves*. Since that time, with a few exceptions (discussed below), women dancers have not worn *ves,* but a modified costume that includes some of its elements.

The basic position of the Kandyan dancer, from which all dances begin, is the *mǎṇḍiya,* a position similar to a deep plié in ballet. The dancer places his feet shoulder-width apart, with his bent knees oriented in opposite directions. The arms are held horizontally at shoulder height, with elbows bent at a little more than ninety degrees. The hands are held palms out, inclined downward, with the fingers together and the thumb outstretched, and the head is tilted slightly upward. While performing, the dancer should always retain some semblance of the *mănḍiya,* even

FIGURE 2.1. I. K. Samaraweera, adorned in the *ves* costume, in the *mănḍiya* position. Photo by Susan A. Reed.

during the fast-paced climactic sections of the dance, when the dancer performs a variety of jumps, pirouettes, and spins. The eyes of the dancers follow the movement of their hands, their facial expressions remaining pleasant but serene. Dancers perform to the powerful beats of the Kandyan drum, the *găṭa bera,* and their movements may be seen as a visual representation of the pitches of drum strokes.[6]

The state dance curriculum, created by government officials and Berava dancers in the mid-1950s, classifies dance into two categories: classical dance (*śāstrīya năṭum*) and folk dance (*jana năṭum*). The Kandyan dances designated as classical are those that derive directly or indirectly from the *kohoṃba kankāriya,* while the folk category includes lighter village forms, such as the harvest (*goyam kăpīma*), stick (*lī keḷi*), and water-pot (*kalageḍi*) dances.

Among the most popular classical dances are the *vannam,* short dance pieces accompanied by song that evoke a particular sacred animal, deity, royal personage, or Buddhist theme. Originally the term *vannam* referred to a group of songs, of both Sinhala and Tamil influence, composed during the Kandyan period (1592–1815) and sung in the courts of the Kandyan kings (Sarachchandra 1966, 12). Later (the precise dates are unknown) dance steps and movements, thought by some to derive from the *kankāriya,* were added. The courtly origins of the *vannam* give the dance the cachet of a regal and aristocratic culture, in contrast to the rustic village folk dances.

The classical *vannam* are traditionally numbered at eighteen, though in the twentieth century three new *vannam* were composed. Among the best-known *vannam* are the elephant (*gajagā*) *vannama,* which depicts the majestic gait of the heavenly elephant; the peacock (*mayurā*) *vannama,* which praises the sacred peacock vehicle of the god Kataragama (Skanda); the horse (*turanga*) *vannama,* which tells of the renunciation of Prince Siddhartha on his horse, Kantaka; and the *asa druśa vannama,* which honors the Buddha and his teachings.[7] Other popular *vannam* include the eagle (*ukussa*) *vannama,* the hare (*musalāḍi*) *vannama,* and the conch shell (*gāhaka*) *vannama.*

In contemporary Sri Lanka, performances of the *vannam* range on a continuum from the "traditional" or pure dance versions to "modern" or "innovated" forms (*nirmāṇa*) that include mimetic movements not found in traditional dancing. The modern elephant *vannama,* for example, includes movements that imitate the waving of the elephant's trunk and the flapping of its ears, while the modern version of the peacock *vannama* includes the movement of a peacock's head and its high-stepping gait. The costumes for some modern *vannam* also incorporate mimetic features. Girls who perform the peacock dance, for instance, often wear shimmering blue and green costumes adorned with peacock feathers.

Both the traditional and modern *vannam* are popular stage dances, though dancers often prefer one style over the other. Those who prefer the traditional *vannam* consider the modern *vannam,* with its mimetic gestures, to lack subtlety, while those who prefer the modern style regard the traditional *vannam* as rather dull and monotonous.

Negotiating Gender and Tradition: Style, Transmission, Repertoire

Lāsya and Tāṇḍava

Lāsya and *tāṇḍava* are terms used by dancers throughout South Asia to characterize two distinct styles of dancing (Vatsyayan 1967, 232). Dances performed in the *lāsya* style are graceful, gentle, and tender, while dances in the *tāṇḍava* style are vigorous, bold, and heroic. Though the *lāsya* style is more closely associated with the feminine, and the *tāṇḍava* with the masculine, male and female dancers may perform either style.[8] Though most of the dances in the *kohoṃba kankāriya* are *tāṇḍava,* there are also a number of important solo dances that are characterized as *lāsya.*

The state dance curriculum which today serves as the foundation of Kandyan dance training does not categorize dances by gender. The Berava dancers who created the syllabus in the early years saw mastery of the dances, songs, and drumming of the *kohoṃba kankāriya* as the ultimate test of a Kandyan dancer, whether male or female. At the most advanced levels of the dance curriculum (advanced-levels and university), girls as well as boys are expected to master a substantial amount of ritual knowledge and demonstrate skill in all of the arts of the *kankāriya.*

Acknowledgment of gender differences nonetheless informs Kandyan dance, and all of the dance teachers that I interviewed—male and female—agreed on the importance of stylistic distinctions in its performance. Some teachers noted that gendered styles of dancing were to a considerable extent "natural." Ransina Jothiratne, one of the most respected and experienced women teachers in the country, told me that for the most part masculine or feminine styles of dance did not even need to be taught, as men and women naturally danced in ways appropriate to their gender (R. Jothiratne, pers. comm., 1992). In general, male dancers were said to be naturally more vigorous and athletic in their dancing, whereas women were said to be naturally graceful and subdued.

Dancers who held this view, however, also mentioned that women could successfully learn to dance in the *tāṇḍava* style. In fact, both male and female dance teachers proudly told me of staged dance-dramas they had directed in which females had skillfully played male roles, even to the extent that their true gender identity was not evident to the audience. These teachers remarked that women's bodies were naturally more flexible than men's, enabling them to perform a wider range of movements.

Beyond a general acceptance of the view that women and men had differing natural tendencies, however, there was no clear consensus among dancers about how gender distinctions should be rendered in movement. At the core of the issue for women's dances was the tension between maintaining the largely *tāṇḍava* character of the ritual-derived Kandyan dances while simultaneously embodying the ideals of Sinhala womanhood. The learning and transmission process illustrates the complexities of negotiating between these two apparently conflicting goals.

Learning and Transmission

Until the 1940s, male Kandyan dance students were trained in the manner of the classic *guru-śiṣya* model found throughout South Asia. The student lived in the home of the teacher, performed daily tasks and errands for him, and took lessons when they were offered. Once a student had mastered the twenty-four basic exercises and the basic elements of the dance, he was taught the major dances. But training was not confined to the teacher's home. Students, some as young as six or seven, also took part in rituals where they performed with their peers and senior dancers.

When I would ask older-generation ritual dancers and drummers how they learned to perform, they would often answer by reciting a standard phrase: *dăka purudda, āha purudda, kara purudda* which can be translated as "learning by seeing, learning by hearing, learning by doing." The Sinhala term *purudda* literally means "practice" or "habit," so the phrase conveys a sense of learning through repeated or habitual exposure and repetition.

This conception of how a performer learns—and its formulation in a standardized phrase—appears to be widespread in South Asian performance traditions. Richard Wolf notes that a *vīṇā* player in Tamil Nadu used the term *kēḷviñāṉam* or "hearing knowledge" to refer to how she learned to develop a particular rendition of a *kriti*. She was referring to the fact that she learned a piece of repertoire not by being taught directly but by hearing it played by others (Wolf, pers. comm., 2007). A highly skilled Kathakaḷi drumming student interviewed by Rolf Groesbeck always responded to Groesbeck's questions about how he mastered a particular drum pattern by saying *kēṭṭa paṭhiccu, kaṇṭa paṭhiccu:* "I learned by hearing, I learned by watching" (Groesbeck, this volume). Phillip Zarrilli notes that observation of one's elders and peers is a major teaching method in all of the arts of India (Zarrilli 1984b, 90).

The practice of observing and learning from one's peers is a well-established training technique in *kankāriya* and Kandyan dance training. *Kankāriya* dancers stress the importance of observing and performing in as many rituals as possible. At ritual performances, the less experienced dancers are positioned behind those more advanced. This method is also used by contemporary Kandyan dance teachers in classrooms, where the advanced students are placed at the front of the class so that others can observe them.

Learning by hearing, observing, and performing suggests a model of knowledge transmission based primarily on mimesis. But what happens when the gender

FIGURE 2.2. Dance class at Tittapajjala village dance school with teacher I. K. Samaraweera. Photo by Susan A. Reed.

of the student differs from that of the teacher? In the next section, I explore how the dynamics of gender (and to some extent class) have affected the transmission process.

Preserving Tradition or "Dancing Like a Man"?

In the late 1980s, during my first major period of field research, I took lessons in Kandyan dance with Peter Surasena, a dancer from a traditional family, considered by many the finest Kandyan stage dancer of his generation. My fellow students were two young women: my Sinhala research assistant and a German friend. Once a week we would meet for a two-hour class, practicing our steps on the unforgiving concrete stage of the Kandyan Arts Association pavilion. Because we were all beginners, we had no advanced women students on whom to model our dancing. Surasena demonstrated the steps for us, and we would do our best to imitate him. If we erred, he would replicate our mistakes, then show us the correct form. Indeed, at times, it seemed he danced almost as much as we did.

After a year of lessons in Kandy with Peter Surasena, I moved to Colombo, Sri Lanka's capital, to conduct research with dance students and teachers at the university-level Institute for Aesthetic Studies. Once a week Surasena came to the city to teach a group of upper-class Sri Lankan women at the home of Sicille Kotelawala, a well-known businesswoman and highly skilled Kandyan dancer. In her youth, Sicille had performed on stage with Peter and his elder brother, Heen Baba, including tours abroad to Europe and the United States.

One day I joined Surasena's class in Colombo, confident that, with my previous experience, I would easily fit in. But from the moment we began warming up with the twelve foot exercises, I was surprised to see that the style of these Colombo women was very different from mine. Their body positions were much more vertical ("Why aren't they in *măṇḍiya?*" I thought), their feet were positioned closer together, and their wrist and arm movements were soft, almost limp. Their movements were languid and graceful. When they jumped, their feet barely cleared the ground. The energy these dancers expended was a fraction of what I was accustomed to in my Kandy lessons. While in Kandy, we would be drenched in sweat after a few minutes' practice, here the dancers barely broke a sweat.

As I watched the Colombo dancers, I wondered if in fact *they* were dancing in the proper feminine style, and if they thought I "danced like a man" (a criticism I had heard leveled against women dancers in another context). It struck me that because I had studied with a male teacher and had spent most of my time observing male dancers, I had little sense of what constituted the proper feminine mode of dancing. If I had continued my classes with these ladies in Colombo, my style of dance no doubt would have been influenced by the process of peer-group immersion (Groesbeck, this volume).

Over many subsequent months of research with women and girl dancers, I came to realize that there was no consensus about a proper feminine style. Some women, including some teachers who were highly revered, danced as I did, in a manner that was closer to the traditional *tāṇḍava* style. Others, like the Colombo ladies, danced in a more gentle, fluid, and graceful manner.

In general, the older-generation Berava dancers (male and female) taught girls and women in the more traditional style. Many of these dancers were reluctant to make changes that in their view would sacrifice the aesthetic integrity of the dance, even as they acknowledged that women's dance should be different from men's. For example, some Berava consider it essential that women maintain a deep *măṇḍiya,* with its wide stance, low center of gravity, and widely outstretched arms. Other dancers consider this position too masculine: they have women take up a more vertical stance, draw their feet more closely together, and hold their arms closer to their bodies.

In interviews, many dancers, especially non-Berava, expressed concern that women were not learning to dance in a properly feminine way. Premakumara Epitavala, a well-known and respected upper-class male choreographer, blamed the teachers in the schools (who at the time of our interview were mostly Berava) for training girls to dance in a masculine way: "What is happening in the schools present day is not very good... in three to five minutes, very virile dancing with ten drums.... Recently I saw on the TV a girl raising her leg over the shoulder and dancing like a man: that is no good. But if the very same thing, the same step was done by a man that would have been very beautiful and more suitable" (pers. comm., 1987). Mrs. Esmee Jayasinghe echoed this view: "I think it is very beautiful when a girl dances like a girl. Sometimes we go to work as proctors in the examinations.... Some girls dance completely like boys.... If we dance beautifully with rhythm, in good form, we should dance slowly. That is gracefulness (*lalitya*).... When we see girls dance like boys at exams we feel sorry for them" (pers. comm., 1992).

Class identity was a significant factor in how dancers articulated what was considered properly feminine. Middle- and upper-class urban dancers were, in general, more concerned about what they viewed as the excessive masculinity of women's dance. Some urban middle-class dancers criticized the Berava, suggesting that they were ignorant of the need to feminize the dance. The Berava dancers, for their part, stressed the importance of maintaining the tradition, contending that the modifications introduced by urban middle-class dancers were destroying the traditional form.

The women dancers I knew who had been criticized for being "too *tāṇḍava*" brushed off the criticisms, asserting that they were dancing in the authentic traditional style. They much preferred the forceful and bold character of the ritual-based dances, and were able to legitimate their choice by referring to the dance's ritual roots.

Masculine and Feminine: Gender in Stage Performance

In the *kohoṃba kankāriya,* male dancers perform in both the *tāṇḍava* and *lāsya* styles. The group dances are danced in the *tāṇḍava* style, while the solo dances, which involve the consecration and offering of specific items to the deities, are performed in the *lāsya* mode. Solo dances are among the most important in the ritual, as signified by the fact that they are performed by the most senior, experienced dancers. Dancers take pride in their performances of these dances, and are highly respected for the grace and subtlety with which they are performed.

In stage dances, however, the meanings of *lāsya* and *tāṇḍava* have come to be defined much more rigidly, reifying essentialist notions of gender. Rather than signifying gracefulness and vigor respectively, *lāsya* and *tāṇḍava* have come to be equated with "feminine" and "masculine." The consequence of this is that dances that are defined as essentially *lāsya* are only performed by women, while those that are deemed to be essentially *tāṇḍava* are only performed by men. Thus, although in the *kankāriya* men perform the graceful betel-leaf offering dance (*bulat padaya*), it would nowadays be unthinkable for them to dance it on stage.

Though most Kandyan dances can, theoretically, be performed by men or women, in practice gender informs which are selected. As a general rule women perform the slower, more graceful dances, while men perform those that are more acrobatic and athletic. Of the popular *vannam* dances performed on stage, experienced dancers told me that the peacock, eagle, and majestic (*udāra*) *vannam* were most suitable for women, while the hare, horse (*turanga*), and conch shell (*gāhaka*) *vannam* were better suited to men.

Performing Masculinity: The Ves Dance

The *ves* dance is the most popular male stage dance, a vigorous and athletic dance typically performed as the climax of a dance concert. As the name of the dance suggests, the dancers perform while wearing the *ves* costume. The *ves* dance is usually an abbreviated version of a *kankāriya* dance, such as *yak ănuma,* "invitation to the deities." Like all *kankāriya* group dances, the *ves* dance includes sequences of competitive dancing. In these competitive segments, male dancers individually demonstrate their virtuosity and prowess by performing intricate patterns of steps, rapid pirouettes, and high jumps. Some dancers also perform acrobatic movements like handsprings and back flips, challenging others to surpass them.[9] Audiences respond enthusiastically to these displays of masculine bravado, showing their appreciation by clapping and whistling after each dancer's performance.

Women's dances, by contrast, do not include competitive sequences, nor do women perform acrobatic movements.[10] However, many young women dancers I interviewed at the Institute for Aesthetic Studies expressed a strong desire to perform competitively, and regretted that women's dances lacked this lively dimension of performance. Several of these students told me that one reason they would like to perform in a *kohoṃba kankāriya* (though they have been barred because of taboos related to traditional conceptions of women's impurity) was because the ritual would allow them to perform the lengthy phrases of improvisational and competitive dancing.

Reproducing the Demure: Pūja and Yuga Dances

The *pūja năṭuma,* or offering dance, is the paradigmatic women's dance, performed as an introductory dance in virtually all Kandyan dance stage concerts. Developed in the mid-twentieth century, the dance, which is derived from the betel-leaf offering dance (*bulat padaya*) of the *kankāriya,* presents an image of women that is in accord with the Sinhala ideal of modesty, restraint, and domesticity. Dressed in white or very light-colored costumes, and carrying small oil lamps cupped in their hands, the women dancers appear as the virginal hostesses of the performance, welcoming the audience, and conveying a warm, domestic image. Dancing slowly on a dimly lit stage, the women make offering gestures with the lamps. Because there is no altar to the deities (as there is in the *kankāriya*) the gestures of offering are made toward the audience. The mood of *pūja* is meditative and reserved.

While the ideal of the modest and demure woman is conveyed in some of the single-sex dances such as *pūja,* mixed-gender dances more vividly depict ideals of female submissiveness and subordination. Mixed-gender dances often display women in less powerful positions than they appear in all-female dances and thus tend to more sharply define gender stereotypes of strong, assertive males and graceful, responsive females. Emblematic of these mixed-gender dances is the modern dance-duet, *yuga năṭuma. Yuga* means "era," and the name of the dance can be translated as "dance of the modern era." Described to me by one dancer as a courtship dance designed to show the complementarity of the *lāsya* and *tāṇḍava* dance styles, the *yuga năṭuma* is considered a modern dance primarily because of its theme; the dance steps and movements are traditional.

The *yuga năṭuma* begins with the two dancers entering from the same side of the stage, performing the same movements, but in the *lāsya* and *tāṇḍava* styles. As the dancers enter, the male dancer is directly behind the female. His position is clearly one of dominance, as he is more imposing physically and his movements cover more territory. The man's stance and position vis-à-vis the woman is one of solicitous protection. His movements appear to contain hers, even as they mirror them.

Although many of the movements in the dance present this kind of mirroring, with the woman in front or dancing beside the man, there are also several moments when they dance apart, performing different movements. In a number of these segments, the woman shows her deference to the man. In one section, while he stands in a static pose, tall and stately, she bends down in a deep, low plié and gazes up at him. In another section, she performs this deep plié four times, twice to the right, twice to the left, while he does not defer to her in the same manner. In a later segment, he dances behind her, with his eyes looking upward, while she bows down her head, eyes downcast. He appears assertive, confident and bold, while she appears modest, subdued, and reserved.

Performing the Powerful Feminine: Vannam Dances

While dances like *pūja* and *yuga năṭuma* cast women in submissive and domestic roles that conform to notions of the conventional feminine ideal, many others, including some of the most popular, convey quite different images of the feminine. *Vannam* dances in particular are often performed by women in an assured and commanding manner. Unlike the *pūja* and *yuga* dances, which were choreographed to demonstrate feminine roles, the gender-neutral character of the *vannam* dances allows women to dance them in a variety of ways.

One of the most powerful performances I observed in Sri Lanka was of a group of advanced women students, all training to become dance teachers, performing the stately, majestic *gajagā* (elephant) *vannama.* One of the women performed the

FIGURE 2.3. Vaidyavathi Rajapakse performing a *vannama*. Photo by Susan A. Reed.

dance in the traditional style, as pure dance, while the others performed in the modern style, with mimetic gestures. All of the performers were highly skilled and danced with precision and presence. The precise figures they created were perfectly in accord with the powerful beats of the Kandyan drum. In the rapid climactic sections of the dance, though they did not jump as high or spin as fast as their male counterparts would have, they nonetheless conveyed an image of strength, agility, and composed confidence.

One of the reasons that the *vannam* provide such scope for interpretation is because they are classical—that is, ritually derived—dances. That women can perform them in a variety of styles, powerful as well as demure, assertive as well as subdued, reveals an ironic aspect to the feminization of Kandyan dance. Because the ritual dance tradition was male, a role for females in performance was not even addressed, much less codified or prescribed. This absence of a role defined as "proper" in the classical dance tradition thus allows women to dance in a style that they choose. Indeed, outside of state contexts, women even perform acrobatics in all-night rituals at Buddhist temples. Thus, the historic absence of women performers and of female roles in dance provides Sinhala women with open territory, the option of pushing the boundaries of what is considered suitable dance for their gender.

Modernity and the Sexualization of Kandyan Dance

The intent of the state in promoting Kandyan dance was to preserve a highly visible aspect of Sinhala culture and tradition as part of a nationalist agenda. In the first four decades of dance teaching in the government schools, from the 1940s to the '80s, the dominance of Berava male teachers ensured that the dance's meaning and form remained closely related to ritual practice. However, beginning in the 1980s, the younger generation of non-Berava dancers became more concerned with "developing," "modernizing," and expanding the dance than with sustaining its ritualistic significance. Though the state still retains much control over dance through the ritual-based curriculum, popular discourses of modernity and sexuality have increasingly come to shape women's dance, introducing new meanings into dance practices.

The state dance curriculum, which has been little altered since the time of its inception in the 1950s, has done much to ensure the continuity of Kandyan dance. The power of the curriculum in shaping the dance world of Sri Lanka can hardly be overstated, since the focus of training is in preparing students for the standardized exams. However, while the repertoire of dances has not changed much, there have been some important innovations in movement style, in particular, the incorporation of sexual movements.

In form and content, Kandyan dance is not erotic. Indeed, much of the success of the dance as a feminine art can likely be attributed to the fact that it lacks overt sexual movements or expression. While much of Kandyan dance—particularly the core classical dances—retains this nonsexual character, in the 1980s and '90s some Kandyan dances by women and by mixed gender groups were becoming increasingly more sexual in their movements, expressions, costuming, and themes.[11]

Tourist performances include some of the most sexualized female dancing. In the late 1980s, I observed a tourist performance in Kandy that included what my research assistant termed "cabaret-style" dancing. In the normally reserved *pūja* dance, for example, the women shook their hips and lifted their legs in a provocative manner. The most sexually charged dance was an eroticized version of the cobra dance, performed solo by a woman. Though there is a traditional classical dance known as the cobra (*nāga*) *vannama,* the cobra dance in this tourist venue bore little resemblance to it. The dancer wore a skin-tight black sequined costume, and slithered and writhed awkwardly on the floor of the stage in a dance that was clearly intended to titillate male viewers.

Choreographers for state troupes have also incorporated sexual movements into Kandyan dances for women and mixed gender groups. At a performance of the Kandy National Dance troupe organized by the Cultural Ministry in the late 1980s, I observed a performance of a modernized duet version of the classical *săvula* (rooster) *vannama* that had been choreographed by a traditional dancer based in Colombo. The dance was performed by a young man and woman, and the theme of the dance, as described by the choreographer, was the behavior of a rooster in the presence of his favorite hen. The piece was danced by the young couple in a highly flirtatious manner, with the hen and rooster provocatively eying each other, with lots of hip-swinging by the hen.

Even traditional *vannam* may now include brief moments of sexualized moves. The most common is hip-swinging by females, which I have seen inserted into performances of traditional *vannam* by even otherwise very conservative choreographers. Some younger-generation dance teachers now include sexualized movements in virtually all of the dances—classical or folk—performed by females.

The incorporation of sexual movements is not restricted to male choreographers. At a remote village dance school in the Kandyan hills, I observed very young girl students—some no more than four or five years old—performing a dance while swinging their hips, smiling flirtatiously, and flashing their eyes at the visitors in the audience. Their teacher, a young urban-educated woman, told me that she favored innovations (*nirmāṇa*) in dance, and that in order for the dance to "develop" (a term in Sri Lanka synonymous with modernity) that it had to be changed from the traditional male style. For her, the inclusion of hip-swinging, smiling, and expressive eyes made the dances more appropriately modern and feminine.

The incorporation of sexual movements suggests that the asexual ideal of Sinhala womanhood is perhaps not as hegemonic as scholars have often assumed. Anthropologist Malathi De Alwis has documented that, as early as the 1920s and '30s, Sinhala commentaries on feminine respectability included discussions of a "managed sexuality that is moral yet feminine and pleasurable" (De Alwis 1999, 186). De Alwis notes that though a woman was expected to be virtuous, she was also expected to "retain the suggestion of sexual attractiveness" and that a woman's dress should accentuate as well as clothe her body (De Alwis 1999, 186). In contemporary Sri Lanka, De Alwis found a similar emphasis on "managed sexuality" and attractiveness at a beauty contest where she had been invited to be a judge (De Alwis 1999, 187). The sexuality that is displayed by women in most dance performances seems to be "managed" in quite similar ways: there seems to be some degree of leeway in allowing to women to reveal their bodies and show their skills in flirtatious play.

The sexual movements that are most commonly performed in the "fun in the village" style of folk dances do not appear to be morally threatening to Sinhala audiences, and women who perform these flirtatious dances do not seem to risk tarnishing their reputations as "good girls."[12] I suggest that this may be the case because the Sinhala women dancers who perform them are seen to be performing in the character of the "village lass" and thus are not seen as expressing their own sexuality, but that of a rustic "other." By contrast, Sinhala women who perform social dances, such as *baila,* in a provocative manner are viewed as expressing their own desires, for which they can be roundly condemned (Hewamanne 2003, 87–90).

While some dancers view the sexualization of Kandyan dance as modernization, others see it as degradation, especially when it occurs in classical dances. When I asked my teacher, Peter Surasena, about some of the innovations younger dancers were introducing into the dance he replied by referring to a version of the *pūja* dance he had seen, and said emphatically "Asking a half naked girl to dance with betel-leaves in her hand is not the modernization of dance" (Surasena, pers. comm., 2000).

Dance, the Marriage Market, and the Fit Body

Another dimension of the sexualization of Kandyan dance is the way in which it has become incorporated into the marriage market. Today, for young women, studying Kandyan dance is seen as a means to become fit and attractive as well as refined and cultured. Mrs. Samarasinghe, a prominent upper-class teacher at one of Kandy's most prestigious girls' schools, told me that the main reason girls were now attracted to Kandyan dance was as a qualification for marriage, and not for "the art" ("Mrs. Samarasinghe" is a pseudonym). When I inquired about why girls dance, she replied: "Going to Kandyan dance classes has become fashionable now. In high-status ('big') families, the parent's ambition is not to have their daughters progress in the field, but to get their 'figures' (Eng.) in shape. Now some elite families say, 'my daughter has learned dancing and has certificates' and it has an influence as a qualification for marriage. In Sri Lanka now, when one says a girl has studied dancing, others would say: 'Ah, then this child's figure would be good and she has a good character'" (Samarasinghe, pers. comm., 1992).

Ceremonial debuts of Kandyan dancing, known as *kala eli mangallaya,* are organized by parents to signal their daughter's availability for marriage. These occasions appear to be modeled, in part, on the elaborate, highly publicized *arangetrams* (T. *araṅkēṟṟam*) of Bhāratanāṭyam sponsored by upper-class Tamil and Sinhala families in Colombo. Indeed, Mrs. Samarasinghe referred to the *kala eli mangallaya* as a "Kandyan dance *arangetram.*"

The goal of these *kala eli mangallaya*s, as one dancer told me, is as much to display the girl's "figure" as her "talent" (these are English terms commonly used by Sinhala speakers). One male consultant told me that, in his view, the main purpose of a *kala eli mangallaya* was to provide an opportunity for prospective grooms and their families to see the girl's body in an outfit that is much more revealing than the everyday dress of saris or skirts and blouses.

The use of dance for fitness rather than "art" is widespread in urban areas, for middle-aged as well as young women. While formerly, the ideal body type for Sinhala women was somewhat fleshy and full-figured, in the 1980s and '90s, the "fit" body emerged as a preoccupation of Sinhala women, at least in urban areas. To improve their figures, women now use Kandyan dance as a form of what Sinhalas refer to as "body exercise." Some middle-aged women students of Peter Surasena told my research assistant somewhat apologetically that their main interest in taking dance lessons was in losing weight.

The increased emphasis on the use of dance to enhance one's physical attractiveness, as well as the incorporation of sexualized movements, raises questions about Kandyan dance as a site of the objectification of women, in which women's bodies have become a kind of commodity on stage and for the marriage market. Though male dancers' bodies are also subject to scrutiny and evaluated for their fitness and attractiveness, women's physical appearance factors in much more heavily than it does for men in determining if they will be selected for advanced dance training or for a national troupe. One state official, for instance, told me that in-person dance auditions were made mandatory at high-level institutions to ensure that the girls who were admitted were attractive. If artistry and skill in the dance had been the sole criteria, students could have been selected based on their scores in the standardized exams.

That physical attractiveness is more important for women than men is exemplified by the comment of veteran female teacher Vaidyavathi Rajapakse referring to the problem of aging. As she told me: "Men can dance even after they lose their teeth. Even if they are old, have wrinkled skin, they can dance after they have tied *ves*. As women, we cannot do that. Only if we have a good body and are somewhat beautiful would people come to see us dance. . . . When a woman reaches thirty, she is considered too old for the stage" (pers. comm., 1992).

Women and Ritual Dance

While the sexualization of dance, the marriage market, and the use of dance for fitness suggest a secular dance world focused on women's bodies, in recent years some women dancers have undertaken a very different project: the expansion of women's dance into the realm of ritual. In November 2001, Miranda Hemalatha, a prominent and highly respected woman dancer, took the radical step of inducting five of her women students in the initiation ceremony of the *ves bǎndīma*, dressing them in the ornaments of the *ves* dancer, including the sacred *ves* headdress.[13]

Another *ves* initiation ceremony was held in 2003 at the Buddhist temple in Bellanvilla, in which seven women students from Mrs. Hemalatha's dance school were ordained. In the evening, at their *kala eli mangallaya*, the women performed traditional dances from the Kohoṃba kankāriya, including the vigorous dance of the invitation to the deities (*yak ǎnuma*), and the seven offering dances (*hat padaya*).[14]

Mrs. Hemalatha has continued to regularly initiate her students in the *ves* ceremony, and by June 2008 she had ordained a total of forty-five women dancers.[15] These women *ves* dancers perform in a wide variety of settings, including on stage, in weddings (as part of the bride's procession), and in major ritual processions associated with women, such as the Sanghamitta Perahăra.[16] Though they have not yet performed in a complete Kohoṃba kankāriya, Mrs. Hemalatha is hopeful that they will be able to do so in the near future.

One of Mrs. Hemalatha's reasons for initiating women into *ves* is pragmatic: as so few men are available to perform traditional dances, women need to take on their roles.[17] She and her students also see the act as an affirmation of women. As she noted in a recent interview, women choose to become *ves* dancers because it gives them a sense of "female pride" (*kāntā abhimānayak*) (M. Hemalatha, pers. comm., 2008). She dismisses as foolish the idea that women are impure, noting that the sacred tooth relic of the Buddha was brought to Lanka hidden in the hair of a woman. Countering the criticisms of those opposed to women wearing *ves,* and highlighting the fact that sexualized dancing has become widespread, Mrs. Hemalatha has remarked that it is better to have women performing in the traditional *ves* costume than dancing on stage "half nude."[18]

While Miranda Hemalatha's revolutionary act has been opposed by some, she and her students state that, overall, the public response has been positive. She has also received support and encouragement from prominent Berava dancers, and Berava drummers have performed at the initiation ceremonies. Although the long-term impact of Mrs. Hemalatha's daring innovation remains to be seen, it vividly illustrates how the practice of Kandyan dance has been used by women in ways that both defy and support Sinhala ideas of the feminine. While women *ves* dancers challenge centuries-old ideas of female impurity and expand women's dance practices into the realm of ritual, they simultaneously support the ideal of feminine sexual modesty.

Conclusion

Though the conventional ideal of the respectable feminine has been a major influence on the ways in which Kandyan dance has developed, it is also clear that both the ideal and the dance tradition have changed over the last several decades since women began performing. Although virginity and domesticity are still highly valued, and though women dancers must be careful to protect their reputations on and offstage, the arena of Kandyan dance has also given women opportunities to push the limits in defining what is considered properly feminine.

As a formerly male tradition, the Kandyan dance has given women wide scope for interpretation and transformation. Women can perform in modes powerful and commanding, modest and reserved, or both in the same dance or performance event. They can play at being flirtatious or they can be made into objects of desire. They can perform in ways that suggest deference to males, or they can dance so skillfully that they put their male counterparts to shame. For women and girls, Kandyan dance is a space of freedom, play, and creativity as well as of restriction and containment: a site for the creation of new modes of objectification and subordination, a means to affirm and expand the idea of the respectable feminine, and a potent resource enabling women to express themselves in new and empowering ways.

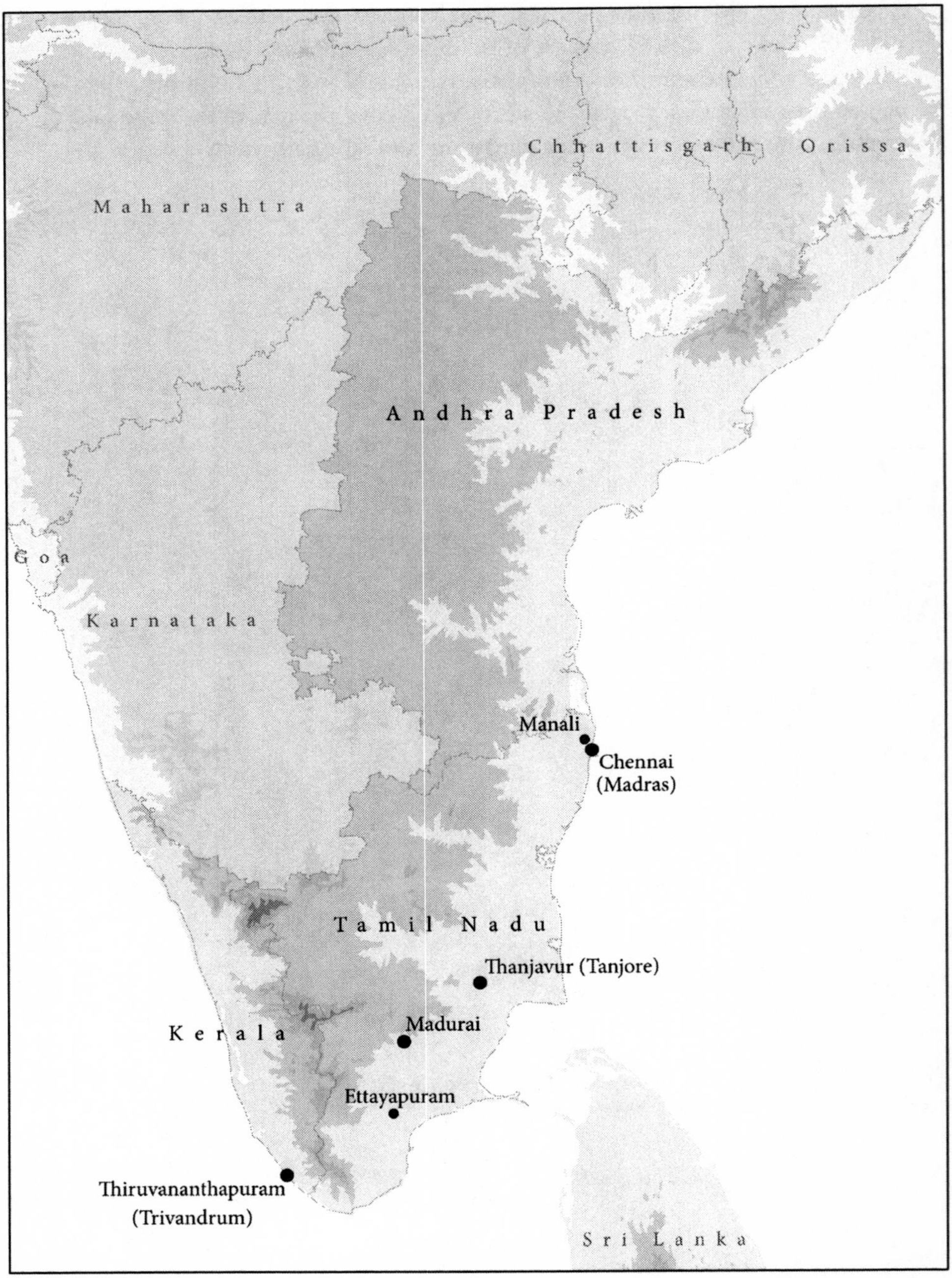

Chhattisgarh
Orissa
Maharashtra
Andhra Pradesh
Goa
Karnataka
Manali
Chennai
(Madras)
Tamil Nadu
Thanjavur (Tanjore)
Madurai
Kerala
Ettayapuram
Thiruvananthapuram
(Trivandrum)
Sri Lanka

CHAPTER 3
Listening to the Violin in South Indian Classical Music

AMANDA WEIDMAN

Two narratives dominate the story of Indian music in relation to the West. One revolves around the idea of "Westernization" or "modernization," in which Western elements and ideas are assimilated into a preexisting Indian musical tradition. The other is a narrative in which Indian music develops on its own, impervious to foreign, and therefore superficial, influences. Central to both of these narratives is a notion of authenticity based on the imagination of an essentially Indian core, on the one hand, and Western or "outside" influences on the other.

One of the problems of "Westernization" narratives is that they oversimplify the dynamics and consequences of the colonial encounter. Such narratives imply that Indian music existed as such before the arrival of "Westerners," and then was selectively impacted by "Western" musical practices and ideas. It suggests that one could presumably strip away the "Western" influences and be left with the pure core of Indian music. The notion of Indian music as basically developing on its own, independent of its circumstances, is reflected in another mode of scholarship that relies on an ideological separation between "actual musical practice" and colonial and nationalist discourse *about* music in India. For instance, Gerry Farrell's *Indian Music and the West* (1997), a book ostensibly about the encounter of the West with Indian music in the nineteenth and twentieth centuries, ironically seems to invest in an idea of "Indian music" as an essentially stable field free from the unstable realm of politics and the whims of "the West." Accordingly, his analysis allows only for the coming together of spectacularly different elements: the use of "Indian" motifs in Western parlor songs for piano; the use of the sitar in Western pop music in the 1960s. Such examples are certainly worth discussing, but Farrell's alignment of them seems to suggest that the story of Indian music and the West can be told adequately in terms of such spectacular misfits, misguided Western appropriations of a preexistent and independent entity known as "Indian music." None of the cases he discusses threaten the integrity of what he calls "Indian music." Although Farrell is critical of the Western notion that Indian music is "in some way deeply unknowable," his own position unwittingly seems to fall within such attitudes (Farrell 1997, 2). His approach preserves a pristine place for Indian music; for him, it is an entity that exists before and after two centuries of "misunderstanding" on the part of the West, going on "developing and adapting as it would, largely impervious" to the debates and appropriations to which it is subjected (1997, 54).

In this chapter I suggest that these narratives are not adequate for understanding the relationship between music in India and music in the West. Because they assume an unchanging, essential core that makes Indian music Indian, they limit our understanding of the historical circumstances under which that "core" has been constructed. I argue here that what we call "Indian music" might be better viewed as a product of colonial and postcolonial encounters through which the categories of "Indian" and "Western" have been created and negotiated. In order to understand the dynamics of these negotiations, it is necessary for us to attend to the ways in which what we now know as "classical music" in India was formed out of local encounters and historical contingencies. Instead of attempting to separate musical practice and discourse about music, looking at how they are intertwined can bring us closer to recognizing the socially constructed nature of musical sound and the affect it produces (cf. Qureshi 2000).

The colonial encounter changed musical practices and discourses about music in south India. What I argue here is that the new practices and discourses that resulted, and that became part of the redefinition of Karnatak music as south India's own "classical" music are specifically colonial in the way they posit both opposition and commensurability between the "classical" music of India and the "classical" music of the West. One of the dominant ways of describing south Indian classical music is that—unlike Western classical music, which is largely instrumental—it is a primarily vocal music. Indeed, this seems only logical. Singing is recognized as the primary way of acquiring musical knowledge, south Indian compositions all have words, and all concerts of south Indian classical music either feature a vocalist as soloist or an instrumentalist whose instrumental technique is built around imitating the sound of the singing voice.

Such seemingly self-evident truths have been used as the basis for a powerful ideologization of the voice in twentieth-century discourse about south Indian classical music. Essential to the largely upper-caste, middle-class project of defining an indigenous "classical" music tradition in south India was the goal of making south Indian music commensurate with the classical music of the West. At the same time as south Indian elites emphasized the comparability of Western and Indian classical music, however, they recognized that in order to be truly Indian, Karnatak music had to be different in reliable and enduring ways. T. V. Subba Rao, a lawyer and one of the founding members of the Madras Music Academy, for instance, imagined music as a safeguard of Indian distinctiveness and difference: "That East is East and West is West and never the twain shall meet is particularly applicable to music," he wrote in his *Studies in Indian Music* (1962, 7). Much of the discourse on music from the early twentieth century revolves around finding and articulating this difference that would set south Indian classical music apart from its counterpart in the West. The voice—the vocal nature of Indian music and its ties to oral tradition—came to stand for this essential difference (see Weidman 2006). In twentieth-century south India, the voice came to be associated with Indianness and not Westernness, originality and not reproduction, humanness and not mechanicalness, tradition and not modernity. The voice came to be privileged as Karnatak music's locus of authenticity, the preserver of its tradition in the face of modernity.

One of the problems with a description of Karnatak music that centers on the voice is what it leaves out, such as the basic fact that there are always other instruments on stage with a Karnatak vocalist. Leaving aside the question of what role the percussion instruments play, I would like to focus on an obvious but neglected presence on the Karnatak stage: the violin. What is a violin doing on stage with the vocalist, and a European violin, at that? What can we learn from shifting our attention from the seemingly central voice to a seemingly marginal accompanying instrument?

In attempting to answer these questions, I place the violin and its role in defining the aesthetics of Karnatak music in a specific historical context. I show how specific styles and instrumental technique embody a socially constructed musical aesthetic. I begin with the early history of the violin in south India. In the early nineteenth century, when it was introduced by the British at Fort St. George in Madras, the violin was mainly an instrument for Scottish jigs and reels, French dancing songs, and English marching tunes, rather than an instrument of Western classical music. In the twentieth century, upper-caste elites interested in what they termed the "revival" of south India's classical music rejected the old "fiddle" image in favor of a classicized "violin" whose counterpart was the classical violin of the West.[1] Around the same time, the violin became the main instrument for accompanying the voice. I discuss the role of the violin as accompaniment, and in doing so show the significance of this generally neglected element of South Asian musical tradition. In the second half of this chapter, I show how changes in violin style in the twentieth century indicate changing aesthetics of the voice. Finally, I consider the central role of the violin in various twentieth-century musical experiments that attempt to rearticulate the relationship between Karnatak and Western music.

The Violin in South India

Unlike the golden age of India, placed in Orientalist accounts in the precolonial era, the golden age of Karnatak music, in conventional south Indian accounts, is usually placed at the peak of British colonialism, the early to mid-nineteenth century. The so-called "trinity" of composers—Thyagaraja (1767–1847), Syama Sastri (1762–1827), and Muthuswamy Dikshitar (1776–1835)—who are said to have revolutionized the sound and practice of Karnatak music were all active during this period. Even more extraordinary is the fact that while they were composing their masterpieces, a new instrument was changing the sound, practice, and repertoire of Karnatak music: the European violin. The violin was taken up and adapted by south Indian musicians shortly after its arrival around the last decades of the 1700s; its tuning, playing position, and technique gradually altered. The alteration of the instrument in present-day south India involves tuning the strings to parallel octaves (for instance, GDGD instead of the Western classical tuning of GDAE), increasing the space between the strings slightly (since double-stops are not generally important), and using a heavier bow. The violinist, like other Karnatak musicians, sits on the floor with the top of the violin resting on his or her shoulder or chest, and the scroll braced against his or her ankle or foot, so that the instrument is at a forty-five-degree angle to the ground. The various playing techniques share an element of sliding along the fingerboard to produce what south Indian listeners identify as a "vocal" sound.

Exactly where the violin first came to south India, and who adapted it first to Karnatak music are matters of some contention. One story is that the violin was brought to Madras in the late eighteenth century, probably by colonial officials with musical hobbies. According to this story, Baluswamy Dikshitar (1786–1858), from a Brahmin family, the younger brother of the composer Muthuswamy Dikshitar, moved with his father to Manali, a village near Madras, around 1800 or slightly before. Attracted by the English band music at Fort Saint George in Madras, Baluswamy expressed the desire to learn European music. Manali Chinniah Mudaliyar, the son of the *dubash* (assistant, ambassador, interpreter) to the governor of Madras, and the trustee of the Manali temple and patron of many musicians at that time (Raghavan 1944, 129), engaged a European violinist from Madras to teach him violin. During his three years of lessons Baluswamy managed to adapt the violin to Karnatak music; although the account doesn't mention this explicitly (Sambamoorthy 1984, s.v. Bālasvāmi Dīkshitar). Baluswamy then returned to Tiruvarur, near the thriving royal court of Tanjavur, the principal "seat" of Karnatak music before Madras (Seetha 1981). Baluswamy's performances made the violin known in south India. The Maharaja of Ettayapuram, a small state south of Madurai, was so taken with Baluswamy's violin music that he appointed him to be a court violinist (*samasthāna vidvān*) in 1824 (Sambamoorthy

1984, s.v. Bālasvāmi Dīkshitar). Later, the composer Muthuswamy Dikshitar came from Tanjavur to Ettayapuram and heard his brother Baluswamy play European music on the violin.

Another story has it that the site of the violin's first transformation was the royal court of Tanjavur, where the Maharaja Serfoji had appointed the Tanjore quartet, four brothers from what is now called the *icai veḷḷāḷar* community, as court musicians and dancers (Subrahmanyam 1980, 47).[2] Vadivelu (1810–68), the youngest of the brothers, was a disciple of Muthuswamy Dikshitar. Vadivelu also studied Western violin with the missionary Christian Friedrich Schwartz, who, having developed a friendly relationship with the royal court of Tanjavur, had set up his headquarters there (Seetha 1981, 103). Muthuswamy Dikshitar later composed songs based on Western tunes Vadivelu had shown him. The composer Thyagaraja used to sing to the accompaniment of Vadivelu and would sometimes ask just to hear the violin by itself (Subrahmanyam 1980, 48). The quartet was dismissed from Serfoji's court when Maharaja Serfoji and the brothers had a disagreement over their rights in the temple at Tanjavur. Not long afterward, in 1830, they found another post in the court of Swati Tirunal (1813–47) at Trivandrum, where Vadivelu became an intimate associate of the composer-king and taught violin to several of his court musicians. In 1834, Swati Tirunal presented Vadivelu with an ivory violin and a bow made of an elephant's tusk, with the eagle, emblem of the Trivandrum royal court, inscribed on it (Subrahmanyam 1980, 49).

A third version of the violin's entry into south India concerns Varahappayyar (1795–1869), the superintendent of court musicians for Maharaja Serfoji of Tanjavur (Seetha 1981, 258) and later his trusted minister. When Serfoji wished to negotiate with the governor of the Madras presidency, he sent his English-speaking minister, Varahappayyar (Jayarama Iyer 1985, 27). A musical negotiation seems to have resulted, whereby the governor showed Varahappayyar the violins and piano in his music room and Varahappayyar played Indian melodies on them. This so impressed the Western musicians that they taught him a few violin techniques: "This news reached the ears of the governor . . . [who] being very music-minded asked him to play before him. In order to please him and have his political mission fulfilled, he agreed to play before the governor (otherwise he would have preferred to play it to his Maharaja first). He took the violin and played some Indian melodies to the pleasure of the governor" (Jayarama Iyer 1985, 27). The governor presented the violin and a piano to Varahappayyar, who returned to Tanjavur and impressed the Maharaja. According to this version, Varahappayyar later taught Vadivelu violin, and it was only after this that the potential of the violin was fully realized and more violins were brought to Tanjavur.

The Western music to which the first Indian players of the violin were exposed was predominantly Irish and Scottish fiddling, rather than what we now think of as Western classical violin. The evidence for this comes from what could be one of the first violin experiments: Muthuswamy Dikshitar's European Airs. In a volume of these "airs" culled from other sources, more than forty compositions of Dikshitar are listed (and notated) with the names of the European songs—such as "Limerick," "Castilian Maid," "Lord MacDonald's Reel," "Voulez-vous Danser?," and "God Save the Queen"—on which they are based (Sankaramurthy 1990, xiv). Muthuswamy Dikshitar probably heard many of these melodies played on the violin by his brother or other court violinists during his travels.

Other composers also show the influence of European tunes in their work. Swati Tirunal, for instance, appointed Western musicians to his court. His *varṇam*[3] in the raga *śaṅkarābharaṇam,* whose pitch intervals are equivalent to those of the Western major scale, includes a passage at the end that sounds distinctly like a European marching band. Unlike the other sections of the *varṇam,* the last section breaks the conventions of Karnatak music by employing large intervallic leaps and a minimum of *gamaka.* One principle of the *varṇam* genre is to lay out possibilities for the permutations of phrases in a raga (see Wolf, this volume). In the early nineteenth century, the possibilities of a raga evidently included tunes that sound almost Western. Meanwhile, several compositions of Thyagaraja suggest strains of Scottish reels or waltzes, composed in unique ragas with suggestive names like *jingla.* Pattnam Subramania Iyer (ca. 1840–1910), a disciple of Thyagaraja, composed his well-known *Raghuvamsa Sudha* in a raga called *katanakutukulam,* which he had invented out of a modified version of the Western major scale. The raga specifies large intervals and almost no *gamaka.* This composition and a variety of other "English notes" or "Western notes," as they are called, are staple fare at the end of many instrumental concerts of Karnatak music today. These items remind us that the violin served, in the mid-nineteenth century, as a potent vehicle for the translation of Western musical forms and aesthetics into a Karnatak form and idiom.

The Violin as Accompaniment

The idea of the violin as the perfect accompaniment to the voice became prevalent in the early twentieth century, when the social context of Karnatak music was shifted to the concert hall.[4] Without amplification, the volume of the voice was no longer adequate for audiences of more than a handful of people in the large, noisy spaces of Madras city. Some kind of accompaniment was needed to make the melodic line audible above the din of the city without jeopardizing its delicacy; the violin, already widely in use in south India, seemed a natural solution. Ramachandra Rao states that the first violinist to accompany vocalists in concerts was Tirukkodikaval Krishna Iyer (1857–1913), followed by a number of other violinists who lived into the first half of the twentieth century (1994, 5). Violin accompaniment provided more opportunities for violinists in the newly burgeoning concert culture of Madras; once it became necessary for vocalists to be accompanied, violinists were in demand. A list of south Indian musicians, compiled in 1917, included more than a hundred violinists, many of whom were described as accompanying artists (Pandithar 1917, 159).

The practice and aesthetic of the instrumentally accompanied voice is pervasive in South Asian musical traditions. The accompanying instrument, however, does more than simply repeat what the soloist sings; not only does it impart a particular sound quality, but the relationship, both musical and social, between soloist and accompanist stages the voice in a particular way. The violin, in accompanying, can influence the soloist's voice. Thus, we might ask: What was the effect of putting an instrument with colonial origins in this role? How did the violin change and/or create the voice it was merely supposed to accompany?

Accompaniment in Karnatak music involves a mixture of support and competition, imitation and creativity, shape-giving and self-effacement.[5] We can get a sense of this from a description of the violinist's duties by P. Sambamoorthy, who became known as one of the great modernizers of Karnatak music.[6] In his 1952 article titled "Kachchēri Dharma" (concert etiquette), Sambamoorthy wrote of the violinist that: "It is his duty to *figurate* [sic] the music of principal performer... by giving judicious emphasis on sangatis and gamakas.... He should not be hasty in deciphering rare ragas and eduppus.[7] He should remember that rare ragas and intricate eduppus are traps set for him by his (not very friendly) chief to catch him unawares.... His responses to his chief's ālāpana and kalpana *swaras* should... not run counter to the train of musical thoughts of his chief" (Sambamoorthy 1984, s.v. Kachchēri Dharma). What is involved in this idea of "figuration"? It indicates precisely the tension between visibility and invisibility, audibility and inaudibility, sameness and difference. At stake here is not representation of the voice, but a kind of partial repetition. The violinist plays something that is not quite the same as what the vocalist sings, but close enough to give the vocalist's sound a greater presence, a recognizable form. In contemporary musical practice, the role of the violinist as accompanist is to "double" whatever the vocalist sings, either in unison, or, during improvised parts, slightly behind. In reality, however, an accompanying violinist has great power over a soloist. For instance, at any point in a section of raga *ālāpana,* a free-time improvised elaboration of the raga, the violinist can choose either to dwell on a single note, reproduce the entire phrase that the vocalist has sung, highlight only the end of the phrase, or play something that the vocalist has not sung at all.[8] What the violinist chooses to play will often determine what the vocalist sings next. Indeed, the best accompanists, one vocalist told me in 1998, make the soloist sound better by covering up "imperfections" and by giving the vocalist ideas about what to sing next. Vocalists often talk of accompanists as inspiring, but also complain that they dominate soloists.

A skillful accompanist is an expert in mimesis, and thus also in dissimulation. My violin teacher, who had worked for twenty-five years as a staff violinist for All India Radio, described her job as the accompanist on call for whichever vocalist might be singing in terms of technological reproduction, using English words to talk about what the violinist had to do. One had to be ready for whatever the vocalist sang and get it "typed" in one's brain after the first line, like a "recording." Often the work meant accompanying compositions the violinist had never heard before; in these cases, it was a matter of knowing the raga and its particular phrases, observing the tala, and being on the ready; one had to "adjust" (the English term musicians often use for faking or fudging something) so that one blended in but sounded confident at the same time. One did not have to know the words of the composition or even remember it afterward, as long as one could imitate realistically enough. Another violinist told me that a certain vocalist preferred her accompaniment because it blended so well that she forgot there was anybody accompanying her at all.

The delicacy and fragility of this accompanying operation stands in contrast to its importance: with poor accompaniment, even the best singer sounds incomplete. If the accompaniment is off-kilter, a concert listener once told me, the whole thing is ruined. In accompaniment, one can't play too much, or the subtlety of the accompaniment is destroyed. On the other hand, the violinist is there partly to provide intonation. Many vocalists, particularly when improvising at fast speed, dispense with intonation and simply belt out the *svara* names, letting the violinist play the actual pitches.

Style and Sound: Three Ways of Imitating the Voice

Musical practice and sound embody social ideologies. Indeed, those elements considered to be the most "natural," "necessary," and "obvious" are often the most highly ideologized. Having the violin accompany the voice in Karnatak music is considered to be utterly natural, and the idea that the violin imitates the sound of the voice so obvious that it hardly merits comment. And yet melodic accompanists do much more than imitate a prior and fully formed voice. This invites us to investigate how interactions between the violin and the voice have, over time, affected the sound of both the violin and the voice. The voice has not been a stable, unchanging referent, but has rather been constructed as part of a complex postcolonial politics of sound.

Three styles of violin playing in south India have come into fashion during the twentieth century. No figure is more emblematic of Karnatak music's modernity than the famous violinist Dwaram Venkataswamy Naidu, who came from an unknown family in Andhra Pradesh to dominate the Madras music world from the 1930s to the 1960s.[9] In 1962, the musicologist B. V. K. Sastry wrote about Dwaram that "his reverence for the classical tradition is tempered with the spirit of inquiry of the scientific age.... Unfettered by *gurukula* traditions, he is subject to few inhibitions and freely avails himself of the best ideas from everywhere, if these harmonize with classical Karnatak traditions" (Sastry 1962, 33). Dwaram was hailed as "the best violinist of the day," universally praised for the imaginativeness and violinistic qualities of his music, often referred to as the "Dwaram touch." Coming not from a family of great musicians, but one of military men and railroad officials, he was largely self-taught. He was greatly influenced by Western violin technique, especially with regard to the bow, which he used to give accents, emphasis, and dynamics. He listened to records of the European violinist Fritz Kreisler and is fabled to have charmed Yehudi Menuhin into letting him play his own violin after demonstrating the gentleness of his touch and respect for Western technique. At the height of his fame in the 1940s and '50s, Dwaram was visited nightly by Indian ministers of parliament and other government officers, who would bring him records of Western classical music and commission him to incorporate them into his playing. If the record was brought at eight in the evening, Dwaram would sit until the wee hours listening to the record one hundred times, counting his auditions with the aid of tamarind seeds. By the next evening, he would have something new in store for the visitors.[10]

A man of eclectic tastes, Dwaram also incorporated many features of Hindustani music into his playing; he said that he appreciated the purity of tone and intonation, and the slow, meditative pace of much Hindustani music. In the 1950s, he stopped accompanying vocalists and played solo until his death in 1964. Dwaram was known for his treatment of rare ragas and his revival of many of Thyagaraja's and others' "Western notes." The characteristics of his playing were described by several as: a judicious use of speed; a generally slower unfolding of elaboration in his *ālāpanas*; a sparse use of *gamakas* "only where necessary," and generally less *jāru* (sliding).[11] A student of Dwaram told me in 1998 that the violin "did not play in his hands; it spoke." When I asked how it spoke, she said it was through the bowing and the trills and *piṭis* (from the Tamil verb *piṭi,* to catch or grab) he used to pronounce the words of the song on his violin.

It is these very characteristics that make Dwaram's playing sound old-fashioned and out-of-style to many south Indian listeners at the turn of the twenty-first century. A young violinist told me in 1998 that the Dwaram style was no longer suitable to Karnatak music: it was too slow and plain and the bowing too rough, all right for solos but no good for accompanying vocalists. From the 1960s on, two more distinct styles had created revolutions in the Karnatak violin world. One was the Lalgudi style, so named after Lalgudi Jayaraman (b. 1930). Born to a family of violinists, Lalgudi Jayaraman moved with his family to Madras in the 1950s, accompanied many vocalists, and began playing solo from 1957 onward. According to one player in the Lalgudi style, the violin should exhibit softness and sweetness, as if the voice were singing and pronouncing ("voice *pāṭaṛa mātiri uccarika mātiri*"). By keeping the bow on the string, the violinist should strive for continuity and avoid *karakkarappu* (a Tamil onomatopoeic term that iconically represents broken up, rough, or discontinuous sound). The words are to be pronounced by means of fewer *piṭi*s and trills and more *jāru;* the sweetness of the Lalgudi style is in the way it reproduces the singing voice without any of the roughness of a human voice.[12]

A third style, known as the Parur style, also became popular in the 1960s and remains the preferred style at present. Its most famous representative, and the one who popularized it, is M. S. Gopalakrishnan (b. ca. 1935; popularly known as M.S.G.). His father, Parur Sundaram Iyer, though originally from Kerala, spent time in Bombay in the 1940s and there studied Hindustani music; M.S.G. himself later studied Hindustani music independently and has given Hindustani concerts. The hallmark of the Parur style is virtuosic speed and range. Here the technique is completely devoid of *piṭi*s; one or two fingers are used in a constant sliding motion along the fingerboard to produce a cascading effect. There is relatively little emphasis given with the bow. The result is a sound that is very vocal but with no vestige of speech: the kind of sound that is more recognizable to contemporary Western ears as "Indian music." M.S.G. gave several public demonstrations in which he showed off a special bowing technique he used—a kind of *spiccatto* in which one long bow is divided into discrete, even units—playing in such a manner for twenty minutes straight. In this style, the use of technique to enunciate the words of compositions gives way to technique developed to exploit the possibilities of speed and virtuosity on the violin. A young violinist in Madras remarked to me in 1998 that the Parur style was the most suited to vocal accompaniment because it captured the speed and cascading effect of virtuosic vocal style.

These three revolutions in violin style reveal a more general change in Karnatak violin playing in the twentieth century: the switch from a *piṭi* style full of trills and catches, where the bow is also used to give emphasis, to a style with wider and more fluid *gamakas* (often called "weepy" by its detractors but *gāyaki*—meaning vocal or voicelike—by its admirers) where the technique relies on sliding along the fingerboard with only one or two fingers, and the bowing is constant.[13] Early recordings of violin playing, from before Dwaram Venkataswamy Naidu's time, reveal a general style that used fingered runs (rather than *jāru*) for speed, as well as numerous trills and catches; the violinists of the 1990s, by contrast, sound much more florid.[14]

In the Madras of the 1960s, the question of which style to emulate was a pressing issue for violinists.[15] That the more fluid, smoother style had become prevalent in the 1990s suggests that something in the notion of the voice had changed.

The reproducible qualities were no longer words and phrases but a generalized, homogenized, virtuosic voice, a voice heavily influenced by the violin. Even in 1939, C. Subrahmanya Ayyar noted that vocalists in south India had begun to increase their tempos in order to match the capabilities of the violin (Subrahmanya Ayyar 1939, 115). Several vocalists remarked to me that much present-day vocal technique—not only the virtuosic speed that many vocalists command today but also the *gamaka*s that define the sound of contemporary Karnatak music—are actually attempts to match the sound and capabilities of this virtuosic violin.

The Violin in Musical Fusions

In addition to being an indispensable accompanying instrument, the violin has, throughout the twentieth century, also been at the center of musical experiments that articulate both its intimate relationship to colonialism and its seeming ability to reverse colonialism's effects. Here I examine several such experimental pieces in which the violin acts as a kind of translator or interpreter, a vehicle through which Karnatak music and Western music can communicate.

In the 1930s and '40s, two violin-and-piano experiments were released in Madras. One was the brothers Muthu and Mani playing the Thyagaraja *kriti* "Nagumomu," for violin, piano, and mridangam. The other was Dwaram Venkataswamy Naidu playing a set of raga *ālāpana* improvisations with the American pianist and composer Alan Hovhaness on the piano.[16] In both, the violin played in traditional Karnatak style, and the piano acted as an accompaniment in the Karnatak sense, trailing and highlighting the main melody. In Muthu and Mani's piece, released on record in the 1930s, the *kriti,* in the raga *abheri,* with its unornamented notes and fast fingered passages, already suggested a Scottish flavor. The piano followed the violin, accompanying the same passage, when it was repeated, with different harmonies. In the *ālāpana* experiment, which was aired over All India Radio in the 1940s, the piano attempted to capture the violin's *gamakas,* particularly its slides and oscillations. The resulting impression, and perhaps desired effect, was that the violin seemed to be pulling the *ālāpana* in the direction of a traditional Karnatak elaboration, while the piano seemed to alight on various harmonies, longing for but never quite reaching resolution. The magic of the violin was its ability to lead the piano, without being dominated by the harmonic laws of Western music.

Since the 1980s these kinds of experiments, or "fusions," have become more self-conscious in the way they articulate Indian music with Western music. In his fusion album "How to Name It?" (1986), the film music director Illayaraja featured a piece entitled "I Met Bach in My House and We Had a Conversation," in which a Karnatak violin "accompanies" Bach's prelude to his third partita for violin. The piece starts with the solo violin's *ālāpana,* beginning in a typical Karnatak way but then building up to a virtuosic pitch, as if the violin is expecting a Western denouement. The Karnatak violin, amplified to a rich tone, contrasts with the orchestra of Western violins in the background, creating a sense of proximity for the listener. This violin answers the orchestrated version of Bach's partita, while, in the second half, actual voices (those of the composer Illayaraja and the Karnatak violinist, V. S. Narasimhan), articulate, or translate, parts of the melody using *sargam* syllables. The effect is as if we are returning, via the wonders of multitrack recording, to a scene of first contact, perhaps the arrival of the European violin in India, but from the perspective of the Karnatak musician. Here is the description in the liner notes:

> "I Met Bach in My House" begins with an invocation that at first is contemplative, introspective, and becomes increasingly importunate; it comes to a climax, and is interrupted by the first notes of Bach's Prelude to his violin Partita III. The Prelude is soon played out in full brilliant dialogue with Indian instruments, a contrapuntal weaving that seems completely natural. Nor does it seem strange when voices break in spontaneously, in rapturous song, and we hear the Prelude articulated at speed in Indian solfeggio, so neatly, so fluently, that a great light dawns—the two musical cultures, Indian and Western—share a common ground, far more than is commonly perceived.

Here, then, the Karnatak violin literally articulates Karnatak music with Western music, providing a magical medium of sound through which the voice can enter and interpret Bach.

In Kunnakudi Vaidyanathan's "Magic Violin" (1998), belligerently subtitled "Everything Personal about It," the object seems to be not so much interpreting as outwitting. Kunnakudi had already used his violin to work other kinds of magic: in the 1970s, he released an album called "Cauvery" (after the river Kaveri, on whose banks Karnatak music is fabled to have been born) in which he, with only the aid of his violin, claimed to capture all the sounds of life along and in the river. Also in the 1970s, he started playing with *tavil* (the drum usually used to accompany the double-reed *nāgasvaram* and therefore exclusively played by non-Brahmins), raising eyebrows in the classical world. This, along with his renditions of film songs on violin, was part of his image as a violinist of the people. In "Magic Violin," Kunnakudi's violin, amplified with echo effects, "takes on" and "conquers" the computer, which is playing flattened, lifeless, synthetic versions of Western chords. The computer, equated with the West, in turn is equated with the world; on the cover of his cassette, Kunnakudi sits, larger than life, astride a cushion floating in space, with the planet earth in the background. The tracks have appropriately cosmic titles: "A Thing of Beauty," "Full Moon," "Eclipse," and "Creation." Kunnakudi's violin, with its bewildering rhythmic effects, dances above the computer, outwitting it every time.

Other uses of the violin in "fusions" abound. A history of the violin in this regard is beyond the scope of this chapter, but a few more recent examples show how prominent the violin has been in making Karnatak music known in the world music market. Experiments that mix Karnatak music with jazz include Shakti, a fusion group active in the 1970s in which L. Shankar played the violin,[17] and L. Subramaniam's collaborations with jazz violinist Stephane Grappelli ("Conversations" 1992) and guitarist Larry Coryell ("From the Ashes" 1999), as well as his album "Global Fusion" (1999). Recent attempts to combine Karnatak music and Western classical music include L. Subramaniam's collaboration with Yehudi Menuhin (1988) on the fortieth anniversary of India's independence, Subramaniam's "Fantasy on Vedic Chants" for Karnatak violin and orchestra, which debuted in 1985,[18] and the album "Resonance" (2001), by the Madras String Quartet, in which Karnatak *kritis* are orchestrated for string quartet. This is of course only a partial list.

Many of the experiments that use the violin seem to have a common logic: through the violin, they rearticulate the relationship between Karnatak music and the music of the West. But in so doing, they comment ironically on the desire, shared by an Indian middle class who look to it as "tradition" and by Western consumers alike, for a recognizably Indian music unaltered by the colonial encounter. Rather, they present in each case a music profoundly affected by colonialism. It is the "magic" of the violin that Karnatak music is not weakened, but rather strengthened, by the encounter; each experiment reenacts and fulfills Karnatak music's stubborn insistence that it be considered on a par with Western classical music.

Conclusion

When the violin became the necessary accompaniment for the voice in Karnatak music, it displayed a seemingly natural ability to reproduce the voice. But what was elided in this transposition from voice to instrument? The Karnatak voice, and the words it pronounced, were supplemented, or replaced, by the tone of the violin and *piṭi, jāru,* and bowing techniques. The development of Karnatak violin technique over the last two centuries has thus been the development of a set of conventions by which the voice could be imitated and/or reproduced. That these conventions change (showing their conventional, rather than natural character), is apparent from the changes in violin style in the twentieth century; as they change, so do notions of the voice.

In imitating the voice, the violin becomes a ventriloquizer. The perfect violin accompanist is one whose playing is so self-effacing and unobtrusive that the vocalist forgets there is anything except her own voice. At the same time, the vocalist cannot be heard without the violin; as the violinist C. Subrahmanya Ayyar wrote in 1944, the violin renders Karnatak music "more articulate." This same power of ventriloquism, effecting a separation between voice and subject, content and form, is perceived as the very magic that saved Karnatak music from destruction in the face of colonialism. "The emergence of the violin in Karnatak music," writes a violinist from Madras, "is a very significant response—a response comprising co-option and adaptation of *just the musical means, not the content, thought, or style* of the colonial music system to the native/indigenous music system. This response, coupled with the high degree of sophistication and complexity that the indigenous musical system had already accomplished, was one of the ways by which the classical music system of South India was able to maintain itself, *quite intact,* in the face of the cultural onslaught" (Parasuram 1997, 40; emphasis mine). By the logic of ventriloquism, then, the site of deepest colonial impact is transformed into the very sign, and sound, of a pure Indian voice. This ventriloquism works through a series of displacements which, as I have shown, have occurred at particular historical moments. The voice is supplemented by the violin, whose sound then becomes a kind of super-voice; this virtuosic sound of a colonial instrument "gone native" is in turn imitated by vocalists. The change in violin styles in the twentieth century from a *piṭi* to a more *gāyaki,* or, depending on your taste, "weepy" sound is indicative not only of a change in vocal style but of a change in the concept of the voice itself. The claim that the latter is the "natural" and "authentic" sound of south Indian music marks a desire to create a distinctively Indian sound, a representative "voice" not in danger of being confused with anything remotely Western. This is a distinctly modern and postcolonial desire.

To say that the voice in Karnatak music is a modern construct is not to say that there was no vocal music in south India before the violin. Rather, the violin, in Karnatak music, stages the voice in a particular way so that the voice becomes available as a metaphor for a tradition, and a self, that have survived colonialism while remaining uncolonized. This staging is a repetitive act, borne through generations of musical practice that have made the violin in Karnatak music a "native" instrument. If we take seriously Regula Qureshi's injunction that "musical meaning and affect need to be considered as . . . historically and socially situated" (2000, 812), then we need to consider how the habitual, repetitive patterns of musical practice—indeed, the very methods of fingering and bowing that I have been discussing—are central to the question of how sound acquires meaning.

This is where I think we can use careful listening and an attention to the details of musical practice and instrumental technique to form subversive interpretations of some of the postcolonial mythologies of south Indian classical music. If we are going to challenge the legacy of orientalist and neo-orientalist claims about South

Asian musical traditions, we need not only to search for what has been marginalized or excluded by processes of classicization; we also need to listen closely to what is now considered "classical music." As I have suggested here, this involves attending to how discourse *about* music can influence the way in which that music is heard, and imagining other ways of hearing. This work represents one step in that direction.

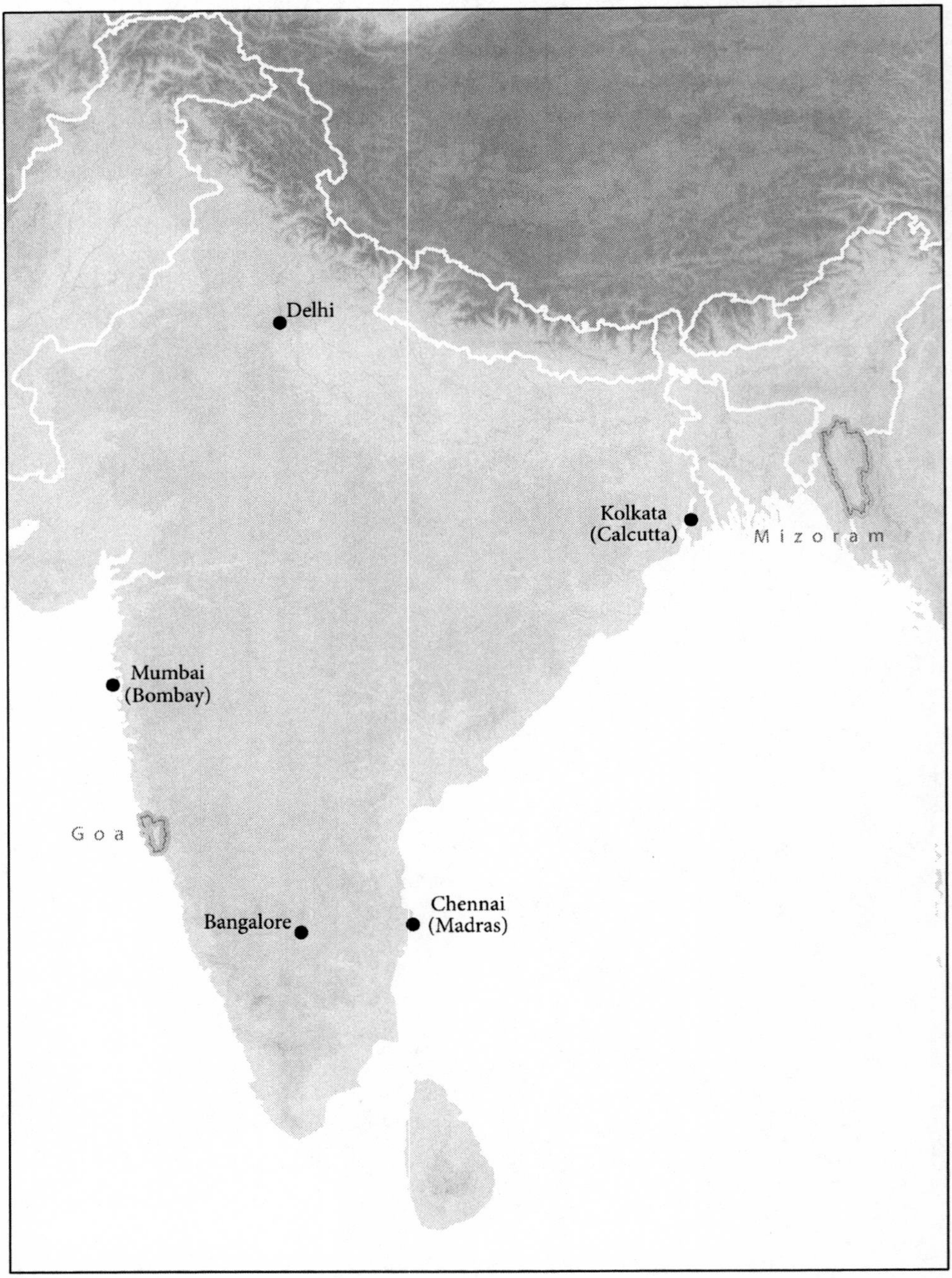
Delhi
Kolkata
(Calcutta)
Mizoram
Mumbai
(Bombay)
Goa
Bangalore
Chennai
(Madras)

CHAPTER 4

Local Practice, Global Network

The Guitar in India as a Case Study

MARTIN CLAYTON

Local Practice? The Paradoxical Location of the Indian Guitar

The guitar is, in India, at once the most global and the most local of instruments. It is firmly rooted in living rooms, churches, and community centers, and is sustained by local networks of enthusiasts; it is also integral to vast global networks in which instruments, recordings, and specialist magazines all circulate. My work on the guitar has addressed both performers of "Western" genres and performers of raga music such as Debashish Bhattacharya and Vishwa Mohan Bhatt. The present chapter focuses on the former, partly as a response to the lack of interest they have received to date. It is also deliberate in that I stress that the most global of instruments and repertoires is theorized locally—the Western is local, too.

This chapter unpicks the location of the guitar with the help of some of its local theorists—musicians and others who explained to me their conceptions of the instrument. In fact, it is constructed as a series of quotations with my supporting commentary, rather than as my argument illustrated with quotations, as a means of highlighting the words of the local theorizers who are its subject. I do, however, make a number of contentions. First, even the most global of instruments is theorized on a local level—that is, people understand it in relation to a local cultural context. Second, understandings of this kind imply theories of three-way connections between instrument, place, and community, in which a global music culture is given a local interpretation. Third, and consequently, the story of the guitar in India can be understood as one of encounter and exchange taking place largely at a local level through negotiations between individuals (even when what is at stake is a globally mediated repertoire or style).

The greater part of the Indian guitar scene remains hidden: Westerners have remained largely uninterested in that part of Indian musical culture that most wants to identify with the West (Clayton 2001, 201). This chapter presents the stories of some of these guitarists and how they conceptualize their musical and social worlds together: the rock star Gary Lawyer, songwriter Leslie Lewis (half of the successful duo Colonial Cousins), Mumbai session musicians such as Dilip Naik and Tushar Parte, Bengali jazz-rock guitarist Amit Dutta and his Anglo-Indian neighbor Carlton Kitto, and northeastern Christians on the metropolitan college scene such as Kennedy Hlyccho. These interviews were recorded during fieldwork conducted with Indian guitarists during the years 1998–99 and 2001. [**Video example 4.1**]

Over the course of this research, hitherto faceless musicians playing in hotel bars and restaurants, on advertising jingles and film soundtracks, became as vividly present to me as any, their musical lives equally bound up in the same questions of value and meaning, history and identity. Their relationship with others in India, people who identified far less, if at all, with the West, was deceptively stable—their skills as performers often in demand even as their histories and cultural expressions were erased or ignored. More self-consciously "Indian" musicians with whom they sometimes mixed had, perhaps inadvertently, become associated with an ideology of cultural nationalism, leaving the "Western" musicians in a kind of accidentally oppositional (anti-Indian? anti-musical?) limbo. Each side seemed to be defined by the other, although their cooperation has been the foundation of India's ubiquitous film music.

The fractured musical world of the Indian guitar was apparent to me early on. As the monsoon of December 1998 broke over southern India—coinciding with the classical music season—I visited the grandly old-fashioned Musee Musical, probably the biggest music shop in Chennai. Musee Musical occupies one vast room, its walls lined with glass-fronted cabinets protecting a wide variety of instruments, harmoniums to tablas, sitars to violins. In the shop's central section is an open display of books—prominently featuring imported guitar tutors and chord dictionaries—and, to one side, an open rack of acoustic guitars. I wanted somehow to capture the ambience, but received mixed reactions, at first, to the idea of documenting with my video camera. Then a technician named Kumar appeared as if from nowhere, dressed in work clothes of shirt and *lungī,* and offered to play for me. He rendered a single melody line with the unusual technique of plucking every note with an upward stroke. "See," said the salesman, "the Indian way of playing. The strumming, they do it in the opposite direction." It took a few seconds for the comment to strike me: who were "*they*"? [**Video example 4.2**]

The industry's consumers offered me overviews of the Indian music scene that were, in their own ways, more sophisticated than those of any musician or musicologist. A theme that played out again and again as I chatted to friends and relations, to taxi drivers, shopkeepers, and waiters was put most succinctly by my driver in Chennai, Ananda Kumar: "I like three language songs: English, Tamil, and Hindi." A popular discourse of local and global culture—or, in non-Hindi speaking areas as here, global, local, and national—is widely employed to make sense of a diverse soundscape. Many people mapped the different levels onto Indian languages; few were comfortable mapping the local or national levels onto English (even though they might use English to perform the mapping).

Musicians painted a picture of a fractured but interlocking system of musical worlds. Millions of listeners were nevertheless able to make sense of their complex soundscapes and to locate the sounds of different guitar styles therein. The taxonomies of Ananda Kumar and others did not, however, include the local-but-Western (such as Chennai-based Anglophone rock or jazz bands). That is, the "Western" or "English" had to either map onto the global level (as in the music of Michael Jackson or Madonna, standing for the presence of the outside world), or be so fully absorbed into the local and national that it was no longer heard as other (as in the countless examples of violins and other Western instruments employed in Indian film music) (see Weidman, this volume).

Guitars and their music cannot be understood without considering local discourses of Indian and Western, traditional and modern (Clayton 2001): what do local theorists consider their own and what is other, what belongs, what is rooted here... and even, who are "we," who counts as Indian? Nowhere are such discourses more fraught with ambiguity than in India's metropolitan centers.

My focus on metropolitan centers is, in part, dictated by my ethnographic experience; but it also makes sense to conduct research in such cities because they (especially Mumbai and, in earlier times, Kolkata) have acted as a magnet for the most talented guitarists from other hotbeds of guitar culture such as Goa, Bangalore, and the northeastern states. This internal migration in response to economic conditions, and the consequent throwing together of musicians with very different social backgrounds but common passions, is one of several levels of encounter between individuals, communities, and localities in the Indian popular music world. Another, of course, is the possibility (or regretful impossibility) of movement to and from the West, which guitarists view variously as the true center of guitar culture, the site of maximum economic opportunity, or a natural home to which one might return. The story of the guitar in India can be cast, therefore, in terms of interactions and encounters of several kinds: between individual musicians, their families, and communities; between musicians of different backgrounds cooperating and competing within the same industry; between "our" music and "theirs" (on various levels); between a national industry and a global market; and not least, between the sensibilities of musicians, the demands of audiences, and the agendas of those in positions of power.

The following sections deal in turn with musicians' origins—guitarists' locales, communities, and family backgrounds; then with discourses of identity—Indianness and language in particular; and finally with musicians' interactions in relation to the Indian and foreign music industries, and music-theoretical and interpretative discourses of Indian guitarists.

Origins and Identities

Even a relatively small sample demonstrates that the backgrounds of Indian guitarists are extremely varied. Historically a high percentage have been born in India as Christians. Guitarists hail from Goa, the northeastern states, cities with large Anglo-Indian communities such as Kolkata and Bangalore, and from Mumbai, Chennai, and to a lesser extent Delhi. Note the preponderance of Portuguese names in film industry veteran Dilip Naik's reflections on his early days as a session guitarist: "I came in the industry in '62, [and] there was, including myself, Castro, Bonnie d'Costa, De Mello, Vaaz, Gomes, [and] Gorakh, Pyarelal's[1] brother, seven or eight guitar players."

Tushar Parte, Naik's student and one of the leading players in the film industry at present, adds:

TP Guitar was used even from the earlier days [of Indian film music], and there were wonderful guitarists in our industry. It was actually a Goan thing, because Western music was all Goa. I remember my teacher telling me at one point that when he was a teenager, it was so synonymous to be a Christian to be able to play guitar that he used to have his hair like the hippies and he used to change his name, just because he could go to the clubs and that kind of thing. Most of the musicians were Catholics, maybe more than 95 percent.

MC Is that still true?

TP No it's not still true. And it was maybe [Pyarelal's] father, he taught a lot of Hindu musicians, and he also gave them a confidence [that they] could also do it, you know, music is not religious.

Dominic Fernandes, one of the film industry's top bass guitarists, was born in Bombay in 1956, into a Goan Catholic family. Fernandes attributed his musical interest to his "Goan blood" (unlike veteran Hannibal Castro, who had emigrated from his Goan birthplace and can actually remember the Portuguese soldiers' guitar playing there). Fernandes has played in hotel bands and on tour with the orchestra of Babla (a percussionist who used to play in the Indian film industry).[2] He pointed out that hotel bands played Western pop music, whereas the Babla orchestra performed Hindi songs. His explanation of why fewer Christians now participate in the film industry differs from that of Parte: "Very few Christian or Goan musicians [in later years] were interested in that kind of music—they preferred doing the outside [non-film] music."

The dominance of Christian musicians, and perhaps the low status of professional musicians in other communities, presented barriers to many non-Catholic guitarists. Dilip Naik, coming from a Hindu family, had to suffer criticism for adopting a "Catholic" instrument: "[My parents] wanted me to play music only as a hobby, because those days musicians were not making money. My father used to say 'You're going to hang that guitar around your neck and sit with a hat somewhere in Bandra and all those Catholics are going to throw some money at you, that's how you're to make a living.'[3] He used to say the filthiest sarcastic things, you know. But I don't blame him, because those days it was unknown for a non-Catholic to play these instruments." The northeastern states are well-known centers of Western music in India, and guitars have long been popular in the region. Many young northeasterners move to other Indian cities and become established as part of college rock scenes; a number are professional musicians in Mumbai. Kennedy Hlychho is a northeasterner, settled in Delhi, who plays on the local circuit. He was brought up in a small town in Mizoram, which he describes as "95 percent, 96 percent Christian." Musical tastes there are split between local guitar-based Mizo-language pop music and Western style rock and pop, as well as hymns, which missionaries teach using tonic sol-fa notation. In Hlychho's Mizoram, with its history of insurgency against Indian rule, Hindi-language pop is possibly more marginal than in any other part of India: "The underground people sometimes [had an] encounter right in the middle of town, with the Indian army. So we grew up thinking that India's a bit, you know, not a part of you. And another thing, because we're so far off and the roads are so bad, we feel geographically cut off. You feel cut off from India as a whole."

Parsi musicians also have a notable presence in the Mumbai music scene in relation to the size of the community. Gary Lawyer, a Mumbai Parsi singer and guitarist, is well known on the local scene and is one of very few to make a good living from performing English-language popular music: "As far as I know, Martin, I'm the only guy really who is surviving doing Western music. And I guess it just stems from the background of a typical Parsi upbringing. One of the things about Parsis is that the background is so purely colonial and Western—you know, the British influence. So everything is geared towards the West. I grew up speaking English, and my influences are just purely Western in terms of music. You know, it's so ironic, I'm 10,000 miles away, and yet it's such a strong influence on me." One could hardly cover the topic of Parsis in popular music without bringing up the late Freddie Mercury (Farokh Bulsara), India's most prominent international rock star to date.[4] Lawyer mentioned Mercury almost immediately: "I can imagine where [Mercury's] coming from, and I hear it in his music, you know, because his music.... I know it's basically rock, but the whole classical influence.... 'Bohemian Rhapsody' is a typical example, I almost believe that only a Parsi could come out with something like that." Lawyer broached the difficult and politically touchy question of the extent to which one might identify with a particular community instead of with the country as a whole—a problem also faced by Christian communities. The tendency of Parsis to be insular did not, in his view, prevent them from identifying themselves as "Indian."

Hindu musicians working in the Indian rock scene told stories not unlike those of Dilip Naik and Tushar Parte, who had reflected on their place in a film music scene dominated until recently by Christians. Amit Dutta for instance, well known in the Kolkata English-language rock scene, associates the tradition of Western music in Kolkata in part to its colonial history, and describes the city in its recent past as a diverse, metropolitan musical center: "This so-called Western music, it's been very much part of Calcutta culture, mainly because of the British Raj. [Around] Park Street, about twenty years back it was buzzing. Everyone would play and then meet up in one place, four o'clock in the morning, and jam, and then go home at six o'clock in the morning. Basically it was like New York, you know, in a very tiny way." Kolkata was also a destination for musicians who sought work in its hotels, theaters, and other venues, although this role has long since been usurped by Mumbai. According to Dutta, the Kolkata scene declined from the late 1970s due to a combination of local government restrictions on live bands, the lure of the Bombay film and advertising industries, and the emigration of many Anglo-Indians. Dutta emerged out of a distinguished family musical tradition, following a rather different path from that of his forbears: his great uncle is Rai Chand Boral, a well-known Indian classical musician.

In virtually every case, Indian guitarists have readily commented on the significance of their place and community of origin to their music. Anglo-Indians and Goans thought it natural that they were the main adopters of Western music styles in India. Younger Hindu musicians found it equally natural that they would break into this Christian-dominated world. For Gary Lawyer, "Bohemian Rhapsody" could only have been written by a Parsi. While this does not suggest a simple mapping of identity and musical style, musicians from all communities nevertheless acknowledge that their social identity matters to their music. Even those who argue that it should not—that "music is universal"—cannot deny that social identity matters to other people. How does that view articulate with the equally widespread recognition that the guitar is a global instrument? How does playing guitar link one into international networks?

Networks

One might expect a process of formal guitar tuition to function as an initiation into the vast international network of guitar culture. Until relatively recently, though, Indian guitarists seem to have managed with little access to tutors, chord dictionaries, or magazines, and with mostly informal tuition. Those neither lucky nor rich enough to obtain a good foreign instrument have also made do with poor equipment. Some of the better current players have had access to formal tuition, especially those who started with contacts in the industry such as Leslie Lewis, whose father P. L. Raj—a dance director in the film industry—set him up with Pyarelal's brother Gorakh Sharma as a guitar teacher.

Tushar Parte, whose father was a music arranger in the film industry, himself started on conga, then shifted to guitar, learning from Dilip Naik and later from a local expatriate American named D. Wood. Parte's father was one of many to have learned Western music formally, taking examinations set by British institutions: Arthur Gracias, for instance, learned through the Associated Board of the Royal Schools of Music (ABRSM). In Mumbai, a number of Christian and Parsi musicians have been trained in Western music to a very high level: Gary Lawyer studied singing with a Parsi teacher who had sung with Zubin Mehta's father and also taught the Goan soprano Patricia Rosario.

Nonetheless, for the older generation, and for those in remote areas even now, the norm has been learning by ear, especially from records. Dilip Naik describes the stages through which he went to achieve competence on the guitar:

> I met a Catholic friend who taught me the first three chords, all open string chords, and we formed a little group. I learned mainly from records. I got a break to go to Kashmir, and play in a band. The band was disgraceful, and unfortunately for us, Nadia Boulanger was vacationing for two weeks in that same hotel, and we were embarrassed. Nadia Boulanger would sit in front of the band. That's one thing I still can't understand, how a great woman, world's greatest composition teacher can sit in front of a disgraceful band and make faces.... we played disgraceful stuff you know. If she liked us or liked a sound she would do, that's good [gestures].
>
> Anyway, in that band everybody was a poor performer so they played the basics, just the tune and the basic chords, so I got to learn a lot of jazz standards with the basic chords. When I came back to Bombay, I had met a friend, Kersey Lord, and he had a lot of modern jazz records, and I heard many of the tunes that we were playing. So I knew the basics, and I said: If the basic is this, what does he play? What is the piano player playing? He's adding some notes to his basic chord, he's playing an altered chord. And that's how I learned a lot from records. Then a couple of books confirmed what I had learned was correct.

Now most professional guitarists in India use high-quality imported instruments. In the past they would use poor-quality local instruments or even experiment making guitars and amplifiers at home. Kennedy Hlyccho recalled his excitement at winding wire for homemade pick-ups. Dominic Fernandes shared similar memories: "Over here it was difficult, because instruments were not freely available. You had to get them from out, anybody who was going out you had to ask them to get them. I remember when I started the rock band, my brother-in-law helped me to make a guitar. He was into carpentry so I'd asked him to make one guitar for me." Overseas travel has for many years been an important aspect of an Indian musician's career. For guitarists it represents not only a chance to earn money, and to increase prestige back home, but also to obtain equipment, recordings, and publications (*Guitar Player* has an avid Indian readership) and to learn new skills. Some, of course, have emigrated or lived abroad for extended periods, and many more have at least considered such a move.[5] Leslie Lewis commented: "I wanted to go to the Guitar Institute of Technology, G.I.T. in Boston to study guitar, and my Dad just thought I was mad. He thought I was pulling his leg or something, so he refused to pay for it, and at that time there was no way for me to pay." Although Lewis did not move abroad, by his account the thought was influential in his later Colonial Cousins project: "Nandu [singer in the band Savage Encounter] said, "But what are you going to go there and do?" I said, "I'll play," and he said, "But they have BB King, why do they need you?" And that got me thinking. While I was in advertising [I started] trying to do what I felt was mine, which is not Indian per se, but was strongly Indian because of my influence." Lewis was able to establish himself as one of Mumbai's leading composers of commercial music. From that base he launched his duet with the singer Hariharan, performing under the name "Colonial Cousins" from the mid 1990s.

MC Who thought of the name, Colonial Cousins?

LL Hari had gone to London, and he's got a Parsi friend over there and they were having tea together. Then he says, "Hari, you know what my British friends and I call each other?—Colonial Cousins." We were looking for a name, and these Sanskrit names just sound too ethnic or too...it's not what we are all about. The blend is always there.

Perhaps the pinnacle of the Colonial Cousins' success was not their albums but their MTV Unplugged appearance in 1996—something that Lewis regards as having the biggest impact on his career. It also offered him an eye-opening experience: he told me stories of American music stores refusing to sell him professional gear... until he told them he had used the same equipment for an MTV Unplugged appearance.

Few of the musicians quoted here have had such an opportunity to record in top London studios. Several have toured abroad and at least two (Gary Lawyer and Dilip Naik) have stayed in the United States for periods of several years. As for younger musicians, Lawyer would recommend emigration at an early stage to escape the limitations of the Indian market: "[If people ask] 'But Gary, where do I go?' I say, 'Listen, do yourself a favour, just catch the next flight, enroll yourself into some music school, either in England or the States. The States has so many of them, you know. And start from there. Don't try doing anything here.'

The other side of the network equation is the penetration of Western pop music into the Indian market. Among musicians I consulted, opinion was divided as to whether the impact is limited by consumer choice or political interference.[6] Lawyer remarked, "India's a huge market. It's proved when Bryan Adams comes and performs here [in front of] 35,000 people in a city like Bombay. I can't think of a single Indian star in India who could draw such a crowd. Similarly when Bon Jovi came here. And it shows that it's there, but it's just being trampled on, I think, deliberately. That 'This is not our music,' 'Invasion of Indian culture.'" Lawyer's own home-grown English songs have had less impact than imported pop: "Every single Indian label is so receptive, they are trying to show the world that they are open, and they *are* open. [The multinationals] refuse to hear it. Why? I said, 'Why won't you hear it?' 'No no, we've been instructed that no Western music is to be entertained.'" Amit Dutta confirms Lawyer's story from his own experience trying to fund a promotional video, although he remains unconvinced by stories of political interference: "I don't know much of politics, or BJP and whatever, but I think it's purely business. It just doesn't sell, so why should they do it? I mean, in fact, the record company I'm talking to now, they're international, big names. Six lakhs [600,000 rupees] is nothing for an international company to pay [to record a video], it's like pocket money. But they say, 'We have strict instructions, not even a penny to any English band in India, because it just doesn't sell.' So why should they?" Although songs are recorded in all India's languages, the overwhelming majority of songs distributed on a national basis are in Hindi (just as Indian films intended to be seen across the country are almost all in Hindi). This means that local musicians who prefer to sing in English are put in a difficult position: English is the language of global, international pop, but Indian pop must be in Hindi; local musicians singing in English may find some work playing for functions or corporate events or in hotel bars, but are almost entirely excluded from the both the film industry and the distribution of commercial recordings.

Colonial Cousins had some success with their first album (1996), singing in a mixture of English, Tamil, Telugu, and Hindi, but by their third album (*Aatma* 2000) they were singing a higher proportion of their songs in Hindi. As Leslie Lewis explained: "They really don't want to hear too much English. They disconnect. Except the slightly elitist crowd which is like . . . they're also our fans, but [the numbers are minimal]. So if you sing in Hindi, you find that the Indian people tend to react a lot quicker to the same song, to the same melody, the same everything. So, since that's how the people like it, let's sing a little more in Hindi this time. We still sing in English, it's not that it's not there. If it was only Hindi then we'd lose what we were about." As Harris Berger points out, "language choice and dialect are issues that can play out anywhere that music and language are combined" (2003, xiii). Indian popular music illustrates the complex play of language ideologies and aesthetic choices, the tensions between the preferences of artists, audiences, and industry gatekeepers. Language choice is not a simple matter of mapping language onto community: it can also be, among other things, an index of the networks to which people claim connection. Frequent code-switching, for instance, as employed by Colonial Cousins, can be taken to imply a claim to familiarity with a variety of both local and international networks.

These stories show how guitarists operate in different, interconnected, local networks; how they learn and respond to Western pop on the Indian market; and how they register their impact abroad with reference to tours, record companies, and MTV. The musical identity of any individual guitarist may reflect his "local" social identity as Goan Christian or Parsi, while also binding him to millions of other guitarists around the world who play the same instrument, read the same magazines, and listen to the same recordings. The intersection of local or communal identities with guitar networks that cut across all of those boundaries is obviously complex and many-layered.

Music

Musicians trained in Indian raga music have been interacting with those with skills in Western repertories at least since the early days of film music in India.[7] Their vast musical production has received a disproportionately tiny amount of academic interest. The following small selection of comments by musicians working in the film industry suggests that they have developed their own theories, terminology, and practical methods for dealing with the juxtaposition of musical systems. In other words, music theory too can be ad hoc and locally configured.

A few key terms will be useful for readers not familiar with the terminology of Hindi film music. First, non-Indian English speakers are often thrown by the usage of the term "music" itself, which usually refers to instrumental music, either background music or instrumental interludes within songs: "music" and "song" are therefore contrasting categories. Songs and music are the responsibility of the music director(s), who work together with producers, directors, and dance directors.[8] Music directors usually delegate much of the work of musical arrangement to arrangers, who also (according to my informants) normally take responsibility for the background music.

The composition process has naturally led to practical decisions about how, if at all, to score the music (most in staff notation, with some Indian instruments' parts written out in Indian *sargam*). Film music arrangements often involve dozens of musicians, some of whom, including guitarists, must write their own parts within a specified structure. Often guitarists with no training in Indian classical music have to work out parts to accompany raga-based melodies. Dominic Fernandes explained:

DF I didn't study any Indian music.

MC So if it's a film song, and the music directors have made a piece in *rāg Bhairavī*, you just listen to the tune and...

DF Exactly. Normally what I do is I ask what raga it is, and the notes that are being used in that *rāg*, and according to that I play bass notes. You cannot just fit any old note into that part, it will sound false.

Fernandes went on to explain that in the day-to-day business of making film music, a curious but practical mixture of terminologies has emerged:

DF [In the 1980s] the whole orchestra used to rehearse together. We used to rehearse the introduction, we used to rehearse the first music and the second music, then we'd go back to the sine line—sine and *antarā* we call it. [*Antarā* is] like a verse. So you have *antarā* 1, *antarā* 2, *antarā* 3; verse 1 verse 2, verse 3, then you got back to the sine, that's the chorus.

MC That's an interesting mix of the Western terminology and the Indian terminology.

DF Yes, exactly.

The reference is to the two main sections of Indian classical compositions, *sthāyī* (the first section, part of which is used as a refrain) and *antarā* (the second section, usually establishing the high *sa* or upper tonic); in pop music *antarā* refers to the verse, *sthāyī* the chorus. (I suspect the term Fernandes spelled "sine" and said could be represented by the letter S is a reference to the *segno* [sign] used in Western standard notation to indicate repeated sections.)

Despite the popularity of film songs, not only critics but even musicians working in the industry are often critical of the quality of music produced. Session guitarist Dilip Naik explains his understanding of the evolution of Indian film music and the reasons for his own critical view:

> From the time film music began—it's a poor fusion of Indian and Western music—the English aspect of it was not handled properly. They somehow managed to fuse it, and the next generation listening to that poor fusion learned from that, and that has been going on for generations now. Now they're maybe [the] third or fourth generation doing the same thing. They are hardly listening to foreign music for the English aspect of it. I keep telling them, "if you want to learn harmony and counterpoint thoroughly you must listen to English music, or American music. Indian music doesn't have that, and this film music has everything wrong."
>
> The Indian aspect of it was neat. Only when they tried to fuse—whenever they needed Western music, when the producer came and said, "I have a night-club scene, and there is a hero and heroine dancing with a piano and I need an English type of song"—the guy didn't know how to compose English music, so he would steal some English record.

Tushar Parte remembers some of the work of his father, the arranger Jay Kumar Parte, with affection and respect. He also raises the question of what musical features count as "Indian," focusing on portamento (see the parallel discussion in Amanda Weidman's chapter in this volume).

> [My father] worked as an arranger, and he introduced a concept of chromatic harmony in our industry. Like, suppose a C major chord is going, my Dad would make a lovely arrangement of strings layering at the top, with the C-sharp, D, E-flat, E, and those clusters were sounding beautiful.
>
> He had a style of playing the violin section and the flute section in an Indian *gāyakī* style.[9] Earlier to his times when the violin pieces were very staccati or without any bends, my father used his own natural style to create that kind of thing so that it merges, and to have the beautiful nuances of the *mīṇḍ,* the bend, as you call it, to incorporate into the violin. To make it sound very Indian.

Film songs and music are not the only context in which different repertories and styles are combined, although in many cases (as in so-called Indy pop) the procedures stay close to the precedents set by the film industry. An exceptional example is that of Colonial Cousins, who have a different conception of their audience. Most music directors and musicians in films expect to reach only Indian audiences. Colonial Cousins set out to appeal to both Indian and Western listeners—or at least, English-speaking Indians with musical tastes primarily in Western music. Leslie Lewis eloquently expressed the view of a composer and producer trying to strike a delicate balance: "What I've managed to get as a producer or a composer or whatever, is to be able to sit on the fence and make the Western listener think that it is an English song with an Asian or with an ethnic overtone, and the Asian guy thinks it's an Indian song with a Western overtone. That balance is something, it's got a lot to do with the way I produce. It's the songs, definitely, but it's also the way we produce it." These encounters involve not only identity, community, economics, politics, religion, and language, but also specifically musical negotiations. The resulting popular and commercial music circulates through film, TV, and sound recordings across South Asia. Thousands of local musicians recreate the popular tunes of the day in brass band performances and in local language versions and so on (see Booth 1990; 2005; Manuel 1993). An important part of this story, then, concerns the way in which that music is put together, the decisions that are made, and the way they are imagined in terms of music theory. The pioneers of film music in India had no rule book to follow. They had to work out their own methods for blending different melodic, rhythmic, and timbral sensibilities, and to figure out how to apply Western-derived harmony to melodies, some of them raga-based, which were not conceived harmonically.

Conclusions and Generalizations

The aim of this chapter has been to provide a perspective on South Asian music through the words of Indian guitarists. To summarize, professional guitarists come from very different backgrounds. Christian and other minority communities have contributed massively to Indian popular music. And people attribute significance to musicians' backgrounds in the popular music realm (as they do in the classical as well). Musicians' communities of origin also relate to the question of linguistic competence, especially in the dominant pop music languages of English and Hindi. Musicians from these different backgrounds are initiated into local, national, and international networks, through tuition, exposure to recordings and publications, and by obtaining instruments and other equipment. Playing the guitar involves one in international networks. Foreign tours, emigration, and exposure to foreign recordings on the Indian market have had different kinds of local and individual impact. Negotiations between individual musicians, particularly in the context of film music production, give rise to new practices and new theories.

The small portion of the discourse of my informants included here is not meant to represent a larger South Asian whole. Rather it is meant as a point of departure for further reflection on broadening the musicological discourse on South Asian music through reference to various kinds of "local theory." The stories some guitarists tell open up areas of South Asian musical practice and discourse that have not previously had much of an airing: far more can and should be said about the role of Christian and other minority communities in Indian musical history, for example. Although most of this chapter has been devoted to the testimony of my informants, I introduced early on a set of three suggestions that form the backbone of my commentary: that even the most global of instruments is theorized on a local level; that this implies theories of three-way connections between instrument, place, and community, in which a global music culture is given a local interpretation; and finally that the story of the guitar in India is one of local encounters and negotiations between individuals. Each of these three points has been amply demonstrated above.

Local theories are also theories of locality—especially in relation to identity, language, and musical style. They implicate global theories, too, since locality and identity are defined in opposition to other localities and other identities: local knowledge is always relative. As Stephen Blum reminds us, theory involves knowing things could be other than they are: "Theorizing starts as we make connections among our thoughts and perceptions with some awareness of alternatives..." (this volume). When a musician suggests that a particular musical style maps onto a community, he or she acknowledges that other styles and other communities exist in a wider musical universe.

Mapping local musical practices in South Asia constantly reminds us of how local practice participates in, and is penetrated by, international networks and markets. Exploring relationships among colonial history and its myths, the South Asian diaspora, and the world music industry is essential for studies of not only popular music but classical traditions too.

If we are to understand the dynamics of Indian music, in all its forms, then more studies of the discourse of musicians and their consumers are needed. Such musical discussions are of particular interest when they clash with received notions of what is and is not Indian. Study of musicians, composers, and arrangers should ideally be combined with studies of the reception of the music in the context of its consumption. More broadly, the relationship between musical imagination, consumer taste, and political ideologies in South Asia needs to be explored in greater depth.

PART II

SPACES AND ITINERARIES

CHAPTER 5

Constructing the Local

Migration and Cultural Geography in the Indian Brass Band Trade

GREGORY D. BOOTH

The bandsmen who play in South Asia's brass wedding band constitute one of the largest musical service trades in South Asia. When brass band instruments first appeared in Indian processional practice, they were evidence of the subcontinent's engagement with the global and with colonialism. In their role as the most commonly used accompaniment for Indian wedding processions, however, bands have become a locally constructed variant on a global theme. At the microlevel of the men who play in them, the world of brass bands is one of India's most socially and musically isolated subcultures, far removed from the global prestige of India's classical traditions and the popular (and profitable) world of the cinema and its music.

This study examines spatial mappings of the commercial brass band tradition in India, in particular, the manner in which bandsmen's structures of professional organization effectively enclose large regions of north and central India.[1] All processional music traditions make some claim to physical space by their presence and through the creation of a public (and usually loud) soundscape. Most mark or enclose local geographies for ritual, political, or social purposes (see Wegner, this volume). The spatial structures I describe here are, in contrast, the results of changes to traditional socio-professional organization in the processional music trade that took place after 1947.

Members of specific social identities (castes) move and control areas of the market according to patterns, thereby creating migratory networks. In these local worlds, competition for jobs in a musical wage-labor market depends upon the social identities of bandsmen and the forces of history. In doing so, it describes an intensely local set of professional behaviors, an alternate view, perhaps, of the "life of music in north India" as Daniel Neuman constructed that term. That this vision of the local extends village or rural based local identities across large areas of central and northern India, into the midst of its biggest cities, adds yet another unique dimension to this professional life of music.

Migrant Musicianship, Social Identity, and Networks

In 1994 in the small Rajasthani city of Bikaner, I met a young bandsman named Salim, who was working as a bandmaster (a musical leader) for a brass wedding band in that city.[2] Salim lived in a nearby village; but had been hired on contract by the Ghaurdan Brass Band's owner to accommodate the greater demand for wedding bands that cities' concentrated populations almost always generate. Perhaps as many as 250,000 musicians like Salim work part- and full-time in the band trade in the northern two-thirds of the Indian subcontinent. The demand for brass bands in wedding processions is huge in many parts of India.

Despite this demand, brass bandsmen are marginalized socially as well as musically in much of contemporary South Asia (Booth 2005), in part because their instruments are explicitly understood to have foreign origins. I have argued—as Weidman argues in chapter 3 of this volume regarding the violin—that the practice of using trumpets, trombones, clarinets, and other brass band instruments in Indian ritual was initially a reflection of a specifically Indian colonial culture. What I suggest here is that brass bands were gradually left behind, so to speak, in the explicitly differenced and somewhat exoticized development of India's postcolonial music culture. In the twenty-first century they are visible reminders of a former colonial culture. For this reason, and because they provide musical services to others, processional musicians in South Asia are generally low in musical and social status.

The traditional connection between social groups with low status and processional music is related to caste-based exchange-economy structures that Wegner and Chaudhuri describe for musicians in Nepal and Rajasthan in this volume. Although processional ritual behaviors continue to enact these structures, professional behaviors and the contemporary rhetoric of both bandsmen and patrons ignores them. In the brass band world, economic exchange is explicitly described by bandsmen and their patrons in terms of fees, wages, and tips. Nevertheless, the majority of Indian brass bandsmen are still drawn from a wide variety of low-status caste groups, both Hindu and Muslim. At the national level, caste changes from region to region and network to network; this contrasts with the smaller-scale interaction among castes reported by Wegner and Chaudhuri.

Professional Structures and Roles in the World of Brass Bands

Band owners, called *māliks* in northern India, own the band's name, instruments, uniforms, and shop. They contract with band patrons to deliver musical services for a specific wedding procession, involving so many musicians, so many hours, such-and-such uniforms, and so forth. Māliks also contract with band musicians to work for so many months at a fixed rate or to play on demand for so much per procession. A named "band" in the northern two-thirds of India is, in a sense, a mālik, his family, perhaps a small permanent managerial and musical staff, uniforms, instruments, and other things; a band does not consist of a fixed group of musicians. The musicians who process in the uniforms of a given band are not necessarily the same from year to year, or even from procession to procession. A bandsman from Saharanpur playing in the Shiv Mohan Band in Delhi one year might play for the Master Band next year (these two shops are almost next door to each other). He might as likely play for the Jea Band in Jaipur or possibly even the Janta Band in Ghaziabad (he would probably not go further east than Ghaziabad, however).

This professional norm based on flexible membership operates within a highly defined labor-management capitalist economic structure developed in India after Independence, and contrasts with the fixed-membership, semi-cooperative ensembles of the colonial era, in which most of the musicians in a given band were related by caste, if not family. It exemplifies what David Rudner has called the "objectification of labor" (1994, 15). As a result, most contemporary māliks are capitalist service providers more than they are musicians or even musical leaders. Indeed, a solely managerial role is a symbol of success in the contemporary band world. As with all trades of this kind, the profits for band owners are found in the difference between what their patrons pay them and what they must pay their musicians.

These changes in practice are tied to the extremes of urbanization that have taken place in India since 1947 and the consequent and growing "imbalance between life chances in the urban and rural sectors" (Smith 1996, 5). Urbanization and the as yet nonnegotiable need for brass bands in the majority of Indian wedding processions have produced professional bandsmen who are mobile or migrant laborers traveling from their villages and towns to work in big city bands.

In our conversation, Salim related a very unusual story. For two years, in his early teens, he had accompanied the man he calls his *ustād* (teacher), an elder band master named Shakur Master, on journeys from their homes in Bikaner to the eastern city of Varanasi, to work for Master Akram, the owner of one of that's city's many brass bands, the Prince Band.

Bandsmen travel considerable distances in their trade, leaving their smaller towns and villages to work in big cities, where demand is quite high (and so are wages). It was not surprising, therefore, that Salim and his ustād had been working in a city other than their own. Varanasi is a much larger city than Bikaner, with many brass band shops, all of which employ migrant bandsmen. The distance from Bikaner to Varanasi (roughly 1,200 kilometers) is not significantly greater than some other distances traveled by migrant bandsmen on a seasonal basis. So this in itself did not make his story unusual.

Like many other Indian bandsmen, Salim and Shakur worked in Varanasi for the wedding season (roughly from December through May or June), returning to Bikaner and their homes each year at the end of those seasons. Hindu weddings (which represent the vast majority of all weddings in India) are timed for auspicious periods of the year (see Eck 1983), and the cycle of auspicious and inauspicious wedding seasons produces corresponding cycles of peak demand for wedding bands. A band that might play three weddings a day in February might well go for weeks without an engagement in August. Seasonality and the highly concentrated markets that major cities represent, create the capitalist, temporary contract-labor system that most modern bands employ. The permanent employment of sufficient bandsmen to meet peak demand would leave a band owner paying salaries to musicians who had nothing to do in the off-season.

Larger and more successful bands in the bigger cites might consequently have a hundred or more bandsmen employed during high season. [**Video example 5.1**] Hira Lal Thadani of Delhi's Jea Band has stated that he routinely has nearly 1,000 bandsmen employed during the wedding season. In August or September, his shop is almost empty; only a small managerial staff remains to take bookings for the following season from the occasional foresighted Delhi resident. Urban costs of living make it difficult if not impossible for bandsmen to afford to live in those same cities on the earnings they can make during the peak season. It benefits both band owners and bandsmen for bandsmen to live in less costly small towns and villages and move temporarily to the cities for the wedding season. [**Video example 5.2**]

Despite the greater sums they must spend on subsistence, bandsmen often earn between 60 and 80 percent of their yearly income in four to six months. In addition, many bandsmen have alternative work to which they can return in the off-season. The professional lives of most contemporary bandsmen in northern India are structured by this village-cost-of-living-versus-urban-wages imbalance. Their patterns of movement and the accessibility of specific urban centers for specific bandsmen are structured by social identity, often expressed as caste.

I have yet to make clear the exceptional nature of Salim's story (and his travels); but to do so, I must consider the interaction of identity and geography in competition for and the control of centers of employment for migrant bandsmen.

A Caste-Based Geography

Richards (1972) and Dandekar (1986) both suggest that migrant labor in twentieth-century India has produced a low-status socioeconomic class of indistinguishable unskilled workers in urban labor markets that have little relevance to any older, village-centered caste-occupation connections. In this context, labor mobility in the band world is distinctive because, although it also involves urban-focused labor mobility, there remains a three-way connection between the specific castes, specific locations, and the processional music trade to which they belong, through a process involving individual choices, economic compulsion, and heredity. Bandsmen come from not just physical places (villages and towns) but also from professional spaces constructed and dominated by specific social identities, many with connections to processional music performance. The professional structures of the band world probably have at least as much to do with caste as with place as such. Caste identity and place, together, made Salim's story (and Shakur Master's choice of destination) exceptional.

Salim, Shakur, and their families belong to a Muslim subset of the broader low-status caste group that they call Dhamānī. They believe that their ancestors were Hindu converts to Islam (probably in the sixteenth or seventeenth century).[3] Bandsmen of Dhamānī subgroups dominate much of the band trade in Rajasthan and migrate, seasonally and permanently, from places like Bikaner or Sardarsher (where job opportunities are rather limited) to bigger cities like Jodhpur, Jaipur, and Delhi. What was remarkable about the trip described by Salim, and what made him quite proud to have accomplished it, was that Varanasi is completely beyond the professional sphere of Rajasthani bandsmen. Salim and Shakur are probably the only bandsmen from any place west of Delhi to have spent two seasons playing in a city so far to the east.

Salim, like most bandsmen, could have expected to spend most of his professional life traveling and playing weddings outside his hometown. His traveling as such was hardly unusual. Nevertheless, and although he was barely twenty years old at the time, Salim understood that his trip to Varanasi *was* unusual because bandsmen from his part of India (and thus from his caste) do not, as a rule, travel east of Delhi in search of work. In the cities to the east of Delhi, other caste groups, with their own histories of involvement, control the brass band trade. When Salim and Shakur traveled to Varanasi in search of work they were actually reducing their chances of successful employment. In Varanasi, there were no caste mates or established socio-professional network to whom they could turn for help or information, or who could recommend them to band owners. They were entering a labor market completely controlled by the Hashimī and Ansārī Muslim castes, as well as by Scheduled Caste Hindus (primarily Bhāngī).

According to Master Akram, the owner of Varanasi's Prince Band, Shakur Master's presence so far from home and in a place where he had no relations or even acquaintances was a reflection of Shakur's somewhat unreliable reputation as a wanderer with a fondness for hashish. For Shakur, distance may have made employment harder at the caste level, but seems to have similarly reduced the chances of his reputation catching up with him on the personal level.

Local Theorizing—Theorizing the Local

The pride that Salim expressed in regard to his travels with Shakur demonstrates his implicit knowledge that journeys to Varanasi are not normal for bandsmen of his caste and place. Bandsmen are well aware of "how things are supposed to be" or "how things work" but rarely enunciate this knowledge, which we must nevertheless identify as theoretical, at least to the extent of its normative and prescriptive nature.

In early December of 1993, I sat on a roof in the small Deccan town of Gulbarga, talking with another young bandmaster named Muhammad Razak, whose home is in a village outside the smaller town of Aland, about 45 kilometers northwest of Gulbarga.[4] Like most Muslims in that area, his family belongs to an artisanal caste who are employed primarily as weavers and bakers, but also as processional musicians. They occupy a middle to lower-middle range of Muslim social hierarchies. Razak was in Gulbarga as a contractual employee of another bandmaster named Manik Rao, who owned the small Santosh Band. Muhammad had negotiated with Manik Rao a salary on the order of one thousand rupees per month for the four to six months of the Hindu wedding season. Although Manik Rao was quite competent as a musician himself, he also had to attend to other business interests. So he employed Muhammad Razak to help lead his band for that wedding season. Like Salim in Rajasthan, this young Deccani bandmaster rehearsed subordinate bandsmen and led the groups sent out to accompany the many wedding parties of the band's customers. Like other migrant bandsmen, Razak would return to his village in late June or early July, having earned a large proportion of his yearly income.

When I left Gulbarga, Razak asked that, when I returned, I should try to find him again. He would surely be, he said, in Hyderabad, which is relatively close to Aland and Gulbarga. If I could not locate him in Hyderabad, however, Razak suggested I look for him in Mumbai or in Ahmedabad, two cities that are considerably more distant.[5] Muhammad Razak was articulating a local understanding regarding the cultural geography of his professional world. Alandi Muslims never travel north of Ahmedabad or south of Hyderabad in their search for work. Within the geographic and professional space that Hyderabad and Ahmedabad enclose, however, they are among the most numerous migrant bandsmen. Salim, if he were making a similar statement of "how things work" relative to his own career, might have suggested I look for him in Jaipur or Delhi, but not in any of the cities named by Razak. Although Bikaner is not much further from Delhi than it is from Ahmedabad, the bands of Ahmedabad are dominated by men from the south and east. There is no advantage to being a Dhamānī bandsman in Ahmedabad.

Networks of migrant bandsmen, organized by social identity and active within definable geographic limits, are theorizable as the result of observable practice, which makes future practice at least partially predictable. Muhammad Bacchan, a bandmaster from Rampur (Uttar Pradesh state), acknowledged his own network structures in pragmatic, quasi-theoretical terms. He was almost totally disinterested in my stories of bandsmen from Jaipur because, "those people don't come over here and we don't go over there." Bacchan's representation of labor migration patterns in the band world is largely accurate; the rare exceptions (like Salim's trip to Varanasi) prove the rule.

The social relations that structure these networks facilitate the movement of migrant bandsmen. Muhammad Razak had never seen any of the big cities he mentioned to me, but knew about them from friends, caste-mates, and extended family members, who had been to those cities to work in bands. He had also observed or met band owners and representatives from Mumbai, Hyderabad, or perhaps Pune, who had come to Aland to recruit bandsmen for upcoming wedding seasons. Had he made the journey to Ahmedabad, Muhammad Razak would likely have gained employment even if no one there knew his name. The māliks in Ahmedabad would be familiar with his home town, which is known for bandsmen; they might know members of his family or many of his caste-mate bandsmen; and they might know local band owners such as Manik Rao for whom Muhammad Razak had worked. Muhammad Razak's origins, locality, and relatedness (Rosen, 1979) would have given credibility to his status as a bandmaster.

In standard band world practice, however, Razak would more likely reach one of these destinations having already agreed on a contract with one of the city's band owners (negotiated either by the owner himself or his representative on a trip made to Aland for that purpose). When Razak reached the city, he would have access to advice regarding which bands had the best reputations, which owners were most reliable, where to find lodging, and so forth. There would be men from his village or region traveling back and forth, to whom he might entrust letters or even bank drafts to be delivered to his family. While he was away, he would spend most of his time with men who spoke his own language and dialect, who knew the people and places with whom he was most familiar, and who shared a common professional and social experience.

Geographer Waldo Tobler's suggestion that "one can infer [geographic] configuration from a behavioral pattern" (1976, 70) applies well to networks of bandsmen. But networks are temporally, socially, and cognitively structured behavioral systems. Each of the two broad networks of migration, which I have labeled Delhi and Mumbai (see pp. 88–89), has somewhat distinctive internal regions, but focuses in some fashion on the city for which it is named.[6] No obvious geographic barrier separates the two networks (in fact, they share a source node); but the border runs through relatively isolated and empty areas of the subcontinent, a belt characterized by desert, hills, and large sections of tribal India: along the Gujarat-Rajasthan border, through the middle of Madhya Pradesh and Chhattisgarh States, and on along the isolated regions of the West Bengal–Orissa border.

The distinctness of these networks is reflected in bandsmen's lack of knowledge about bands outside their own professional world and also helps explain that circumstance. As such, these networks "represent the manifestations of a myriad of past and present decision-making behaviors by individuals, groups, and institutions in society" (Golledge and Stimson 1997, 6). It is worth noting in this context that among the myriad decisions are the political events of 1947, which have had an impact on the brass band world.

Local Rajasthani bandsmen (like Salim) were once active in a different kind of socio-professional network extending well into modern-day Pakistan and throughout the Panjab and Rajasthan. In an earlier, "proselytizing" period of colonial "evolution," big city bands were images and models of colonial modernity. As symbols

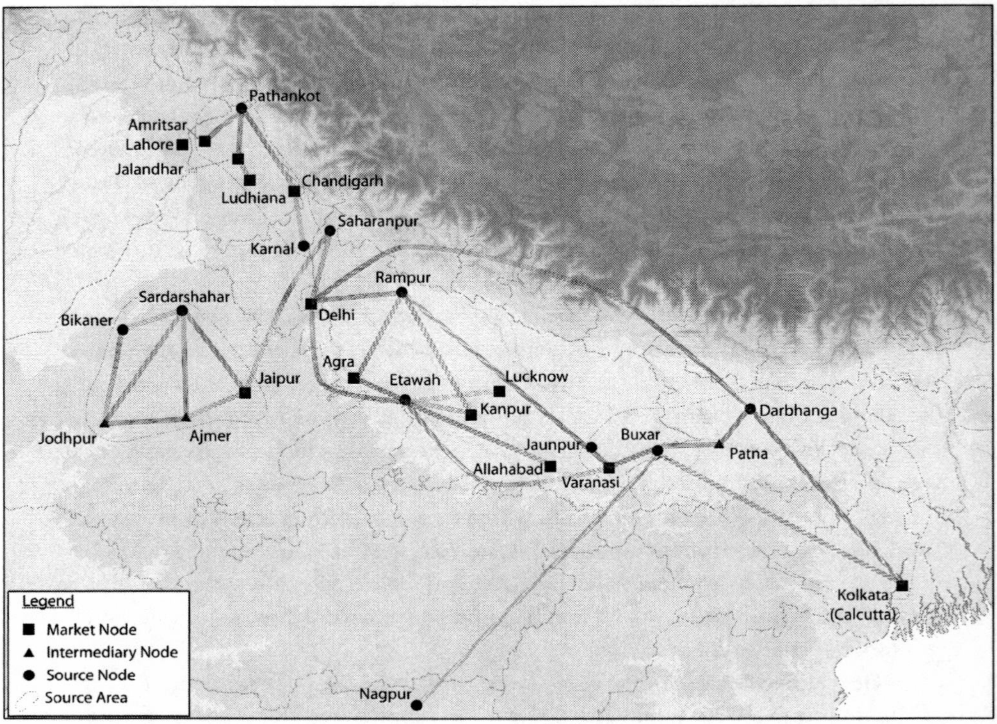

The Delhi networks of migrant bandsmen

of prestige they were sometimes engaged by rural, wealthy families who were attempting to construct similarly modern images of themselves. In northern rural Rajasthan, during the 1930s and '40s, wealthy families competed to hire the most important urban bands (usually from Lahore, but occasionally from Amritsar as well) for local prestigious weddings. When demand in these rural settings exceeded supply, the Muslim owners of these big-city bands found it more convenient and economical to hire additional musicians locally rather than to bring enough musicians with them from the city to meet every contingency. Local, low-status Muslim musicians were, thus, initiated into the band trade by working part time in these larger Panjabi urban bands.

The importation of urban bands into the countryside was a part of the process that spread brass bands throughout India and was not limited to Rajasthan and Panjab. However, the network of professional interactions between rural Rajasthan and urban Lahore (especially) was destroyed by the partition of British India in 1947. Thereafter, rural Rajasthan reoriented itself to the bigger cities of southern Rajasthan and to the national capitol, Delhi. Cities like Bikaner and Sardarsher were now more peripheral than ever; they began exporting musicians to the urban centers as I have described here; but not, of course, to the city (Lahore) that had

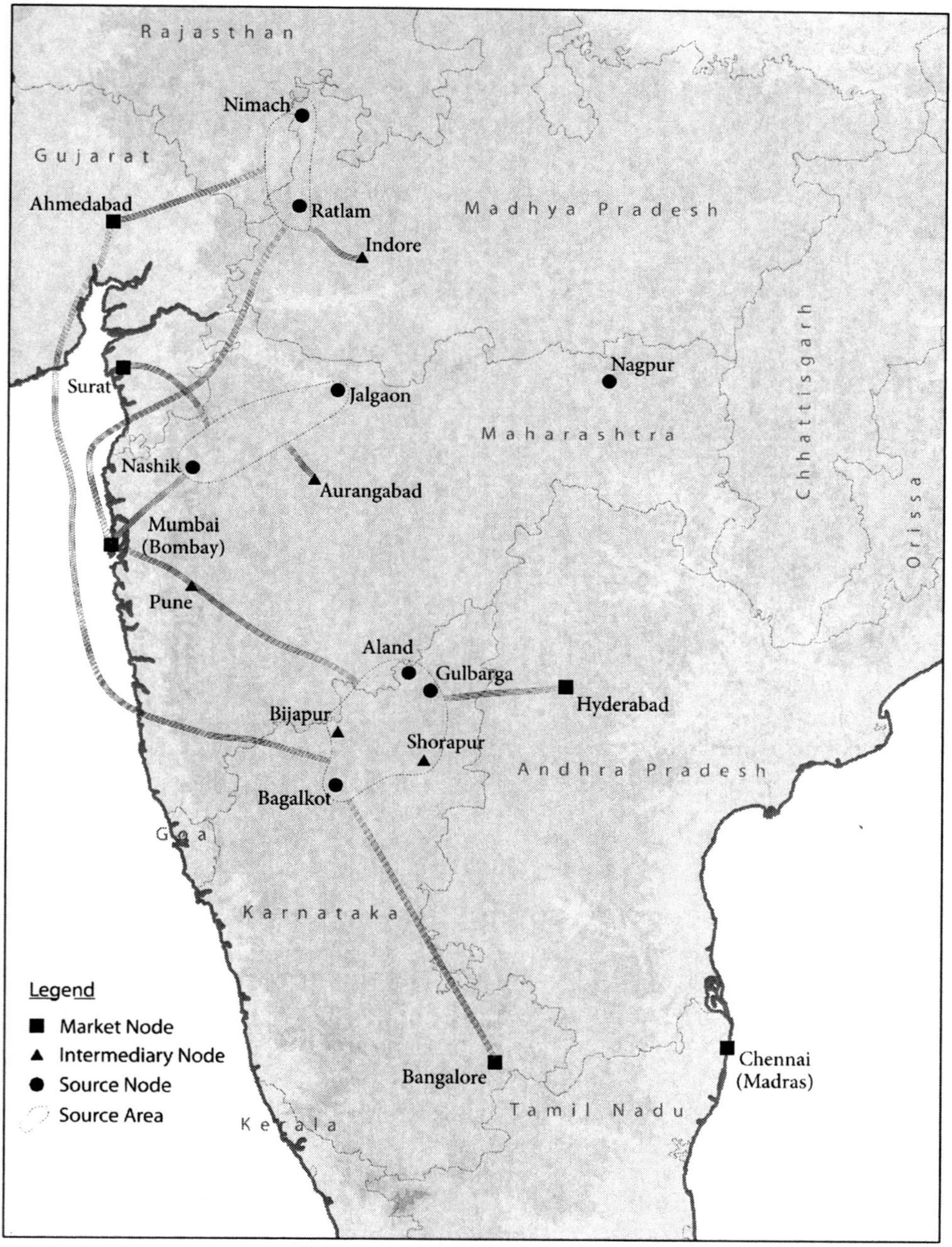

The Mumbai network of migrant bandsmen

been, up to that point, this region's urban source of professional knowledge about a colonially fashionable industry.

Decisions of all kinds, then, and at all levels of society, define and redefine invisible but very real "areas" in which social relations and seasonal market demand produce seasonal movements, which are forms of "goal directed spatial and temporal behavior" (Golledge and Stimson 1997, 5–7). Individual bandsmen all make individual choices; but those choices are constrained and shaped by the social groups to which they belong and the social institution of the Indian brass band in the wedding procession tradition.

Theorizing Migratory Networks in the Indian Band World

Delhi and Mumbai are the central urban nodes of their networks; but both networks also have secondary urban nodes. A city is normally conceptualized as a "central place," functioning as the site of "activity . . . that derives at least part of its support from people living in the rural area around the place" (King and Golledge 1978, 119). Both networks of migration read, in one sense, like lists of greater and lesser market nodes.

While Indian cities are central places for customers, for bandsmen (and in the understandings of professional network members) the nature of urban centrality is actually reversed. The trade derives the vast majority of its income from the people of the urban center; but "people living in the rural area around the place," that is, bandsmen, come to take advantage of the economic surplus that cities accumulate. For bandsmen, the major cities of northern India are thus market nodes, hubs of intense professional activity and economic support. The biggest cities are also the places in the band region's socio-professional structure where smaller segments of the network connect.

Mumbai represents the geographic and socio-professional center of the southern network. This is due in part to the city's general economic vitality and also to its historical prestige in the development of the brass band trade. In the contemporary band world, the prestige remains, as does the pay; but the urban core of this huge city is too crowded, busy, and businesslike to accommodate street processions easily on the scale of the less crowded streets of its northern suburbs or of cities like Ahmedabad or Hyderabad. In consequence, the number of bands and bandsmen in Mumbai is slightly lower per capita than in other major urban markets. By this I mean that in high-season terms, instead of roughly one bandsman for every thousand residents of Delhi, in Mumbai there would only be one for every two or three thousand persons. The sheer size of Mumbai makes it difficult to speak definitively; certainly the ratio increases as one includes more and more of the outer suburbs (such as Navi Mumbai) in the equation.

The Delhi network differs from the Mumbai network in a number of ways. A cultural preference for bigger, flashier bands is pronounced in the north, leading to greater demand and consequently a larger band population. The capitalist features of the band business are more clearly articulated in Delhi than anywhere else in India. The shape and workings of the Delhi network have also been affected by the events of Partition in 1947, as I have described above.

The core of the Delhi network is formed by that city together with the central market nodes located on the riverine plains of central Uttar Pradesh: Agra, Kanpur, Lucknow, Allahabad, and Varanasi. These core markets are somewhat interchangeable as far as bandsmen are concerned, although generally speaking, the pay is best in Delhi. While it is unremarkable that a musician in Allahabad one season might appear in Delhi the next, as one moves east, the proportion of common personnel declines. Delhi is also the meeting point for men from source nodes to the north, east, and the west of the city, who would otherwise have no markets in common. In the south, Hyderabad and Ahmedabad are the major secondary market nodes; but geographically, they represent the northern and southern limits of their network, rather than a core.

There is no clear core in the southern network—other than Mumbai, if we could describe that city as southern. Instead, such intermediary nodes as Pune, Sholhapur, Surat, and Indore separate Mumbai from the two secondary market nodes, Hyderabad and Ahmedabad. Muhammad Razak, for instance, would have earned more in any of these cities than he did during his year in Gulbarga, but would not have considered them signs of professional success. These smaller urban centers act simultaneously as markets to which local rural bandsmen may migrate and (sometimes) as source nodes from which bandsmen, often those who are better trained and more highly skilled, may move on to major urban centers. Bandsmen who are just beginning, or in some cases winding down, their careers will seek employment in the intermediary nodes. Southern migrants may choose to bypass Mumbai altogether, traveling an extra day to get to Ahmedabad; from the Deccan source nodes they may choose to move in the opposite direction altogether by migrating to Hyderabad. Although its history makes it the primary city of the network, one cannot argue that all roads lead to Mumbai.

In many smaller urban nodes, the proportion of migrant bandsmen to locally resident bandsmen swings slightly more in the direction of the residents. In such cities, the demand is limited by size or other factors. Bangalore, for example, has limited demand for its size; relatively large numbers of northern immigrants create a somewhat artificial demand. Bangalore is also in the wrong direction, beyond the normal limits of southern bandsmen migration. These factors mitigate the attractiveness of Bangalore as a market node for migrant bandsmen. Instead, Bangalore is served primarily by Bagalkot, a source node from the network. Chennai is both geographically and culturally isolated from the bandsmen networks, so local labor must meet the limited demand for wedding bands there. Chennai offers neither the jobs, nor the connections, nor the wages to make possible or productive the considerable travel that would be required.

Some cities are simply not part of the network system, although it is not clear why. Kolhapur, rather small and rather off the beaten track, is one such city. Jabalpur is neither small nor out of the way, but is nevertheless dominated entirely by resident bandsmen. Many of them work in regular "day jobs" that augment the earnings from their band work and are apparently flexible enough to allow time off during the wedding season.

By definition, migrants live in source nodes. Although these are sometimes physically distant from the urban markets, their peripheral nature is more consistently structured by socioeconomic and cultural factors than by distance as such. Migrant bandsmen live in small towns and villages that are characterized by low costs of living, few economic opportunities, and relatively underdeveloped economic infrastructure. Because the motivation for migrant labor in the band world is based on cost-of-living differences between market and source nodes and a high concentration of demand, market nodes are definable as places with high demand and a high cost of living. In most, but not all, cases this means a large city. Source nodes are similarly but conversely definable as regions with a low cost of living and low demand. Source nodes have one other characteristic, which is that they are dominated by a small number of caste groups who are most active in providing musicians for the band trade. Usually, these are low-status groups; most (but not all) have a traditional association with processional music. The town names I use to identify source nodes are those commonly used by bandsmen; but it should be understood that source nodes can be areas in themselves comprising many smaller villages that surround the named town.

As cultural places, market and source nodes represent locations of dominance by different social and professional identities. Cities are the home of the bands and band owners. Fewer generalized comments can be made about this smaller population than about the bandsman population; but in each city a relatively limited number of social identities are prominent in band ownership. Normally multiple bands are owned by members of any given social identity; those identities represent either minority populations within that city, refugee populations, or populations from low-status castes. In many instances, relations based on caste or religions may exist between groups of band owners and migrant bandsmen whom they recruit. Nevertheless, this is a business; more than caste, it is economics that drives the individual decisions of both owners and laborers.

Similar kinds of comments can be made with regard to migrant bandsmen from various source nodes, although one must look at very small areas to find single identity sources. Whereas Rampur city and Saharanpur district are dominated by a small number of Muslim castes, Rampur bandsmen are all Sheikh-Siddiqī, while those from Saharanpur are predominantly so. The Bijapur/Bagalkot area is completely dominated by Mane-Jādhav bandsmen; but while Nimach/Ratlam is dominated by Sheikh-Masūdī bandsmen, Dhar, immediately adjacent, is a source for low-status Hindu bandsmen. [**Video example 5.3**]

Bandsmen often travel in fairly homogeneous groups; but again, while the professional structure effectively produces intergroup competition, such competition is not expressed at the individual level. I must make clear that there is no verbalization, nor really any sense of, an "us-against-them" mentality within the migrant bandsman population (except conceptions of bandsmen in relation to band owners). A Hindu bandsman from Dhar and a Muslim bandsman from Ratlam would still have a regional and experiential solidarity that would normally override any social differences.

The Delhi network is distinctive in the extent to which its outer reaches are indistinct and difficult to represent. The developing professional structures in these regions and the cultures that surrounded and supported them were profoundly disrupted by Partition, as I have described above for bandsmen in Rajasthan and Panjab. Rajasthan now provides a nested nodal hierarchy within the larger northern network. Jaipur is the local center of the Rajasthani subnetwork; but smaller Rajasthani cities such as Jodhpur and even Ajmer are intermediary nodal centers. All the Rajasthani markets recruit local bandsmen, but also depend on mobile laborers, who come almost exclusively from smaller cities in northern Rajasthan such as Bikaner or Sardarshahr. As a peripheral center, Jaipur is the point of contact between its own area and the greater Delhi network. The cities of the Indian Panjab form another subnetwork.

Although Kolkata was home to very early developments in the band business, the economic downturn that followed the shifting of the Indian capitol to Delhi (in 1933) and the severe crises that followed Partition and, later, the Bangladesh war, all weakened the city's ability to support a large number of bands. Since much of the colonial-era band trade was supported by patronage from wealthy Marwari business families, the gradual decline or flight of these families to other cities also weakened Kolkata's position as a major market node. As with Rajasthan, Partition also relocated Kolkata on the national borders, in an increasingly isolated position geographically. Finally, the contemporary trade has been under intense pressure for many years because of the physical difficulty of mounting private processions in the streets. Tenuous social and professional links nevertheless connect Kolkata at least as far as Patna. Patna becomes a common market and source node linking Kolkata with the eastern side of the Delhi network, since bandsmen do move between Bihar and Uttar Pradesh, especially Varanasi.

The distances separating rural villages, intermediate towns, and large cities of India and the transportation infrastructures that connect them are factors that influence movement between nodes. More significant than physical factors, however, are the patterns of group identity in South Asia, which are the real forms of connection that keep individual bandsmen moving from small villages to big cities.

Social relations in the band world range widely from the sometimes powerful bonds of immediate family or extended family to the more diffuse sharing of tribal or religious identity. Karen Leonard's ethnography of Kayasth-caste families in Hyderabad (1978) shows that caste members organize professional activity across a range of levels. In the band world, professional decision making by band owners regarding hire, fees, wages, conditions of employment and control of particular markets does in fact, take place within the context of this range of social relations engendered by family and caste. The interplay of caste and patterns of market control appears with regularity in particular networks and market nodes throughout India.

David Rudner has argued that "caste identities... constitute a form of what Bourdieu called *symbolic capital*" (Bourdieu 1989, 18). In a similar vein, Gurcharan Das (2002) has pointed to the specific abilities of caste structures to support private economic developments. Like Das, I would argue that, in the arenas of labor and economics, caste relations embody a potential form of actual capital. Inheritable and sometimes inescapable, caste provides a social mechanism whereby individuals may gain access to a particular trade and through groups may attempt to exert total, or near total, control over particular labor networks or patronage markets. Related groups organize behavioral systems across space as part of strategies designed to ensure access to markets for their members.

Specifically, caste identities engender relationships among bandsmen and sometimes between bandsmen and band owners that encourage the development of network structures. On the level of the individual, this means that for bandsmen such as Muhammad Razak, membership in his particular social group offers an entry into a particular market or trade. This is only so, however, if Razak chooses to take advantage of the economic potential represented by his membership in a caste with suitable connections, and if he wishes to become a mobile musician, leaving his family and his small village each wedding season for one of the better-paying urban markets.

The structures that organize the movement of bandsmen to and from urban markets are informed largely by relations that are familial, social, professional, and to a limited extent historical. As behavioral systems, these mobile labor networks and patterns demonstrate the adaptive results of an interrelated set of cultural "zations." The processes of colonization and urbanization have been the most influential; but not paradoxically, these phenomena also reflect aspects on both ends of the globalization-localization continuum. There are, in effect, two fundamental raisons d'être for the existence of these networks. First, they create, as in my story about Muhammad Razak, a mobile "locality" for bandsmen, where they are known, and have friends and support. This is an important consideration for men who may spend as much as six months away from their homes and families. The migration pathways create a geographically flexible locality within which bandsmen may travel from their homes to the city for work and back, all the while in the company of others from home.

In 1989 I met an elderly bandsman named Bashir'uddin who worked regularly for a band in Mumbai, traveling each year from his village near Aland in

Andhra Pradesh. When I returned there in 1995, and again discovered him working there, I mentioned that I had met another elderly bandsman named Abdul Jaffar (but called Nanhe Mia) from Bashir's village at a wedding in Gulbarga a few years before. Bashir'uddin happily informed me that Nanhe Mia was his elder brother. Despite the roughly 600 kilometers of physical distance, Bashir and his brother were part of a unified cultural world, much more relevant to them (and to me) than the world inhabited by the many Mumbaikars walking past the shop that day. A geographically dispersed group of bandsmen, spread from Ahmedabad to Hyderabad, had a set of shared acquaintances and experiences that was very much part of their cultural locality, but that was not tied to the particular place they happened to be that particular wedding season. Migratory bandsmen travel within a culturally constructed professional locality out of which they rarely step. They do not normally know the families for whom they play, or much about the cities in which they reside temporarily.

The socio-professional networks of the north and central Indian bandsmen offer a valuable perspective on the interactions among cultural expression, geographic place, and social identity. They may also provide insights into other areas in which professional or economic competition has been more carefully cloaked in cultural terminology. The *gharānā* phenomenon in Hindustani classical music, for example, to whatever extent it existed as a concrete social reality, seems to have focused on control of repertoire, although we might perhaps imagine a point in time at which the forbearers of the *gharānā* structure did, on a local level, try to restrict access to royal patronage to their own family and students. Bandsmen may have no control over their repertoire; but they can control markets to some extent, at least at the level of caste.

The migratory behaviors of Indian bandsmen are professional and social responses to a changing market place and patronage structure. As those economic realities changed, with the growth of India's big cities, bandsmen found ways to organize, along traditional lines, the economic potential of these growing markets. Similarly, that demand allowed many band owners to move beyond their traditional roles to truly managerial roles. Almost coincidentally, this view of these behaviors adds a further dimension to the notion of cultural locality. The picture that comes from their behaviors adds considerably to our understanding of how social and professional groups and group behaviors construct socio-professional space in specific ways and for specifically pragmatic ends. Their rare statements about these localities are more routinely expressed in behavior, but nevertheless demonstrate a clear understanding of "the way things are supposed to work."

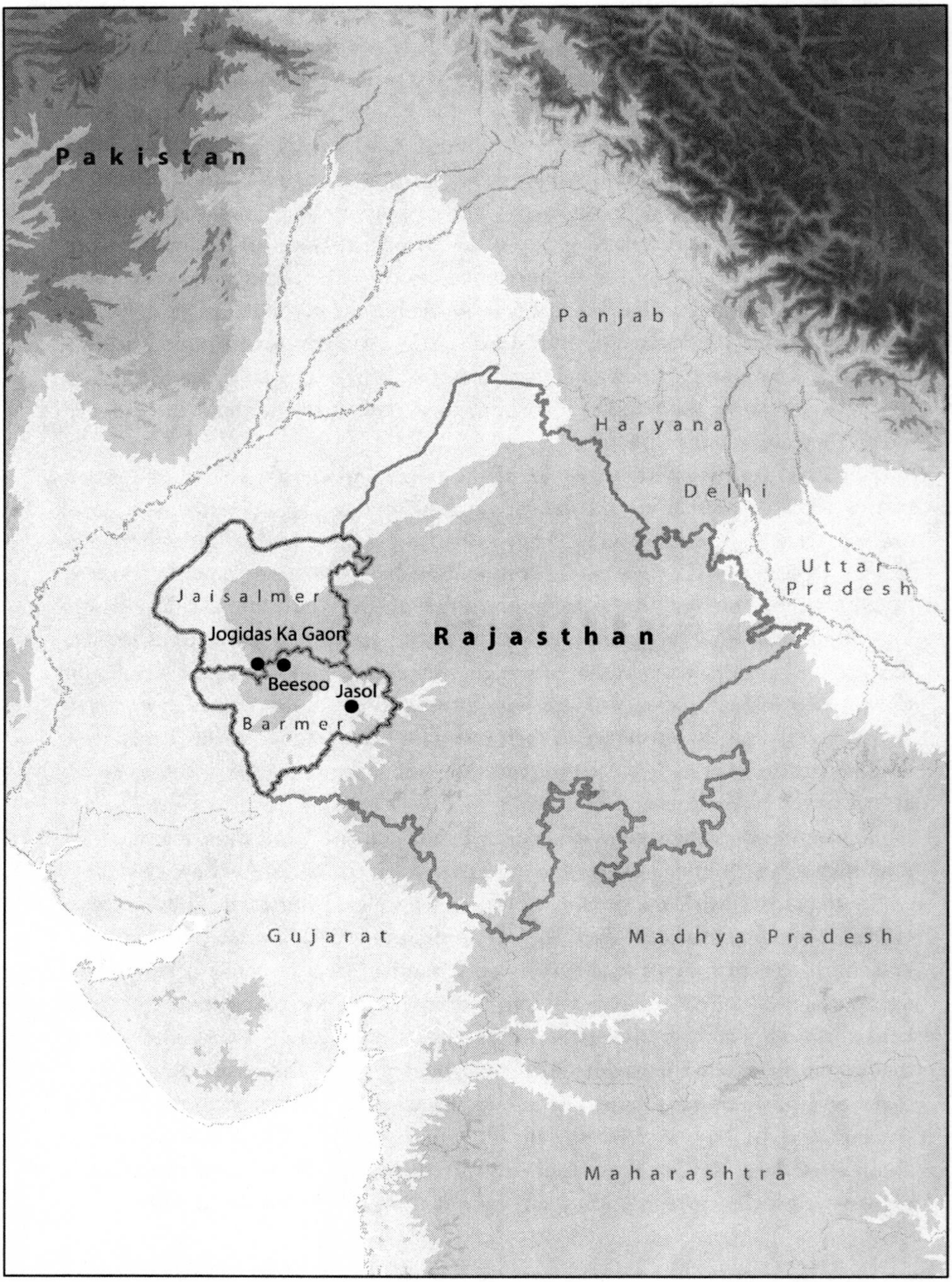
Pakistan
Panjab
Haryana
Delhi
Uttar Pradesh
Jaisalmer
Jogidas Ka Gaon
Rajasthan
Beesoo
Jasol
Barmer
Gujarat
Madhya Pradesh
Maharashtra

CHAPTER 6

The Princess of the Musicians

Rāni Bhaṭiyāṇi and the Māngaṇiārs of Western Rajasthan

SHUBHA CHAUDHURI

Musicians and Patronage

The Rājput-Māngaṇiār Relationship

Among the hereditary musicians of western Rajasthan are the Māngaṇiārs. As is the case with all hereditary castes in Rajasthan, the Māngaṇiārs have another caste as their patrons. This relationship is part of the *jajmān* system, where hereditary groups provide customary services to other groups. Māngaṇiārs (a word derived from *māngnā* or to "to beg") are one of the dependent castes of the Rājputs, along with a few other Hindu communities. They provide musical services at the time of births and weddings as well as any important life-cycle event of the patron families, in return for which they are supported in various ways. They are expected to attend the funeral and mourning rites of the patron families as well, though there is no music performed at that time. The rights of the musicians include gifts of clothes and money, and also extend to a share in the agricultural produce. Patrons even contribute to ritual events in the musician's family such as weddings and funerals.[1]

One of the many complexities of this relationship is the fact that Māngaṇiārs are Muslim and belong to the larger group of Mīrāsīs—and have as their patrons Hindu Rājputs. Rājputs are considered the ruling caste of Rajasthan, and indeed historically Rājputs ruled many other princely states of India. An analysis of this relationship, which is very alive in western Rajasthan even today, reveals many of the intricacies of the social order and of the status of musicians and the changes that they are undergoing.

The subject of this chapter, however, is the relationship of hereditary musicians to local shrines, which is explored through the relationship of the Māngaṇiārs to the deity known as Rāni Bhaṭiyāṇi. This lesser-known extension of the patronage system is connected with a story or myth that encapsulates the fabric of the musical culture of western Rajasthan: the relationship of the musicians to their patrons, the concept of sati in western Rajasthan, and the role that musicians play in shrines. Māngaṇiārs and their patrons alike continue to theorize their local through variations in this story. These variations raise further issues of patronage, gender, narrative, and the impact of all these on musicians in this part of Rajasthan.[2]

Creation of a Myth: The Story of Rāni Bhaṭiyāṇi

This is the story of a Rājput princess called Svarūp, popularly known as Rāni Bhaṭiyāṇi, from a small state in the Jaisalmer district of Rajasthan.[3] She is called Bhaṭiyāṇi as her father belonged to the Bhaṭi clan of Rājputs, who are the ruling caste of Rajasthan. She was married to Kalyan Singh—a Rāṭhor of the royal family of Jasol in the district of Barmer (according to another version of the story discussed below, she was his second wife). Rumor had it that she was having an affair with her brother-in-law Sawai Singh. This obviously did not endear her to her in-laws. Once, when Kalyan Singh and Sawai Singh went to fight in battle, word reached Rāni Bhaṭiyāṇi that Kalyan Singh had been killed, and she decided to commit sati by immolating herself on his funeral pyre.[4] However, the body that arrived was not her husband's but that of Sawai Singh. Rāni Bhaṭiyāṇi went ahead to commit sati nevertheless.

Not knowing of her death, a Māngaṇiār musician from her father's village in Jaisalmer came to Jasol to visit her at her married home. When he asked after her, the in-laws sarcastically told him to go and meet her in her palace on the hill. While he was on his way, he met her on the path. He did not know that it was her ghost or spirit; she gave him all her jewelry and told him not to show it to anybody, and that the gold would serve to support his family for life. On his way back, the Māngaṇiār was tempted to show the in-laws what he had received from Rāni Bhaṭiyāṇi in the hope that he would get more from them. They, however, recognized the jewelry and thinking that he had stolen it, took it from him and sent him away with a beating. On his way home, Rāni Bhaṭiyāṇi met him once more. She berated him for not obeying her. She said, however, as compensation, and as he was her musician, he and his community would be able to sing about her and earn their livelihood.

After the death of Svarūp, her husband Kalyan Singh remarried. A spate of bad luck and years of drought later forced the family to relocate to the nearby town of Balotra. Eventually a temple was built to honor Rāni Bhaṭiyāṇi at Jasol, at the site of her cremation. This ended the phase of bad luck, and she was worshiped as a *satī mātā* ("sati mother"). The cult of Rāni Bhaṭiyāṇi grew as fame of her miraculous "powers" spread throughout western Rajasthan and beyond Rajasthan. True to her boon, Māngaṇiārs (and other musicians as well) have been able to earn a livelihood singing about her.

Musicians and Shrines Trance/Possession and Music

The story of Rāni Bhaṭiyāṇi illustrates, among other things, how shrines of local deities are established in western Rajasthan. Shrines are built for those who died unnatural, often heroic deaths, or died before their time.[5] However for a shrine to be built the person who has died must appear as a vision or in a dream. This is taken as a sign of their supernatural powers. Often they ask for a shrine to be built in the dream. Shrines in memory of satis are normally made on the sites of their deaths.[6]

Offerings or *caṛhāvās*, as they are called at these shrines (unlike mainstream Hindu shrines), consist of alcohol, tobacco, and incense. Another feature of these local shrines is that they are not attended by traditional Brahman priests but by *bhopās* (f. *bhopī*).

A person becomes a *bhopā* by choice or calling, and is attached to a specific deity. Possession and trance play a critical role here, as the deities manifest their powers and presence through the medium of the *bhopā*. A shrine is considered active only when the deity is seen to intervene in people's lives through this possession or trance state. Miracles, powers of healing, or granting wish fulfillment are attributed to such deities, who can even demonstrate malevolent powers that need appeasement. It is here that the role of musicians becomes important.

Music, especially drumming, is connected with trance and possession in many parts of the world (see Rouget 1985). Musicians sing invocatory or panegyric songs called *oḷakh*s and play a large, cylindrical *ḍhol* drum to bring the *bhopā* or even devotees into a state of possession.

The strong association of the *oḷakh*'s melody (they are all similar) with the context probably creates the trigger for possession. The association is so powerful that once Nagge Khan, a Māngaṇiār, simulated the situation at a shrine in jest for me by singing a fragment of an *oḷakh* and making sounds of drumming. A young woman in the vicinity, who turned out to be a *bhopī* of Rāni Bhaṭiyāṇi, went into a state of possession, insisting that he beg forgiveness for insulting her.

All musician communities in western Rajasthan have a relationship to local shrines and sing *oḷakh*s to local deities. For example, at the main shrine in Jasol, the resident musicians are from the Ḍholī community that serve that area.[7] The musicians who attend the shrines receive financial offerings made by the pilgrims who visit the shrines. Whether one is a Māngaṇiār or a Ḍholī, the right of performing at a shrine is hereditary and limited to particular musician families. They can also be called upon to sing at any place where a person is known to come into trance, or is believed to be possessed by a particular deity.

The *ḍhol's* ritual significance in the shrine is also reflected in the fact that it is communally owned, in the custody of the head of the village or the *bhopā*.[8] Of the various Māngaṇiārs who are attached to Rāni Bhaṭiyāṇi shrines, some also function as *bhopā* priests.

The Māngaṇiārs' special relationship to Rāni Bhaṭiyāṇi rests on the fact that she first appeared to one of them in a vision. It is this first manifestation in the spirit form (*parchyo*) that is significant.

The Changing Versions of the Story

In 2003–4, I collected no fewer than six versions of the story being told at the time. In just over a decade the story that was popularly accepted seemed to have changed dramatically.

In some versions of the popular story, Kalyan Singh is portrayed as having married a woman named Devri prior to marrying Rāni Bhaṭiyāṇi. Devri is said, in these versions, to have poisoned Rāni Bhaṭiyāṇi, Rāni Bhaṭiyāṇi's son, or even Sawai Singh. Rāni Bhaṭiyāṇi's identity as a sati seems to be growing less popular. Sawai Singh is variously cast as her brother-in-law or her grandson, and there is no mention of any romantic relationship between Rāni Bhaṭiyāṇi and Sawai Singh. It is perhaps interesting to note that just a few years earlier a young Māngaṇiār had told me that the story was that she was not a sati—but that she and her lover Sawai Singh had been murdered by the in-laws and they had later tried to cover this up by proclaiming her a sati.

A publication being sold by the Rāni Bhaṭiyāṇi Trust at the Jasol temple is perhaps the source of the changes in the so-far orally transmitted story.[9] This version claims that Rāni Bhaṭiyāṇi died in sorrow over her son's poisoning. The recent versions of the story also name the Māngaṇiār to whom she appeared—Shankar Māngaṇiār.

In a couple of versions, Rāni Bhaṭiyāṇi performs miracles to substantiate the claims of the Māngaṇiār. There are overall more miracles in most of the recent versions; for example, a feast that appeared accompanying the gifts to the musician, or lamps that appeared magically at the site of her cremation.

It is also interesting that in the Jasol pamphlet, Sawai Singh appears as a *bhomiya* (a person who becomes a village deity after sacrificing his life for the cows of a village) and does not enter into the tale of Rāni Bhaṭiyāṇi's death at all. This story, however is not yet in circulation among the Māngaṇiārs. Shirley Trembath (1999 and pers. comm.) cites a 1997 interview with Nahar Singh, the current descendant of the Jasol Rāñhor family, in which he denied all stories of an affair between Rāni Bhaṭiyāṇi and her brother-in-law Sawai Singh, saying it was invented by the Māngaṇiārs. But he did not deny that she had committed sati for him, for, according to him, in those days it was not uncommon for a woman to commit sati for a younger man, especially if he was not married. He and other members of the family did believe, he said, in her ability to perform miracles. Shirley Trembath also found a version of the story in a pamphlet in which Devri, the first wife of Kalyan Singh, poisoned Rāni Bhaṭiyāṇi and her son Lal Singh because she was jealous of Rāni Bhaṭiyāṇi (the second wife) and did not want Rāni Bhaṭiyāṇi's son to gain the throne.

Appropriation of a Myth and a Deity

In the Rāṭhor Rājput's appropriation of the Rāni Bhaṭiyāṇi story, her image changes from a sati of perhaps dubious reputation to a *camatkāri devī* (one who performs miracles) more like a *kul devī* (an ancestral goddess)—from a negative force that had to be appeased to one that they now own, carrying with it cultural power and the money that goes with it. The Rāṭhor family of Jasol is now credited with having been the first to institute a shrine to her and the first to realize her powers. It is significant, however, that the musician retains his presence through all the variations of the story.

A local myth or story grows into to an epic as the fame and power of a deity grows beyond the immediate area. The stories grow as they spread, absorbing other local elements. Sometimes they get linked to other myths and deities and, in some cases, to the major epics of the *Rāmayāṇa* and *Mahābhārata*. Local deities also start being related to Hindu gods and goddesses, as avatars. Elements of these processes have also begun with the Rāni Bhaṭiyāṇi story.

The published pamphlet found in Jasol contains an additional story, not corroborated in oral interviews with musicians, that links Rāni Bhaṭiyāṇi to Rupānde and Māllināth, local deities of the Rāmdev cult. Rāni Bhaṭiyāṇi is now cast as a reincarnation of the first wife of Māllināth. The story of this new relationship has economic implications for the Rāni Bhaṭiyāṇi Trust, which now controls shrines in the surrounding area of Khed, including the shrines of Māllināth and Rupānde. Various appropriations of the Rāni Bhaṭiyāṇi story, then, marginalize the role of musicians regardless of whether these are alterations of the story supported by the media, published pamphlets, cassettes, and films, or the creation of trusts that control shrines and the revenue that is generated.

The Growing Fame of Rāni Bhaṭiyāṇi

The cult of Rāni Bhaṭiyāṇi has grown immensely in the past decade. Māngaṇiārs say that there are now numerous shrines in each village. More shrines and temples are dedicated to her than ever before. Cassettes of songs about her magical powers proliferate, and even a film has been made about her. The local cassette and CD industries find ready markets at the many shrines where crowds throng in busloads on auspicious days. This is probably part of the general growth of shrines and temples in Rajasthan. In and around Barmer, Mājisā (meaning "mother"—one of names Rāni Bhaṭiyāṇi is called) is well on its way to being a brand name with shops, and autorickshaws advertise various goods bearing her name.

In the following case studies of three shrines of Rāni Bhaṭiyāṇi—the primary one at Jasol, the shrines at Jogidas, her birthplace, and a *thān* at Beesoo—I explain further how music functions in local religious contexts and how tensions between the patron communities and marginalized musicians get played out.

Jasol 1990–2004

The shrine of Rāni Bhaṭiyāṇi at Jasol, with its special significance of being the first such shrine, provides perhaps the clearest profile of change. Though the cult of Rāni Bhaṭiyāṇi was fairly widespread all over Rajasthan and beyond, when we visited the shrine in 1990 it was a small and fairly quiet shrine, which had a reputation of curing crippled and paralyzed people.

Ḍholī musicians performed inside the temple at the time. We were told that four Ḍholī families in Jasol took turns performing inside the temple. Ḍholīs also sang in the courtyard of the temple. A Hindu priest officiated there then, instead of a *bhopā;* and an electrically run machine played drums and cymbals. A locked chest bore the name of the trust that ran the temple.[10] Devotees put money into the locked chest and made cash offerings directly to the Ḍholīs who sang there. This ensured the Ḍholī families a constant source of support. The priest officiated without highly controlling the atmosphere; people were free to carry out their own forms of worship. We were able to witness the offering of alcohol, which is considered one of the traditional forms of offering.[11] Neither the lack of a *bhopā* nor the presence of a drum-playing machine in 1990 had threatened the presence of musicians.

Komal Kothari reported in the 1970s that the offering box was opened once a month and the money distributed equally between the four Ḍholī families who served the temple. By 1989–90, the introduction of the trust had caused a power shift in which the economic benefits then had to be shared with the trust, as well.

In 2004, the shrine had turned into a huge temple, along the lines of many temples being constructed today with elaborate carvings and domes. The rebuilding was obviously used to put a new order in place. Not only were musicians not performing there, but Ḍholīs were not even allowed to sing and play in the temple. Prior to this, the Ḍholīs had been moved out of the temple and were allowed to sing only in the courtyard. Today, the playing of the *ḍhol* is forbidden, as is the offering of alcohol, tobacco, and animal sacrifices. The offerings are now more traditional: sweets, coconuts, and auspicious items (*suhāg*) such as bangles, henna, and

FIGURE 6.1. Traditional Rāni Bhaṭiyāṇi idol at Jasol. Photographed by Daniel Neuman, 1990.

bindīs, that are associated with the status of a married woman. Policemen keeping vigil amid the huge crowds, and no photography is allowed.[12]

The idol in the temple has been made more classical, like the white marble ones of mainstream Hindu temples. The old idol, typical of sati shrines, lacked explicit and recognizable features except for large eyes; it was dressed in red and gold.[13] So even iconography reflects the desire to create a more mainstream goddess who perhaps in the future will be seen as related to a Hindu goddess.

Jasol today is important as the center from which changes are being propagated through a printed pamphlet. The undated pamphlet, which claims to be an authoritative historical account of the life of Rāni Bhaṭiyāṇi, reinforces the dominant power structure by acknowledging the support and help of the ruling families of Jasol.

The temple at Jasol, now a major pilgrimage site, has a market that has grown around it selling sweets, flowers, and other offerings. Companies with such names as Mājisā Audio and Video company produce cassettes sold there.

* * *

Elsewhere, too, trusts consolidate power and finances of temples and other places of worship and move musicians away from being beneficiaries. A study of the changing relationship of musicians to shrines on a wider scale would have to be undertaken to see the larger implications of these takeovers. The relationship of musicians to shrines is in this sense an extension of the patronage system. Nevertheless, even though musicians no longer have the same support, they retain a place.

The sanskritization (if one may use the word in a context of shrines such as Jasol) leads to a change in the form of worship; this does away with the *bhopā* and the need for trance possession, and thus the presence of the musician. However, this is not cut and dried. Since the beliefs surrounding deities, possession, and music persist, musicians perform outside the gates at night for pilgrims who participate in trance possession. Even though it is not played, the *ḍhol* remains in the temple and retains its importance as a ritual object. I was told that the atmosphere changes at night outside the official hours of worship.[14] Devotees come from other towns and camp outside the gates at night. As Ḍholīs sing and play the harmonium and *ḍholak* (a barrel drum smaller than the *ḍhol*), some devotees become possessed (experience *bhāv*).

As has been mentioned, the growth and establishment of shrines is an organic one in western Rajasthan. Changes that have come about in the worship of Rāni Bhaṭiyāṇi owing to her increased popularity have not shaken the belief that Māngaṇiārs have a strong historical connection to her. The implications for the status of musicians in this changed scenario are suggested in the following consideration of the shrines at Jogidas and Beesoo.

Jogidas ka Gaon

The village of Jogidas ka Gaon is the birthplace of Rāni Bhaṭiyāṇi. According to all local sources, it was practically abandoned for many years. The shrine of Rāni Bhaṭiyāṇi there was practically unknown, and was "attended" by Ramzan Khan, believed to be the descendant of Shankar Māngaṇiār, to whom Rāni Bhaṭiyāṇi had first appeared as a vision.

Now there are three shrines of different levels that involve Māngaṇiārs. Today, Jogidas has a rebuilt shrine, and a new shrine created on the ruins of the house in which it is believed Rāni Bhaṭiyāṇi was born. Nearby is the small "Māngaṇiār

FIGURE 6.2. The new Rāni Bhaṭiyāṇi idol at the shrine at Jogidas ka Gaon. Photographed by Jyoti Rath, 2003.

shrine," which Ramzan Khan's wife, known to be a *bhopī* of Rāni Bhaṭiyāṇi, attends. Separate from this is a fourth a shrine built by the Darji (tailor) community. The main shrine has an idol, which is different from the older one at Jasol, and seems to be more like "mainstream" Hindu goddesses.

I visited the shrines on the thirteenth night of the bright phase of the Magh month, known to be one of the most auspicious nights for wish-fulfillment from Rāni Bhaṭiyāṇi. Māngaṇiārs Niyaz Khan and his brother (brothers of the famous musician Anwar Khan from the nearby village of Baiya) were singing as forms of offering in the main shrine at the time. The singers accompanied themselves on a

FIGURE 6.3. A stall at Jasol selling photos of Rāni Bhaṭiyāṇi, playing recordings of Rāni Bhaṭiyāṇi songs, as is seen by the loudspeakers. Photographed by Jyoti Rath, 2003.

ḍhol and a harmonium. The singing of *oḷakh*s in this context is called *oḷakh bharni*. They were followed by singing of the *bhopī* of the Māngaṇiār shrine, the wife of Ramzan Khan. The singing goes on through the night as other Māngaṇiārs arrive. A priest officiated over the offerings part of the time, and people put cash offerings into a locked chest. A few people also put money on the *ḍhol* and harmonium of the musicians. [**Video example 6.1**]

The Māngaṇiārs also visited the shrine at the nearby birthplace of Rāni Bhaṭiyāṇi. That shrine has neither an idol nor a priest, but rather a carving of footprints and an icon of a horseman which is supposed to represent Sawai Singh, the brother-in-law. The *ḍhol*, sitting in an empty courtyard, was considered significant here (as at other such shrines) and was maintained by the local community around the shrine. Niyaz Khan sang a few *oḷakh*s, each one ending with the *shubhrāj* of the Bhaṭi Rājputs, invoking Rāni Bhaṭiyāṇi's grandfather and father. The *shubhrāj* is a geneaology recited by the musician of the patron family, which includes great deeds of some of the ancestors. Reciting the *shubhrāj* is one of the duties of the musicians toward their patrons.

A trustee of the newly formed trust there corroborated the importance of the Māngaṇiārs in the worship of Rāni Bhaṭiyāṇi and the fact that this community is particularly dear to her. Ramzan Khan, the Māngaṇiār who lives in Jogidas, has the hereditary right to the offerings made at the shrines. He claimed that all the money collected that night would go to Ramzan Khan, even though he was not even present in the village that particular night.

As the cult of Rāni Bhaṭiyāṇi spreads, the importance of Jogidas as her birthplace is also seen as increasing. The shrines at Jogidas have today become a major pilgrimage center for the Māngaṇiār community. This relatively recent development may be due to the proximity of the shrine to many Māngaṇiār villages, or to control by Bhaṭi Rājputs, who are patrons of many Māngaṇiārs. This situation provides an insight into a different state of the change at Jasol. The increase in Rāni Bhaṭiyāṇi's popularity has led the Rājputs to highlight their relationship as her descendants and to her place of birth.

* * *

As shrines to Rāni Bhaṭiyāṇi were built in various parts of Rajasthan, the musicians who sang at those shrines have not necessarily been Māngaṇiārs. At the same time, Māngaṇiārs attend shrines of other deities and sing *oḷakh*s for them, as well. What, then, are the unique features of this story in which musicians figured and how do the Māngaṇiārs perceive their relationship to Rāni Bhaṭiyāṇi? According to the Māngaṇiārs, they have a special relationship with Rāni Bhaṭiyāṇi because she appeared to a Māngaṇiār and displayed her divine powers. According to them it is necessary for a Māngaṇiār to be present for wishes to be granted. Their privilege of being selected first to witness her divine form is widely acknowledged. The Māngaṇiārs as well as many others in the area surrounding Jaisalmer refer to Rāni Bhaṭiyāṇi as Mājisā (mother) or Bhuāsā (paternal aunt).

All Māngaṇiārs whom I interviewed related instances of cures they had experienced by praying to her, commissioning all-night *rāti jāga* ceremonies of singing for her, and making offerings at her shrines. Though such examples of the powers of Rāni Bhaṭiyāṇi are not unique to the Māngaṇiārs, they underline the fact that she has a special place among deities for them. Many Māngaṇiārs say that children are brought to the shrine after their birth or that they visit the shrine to make offerings after the birth of a child. Some said they also pray to her in times of trouble, illness, or any difficulty, as they feel she cares for them.

Many Māngaṇiārs individually are devotees of other *devīs* (goddesses) but as a group Māngaṇiārs see themselves as special devotees of Rāni Bhaṭiyāṇi. In the districts of Barmer and Jaisalmer where the Bhañi Rājputs were the ruling clan, the Māngaṇiārs consider themselves to be Rāni Bhaṭiyāṇi's family's musicians and recite the *shubhrāj* as part of their worship. It is not so much that they see her as a Hindu deity who they as Muslims are worshiping but as the daughter of a Bhaṭi Rājput family, who, as their patron and protector, is worthy of their attention and respect.

Māngaṇiār women also feature in this relationship, and there are numerous women who function as *bhopīs* of Rāni Bhaṭiyāṇi, and get possessed by her. The issues of gender, possession, and female deities that are involved go beyond the scope of this discussion. Nevertheless, it is tempting to speculate that women have access to power only through supernatural means as *devīs*, or vehicles for *devīs*

FIGURE 6.4. Māngaṇiār musicians framed in the doorway of the birthplace of Rāni Bhaṭiyāṇi at Jogidas ka Gaon. Photographed by Jyoti Rath, 2003.

through possession. However it seems to be the unnatural death, sacrifice, or valor that provide this status, whether it is a male or female deity.

All-night performances (*jāgarans*) are held at shrines of Rāni Bhaṭiyāṇi on days considered special for her. When Māngaṇiārs attend shrines of Mājisā as devotees and not as professionals serving the temple, they sing *oḷakh*s as musical offerings. They also attend the shrines for making a *pheri* (attending the night-long singing in thanksgiving after a wish has been granted). In these night-long sessions, unlike the *rāti jāgas* that may be commissioned, musicians come, sing for a while, and go. It is not necessary for them to stay for the entire night, and the singing goes on in rotation.

Changes in patronage and shrine behavior are influenced by economic and social parameters, but the changes are not absolute, and various systems coexist on different levels.

A miracle or manifestation of a spirit is required for a shrine to be established. As Rāni Bhaṭiyāṇi manifests herself to an increasingly large number of believers many new, small shrines are established and need to be attended to by Māngaṇiārs. These small shrines, often called *thān,* can be within the home or a courtyard and are not necessarily separate structures. This is a new, growing layer of shrines being maintained by Māngaṇiārs, in a spontaneous and unorganized manner.

Thān at Beesoo

Nagge Khan, a Māngaṇiār of the village Beesoo, has a *thān* of Rāni Bhaṭiyāṇi. I am told that it is one of eight in the village, though there was only one a few years ago. The shrine is built in the courtyard of his home. It has photographs of the idol from other shrines, and footprints carved in stone, which are meant to be the footprints of Rāni Bhaṭiyāṇi.

Nagge Khan tells me that he inherited this shrine from his mother, who was a *bhopī* and used to get possessed by Rāni Bhaṭiyāṇi. He wears a *phūl,* a silver amulet

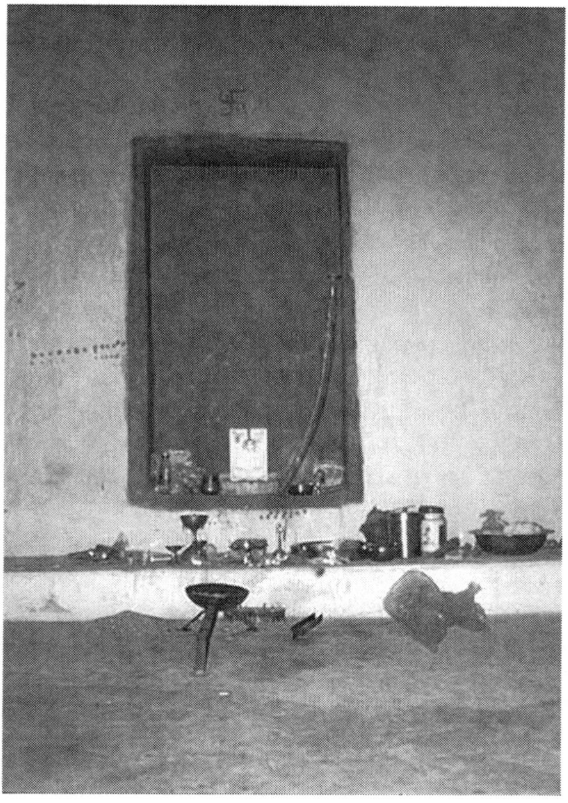

FIGURE 6.5. A *thān* of Rāni Bhaṭiyāṇi. Photographed by Jyoti Rath, 2003.

that was given to him by his mother, and relates miracles that he has witnessed. He says that people from the village come to his shrine for solutions to problems.

The story of Rāni Bhaṭiyāṇi he relates shows unmistakable influences from the printed Jasol version. He also knows and recites contemporary poems written in praise of Mājisā, and is developing a repertoire around Rāni Bhaṭiyāṇi.

The Songs of Rāni Bhaṭiyāṇi

The body of songs associated with Rāni Bhaṭiyāṇi consists of *oḷakh*s and *ghūmar*s. *Oḷakh*s can be divided roughly into those that are specifically about Rāni Bhaṭiyāṇi and more generic ones. In these, the text and the melody are not specific to a particular deity but are "customized" by the insertion of names of individuals and places associated with the deity in the text. The *ghūmar* is a standard melody that is sung to various goddesses and is for dancing the slow whirling dance by that name performed in Rājput homes. Māngaṇiārs perform a *ghūmar* with a different melody as an *oḷakh,* although the text is practically the same as other *ghūmar*s. When Ḍholīs sing *ghūmar*s to Rāni Bhaṭiyāṇi they use the standard dance melody.[15] [**Audio example 6.1**]

The more commonly sung *oḷakh*s and *ghūmar*s are invitations to Rāni Bhaṭiyāṇi to join in the *ghūmar,* to manifest herself. These are cues for possession. She is addressed as mother, princess of Jaisalmer, and the daughter of Jogidas. Some of the songs of Rāni Bhaṭiyāṇi deal with her malevolent aspect, of the harm that may prevail if she is not respected and worshiped (this again is a kind of standard text).

The style of singing by the Māngaṇiārs in the shrine also seems different from when they perform for patrons in other contexts, such as weddings and concerts, and is accompanied by the *ḍhol.* The context of performance is also different, as there is no formal audience and musical artistry seems to have no place. [**Video example 6.2**]

Shirley Trembath (1999) collected and commented on the body of Rāni Bhaṭiyāṇi songs sung by Rukmā, a Māngaṇiār woman singer, at the Bhuāsā temple at Jaisalmer.[16] A large body of song texts and melodies appear to be based on songs of such genres as *kallali* (drinking songs) and wedding songs, which are not necessarily devotional. Names associated with Rāni Bhaṭiyāṇi, including her own various names, that of her husband Kalyan Singh, her brother-in-law Sawai Singh, and names of places like Jasol and Jaisalmer are included in the text. The rest of the text remains the same as in the source genre, and thus might appear to the casual observer as incongruous and unrelated to a devotional song addressed to Rāni Bhaṭiyāṇi. However, Trembath remarks on the emotion with which Rukmā sang these songs in comparison to the rest of her repertoire. The role of music and musicians seems more significant than the source of the music and some remaining elements of text.

Mājisā and Her Musicians

The changes in the story and at the major shrines have a few underlying features. As the cult grows, Rāṭhor Rājputs have attempted to suppress the story of Rāni Bhaṭiyāṇi's extramarital relationship with Sawai Singh. The Rāṭhor family of Rāni Bhaṭiyāṇi's in-laws now want to own her and thereby promote Sawai Singh, her brother-in-law, and Lal Singh, her son—both of the Jasol Rāṭhor family—as deities. Controlling the temples provides clear financial benefits and power.

Why the changed story is also circulating among the Māngaṇiārs is less obvious. They may be supporting this version of the story to please their Rājput patrons. They might also fear saying anything that could be construed as negative, for they both believe strongly in her magical powers and fear her wrath.

As the Jasol temple now has succeeded in removing musicians entirely, and as the trusts grow more powerful, the relationship of the musicians to this temple is clearly changing. At Jogidas, where there are new shrines, there is also the beginning of a trust, which may take over the shrine in much the same way as at Jasol.

The popularization of the cult, nevertheless, also offers new opportunities to some musicians such as Ramzan of Jogidas, where the rising importance of Rāni Bhaṭiyāṇi's birthplace benefits him directly. So too does Nagge Khan of Beesoo benefit, probably one of the many who are setting themselves up by establishing a *thān*, accruing benefits from Rāni Bhaṭiyāṇi's rising popularity.

The temple at Jasol also offers an insight into the process by which a local deity loses specific features and grows by being associated with other deities as reincarnations and avatars. There are social, economic, and political factors that enter the process of these changes. Whether the Mājisā of the Māngaṇiārs will continue to protect them in this milieu remains to be seen.

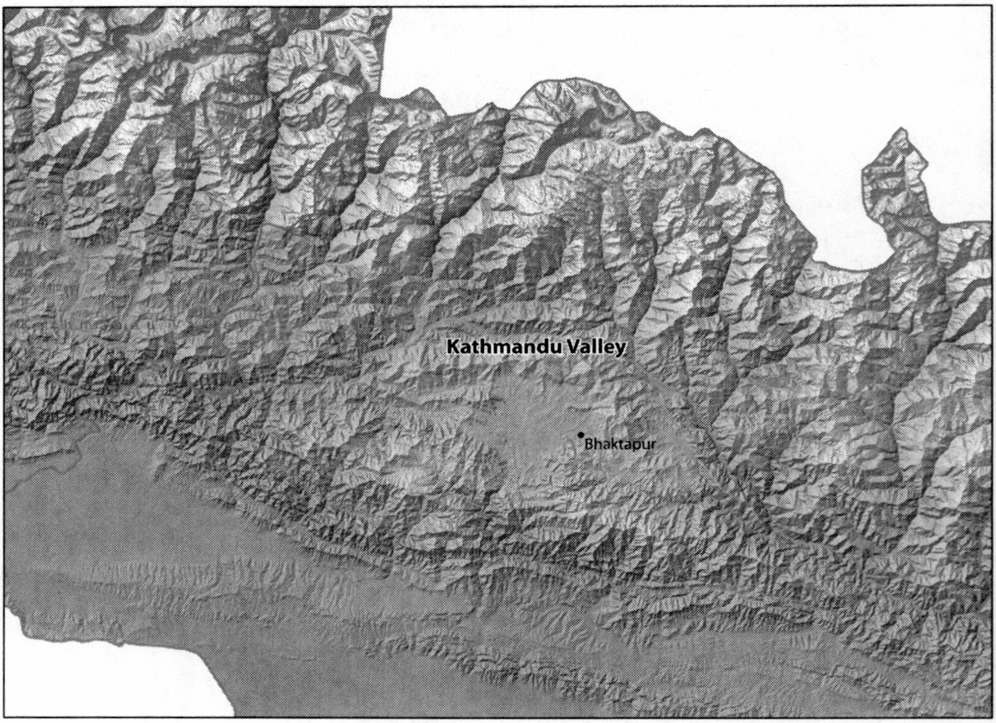
Kathmandu Valley
Bhaktapur

CHAPTER 7

Music in Urban Space

Newar Buddhist Processional Music in the Kathmandu Valley

GERT-MATTHIAS WEGNER

This chapter examines how the Buddhist processional music called *gūlābājā* (lit., music performed during the Buddhist month of *gūlā*) of the Bajrācarya, Sākya, and Sāymi castes in the town of Bhaktapur, Nepal, relates to Hindu-Buddhist concepts of sacred time and space, and how these concepts and rules influence musical performance. I focus on ways in which performers integrate music and dance in the ritual and agricultural calendar, and on local forms of social organization and urban space. In particular, I show how the location in which pieces are performed serve as keys to musical meaning. This is part of a larger, ongoing project examining the drumming traditions of Bhaktapur that are performed and transmitted as part of the living social and religious culture of the town.[1]

The Newar people of the Kathmandu Valley are known for their achievements in the arts and architecture, which developed during the five hundred years of Malla rule (thirteenth to eighteenth centuries) in the three rival kingdoms of the Kathmandu Valley, Kathmandu, Patan, and Bhaktapur. Despite pressures of modernization and changing political and economic conditions, Newar musicians continue to perform many long-standing genres of music that articulate important dimensions of social and cultural life.

Newar culture unfolds in a contact zone between Hinduism and Buddhism. Over the centuries, both religions have incorporated Tantric practices and local cults, resulting in a special Newar blend of religious practices. Each occupational caste carries out different ritual and musical duties and functions (Gutschow and Kölver 1975). Some of the numerous Hindu castes exhibit strong Buddhist

FIGURE 7.1. Sāymi oilpressers from Tekhācva, Bhaktapur.

tendencies, and the few Buddhist castes (3.6 percent in Bhaktapur, according to the 1981 census) observe Hindu rituals and festivals along with their own.

The research is based on my ongoing fieldwork in Nepal, where I lived from 1982 until 2003. During these years I learned the entire drumming repertoire of Bhaktapur orally, through apprenticeships with master drummers.[2] I transcribed the complete drumming repertoire, took part in countless processions and ritual events, and taught many local drumming students. Surveys were carried out on each musician in town in order to obtain information on performance schedules and locations, and social and ritual implications, and economic support of music.[3]

Sacred Space and Sacred Time

In his ground-breaking study on urban space and ritual in the Newar towns of the Kathmandu Valley, Niels Gutschow (1982) has revealed how the complex order of space and time rules all aspects of life among the Newars. By relating the geography of the Kathmandu Valley to traditional models of cosmic order, Newars have created what Robert Levy (1990) calls a "mesocosm," or what Mary Slusser (1982) identifies as a *maṇḍala:* a sacred habitat to live in, under the protection of numerous gods and goddesses that inhabit shrines, temples, rivers, trees, stones, and other artifacts. Mortals offer their prayers and other gifts, expecting the gods to respond with their blessings and continuous protection. The realm of the gods and the world of humans are connected through such activities as rituals, processions, circumambulations, offerings, and music. All this happens at a proper time determined by phases in the ritual and agricultural calendars and in the human life cycle.

Figuratively, Newar musicians proceed in their routes on an elaborate *maṇḍala* that represents their ritual townscape. Whenever passing a key point of the *maṇḍala,* they erupt in loud musical invocations that address the divine power residing in those places. These *dyaḥlhāygu* ("calling the god") invocations function like telephone numbers: while concentrating on the correct production of the sacred composition, the players focus on tapping the divine energy residing in the monument. These compositions, then, help the musicians establish a connection with the gods and reaffirm the order of ritually used urban space. However, the continuing processional music and the simultaneous roar of the invocation may appear to be musical chaos to the uninitiated. Locals make sense of the music in terms of where it is played. Newar settlements are like musical scores to those who know how to read them.

Although the Bhaktapur musical scores read by Buddhist and Hindu musicians differ, both groups agree upon the essential importance of the music gods Nāsaḥdyaḥ and Haimādyāḥ. Unlike Hindus in the rest of South Asia, Newars have the concept of the linear progression of divine energy ("flight lanes"), manifested through specific holes in walls that connect throughout the town.[4] The major shrines and flight lanes of these music gods receive musical offerings from members of both religions, as musical apprenticeship of any kind is closely linked to the cult of Nāsaḥdyaḥ and his destructive aspect, the god of mistakes in music, Haimādyāḥ.

Following my drumming apprenticeship, I played in processions of oilpressers and gold- and silversmiths, circumambulating every Buddhist monument en route. When the processional month was over, every musician had the musical score engraved on his mind, with each key locality inducing specific musical patterns.

Gūlābājā

Gūlābājā is processional music performed by Newar Buddhists in the cities of the Kathmandu Valley, namely Kathmandu, Patan, and Bhaktapur, and in a smaller town outside the valley, Banepa, in order to accumulate religious merit and repel negative influences. The Buddhist processional month of *gūlā* starts on the day of the new moon in July/August and ends one month later. According to Buddhist lore, this time of year is beneficial for processions and almsgiving; musical activities of the Newar Buddhists in the Kathmandu Valley reach a monumental scale. Every morning, the men walk along processional routes to visit Buddhist monasteries (*bāhā, bāhī*), and circumambulate Buddhist monuments (*caitya*), shrines, and other places of worship in the Kathmandu Valley and beyond.[5]

In Bhaktapur, the following story about the origin of *gūlābājā* was recalled by an ancient member of the Gvaḥmādhī oilpressers' group. Once there was a continuous drought for twelve years. People were starving. They wanted to call Bhagvān (god) for help and tried to wake him up from his deep meditation with a friendly fanfare of natural trumpets (*pvaṅgā*). No response. Finally the oilpressers were asked to come to the rescue with their horns. The god awoke, and so did the rain clouds. Since then, this effective horn blast is recalled during visits to *Kasti-Bhagvān*.

Another reason for pious merit gathering during *gūlā* could be the approaching "end of the world." When the *kaliyuga*, the last and shortest of the four world-cycles (*yuga*) ends, all of creation will be destroyed. This present world cycle consists of 432,000 years. The final month of each *yuga* year coincides with the month of *gūlā*. So this month is predestined to lead men to face the inevitable not with despair or sensual excesses but with pious activity, leading to a favorable rebirth in another existence.

Today, there are two different genres of *gūlābājā*, those of the Sāymi oilpressers and those of the Sākya and Bajrācarya gold- and silversmiths and Tantric Buddhist priests. Both of these groups require the participation of low-caste Hindu Jugi tailor-musicians, who are the only shawm players among Bhaktapur's eighty-two castes.[6] In contrast to all other music makers, they are professional musicians who receive payment for musical services.

Music Ensembles of the Oilpressers

Gutschow and Kölver (1975) counted 129 Sāymi oilpresser households in Bhaktapur. These families live in three parts of town, Sākvalā/Kvāthādau, Ināсva/Gvaḥmādhi (both located in the Upper Town), and Tekhācva/Bharbacva/Baṃśa Gopāl (Lower Town), where they pursue their traditional occupation of producing and selling mustard oil and generate additional income by distilling *aylā*, a fiery beverage required for every Newar feast. It is not uncommon for oilpressers to start the day with an inspiring peg or two.

The three Sāymi *gūlābājā* ensembles in Bhaktapur are named after the residential areas Sākvalā, Gvaḥmādhi, and Baṃśa Gopāl. For the past two decades, oilpressers have found it increasingly difficult to organize processions annually. Most of them try to maintain a routine of every two to four years. Usually this is a question of funds, and/or identifying the required *dhalāchẽ*, a house where the daily rituals take place during the processional month. The groups finance their *gūlābājā* activities themselves. One wealthy group member provides the major section of his home to be temporarily transformed into a *dhalāchẽ*. Owing to the usual quarrel among Newar brothers who demand partition of their inherited home into equally small fractions, very few houses have rooms large enough to carry out the rituals.

FIGURE 7.2. Oilpresser boys with horns.

Oilpressers call the kind of *gūlābājā* they perform *ṅakha dhalā,* literally, "collective worship with horns." The smallest oilpresser boys blow buffalo horns called *ghulu,* and the older ones play two varieties of goat horns, *cāti* and *tititālā.* Their fathers and uncles play nine different drums, cymbals, and natural trumpets (*pvaṅgā*).[7] The complete oilpresser ensemble consists of four functionally different groups described here in their processional order.

1. Small boys with buffalo horns (*ghulu*) alternating with bigger boys and men with goat horns attached to bamboo tubes (*cāti* and *tititālā*).
2. An ensemble of double-headed *dhā̃* drums and thin-walled brass cymbals (*sichyāḥ* and *bhuchyāḥ*), playing invocations in combination with horns, or processional patterns.
3. Tailor musicians playing shawms along with either one of the double-headed *pachimā* or *dhalak* drums, brass cymbals (*sichyāḥ*), and thick-walled bronze cymbals (*tāḥ*).
4. An ensemble of natural trumpets (*pvaṅgā*) playing together with *tāḥ* and the *pastā,* a compound drum comprising two drums tied together, enabling the drummer to play three heads.

Musicians walking in the middle of the procession (ensemble three) play processional music; those walking at the head and tail of the procession sound loud blasts whenever the procession passes a Buddhist monument.

FIGURE 7.3. Oilpressers play an invocation while passing a *caitya*.

FIGURE 7.4. Oilpresser playing *kā̃tā̃dabadaba*.

FIGURE 7.5. Oilpressers from Banepa visiting Baṃśa Gopāl, Bhaktapur.

At the commencement of the procession several other drums are required, which are only carried along the route if the procession includes a visit to a sacred site of exceptional importance (such as Namobuddha, Svayaṃbhūnāth, etc.), or to a ritual offering of five kinds of grains to the group of musicians. Such a *dhalā* (religious vow) offering requires the performance of auspicious music with all the available instruments, including an hour-glass drum accompanied by fipple flutes.[8]

Except for some minute details, the musical repertoires of the three oilpresser groups of Bhaktapur do not differ. During *gũlā,* the oilpressers from Banepa (ten kilometers east of Bhaktapur) visit Bhaktapur for a day to play in the three Sāymi residential areas Sākvalā, Gvaḥmādhi, and Thāpālāchẽ; during this occasion, it is possible to listen to a different set of *gũlābājā* compositions from another locality.

Music Ensembles of the Buddhist Priests and Goldsmiths

Gutschow and Kölver (1975) counted 209 households of Buddhist priests (Bajrācarya or Gubhāju) and goldsmiths (Sākya) in Bhaktapur. Bajrācarya and Sākya are householder Buddhist monks. As Buddhists, they are technically outside the caste hierarchy but, as Gellner argues, "in their life as householders, they are inevitably concerned with their caste status" (Gellner 1992, 59). Bajrācarya and Sākya intermarry. Some Bajrācaryas are family priests and perform rituals for other castes. Most Bajrācaryas work as goldsmiths, artisans, and shopkeepers and in this respect are not distinguishable from the Sākyas, who cannot be family priests. Their disposition is that of an old élite now dominated by others, but still knowing exactly what they are worth. The expensive and elaborate processions and rituals bring about immense physical and financial problems. They are a demonstration of an ancient minority's identity and wealth.

As has been said, Bhaktapur's Bajrācaryas and Sākyas organize three *gũlābājā* groups in the localities of Inācva, Yātāchẽ (Upper Town) and Tekhācva/Baṃśa Gopāl (Lower Town). The three ensembles use similar instruments and play a similar set of compositions, which are taught to the youngest group members during the weeks before *gũlā*. The final *pūjā* demarcating the end of the drumming apprenticeship is performed on the day of the new moon (*aũsi*), just before *gũlā* starts.

During *gũlābājā* processions, Bajrācaryas and Sākyas play only two kinds of two-headed barrel drums, *dhā̃* and *nāykhī* (lit., "butcher's drum"). Usually, there are many *dhā̃* drums and at least one *nāykhī*. These drums do not play the same musical patterns but they do play concurrently at specific localities. This happens when one group plays a long composition with processional patterns and the other group plays a phone-number-like *dyaḥlhāygu* invocation to a god on the route. The *dhā̃* group includes two different pairs of cymbals called *bhuchyāḥ* and *tāḥ*. The butchers' drum *nāykhī* is accompanied by a pair of light brass cymbals called *sichyāḥ*. Either one of the two drumming groups can play processional compositions, leaving the playing of *dyaḥlhāygu* to the other group. Usually, the much louder *dhā̃* group starts the processional music. When these drummers get tired, they ask the *nāykhī* players to take over, and they carry their silent drums until it is their turn to play an invocation.

FIGURE 7.6. Sākya boys with their drums.

FIGURE 7.7. Jugi tailor-musicians playing trumpets and clarinets while accompanying Yātāchē Sākya *gūlābājā.*

Only the group playing processional music is accompanied by two or three tailor-musicians playing Western trumpets and clarinets. They walk in front of the drummers, smoke cigarettes, and play the same serene Buddhist tunes every day. As professional musicians, their minds remain fixed on the meager remuneration awaiting them at the end of the month: a feast and rice or, more commonly, cash. During the final feast, the Bajrācarya and Sākya would be utterly shocked and vehemently protest if a low-caste tailor-musician expected to have food in the same room as themselves. Tailors have to sit outside or down on the ground floor, next to the toilet.

During the late 1990s, some Bajrācarya and Sākya groups started to include girls as drummers during processions. This happened after I taught the first girl in town to play *dhimay,* the Newar farmers' processional drum. Indira Machimasyu's appearance as a drummer caused quite a sensation, encouraging many girl groups to emerge and conquer ground hitherto held by men alone. Some colleagues may interpret this as a result of foreign interference. In fact, after the initial step, everything happened quite naturally. Perhaps the time was just ripe.

Music in Space and Time

The wet month preceding *gūlā* is the most work-intensive time of year for Newar farmers. This is when they transplant the young paddy plants. Neither oilpressers, Buddhist priests, nor goldsmiths are concerned with field work. They make use of the weeks to teach their boys how to play *gūlābājā* music.[9] Any Newar musical apprenticeship is closely linked to the cult of Nāsaḥdyaḥ, Lord of Music and Dance. In Bhaktapur, both Nāsaḥdyaḥ and his destructive aspect Haimādyāḥ (responsible for mistakes in music), are transferred from their shrines into the room where music is taught and practiced. At the end of the apprenticeship, the gods are transferred back to their shrines, and the apprentices play the compositions in public for the first time, in front of the shrine of Nāsaḥdyaḥ. Usually, this happens on the day of the new moon *(aũsi)*, one day before processions start.

Processions of the *gūlābājā* ensembles run on similar lines with similar schedules. As maps on pages 123 and 128 illustrate, each group starts their procession near their residential area and pass Buddhist artifacts and monasteries in the vicinity by following a standard route for most weekdays. On Wednesdays and during weekends, these relatively short processional routes are expanded—even beyond the borders of the Kathmandu Valley.

During their daily processions, the oilpressers living in Sākvalā/Bhaktapur gather at six a.m. at the nearby shrine of the Lord of Music and Dance, Thāthu Nāsaḥdyaḥ. One of the elders places offerings of grains and flowers at the shrine. These offerings are almost instantly consumed by stray dogs or chickens. A vermilion mark is applied to every participant's forehead. While musicians gather, a small group of old men sing Buddhist unaccompanied hymns (Sanskrit: *stotra,* Newari: *tutaḥ*), from a songbook containing handwritten texts.

Another senior oilpresser asks the arriving Jugi tailor-musicians to accompany him with their shawms, to lend dignity to the ongoing *pūjā.* He plays a piece called *pūjāmālī* on a small double-headed *nāykhī* drum. When everyone has arrived and the prayers and offerings in kind for the music god have been completed, Nāsaḥdyaḥ receives a series of musical offerings called *dyaḥlhāygu* (lit., "calling the god").

The player of the thick-walled, small, bronze *tāḥ* cymbals rings out the first notes by striking these together three times, leaving just enough time after each stroke for everyone present to raise their right hand to their forehead, in a salute to the music god. Three powerful *dyaḥlhāygu*s on *dhā̃* and horns follow, alternating with three *dyaḥlhāygus* on *pastā* drum and natural trumpets. After this, each of the other drums (*nāykhī, dhimaycā, dhalak, pachimā, kvakhīcā,* and *kā̃tā̃dabadaba*) plays a short *dyaḥlhāygu* for Nāsaḥdyaḥ, each with the accompaniment of cymbals.

As soon as all invocations for the music god have been completed, the procession starts taking shape, first circumambulating the Nāsaḥ shrine with a piece called *dyaḥ cākā hulegu* ("circumambulating the god") before proceeding with processional patterns to the monastery where the Dīpaṅkara Buddha resides, and further via Kvāthādau, Gaḥchẽ, Sujamādhi, and Tacapāḥ to Sākvalā, where the procession ends in the *dhalāchẽ* house (see map, p. 126, no. 17). Every Buddhist artifact on the way receives loud musical offerings with horns and drums. As the morning air resounds with their powerful fanfares reflected by the brick walls, the oilpressers alert all the

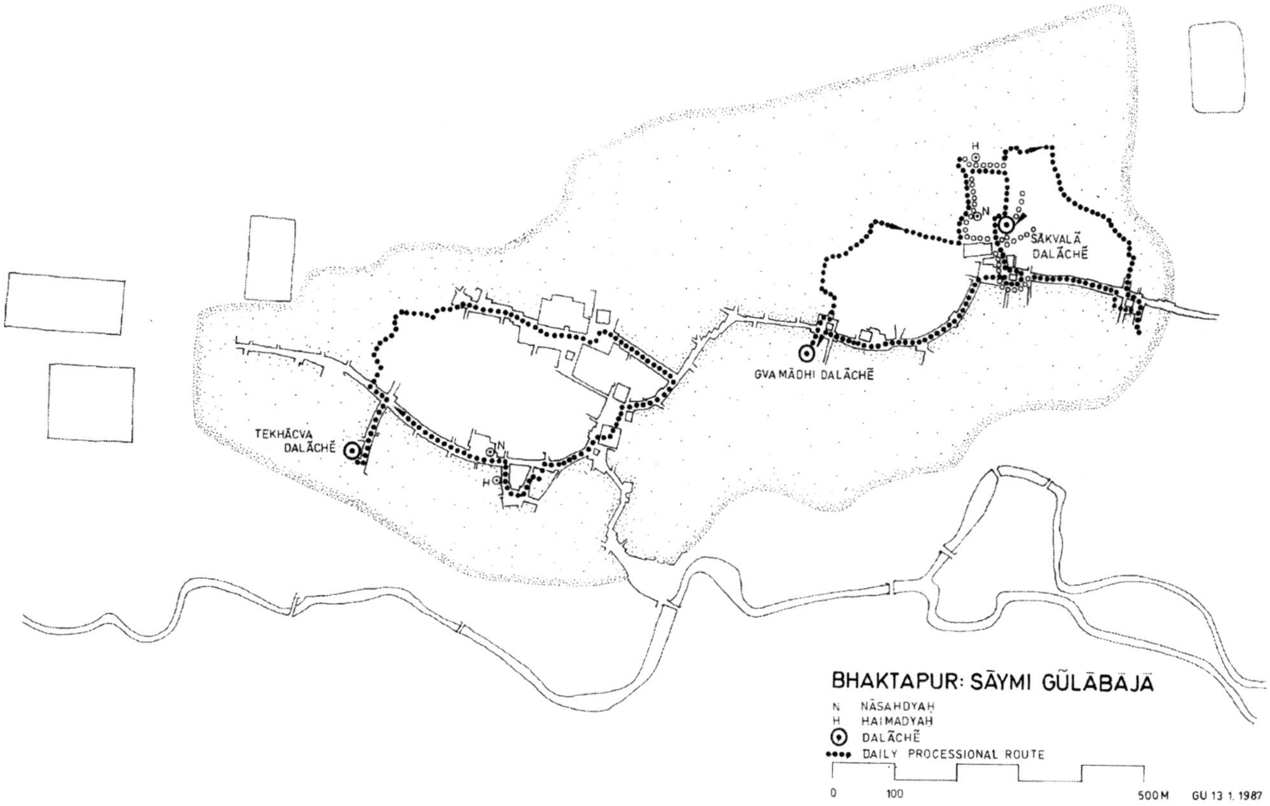

Daily processions of the three oilpresser groups of Bhaktapur

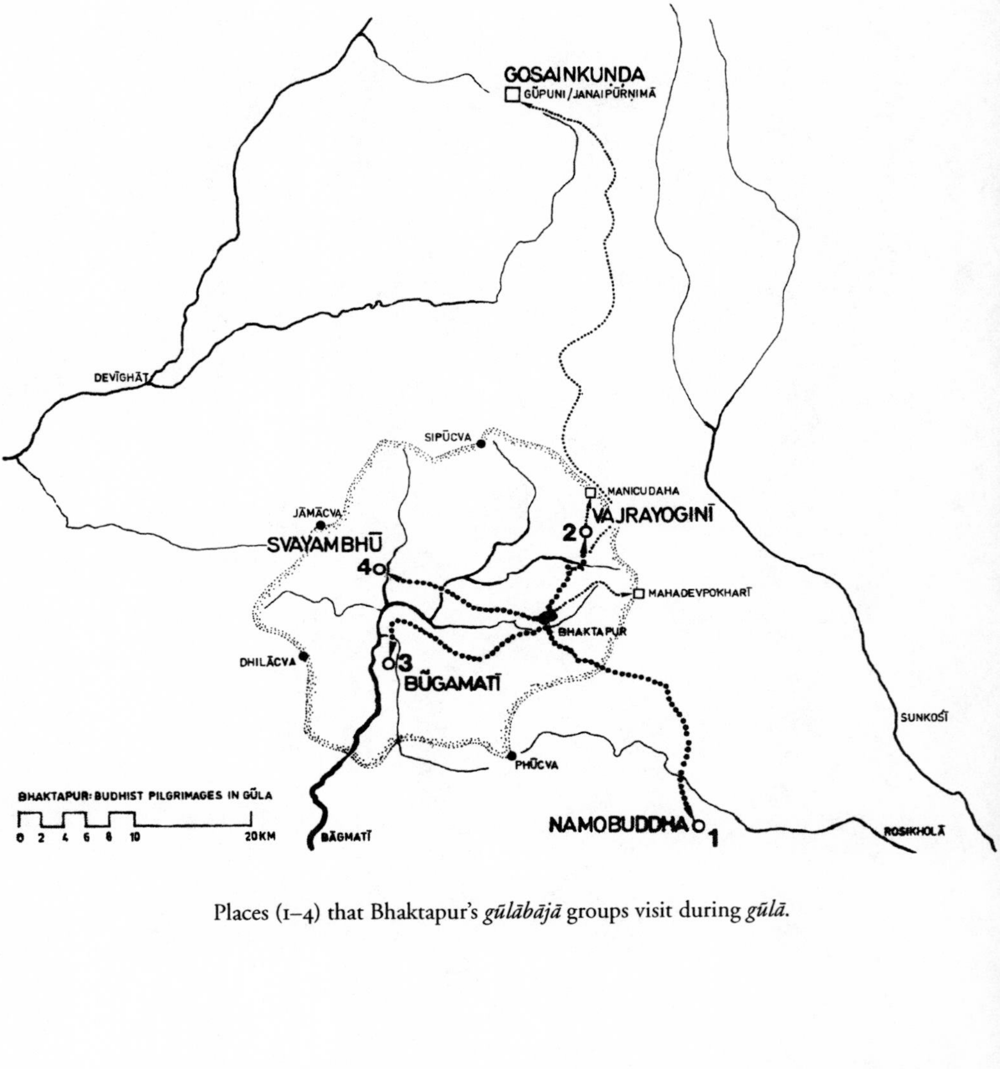

Places (1–4) that Bhaktapur's *gūlābājā* groups visit during *gūlā*.

Buddhas in their vicinity and consciously activate the protective *maṇḍala* around their residential area, Sākvalā.

On arriving at the *dhalāchẽ* house, the musicians announce their arrival and climb the stairs while playing the piece called *dhalāchẽ sidhaykegu dyaḥlhāygu* ("arriving at the *dhalāchẽ*"). The next piece is *svanā thā̃ vānebale* ("approaching a consecrated area where ritual objects are kept"). The procession ends on the first floor of the building in front of those ritual objects, thousands of tiny clay *caityas* (Newari: *cibhā̃*), produced by oilpresser women.

Around six A.M. the Bajrācaryas and Sākyas of Inācva start their daily processions outside the Indravarṇa Mahāvihāra monastery with all *dhā̃* drummers

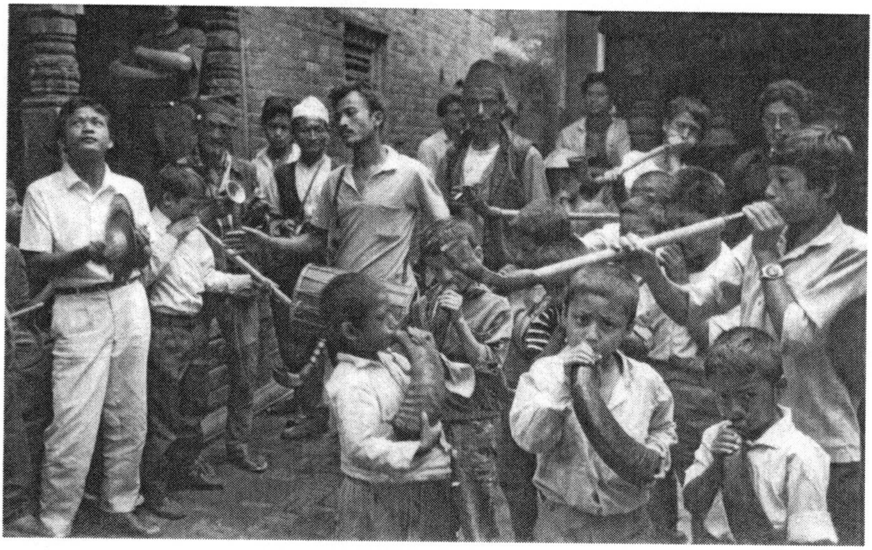

FIGURE 7.8. Sākvalā oilpressers playing *dyaḥlhāygu*.

playing three *dyaḥlhāygu* invocations, followed by one invocation played by *nāykhī*. As the *dhā̃* group starts with the first pattern of the processional piece called *calti* ("going"), the Jugi tailor-musicians join in with their trumpets and clarinet, accompanying the drummers while heading west along the main road to the Jhaurbahī monastery (see no. 1 on map, p. 128). The procession walks into the courtyard and continues with processional music, as the *nāykhī* drummer plays his *dyaḥlhāygu* for the Buddha residing on the first floor. This distribution of two different musical functions among *dhā̃* drummers and *nāykhī* continues up to the Caturvarṇa Mahāvihār in Sākvathā (see no. 4 on map, p. 128). Here, on completion of the third processional *dhā̃* piece, roles reverse. From now on the *nāykhī* drummer plays processional music and the *dhā̃* group becomes active only when they have to play invocations. At the Ādīpadma Mahāvihār in Sujamādhi (see no. 6 on map, p. 128), the *dhā̃* group takes over the much more strenuous part of playing yet another processional piece, leading the procession back to Inācva. The map shows this standard route of the Inācva *gūlābājā* group. The bold numbers stand for seven different processional pieces accompanied by trumpets and clarinets. The small numbers point to invocations played on the way.

During invocations, both drumming activities occur at the same time, but their respective musical patterns, tempi, and instrumentations are totally separate. Nobody seems to mind. In fact, this is what everyone expects. The music makes sense because of the locality. Newari language does not have a word for "disturb."

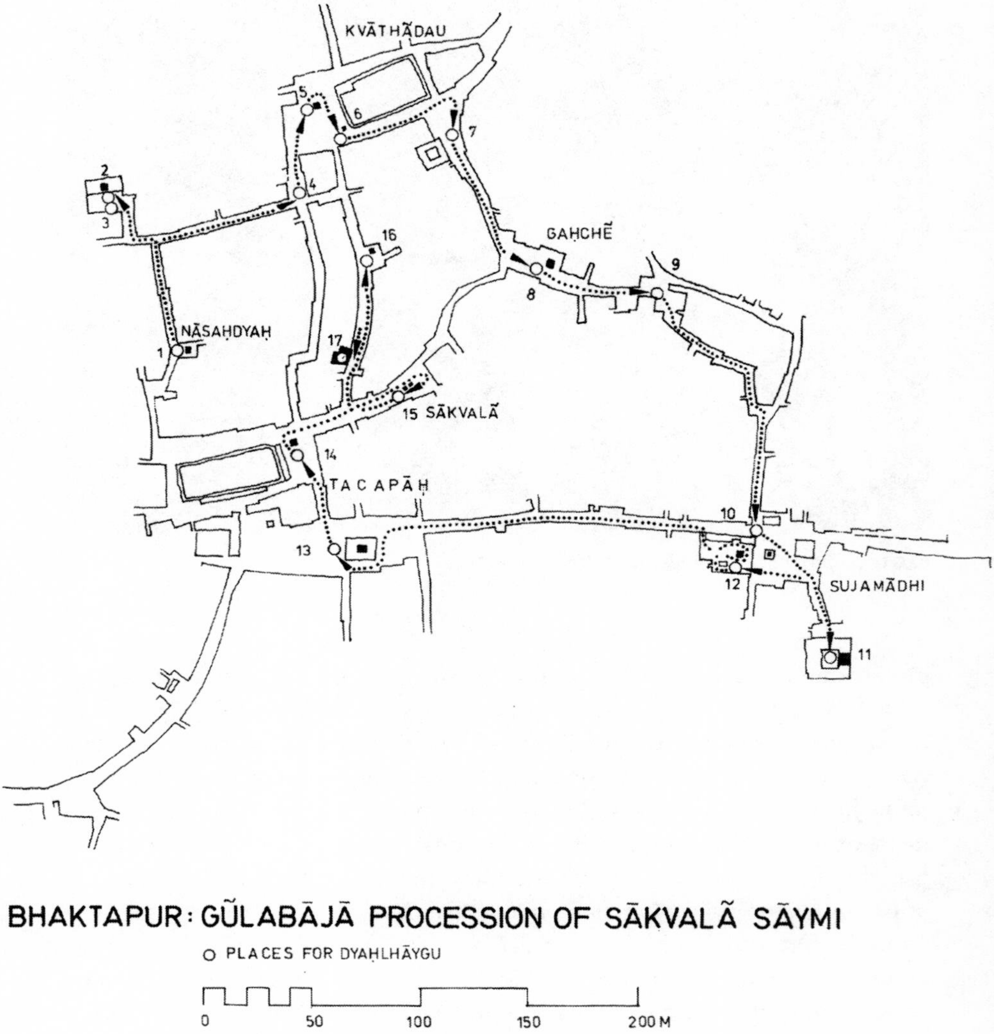

Gūlābājā processions of Sākvalā oilpressers.

This appears to be an alien concept to people who accept that life unfolds like a song with many different voices. Any sounds others make are welcome sounds, because they are there.

With the exception of their different starting and ending points, the three Sākya and Bajrācarya groups of Bhaktapur use the same standard processional route. The Sākyas from Inācva start at Indravarṇa Mahāvihāra and proceed via Pasi Khyah (Gvaḥmādhi), Sukul Dhvakā (Bhimsen), Taumādhi Nārāyaṇa Caukh (no. 2 on map, p. 128), Bvalāchẽ Bahī, Bārāhi, Baṃśa Gopāl (Jethvarṇa Mahāvihār),

FIGURE 7.9. Sākvalā oilpressers circumambulating Thāthu Nāsaḥdyaḥ. The hole in the brass plate at the shrine indicates the flight lane of the Lord of Music and Dance.

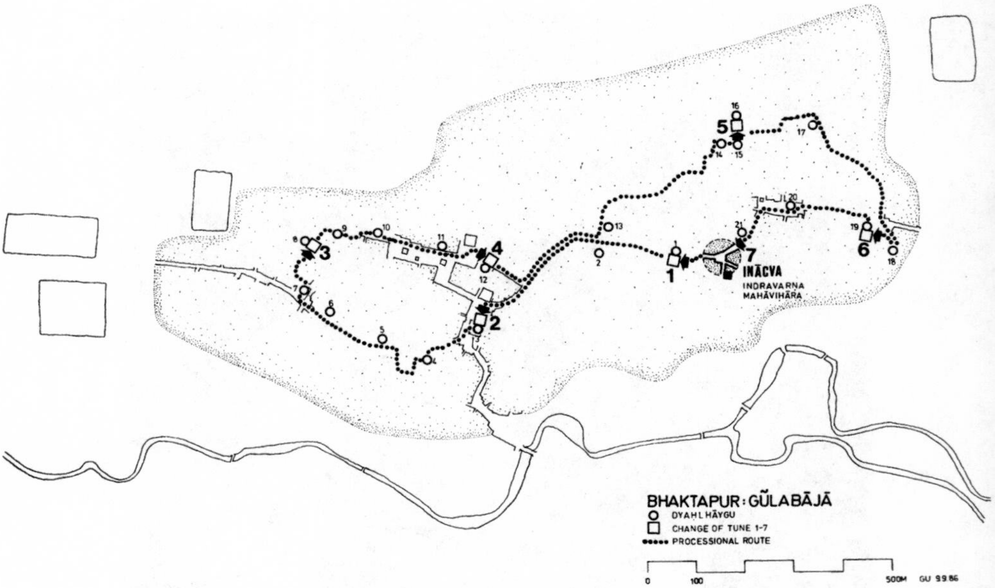

Standard processions of the Inācva Sākya *gūlābājā*.

Lokeśvar (Khauma Bahā, no. 3 on map above), Caturvarṇa Mahāvihār (no. 4 on map above), Sukul Dhvakā, Yāchẽ, Nāg Pvukhu and Thālāchẽ, Dīpaṅkara Buddha (no. 5 on map, p. 132), Kvāthādau, Gvaḥchẽ, Sujamādhi (Ādīpadma Mahāvihār), Vākhupati Nārāyaṇa and Dattatreya back to Inācva. This group collects holy water for the rituals at Hanuman Ghāt and black clay at Bhvutti Pakva. The Sākyas from Bikumāchẽ (Yātāchẽ) start at Paṣu Bahī and proceed via Dīpaṅkara Buddha (no. 5 on map above) and all other stations, back to the starting point Paṣu Vihāra and up to the *dhalāchẽ*. This group collects holy water for the rituals at Hanuman Ghāt and black clay at Bhvutti Pākva.

The third Bajrācarya and Sākya group, from Tekhācva, follows the same route. Their starting and ending point is Jethvarṇa Mahāvihār. In 1986 they did not have a *dhalāchẽ*. They collect holy water from Hanuman Ghāt and black clay from Khāpī (south of Yātā).

While following their standard route, all Bajrācarya and Sākya groups circumambulate a much larger area than the oilpressers, who restrict their rounds to Buddhist artifacts in the vicinity of their residential area. With a few deviations, their daily standard route follows the *pradakṣiṇā*, Bhaktapur's processional route for town rituals, including circumambulation of the town. On the other hand, Bajrācaryas and Sākyas appeared keen to stay in their workshops rather than make day-long pilgrimages to such sites as Namobuddha, Vajrajogini, Nilbārāhi, Karuṇamaya (Buṅgadyaḥ) of Buṅgamati, Ādināth Lokeśvara of Cvabahar, and Svayaṃbhū.

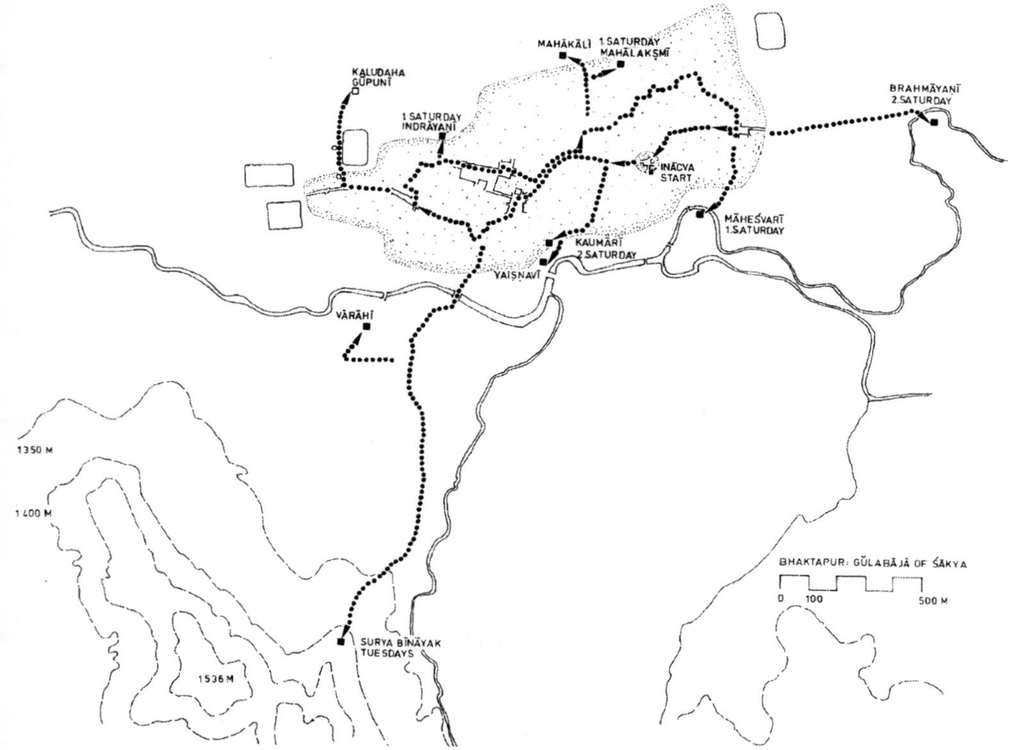

Inācva Sākya *gūlābājā* visiting the Aṣṭamātṛka and Sūrya Bināyak Gaṇeś.

The procession schedule includes the eight Tantric mother goddesses (Aṣṭamātṛka)—Barmayāṇī, Maheśvarī, Kumārī, Badrakālī, Bārāhī, Indrayāṇī, Mahākālī, and Mahālakṣmī—residing in their shrines at the periphery of Bhaktapur. They constitute the outer circle of the Bhaktapur *maṇḍala* of gods and goddesses. Their importance as protectors of Bhaktapur makes their inclusion into otherwise Buddhist-oriented processions mandatory. This applies also to Sūrya Bināyak Gaṇeś, one of the four guardian Gaṇeśa gods of the Kathmandu Valley.

During the final five days of *gūlā,* ritual activities accelerate. The evening procession on September first, called *mātā biyu vānegu* ("distributing oil lamp wicks") combines the Bajrācarya and Sākya men and their *gūlābājā* music, with the women distributing rice grains and burning oil wicks at all Buddhist artifacts in town. Stone *caityas* in the streets and courtyards are decorated with oil lamps donated by Buddhist households of the neighborhood. Every single Buddha is activated and alive, highlighting the three jewels of Buddhism: awakening (*buddha*), religious duty (*dharma*), and community of initiates striving for enlightenment (*saṅgha*)

Pañcadān carhe is the last day before new moon.[10] Almost the entire population of Bhaktapur is involved in hectic alms giving and receiving. In the morning,

FIGURE 7.10. Bhaktapur *maṇḍala* (painting by Madhu Chitrakar), with eight Aṣṭamātṛka dominating the outer section. In the center of the *maṇḍala* resides the Tantric mother goddess Tripurasundarī. Cremation sites are depicted at the riverbanks outside the *maṇḍala*.

the five Dīpaṅkara Buddhas are decorated and leave their monasteries to gather on a stone platform in Sujamādhi, where they receive offerings of grains, fruit, flowers, yoghurt, and music from a vast crowd of devotees, both Hindu and Buddhist. Some Hindus identify the five Buddhas as the five Pāṇḍava brothers from the *Mahābhārata* epic on this occasion. The leading Dīpaṅkara Buddha appears

FIGURE 7.11. Dīpaṅkara Buddha walking from Yātāchẽ to Sujamādhi to meet the other four Buddhas on Pañcadān *carhe*.

to look down at his feet as if overcome with shame. This head posture exposes him as Yudhisthira, eldest son of King Paṇḍu, who lost his kingdom and finally his wife to his gambling opponent. He is also called Ajajudyah, the grandfather god. The Dīpaṅkara Buddhas are escorted throughout the town by *nāykhībājā*, including the *nāykhī* butcher's drum and a pair of *sichyāḥ* cymbals, to receive

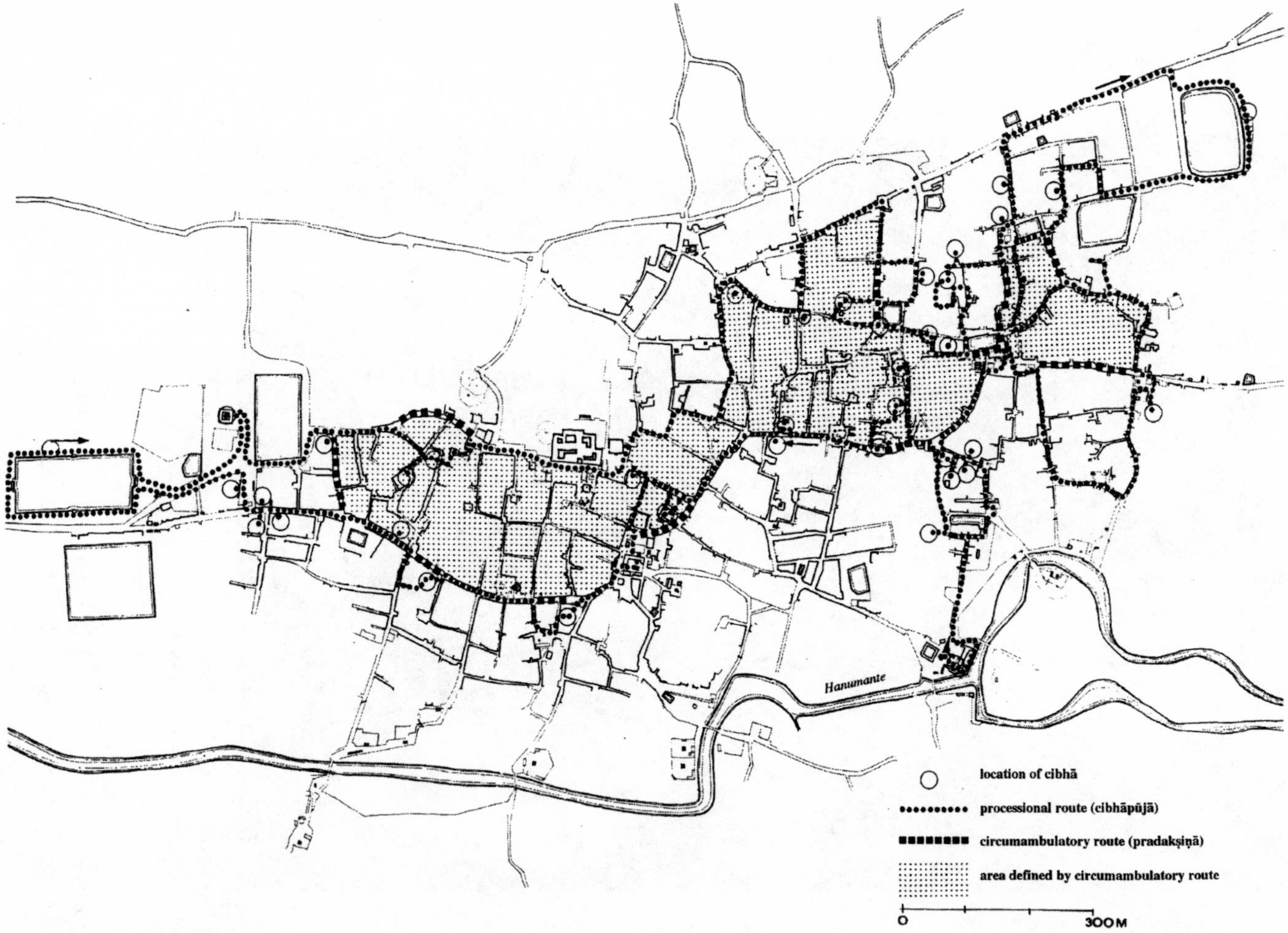

Cibhāpūjā: Bhaktapur Buddhists offer lamp wicks and mustard oil to all stone *caityas* in town. *Gūlābājā* leads the procession.

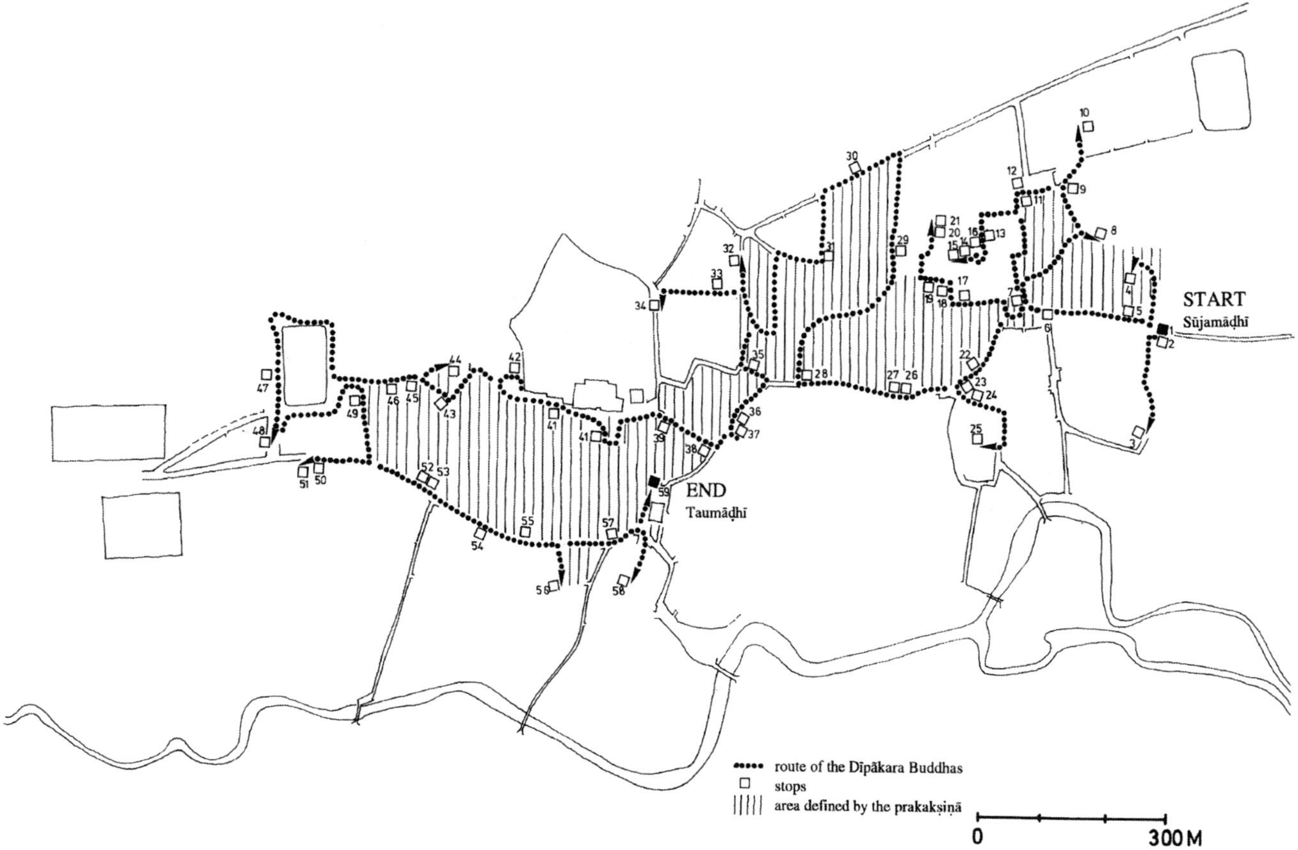

Processional route of the five Dīpaṇkara Buddhas.

offerings in all the areas where Buddhist families live. A drummer of the butcher caste plays a special pattern called *bāre dāygu* exclusively reserved for this procession (see Wegner 1988). Members of the Gāthā caste (gardeners and Navadurga dancers) carry baskets with offerings first received by the five Buddhas. At the end, the gardeners are allowed to keep the fruit and vegetables. The Sākyas and Bajrācaryas keep the grains.

Only on the day of Pañcadān *carhe,* Sākyas and Bajrācaryas eat a nourishing soup (*kvāti*) prepared from nine kinds of boiled pulses, flavored with red chilies and *imu* seeds fried in oil.

Around sunset, the five Dīpaṅkara Buddhas gather on a stone platform in Taumādhi, where they receive a climactic volley of musical offerings from all *gūlābājā* groups combined. Taumādhi Square is a fantastic arena surrounded by temples and traditional houses. During this hour, their walls echo and amplify the immense roar and clashing into the acoustic climax of the processional month.

Rituals in the Dhalāchẽ

A *dhalāchẽ* house must have a small room (*nyāchī kvataḥ*) for storing holy water, a room on the ground floor (*cā kvatāḥ*) for keeping black clay, and a very large room for gatherings. This large room has a secluded area with a temporary shrine (*dyaḥkuti*), guarded and kept in a state of purity by six attendants (*dhyaḥbāris*). These young oilpresser males who during the month of *gūlā* observe a fast (that is, eat only one vegetarian meal per day after finishing the ritual duties), abstain from sex, and have their heads shaved. If they are defiled by touching a dog or in some other way, they have to bathe and shave again. People place donations of rice grains for the attendants into the silver crown (*kikāpā*) of Lokeśvar at Thāpālāchẽ.[11]

The temporary shrine (*dyaḥkuti*) contains the hill of small votive *caityas*, molded by oilpresser women, which grows daily. The women aim to produce a total of 125,000 such votive miniature *caityas* to be submerged at the confluence of two rivers (*triveṇi*) with the Hanumante River at Hanuman Ghāt. At this confluence there resides a mighty Nāgarājā, snake guardian of all springs and rivers. He is present in the main room of the *dhalāchẽ* as a paper effigy (*nāgva*), prepared by a member of the Chitrakār painters' caste, looking like many intertwined snakes with a single split tongue in the center. The *nāgva*'s presence ensures a peaceful atmosphere in the house where so many people gather during the month of *gūlā*.

During morning hours, a pleasant atmosphere of pious business prevails. Enveloped by fumes of aromatic shrubs and incense and by the sounds of the chanting and bell-tinkling of the Bajrācarya priest, the oilpresser women engage daily in the month-long *caitya* production. The procedure is simple but requires total concentration. Every woman uses a *caitya*-shaped brass mold, which is approximately two inches

FIGURE 7.12. *Dyaḥbāri* in attendance of the temporary shrine containing the growing hill of miniature clay *caityas*.

FIGURE 7.13. Oilpresser women preparing clay *caityas*.

high. Under the supervision of a Bajrācarya priest (*gubhāju*), she rolls the black clay, oils it, stuffs it into the mold and inserts a grain of uncooked rice into the clay, giving it life. The emerging clay *caitya* is carefully placed on a tray, decorated with flowers, and later transported to the guarded shrine kept next to the eastern wall of the room. The growing hill of clay *caityas* in the temporary shrine receives daily offerings of red powder and, after the arrival of the *ṅakha dhalā* procession, a musical offering.[12]

On the last day of *gūlā*, the *caityas* receive further blessings by way of an elaborate ritual carried out by the leading Tantric Buddhist priest, who supervises all ritual aspects of the oilpressers' activities.[13] After this, the *caityas* await their submersion at Hanuman Ghāt (in Newari: Khvāre)—the most auspicious place for any Bhaktapurian to leave this world, which the Buddhists among them view as one of suffering and misery. On this final day, the 125,000 clay *caityas* are arranged in baskets with a few spectacular big ones on a palanquin, and carried to the river. They are preceded by the *nāgva* effigy of Nāgarājā, the snake guardian, which is tied to a long bamboo pole. *Dyaḥbāri* attendants carry the remaining holy water. The entire music ensemble follows, as does the priest and the women with all the *pūjā* leftovers. At the *ghāt* the men undress and enter the shallow river. The bamboo with the effigy is placed at the exact point where Nāgarājā resides at this confluence. The palanquin is put down on the stone steps leading into the water. The musicians play their final invocations of the year while the men in the river splash water on the big *caityas* in the palanquin and empty all the baskets into the river. When everything is over, the procession returns to Sākvalā with the music of the *pachimā* drum and shawm accompaniment. This is the end of *gūlā*.

Dhalāpa

A *dhalāpa* is an offering of prescribed gifts to a Sāymi *gūlābājā* group, under supervision of a Bajrācarya priest. After the full moon, any Buddhist donor can arrange this elaborate offering to an oilpresser group and gain tremendous merit through doing so. In 1986, the Sākvalā Sāymi *gūlābājā* group received three such offerings in Banepa, six in Bhaktapur, and three in Thimi.

A *dhalāpa* offering includes five kinds of grains in large quantity, among other things. Impressive heaps of five kinds of grains are displayed in the donor's house when the group arrives. The musicians play a series of *dyaḥlhāygu* invocations before attending to the inspiring drinks offered by their hosts. These are exactly the same succession of musical offerings as during the daily morning start of their procession at the shrine of the music god, Nāsaḥdyaḥ. The Bajrācarya priest invokes Nāsaḥdyaḥ, the five Buddhas, the four Taras, and other important gods before blessing the musical instruments, the songbook of unaccompanied hymns (*tutaḥ*), and the oilpresser musicians.[14] When all offerings are assembled, the priest asks the musicians three times to play the auspicious *pūjāmālī* piece on the *nāykhī* drum accompanied by shawms. He places orange powder marks (*sinā tikegu*) on the

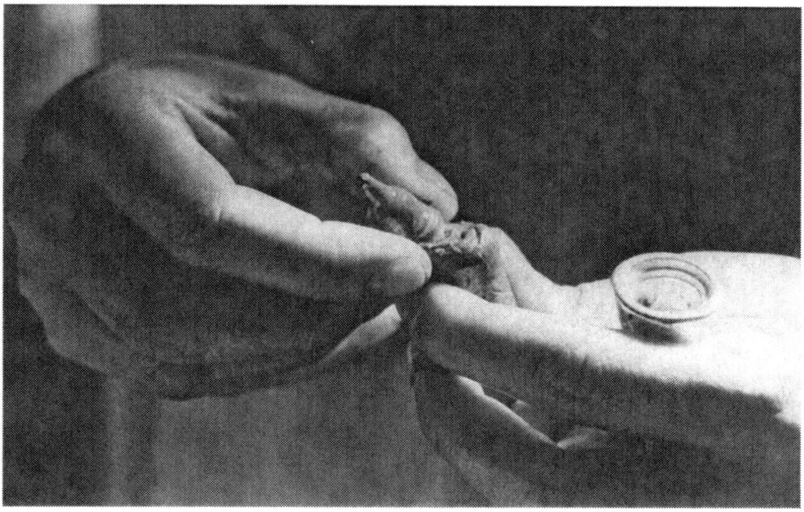

FIGURE 7.14. Clay *caitya* emerging from a brass mold. The *caitya* is pulled out with the help of a piece of clay stuck to its base.

FIGURE 7.15. Submersion of 125,000 *caityas* at Hanuman Ghāt.

musical instruments, adds flowers and cotton threads (*jalākhvakhā*), and sprinkles unhusked rice grains over them, before placing marks of wet orange *sinā* and red *abīr* powder on the musicians' foreheads. The musicians receive a (*samay*) meal.

An elaborate program of music follows, starting with the *pastā* drum playing the pieces *nhyāḥ* and *khīpvu dhādiganā,* and the *dhā̃* group playing *nhyāḥ* with shawm accompaniment. All these *dhā̃* pieces conclude with powerful horn incantations of the *mantra* "*ārya tārā tā—rā—buddha dharma saṅ—gha* " played in unison with the drums.

After this, each drum plays one or two long pieces with shawm accompaniment.[15] *Dhalak* or *dhā̃* conclude with *cavā̃,* the piece that is most auspicious and said to have healing properties.[16]

After playing a final round of *dyaḥlhāygu* invocations, the oilpressers carry the offerings home, into the *dhalāchē*. The grains are sold, the money spent on feasting, drinks, and *pūjā* expenses.

Conclusion

This paper describes, through the medium of Newar Buddhist processional music, the fundamental Tantric concepts of actualizing static urban space through the dynamics of town rituals. As Gutschow states (1982), Hindu towns, landscapes, and even the entire Indian subcontinent have been superimposed by multiple *maṇḍala* patterns. Wherever the *maṇḍala* concept is anchored in annual rituals, it does not remain an esoteric attempt of certain priests to relate the elements of their environment but becomes general knowledge and practice. The experience of urban space as a *maṇḍala* is made possible by way of town rituals (*jātrā*), offerings (*pūjā*), and circumambulations of sacred objects or areas (*pradakṣiṇā*). During circumambulation, the venerated object remains at the right side of the practitioner. Newar processional musicians in Bhaktapur actualize the outline of the *maṇḍala* by the playing of processional music. The key points of the *maṇḍala* are usually manifest as religious monuments and given special attention by playing musical invocations *(dyaḥlhāygu*). These invoke the gods who are perceived to reside at these key points. The playing of an invocation focuses the mind of the player and actualizes the divine energy of the locality. The attention that Newar processional musicians pay to the locality, inducing them to play specific music at specific places, resembles the reading of a musical score named Bhaktapur. To the Tantric practitioner, these dynamic town rituals are nothing but a cosmic actualization of the *maṇḍala* which he arranges with cult objects or draws on the ground.[17] The detailed descriptions of processions and rituals above confirm this world view precisely.

Appendix

The total repertory of the oilpressers includes the following drumming compositions.

Pastā: 2 *dyaḥlhāygu* (invocations)
nhyāḥ (walking)
dhādiganā
dyaḥ cā hulegu (circumambulating)
bājā kvacāya kigu (completion)
svanā thā̃ vānebale (arriving at a consecrated area)
dhā̃: 5 *dyaḥlhāygu* (invocations)
2 *dyaḥ cā hulegu* (circumambulating)
3 *nhyāḥ* (walking)
dhalāchē sidhaykegu dyaḥlhāygu (arriving at *dhalāchē*)
cavā̃ (auspicious piece for *dhalāpa*)
dhimaycā: dyaḥlhāygu (invocation)
nāykhīca: dyaḥlhāygu (invocation)
2 *pūjāmālī* (to be played during *pūjā*)
dhalak: dyaḥlhāygu (invocation)
cavā̃ (auspicious piece for *dhalāpa*)
navabājā pieces: *partāl*
calti
dehrā
rikhā
sācalā
dhamāk
kharjati
brahmatāl
pachimā: dyaḥlhāygu (invocation)
navabājā pieces: *partāl*
calti
dehrā
rikhā
sācalā
dhamāk
kharjati
brahmatāl
kvakhīcā: dyaḥlhāygu (invocation)
navabājā piece: *calti*
nagara:navabājā pieces: *partāl*
calti
dehrā
rikhā
sācalā
dhamāk
kharjati
brahmatāl

The total repertory of the Sākya and Bajrācarya includes the following drumming compositions.

Dhā̃: 8 *dyaḫlhāygu* (invocations)
calti
partāl
lātā
jati
paliman
nṛtyanāth gvarāḫ
Srī Kṛṣṇa *gvarāḫ*
nāykhī: 2 *dyaḫlhāygu* (invocations)
calti
partal
lātā
jati
tatali—with *rāg* (introduction)

PART III

LEARNING AND TRANSMISSION

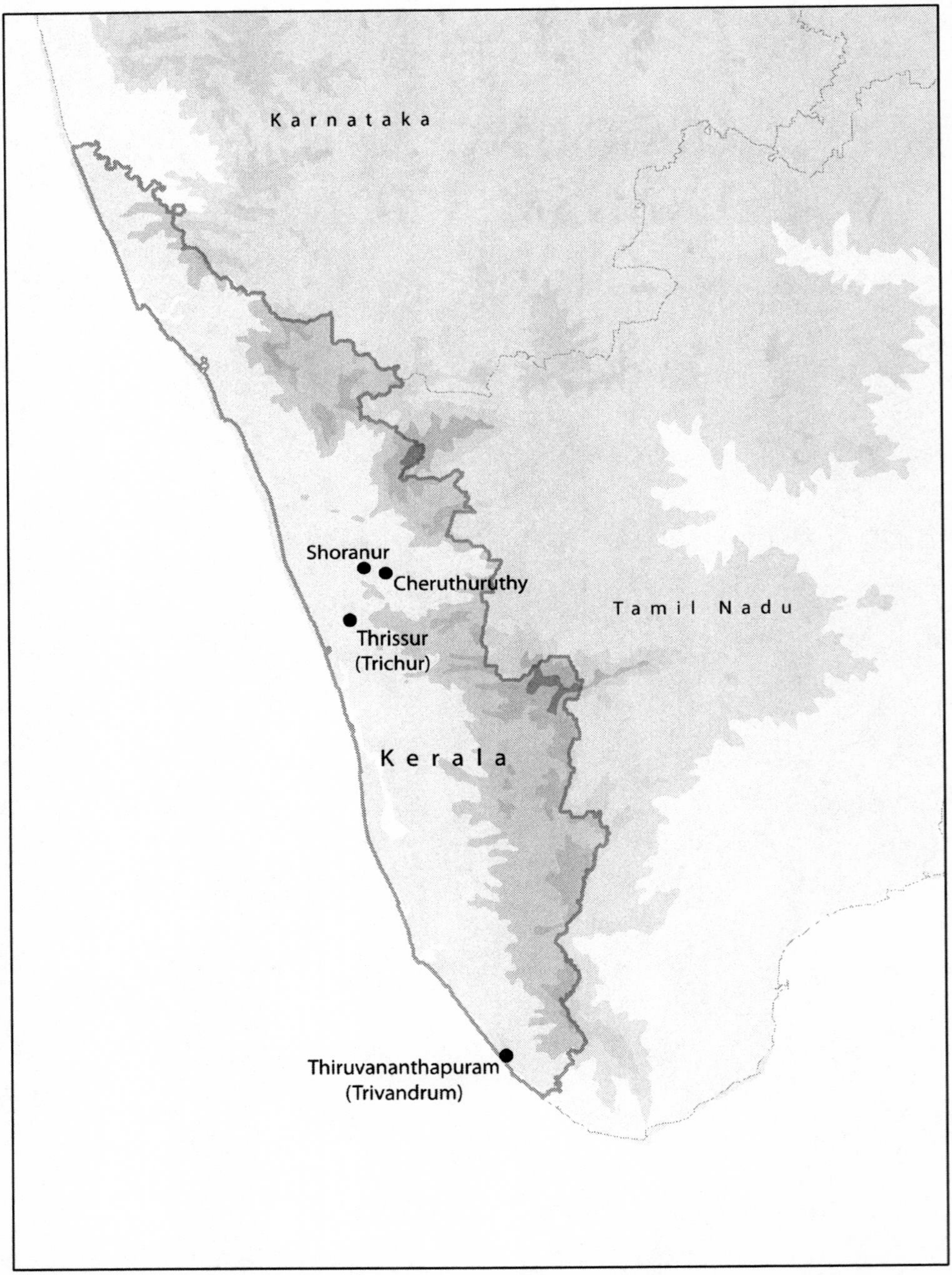
Karnataka
Shoranur
Cheruthuruthy
Tamil Nadu
Thrissur
(Trichur)
Kerala
Thiruvananthapuram
(Trivandrum)

CHAPTER 8

Disciple and Preceptor/Performer in Kerala

ROLF GROESBECK

The observation that one learns in part by mimicking one's teacher forms one of the ubiquitous themes in the literature on the transmission of knowledge in South Asian performance. One ideally assimilates the influences of one's preceptor through bodily imitation over time, and in this way a canon regenerates itself. Knowing bodies beget other knowing bodies. Phillip Zarrilli illustrates this perspective in his discussion of the initial stages of pedagogy in *kaḷarippayaṯṯu*, a Kerala martial art: "The how is learned only from the [preceptor] and from practice.... the specific steps of physical behavior embodied in the exercises must be learned physically, through repetition....The student first tries to follow the teacher... mimicking his every move.... Observation is the single most important mode of informal learning" (Zarrilli 1984a, 197–98). One way to interpret the disciple's attempts to approximate the guru's actions would be to infer that a guru is really an older version of a disciple; a disciple is an incomplete guru. For instance, Stan Scott's *k̲h̲yāl* guru exclaimed, "I have made you into myself!" after Stan's initial successes in his lessons (Scott 1997, 48), and Ravi Shankar compared his teaching of improvisation to the programming of a computer (Slawek 1987). One purpose of pedagogy would seem to be to enculturate a disciple into guru-ship; as the guru projects his own bodily experiences onto a disciple, he or she ensures (among other things) stylistic continuity in a tradition.[1]

Pedagogy in at least one part of South Asia, however, can combine corporeal reproduction of selfhood with a complementary process of peer-group immersion. This results in transmission of different types of knowledge. Since this peer-group immersion may introduce a disciple to influences beyond that of his or her preceptor, the disciple may develop a degree of individuality that is greater than a model of mere rote repetition might suggest. The presence of individuality within a group of disciples who share a common pedagogical lineage problematizes the idea that knowing bodies are merely replicated. The sort of person the student eventually becomes would seem to result from a variety of factors, not just his or her relationship to his or her preceptor.

Preceptor-disciple transmission and peer-group immersion could characterize two stages in a pedagogical curriculum. In the first stage, disciples may learn by copying their preceptors' bodies, performance styles, beliefs, and verbal and physical behavior, inside and outside of the pedagogical arena. In group environments, they could also define themselves in relation to their fellow students. In this first stage, peer-group immersion would reinforce the power of the preceptor and the centrality of preceptor-disciple transmission, since all students in a group would be studying with the same preceptor.

Later in their development, however, students in some environments could define themselves more and more in terms of their peer-group interactions. As the preceptor's role diminishes, peer-group learning could potentially generate new types of knowledge. Students might emphasize this second stage and define themselves more in relation to their peers than as disciples. A group of advanced students might adopt and share a performance style that differs in some respects from that of their preceptors. Even when the role of the preceptor is strong, the student's exposure to other students and stylistically related preceptors allows him or her to develop a strong sense of individuality (see Wolf 1991, 126, on *vīṇā* pedagogy in Karnatak music). This generates considerable stylistic diversity within a given school or lineage.

Regula Qureshi's discussion of discipleship in Hindustani music (Qureshi 2004) illustrates such a two-stage model. A stage-one attitude is represented by the ustād Vilayat Khan, who sneers at an early-stage disciple for showing too much individuality: "What, the boy has decided to think?" A stage-two view is suggested by the *sārangī* ustād, Sabri Khan, who tells Qureshi (his *sārangī* student at the time), "Imitation generates creativity." Imitating one's ustād at an early stage paves the way for creativity later.[2]

This model could help explain the dichotomy, frequently found in South Asia, between memorized fixed items and improvised sections learned through observation in the course of performance, and during advanced informal training. Aspects of Karnatak concert music exemplify this phenomenon; thus, whereas the student learns the *varṇam* as a fixed item from the preceptor through rote repetition, he or she often picks up the improvised *svara kalpana* and *ālāpana* sections more informally from this preceptor, or by observation as a performer, several years after the commencement of study (Viswanathan 1977; Cormack 1992).[3]

At first, then, disciples learn via their asymmetrical relationships with their preceptors and their somewhat more egalitarian relationships with fellow disciples. In the second stage, as students define themselves more in relation to their peers, they gain the ability to innovate, individually or collectively. When students become gurus, they continue to interact with and define themselves in relation to their peers, who are now gurus themselves. Thus, in some South Asian traditions, pedagogy not only prepares today's disciples to be tomorrow's preceptors and performers, it also trains the student to be a student and the guru to be a guru.

Here, I would like to consider this model in light of Kathakaḷi drumming pedagogy among males in Kerala.[4] Kathakaḷi is an all night dance-drama whose stories are usually derived from the Hindu epics.

Two men sing in accompaniment as well as keep the metric cycle (tala) on idiophones; one plays a flat gong and the other cymbals. Kathakaḷi percussion also includes the *maddaḷam,* a barrel drum, and the *ceṇṭa,* a cylindrical stick drum.[5] I participated in and observed drumming lessons at the Kerala Kalamandalam between 1988 and 1990, in 2000, and very briefly in 2006. The Kalamandalam, founded in 1930, is the primary state institution for the instruction of Kerala performing genres (Kathakaḷi and several others) and is located in Cheruthuruthy in central Kerala. It is by far the largest of the Kathakaḷi institutions in Kerala, and it became an academic high school in the early 1990s and a university in mid-2006.

FIGURE 8.1. Kathakaḷi, *Puṟappāṭu,* Kerala Kalamandalam, August 1989. The *maddaḷam* player is in back to the far left; the *ceṇṭa* (played by the author) in back toward the center, and in back at the far right is one singer.

I also conducted interviews and observed students in other institutions. At the Kalamandalam I was generally placed in groups of three to eight *ceṇṭa* drum students, most of whom were teenaged Malayali boys (one was an older French man).[6] Although most of my study of Kathakaḷi focused on preliminary pieces intended for beginners, in 2000 I learned a number of *kalāśams* (more advanced fixed compositions) and became one of the first Westerners ever to accompany actor-dancers on the *ceṇṭa* (outside of the preliminaries) in the group rehearsal studio. That said, my Kathakaḷi *ceṇṭa* skills, particularly with regards to performance in the group rehearsal studio, are still extremely rudimentary.

Although most of the leading performers of many Kerala musical genres train privately, almost all professional Kathakaḷi artists learn in the Kalamandalam, or in one of a number of other, smaller Kathakaḷi institutions, which have been founded more recently.[7] This emphasis on institutional training of pre-professional artists contrasts strikingly with data from much of the rest of South Asia.[8]

In Kathakaḷi drumming, the "performer/preceptor/advanced disciple" and the "beginning disciple" can be distinguished on the basis not only of skill but also of musical style. A stylistic dichotomy exists between certain types of fixed composition learned relatively early in the training period (*kalāśams* and a few others), and a particular process of improvisation practiced later on. While lower-level disciples learn the aforementioned fixed compositions by mimicking their primary drum teacher in group drum classes, more advanced disciples absorb improvisatory procedures by observing and interacting, mostly with their peers, in a studio that joins drummers, singers, and actors together in group rehearsal (*colliyāṭṭam,* "spoken dance"). A dichotomous musical structure thus reflects the distinction between the two stages of pedagogy. As the beginning disciple advances, rote repetition of the preceptor's patterns recedes in relation to what anthropologist Jean Lave calls "legitimate peripheral participation" (Lave and Wenger 1991) in the activities of the group rehearsal studio. Not only does the student learn different patterns but he also accumulates them through a process that encourages self-definition more in relation to his peers than to his primary preceptor. A secondary drumming preceptor, who is present in this studio, is one influence among many. As advanced disciples grow to manhood, they may develop musical identities that are distinct from those of their preceptors. The continuity of tradition fostered by the guru-disciple relationship remains in tension, then, with other generationally based style changes deriving from other influences in the pedagogical arena.

Kathakaḷi *ceṇṭa* drumming pedagogy at the Kalamandalam consists of two stages. Initially, beginning disciples learn relatively fixed segments, compositions, and exercises from their primary preceptors (*āśāns*) in the drum *kaḷari* (open-air pedagogical arena). The first of these is a set of exercises required of *ceṇṭa* students everywhere (not just in Kathakaḷi schools) collectively called *sādhakam* (lit., "accomplishment," "expertise," in this context "technical exercise"). A given brief *sādhakam* exercise is repeated several thousand times by all students in a group, in four or five tempi, each twice as fast as the previous one, continuously from roughly 4:30 A.M. to 6:30 A.M. Participation in *sādhakam* develops the right-stick technique necessary for *ceṇṭa* proficiency.[9]

Beginning disciples also learn an elementary version of the solo *ceṇṭa* genre *tāyampaka;* although *tāyampaka* is separate from Kathakaḷi *ceṇṭa,* it is a necessary prerequisite for the latter. After having mastered beginning *tāyampaka* and *sādhakam,* they can learn the fixed segments performed for Kathakaḷi.

Some of the fixed segments are the drum part for a dance for beginning students, performed at the outset of a Kathakaḷi play (called *puṟappāṭu,* lit., "starting out"); a *mēḷappadam* ("instrumental performance and song") recital for singers and drummers, performed immediately after *puṟappāṭu* during the play's preliminaries, and which, like *puṟappāṭu,* is learned within the first two years of study; and the *tiranōkku* (lit., "curtain look"), the drum part for a dance performed by certain fearsome characters when they appear from behind a curtain at scene beginnings. But most of the fixed segments are cadential patterns, called *kalāśams. Kalāśams* conclude segments of the Kathakaḷi play's sung verses (*padams*) and are usually short. In most *kalāśams* the singers do not sing, but rather keep tala (metric cycle) for the *ceṇṭa* and *maddaḷam* drums on their gong and cymbals, while the actors perform *nṛttam,* dance moves that have no mimetic component.

Next, they move on to the aforementioned *colliyāṭṭam kaḷari,* where they accompany actors and singers and work with performers of barrel drums (*maddaḷams*). In the *colliyāṭṭam kaḷari* the students supplement the fixed segments with improvisational parts that respond directly to the actors' movements; this is sometimes called Kathakaḷi *koṭṭu,* or "beating" the drum for Kathakaḷi. During my time at Kalamandalam I knew of no instance in which Kathakaḷi *koṭṭu* was taught in a drum *kaḷari.*

The two stages of pedagogy are not completely discrete; at Kalamandalam an advanced student may go to the *colliyāṭṭam kaḷari* early in the class and return to the drum *kaḷari* later, where he practices *kalāśams* and other fixed segments with his fellow drum students. But first-year students do not typically go to the *colliyāṭṭam kaḷari,* and very advanced students spend little time in the drum *kaḷari.*

The *kalāśam* in figure 8.2 is one of a great many called *vaṭṭam veccu kalāśam* ("*kalāśam* kept in a circle"), so named because the actor traces circles on the stage while dancing. [**Audio example 8.1**] He traces one circle per cycle of tala, which consists of fifty-six counts in this case.[10] This particular *kalāśam* is four cycles long; the *ceṇṭa* part for each of the first three cycles repeats a different rhythmic motif. The rhythmic pattern played by the tala-keeping gong and cymbals remains the same from one cycle of tala to the next (as in many comparable genres of south Indian music), the fifty-six counts being divided 8 + 4 + 4 + 4, 8 + 4 + 4 + 4, 8 + 8. In the fourth cycle of tala the *ceṇṭa* starts to repeat another motif, then breaks off to play a final cadence in which yet another motif expands from three to five counts, contracts to two, and expands back to five again and closes. Thus, in this particular

FIGURE 8.2. Kathakaḷi, *Vaṭṭam Veccu Kalāśam, Aṭanta tala*, first *kālam* (*ceṇṭa* and idiophones only). As learned by the author at Kerala Kalamandalam, summer 2000. In the *ceṇṭa* part: notes on the center line denote strokes in the center of the drum (both right-stick and left-stick strokes); notes just above the line denote right-stick strokes on the edge; and notes just below the line denote left-stick strokes on the edge. In the last tala cycle, in the *ceṇṭa* part, 8 + 8 + 3 (2 + the rest) + 4 (3 + the rest) + 5 + 5 + 4 + 3 + 2 +2 + 3 + 4 + 5 = 56. In the tala part, 8 + 4 + 4 + 4 + 8 + 4 + 4 + 4 + 8 + 8 = 56 (as in every tala cycle in this *kalāśam*).

FIGURE 8.2. (Continued)

(Continued)

FIGURE 8.2. (Continued)

kalāśam, an extraordinary level of tension with the underlying tala is present, as the drum part seems to separate itself from the tala (as demarcated by the gong and cymbals) before returning to it.[11] This particular type of tension is specific to this and a few other *vaṭṭam veccu kalāśams*, but the overall principle of separation between tala and drumming applies generally. The actor's steps, which I do not have time to discuss here, are extremely closely related to the drum strokes, not as much to the strokes of the tala-keeping instruments.[12]

Again, at Kalamandalam the *ceṇṭa* disciple (Indian and Western) learns all of these *kalāśams* from the primary drum preceptor in the drum *kaḷari*. Typically second- and third-year students learn these (as of 2000), while the more junior students learn more elementary fixed compositions (*puṟappāṭu, mēḷappadam,* and *tāyampaka*), and while the more advanced students are in the *colliyāṭṭam* studio.[13] The preceptor initially directs a relatively advanced student in the group to beat the tala (on a block of stone or wood), and the preceptor then plays each segment of the *kalāśam* on a wooden table, behind which he is sitting. Each student repeats a given segment until he can do so flawlessly. Then students go down the line: the first plays the *kalāśam* on his block while the others keep tala on theirs; then a second one does so. This goes on until, ideally, every student has played the *kalāśam* without mistakes. When all students have learned all *kalāśams* in a tala, the down-the-line process repeats, without a break, for each of these *kalāśams*. This process often lasts up to two hours, and repeats in successive classes throughout the academic year (June to March). *Kalāśams* take up a great deal of class time, although the preceptor also spends time in the drum *kaḷari* teaching *tāyampaka* (the solo drum composition) and other Kathakaḷi fixed compositions. He will also occasionally quiz students about Kathakaḷi plays with such questions as, "In which play does Bhima fetch flowers for Draupadi"?

The idea is to instill the knowledge of *kalāśams* so thoroughly that students cannot forget how to perform them. The process resembles the "first stage" of my model: through tactile and aural means, the preceptor transmits his embodied experience to the disciple, enabling the disciple to reproduce patterns exactly as he is taught them—in essence, to become a smaller, junior version of the preceptor. The preceptor corrects the disciple by clutching his right wrist and rotating it (this movement is necessary to play the *ceṇṭa*), or by moving his arm; knowledge is firmly embodied into the disciple. Disciples also learn how their identities differ from those of their preceptors. The preceptor, for instance, sits in the *kaḷari* in a chair behind his wooden table, while the boys sit on mats on the floor and beat the patterns on their wooden blocks or stones (dummy instruments). The preceptor can wear a shirt, make small talk with colleagues (who walk by the *kaḷari* to visit), arrive late to the *kaḷari* or leave early, or chew betel nut; the disciples, huddled on the mats next to the wall, may do none of these things. So, in the drum *kaḷari,* students learn their social roles by observing their peers and by submitting to the preceptor. Yet as much as the disciple is learning to be a disciple, he is also starting

FIGURE 8.3. *Ceṇṭa kaḷari,* Kerala Kalamandalam, August 2000. Note the blocks of stone in front of three of the students (the two on the extreme left and the one on the extreme right), and the circular blocks of wood in front of the other five students. All of the students are holding the tamarind wood sticks with which they play. At the extreme right and front, note the wooden table with the stick upon it, the preceptor normally sits here. The mats upon which the students normally sit are missing. Photograph by the author.

FIGURE 8.4. *Ceṇṭa kaḷari,* Kerala Kalamandalam, June 2006, outside view. *Ceṇṭa kaḷari*s are located at the top of the hill in the back of the Kalamandalam campus. Behind them are the preceptors' quarters; down the hill and to the front of the campus are the *colliyāṭṭam kaḷari*s and the students' quarters. Photograph by the author.

to incorporate the embodied musical knowledge of the preceptor, and thereby learning to become a (future) preceptor as well.

Only after a disciple has mastered the *sādhakam* exercises, the elementary version of *tāyampaka,* the preliminary items for the Kathakaḷi play (*puṟappāṭu, mēḷappadam,* and a few others not mentioned here), a great number of *kalāśams*, and a few other advanced fixed compositions in the drum *kaḷari,* including *tiranōkku* (the "curtain look"), is he ready to rehearse *padams* (the vocal/dance-drama compositions that make up the core of a Kathakaḷi play) with the *maddaḷam* drummer, the singers, and the actors in the *colliyāṭṭam kaḷari* (group rehearsal studio).

The *colliyāṭṭam kaḷaris* at Kalamandalam are located some distance from the drum *kaḷaris*. At the former, the primary preceptor is the dance-drama preceptor (*vēṣam āśān*), who also teaches his own students in a separate dance-drama *kaḷari;* singing and drumming preceptors also rehearse with the ensemble in the group rehearsal studio, or more frequently watch their own students rehearsing. The dance-drama preceptor normally observes his own students' performance in the group rehearsal studio, but sometimes interrupts the rehearsal to re-demonstrate the movements and gestures of the *padam* to a dance-drama student, especially when the student errs. (The dance-drama students will have already learned their roles in the *padams,* without music, in group "sitting classes" in the dance-drama *kaḷaris*; in theory they would have to perform these *padams* in sitting classes perfectly before rehearsing with musicians in the *colliyāṭṭam* studio. In sitting class the dance-drama preceptor beats the tala with a wooden stick on a table.)

In the drum *kaḷari,* my main preceptor had told me to play the *kalāśams* he had taught me, as short cadential patterns at the ends of segments of *padams*, when I reached the *colliyāṭṭam* studio.[14] In the *colliyāṭṭam* studio, however, another *ceṇṭa* preceptor, who was observing a more advanced *ceṇṭa* student, told me to watch that student and imitate him.[15] I was surprised to discover that the advanced *ceṇṭa* student played *kalāśams* only occasionally; he far more frequently provided soft improvisation under the sung lines of the *padam,* responding to the actor-dancers' movements with Kathakaḷi *koṭṭu*. During these *padams*, the actor-dancers interpreted the singers' lines with meaningful hand gestures called *mudras*.[16]

I had not learned this Kathakaḷi *koṭṭu* from my *ceṇṭa* preceptor in the drum *kaḷari*.[17] Nor could I infer it from my knowledge of the *kalāśams*, since it was musically quite different. First, its dynamics were in general much softer: drummers subordinated themselves to the singers, who were not amplified in rehearsal. Second, it involved the use of a crushed right stick stroke, which never appears in the *kalāśams*. This is illustrated in figure 8.5 (the second cycle of tala in particular), a transcription of a minute-long excerpt of the *ceṇṭa,* vocal, and idiophone parts of a *padam* from the Kathakaḷi play "Lavanasura Vadham." [**Audio example 8.2**]

FIGURE 8.5. Excerpt from "Sukhamō Dēvī" ("Are you well, Devi?"), a *padam* from the Kathakaḷi play "Lavanāsura Vadham." *Nāṭakuranji* raga, *cempaṭa* tala (eight counts per cycle). Tala-keeping idiophones (cymbals, gong); *ceṇṭa* and vocals only (actors and *maddaḷam* not transcribed). Transcribed by the author from CD "South India: Ritual Music and Theatre of Kerala" (1990), recordings and commentary by Pribislav Pitoeff, with the collaboration of G. Venn, Centre national de la recherche scientifique/Musée de l'Homme, Le chant du monde LDX 274910, first track ("Théâtre dansé Kathakali"). Kalamandalam Sankaran Embrantiri and Kalamandalam Surindren, voice and idiophones; Ayamkutty Kuttapa Marar, *ceṇṭa;* Kalamandalam Appukutty Poduval, *maddaḷam*. The vocal part is divided, with some overlap, between two singers (ponnani and śiṅkiṭi). One sings tala cycles 1–2, 5–6, and 9–10; the other sings cycles 3–4, 7–8, and 11–12. In the *ceṇṭa* part, the top space in the staff represents a right-stick edge stroke; the second space a right-stick center stroke; the second to bottom space a left-stick center stroke; and the bottom space a left-stick edge stroke. *Putra rute parakrāmam* means "Thy sons' deed." Hanuman speaks here to the princess Sita; "tr" denotes quick *gamaka*s in the vocal part and quick crushed strokes on the *ceṇṭa*.

FIGURE 8.5. (Continued)

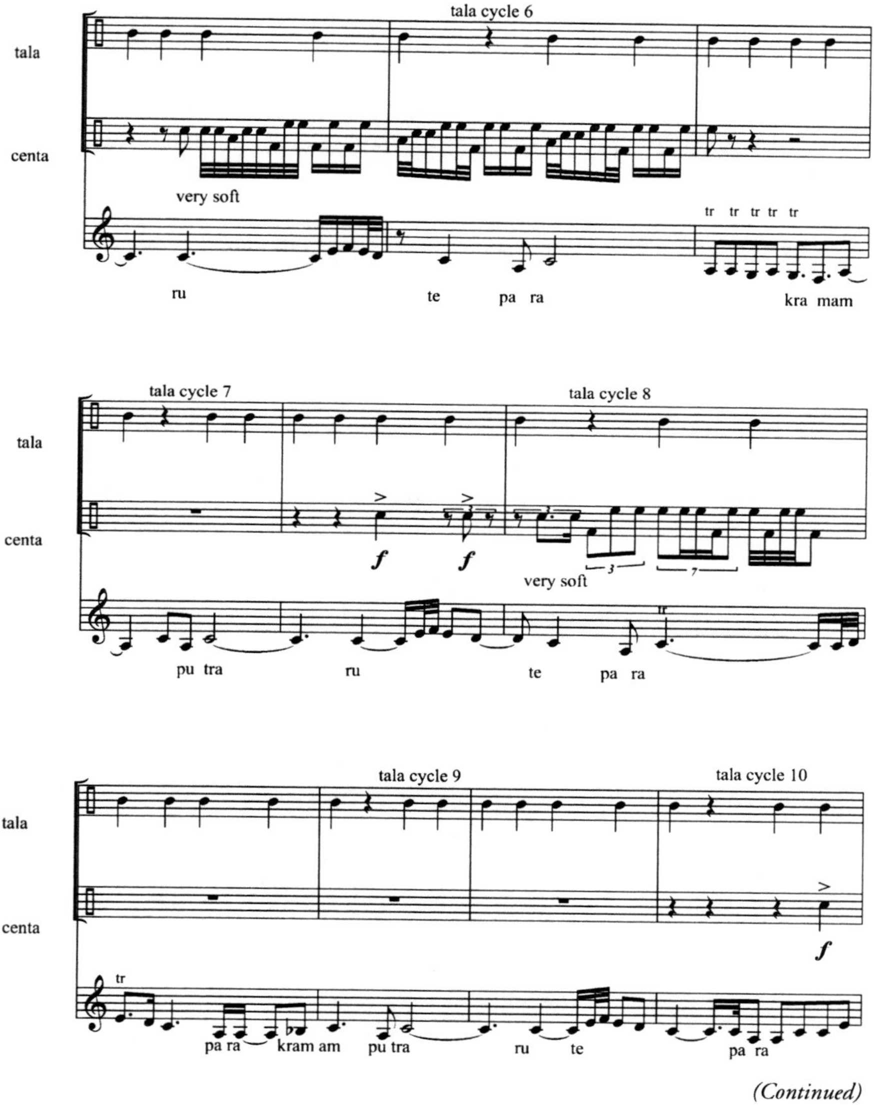

(Continued)

FIGURE 8.5. (Continued)

Third, the separation of drum from sung lines and tala is remarkable, as the *ceṇṭa* does not generally reinforce the eight-count *campaṭa* tala but rather plays highly scattered motifs, at times separated by considerable periods of silence. In the *kalāśams*, by contrast, in general the drummer plays throughout, even though, as noted, the *ceṇṭa*'s phrases do not always coincide with the flow of the tala.

Finally, the logic underlying the drum's performance of Kathakaḷi *koṭṭu* lies in its relationship to the actor's movements (not transcribed here); many motifs highlight the actor's arm, leg, hand, or facial gestures. Since the rhythmic organization of these does not reinforce the tala, neither does the drum part (see especially tala cycles seven and eight in fig. 8.5). Note that the nature of the drum's divergence from the tala in *Kathakaḷi koṭṭu* differs considerably from that of the *kalāśam* transcribed in figure 8.2. In the last tala cycle of that *kalāśam* a drum motif expanded from three counts to five, back down to two, and finally up to five again. Thus the last 40 counts of the tala cycle were organized: 3 + 4 + 5 + 5 + 4 + 3 + 2 + 2 + 3 + 4 + 5; while the tala-keeping gong and cymbals continued outlining a 56-count cycle divided 8 + 4 + 4 + 4, 8 + 4 + 4 + 4, 8 + 8. But in the Kathakaḷi *koṭṭu* transcribed in figure 8.5, no regular arithmetic progression explains the departure of the drum patterns from the structure of the tala; rather the drum patterns are direct responses to the actor's movements. Thus, Kathakaḷi *koṭṭu* and fixed *kalāśam* constitute two quite different subgenres of drumming, and the emphasis on the latter in the drum *kaḷari* did not prepare me for my introduction to the former in the *colliyāṭṭam* studio.[18]

So, how to master it? Three routes seemed to be available. First, the *colliyāṭṭam* drum teacher (not my primary teacher, who was in the drum *kaḷari*), sitting behind me observing, sometimes grabbed me or the more advanced student next to me and motioned for one of us to step aside so that he could accompany the *padam* himself. He did this especially when he was irritated at the incompetence of myself or the other student. Observing him and almost inaudibly trying to replicate his performance, I began to pick up the correct techniques.

Second and more frequently, the advanced student would play for the *padam* (with me following along quietly), so that I found myself learning by observing my fellow student. The *colliyāṭṭam* drum teacher would sit and observe, but did not always play an active role. Third, both the advanced student and this drum teacher would implore me, when I was playing, not to look at my drum, but rather to listen to the singers (and their tala keeping) and, much more important, watch the actors. As noted, some of my Kathakaḷi *koṭṭu* improvisations had to match their hand gestures, or their other arm and leg movements. By watching the actors, I was told, I would understand. At one point, the *colliyāṭṭam* drum teacher took me aside to teach me the meanings of many of the actors' *mudra* hand gestures, so that I would be able to figure out how to accompany them better. However, I was mostly learning by observing my fellow students (a *ceṇṭa* student in the second instance, dance-drama students in the third) rather than repeating patterns I had learned in the drum *kaḷari*.

The older drum students quickly figured out how to accentuate the actors' movements in *colliyāṭṭam*, using techniques they would not have learned in the drum *kaḷari* from their primary teachers. Since they lived in the Kalamandalam's dormitories in close proximity to the dance-drama and singing students, perhaps they intuited the mysteries of Kathakaḷi *koṭṭu* by practicing with their housemates after their official classes ended. A number of *ceṇṭa* students typically stayed in one dormitory room, *maddaḷam* students in the next, dance-drama students in the next, and so on.

Students would join together to eat, play cricket, or, on weekends, go into town. Also, many of them had grown up where Kathakaḷi was performed frequently, so perhaps they had observed some of these techniques as children. This situation may mark a continuity with Kathakaḷi's preinstitutional period (before 1930), in which disciples often lived with fellow disciples, as well as with preceptors, in or near the house of a wealthy landlord, who would take responsibility for patronizing a *colliyāṭṭam kaḷari* (and thus a Kathakaḷi troupe) in that house (Menon 1957).

When I asked one especially adept older (late teens) drum student at Kalamandalam how he had mastered a Kathakaḷi *koṭṭu* pattern, the answer would always

FIGURE 8.6. Students' quarters, Kerala Kalamandalam, 1989. Photograph by the author.

be the same: *kēṭṭa paṭhiccu, kaṇṭa paṭhiccu* ("I learned by hearing, I learned by watching"). This process really constituted the bulk of Kathakaḷi drumming, more so than mastery of *kalāśams*. As my *colliyāṭṭam* drum teacher put it, "If you want to learn the *kalāśams*, two or three months is enough; if you want to learn Kathakaḷi *koṭṭu,* two years is insufficient."[19]

One could argue that *colliyāṭṭam* is more central to the training of Kathakaḷi drummers because its format is closer to that of professional performances at temple festivals, in concert halls, and on tours. An ideal *colliyāṭṭam* rehearsal consists of an advanced group of student performers, some intermediate students, preceptors who observe and sometimes perform themselves, and perhaps some peripheral observers. The ensemble is rehearsing the *padams* that will eventually be performed in public. Whereas the drum *kaḷaris* prepare one for rehearsal by teaching a small percentage of what is actually played on the Kathakaḷi stage, *colliyāṭṭam* is that rehearsal. The groups that perform in *colliyāṭṭam* are "communit[ies] of practice" (Lave and Wenger 1991, 29) engaged in "legitimate peripheral participation." Jean Lave, who critiques the idea that schooling should be viewed as normative and diametrically opposed to apprenticeship or informal learning,[20] argues that legitimate peripheral participation (especially within a context of informal learning) provides a community of doers into which the novice can gradually enter and eventually become a full-fledged member. Apprentices proceed via "way[s]-in" and "practice," "from a state of high ignorance about how to do something to a state in which one can make a first approximation to it." Certain activities "move the apprentice from a first approximation to a high level of skill" (Lave 1982, 184). Learning, even in some schooling situations, takes place when problems are not decontextualized and abstracted (as they so often are in schools), but rather arise as an individual enters into a community of practitioners (Lave 1982). A *colliyāṭṭam kaḷari,* at its best, even when it is part of a formal institution, epitomizes this idea of a "community of practice"; the "ways-in," for drummers, are to play the *kalāśams* and observe the more advanced students improvising Kathakaḷi *koṭṭu.* Later they should be able to mark the actor-dancer's gestures with Kathakaḷi *koṭṭu* themselves. They gradually understand how to accompany the dance-drama without having been told explicitly what to do. Rote repetition of fixed patterns in the drum *kaḷari* is an important beginning, but becoming a full-fledged participant in the *colliyāṭṭam kaḷari* over time is the crucial way-in. At the Kalamandalam, this process involves hearing and watching one's fellow students as much as one's primary preceptor.

I do not want to overstate these points. Fixed compositions like *kalāśams* are not completely marginal to Kathakaḷi performance. They form much of the foundation of the training of the Kerala drummer, and certainly no drummer could dream of entering *colliyāṭṭam* without having first mastered the *kalāśams.*

It is also possible that those pedagogical issues related to peer-group immersion apply more to Kalamandalam than to other Kathakaḷi pedagogical sites. In smaller institutions, for instance, the primary *ceṇṭa* teacher sometimes accompanies daily *colliyāṭṭam* rehearsals, rather than staying in the *ceṇṭa kaḷari,* and the dance-drama teacher sometimes acts his *padams* in the *colliyāṭṭam kaḷari* rather than merely observing.[21] The student would thereby learn Kathakaḷi *koṭṭu* through "legitimate peripheral participation" in a "community of practice" consisting more of his preceptors than of his fellow students. This would tend to strengthen the preceptor–disciple bond. Defenders of these smaller institutions (see Zarrilli 2000, 30–38) contend that they closely approximate the older *gurukula* system in which Kathakaḷi thrived in the preinstitutional period (pre-1930). The distance between disciple and preceptor in the preinstitutional period and in certain smaller institutions may be much less than in the Kalamandalam.

The situation at Kalamandalam may exacerbate this sense of distance for several reasons. First, beginning sometime after Krishna *jayanti* (Krishna's birth holiday, mid- to late August) the general demand for preceptors' performances increases, especially in the village temples where many Kathakaḷi performances take place. As the performance season wears on and preceptors accept invitations to perform in these village temple festivals as well as abroad, preceptors become scarcer at Kalamandalam, even though students are required to continue attending classes. (This was especially true during my first stay at Kalamandalam, in the late 1980s.) Advanced disciples may take a more central role during the absences of their preceptors.

Second, many Kalamandalam preceptors stay in houses in the woods behind the institution, a considerable distance from the drum *kaḷari*s, and further still from the student dormitories. In some cases, preceptors even live in houses in town or in one of the neighboring towns. In an ideal *gurukula* situation, students would live with their teachers. Additionally, students and preceptors eat at the institution's canteens at separate times. Finally, students perform the technical exercises (*sādhakam*) together early in the morning in the drum *kaḷari*s. The drum preceptor who oversees these exercises typically arrives later and leaves earlier than the students. Students occasionally take advantage of this absence to attempt to gain some control over their training; for instance, I recall on one occasion the students practicing a technical exercise that was not the one normally performed on that day, and I asked one of them why. He said that an unusually strict preceptor was to monitor *sādhakam* that day and so the students had decided to play a less taxing exercise (preceptors never participated in student *sādhakam* themselves, rather they sat behind their wooden tables and observed).

These aspects of separation and distance between preceptor and disciple may stem from the phenomenon of institutionalization in general and from the large size of Kalamandalam in particular.[22] The great number of students and courses of study available requires many rooms for practice and necessitates a division of labor among faculty. This is why some *ceṇṭa* preceptors are assigned to the drum *kaḷari*s, and others observe at *colliyāṭṭam*. Institutionalization may cause the bonds between preceptor and disciple to weaken and those among members of the student peer-group to strengthen in compensation.

The Kalamandalam experience, central to many Kathakaḷi performers' backgrounds, involves, then, separation of disciples from preceptors, absence of primary drum teachers from *colliyāṭṭam,* and importance of peer-group immersion in *colliyāṭṭam*. This way of training suggests that the core of Kathakaḷi drumming is rather distant from the fixed compositions the primary drum teacher imparts to the student. Some of these are rarely played on stage in any event. To master Kathakaḷi drumming one must learn things that a preceptor does not normally teach by rote. One frequently learns by imitating a more advanced student or by trying Kathakaḷi *koṭṭu* out on one's own. The learning process is as much horizontal—peer-to-peer—as vertical—preceptor-to-disciple.[23] The disciple's transformation into a future preceptor and performer couples with his discovery of how to be a disciple, and the preceptor's of how to be a preceptor. Different rhythmic patterns and processes are associated with different discipular and career stages: *kalāśam*s and other fixed compositions with early discipleship, rote repetition, the drum *kaḷari,* and mimicry of the guru; and Kathakaḷi *koṭṭu* with advanced discipleship and preceptorship, observation and gradual entry into a community of practitioners (gurus and advanced students), and the *colliyāṭṭam kaḷari.* As noted in different places earlier in this chapter, this two-stage model for pedagogy, musical content, and musical process could apply also to Karnatak music (the fixed *varṇam* versus the observed, informally learned *svara kalpana* and *ālāpana*); drumming in the Karnatak tradition (learning of patterns used in the drum solo from the primary teacher versus the "way-in" to accompaniment of vocal and melodic instrumental concerts); and the Kerala drumming genre *tāyampaka* (fixed *eṇṇams* in the drum *kaḷari* versus improvised, informally learned *manōdharmam* in concert performance), among others.

Differences between the Kerala and Karnatak music data may focus on the continued centrality of the preceptor in the latter; for instance, Nelson describes the Karnatak drummer as learning to accompany "by listening: *first to the teacher,* then to other senior drummers" (Nelson 2000, 157, emphasis added). In Karnatak music, vertical learning may prevail in both stages of pedagogy, instead of prevailing more in the first stage.

Indeed, I am struck by the contrasts not only between these data and Nelson's but also with those presented by Henderson and Qureshi in this volume. If horizontal (*birādarī*) and vertical (*sīna ba sīna*) learning reinforce and complement each other in Ustad Sabri Khan's home, where Qureshi studied—the former usually subordinated to the latter—vertical learning at Shambu Prasad Mishra's house (where Henderson studied) is itself horizontal. Henderson's description of his lessons with the latter calls to mind a rhythmic conversation between two social equals (despite the vast age gap). Both preceptor and disciple simultaneously explore new variations and potential innovations, the former generally taking the lead, but within an atmosphere of partnership. Such a relaxed environment is unimaginable in the drum *kaḷari* at Kalamandalam. This underscores the present focus on locality; my task here is not to illuminate a pan-Indian system of pedagogy (*guru-śiṣya*), nor to claim an unusual exception to some putative pan-Indian system, but to define pedagogy locally—not for Kerala as a whole, but within the confines of the Kalamandalam alone—so that it can be compared and contrasted to that in other South Asian sites. Local theory in Kerala, rather than deriving wholly from Sanskritic pedagogical concepts, manifests itself partly as the "I learned by hearing, I learned by seeing" aphorisms used in casual conversation by drum students, and in the "legitimate peripheral participation" characteristics of the group rehearsal studio. As Wolf insists in the Introduction to this volume, "individual practices serve as guides to inchoate theory or as challenging counterpoints to prevailing explanatory discourses among participants in a tradition." The prevailing explanatory discourse here—the *guru-śiṣya* model—is certainly relevant, as every disciple at Kalamandalam defines himself in part in terms of his preceptor, and all use the *guru-śiṣya* terminology to refer to themselves and others. But this model is only part of this locality's indigenous theorization of the praxis of pedagogy.

The process I have outlined could help explain why connoisseurs and performers alike describe some aspects of Kerala music's recent history in terms of style development and the achievements of heroic individuals—almost in the way that Westerners commonly understand histories of Western musics such as classical music, jazz, and rock. Kathakaḷi connoisseurs highlight the many achievements of the *ceṇṭa* player Moothamana Kesavan Nambutiri and the *maddaḷam* player Venkicchan Swami, who were born in the late nineteenth century (around 1880–1890). Connoisseurs credit Moothamana, for instance, with introducing the one-stick-and-one-hand technique of performing the *tiranōkku* ("curtain look") piece, which had been and still is usually played with two sticks. Venkicchan Swami is credited with developing the role of the *maddaḷam* barrel drum in the modern *pañcavādyam* temple drumming ensemble (Rajagopalan 1972)

These connoisseurs also focus on another pair of brilliant drummers born roughly thirty years later, Krishnankutty Poduval (*ceṇṭa*) and Appukutty Poduval (*maddaḷam*). Krishnankutty Poduval is credited with having invented the *drīm* stroke, which he used, in particular, in the Kathakaḷi play "Nala Caritam, Second Day."[24] He is celebrated in particular for his accompaniment of the actor Ramankutty Nair, with whom he worked for most of his career, in the play *Ravanodbhavam*. Connoisseurs marvel at the reputed connection between the two artists, as if one creative spirit had simultaneously animated two bodies.

In thinking about the great maestros, most *rasika*s (connoisseurs) bemoan the state of Kathakaḷi drumming today; some, however, see hope in the playing of Balaraman, my own primary preceptor, and Unnikrishnan, who were both born in the 1950s. This pattern, whereby a new group of innovative giants is born once in a generation, also applies to the tradition of the drum solo *tāyampaka*. Leading performers like Malamakkavil Kesava Poduval, Tiyadi Nampiyar, and Atanta Konta Swamy, all born about 1890, preceded a group born in the 1920s, including Pallavoor Appu Marar, Aliparambil Sivarama Poduval, and Trittala Kunnikrishnan Poduval, and the legendary Mattannoor Sankarankutty, born in the 1950s.

Performers born in decades other than the 1890s, the 1920s, and the 1950s also contributed to Kerala's performing arts. However the perception of a stylistically dynamic history demarcated by generationally based (once every thirty years) transformations continues to persist, as does the image of each generation's masters having worked closely with each other, their creative inspirations having drawn upon the richness of these relationships. I contend that this perception could result from a culture in which performers define themselves in terms of their immersion in their generational peer groups as well as their relationships to their preceptors.

The importance of the preceptor-disciple relationship in Kerala is undeniable. One could easily emphasize the importance of many preceptors in the lives of their disciples, even long after the teaching period has concluded (see Groesbeck 1995, 469). The preceptor-disciple relationship is in many ways central here, as it is throughout South Asia. I have rather tried to indicate that an understanding of the horizontal as well as the vertical aspects of musical transmission, and of separate generational identities resulting from peer group immersion, can illuminate aspects of musical transmission in South Asia that have, heretofore, not been thoroughly studied.

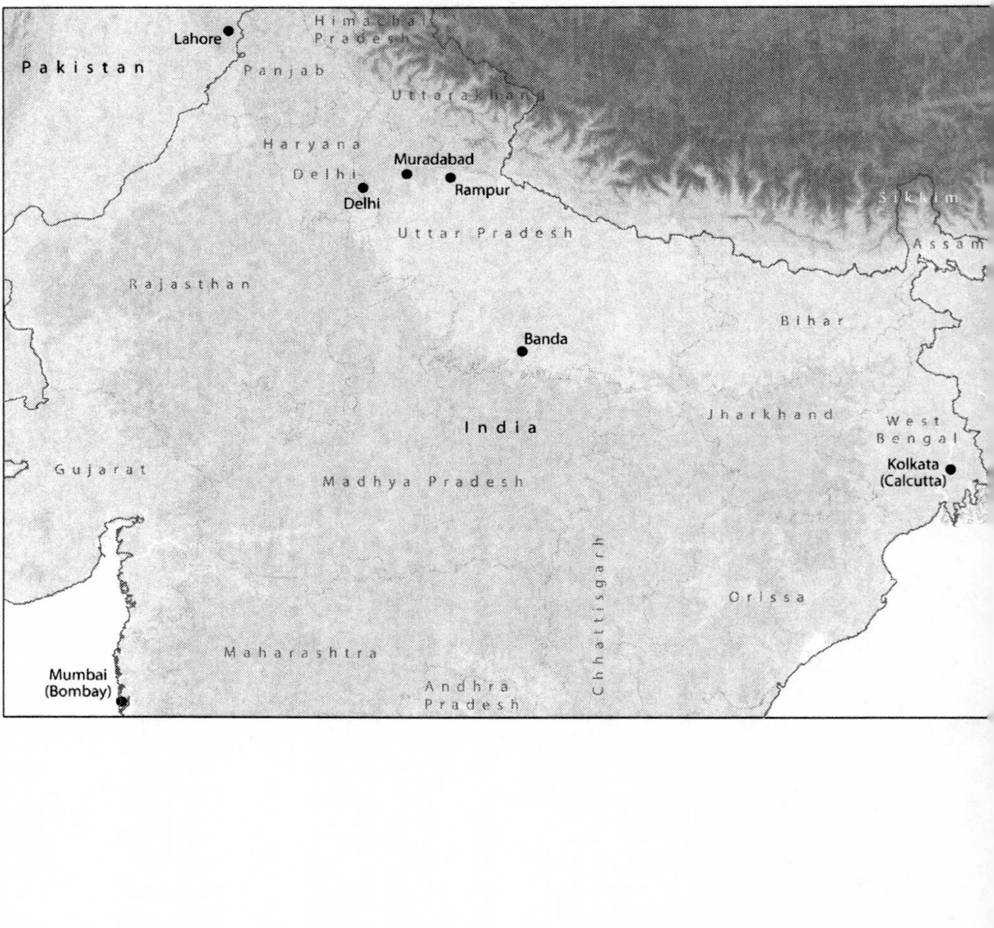

Lahore
Pakistan
Himachal Pradesh
Panjab
Uttarakhand
Haryana
Muradabad
Delhi
Rampur
Delhi
Sikkim
Uttar Pradesh
Assam
Rajasthan
Bihar
Banda
India
Jharkhand
West Bengal
Gujarat
Kolkata (Calcutta)
Madhya Pradesh
Chhattisgarh
Orissa
Maharashtra
Mumbai (Bombay)
Andhra Pradesh

CHAPTER 9

Sīna ba Sīna or "From Father to Son"

Writing the Culture of Discipleship

REGULA BURCKHARDT QURESHI

Hindustani music has for centuries been a hereditary specialization among communities of musicians who serve landed patrons, including princes and royalty. Children are born into an environment of musical immersion and taught to become professionals by their father or a family elder. In a process of transmission that is entirely oral, they learn the musical system informally, like a language, as well as formally. This training continues as students become masters who in turn teach their children and, rarely, students from outside the community.

Today, hereditary musicians and their disciples continue to maintain the highest level of musical competence, but under conditions of reduced or fundamentally altered public patronage by the Indian state. This state patronage has attracted a vast contingent of middle-class performers, many of whom have themselves become disciples of hereditary masters. The new performers recognize the value of the oral hereditary milieu, even as its existence is threatened with extinction. At the same time, hereditary Hindustani musicians have gained increasing access to patronage abroad, extending their reach across continents into the expanding sphere of world music.

Sonically, the global success of Hindustani music clearly lies in this combination of a highly elaborated, aestheticized, theorized, and professionalized musical language of melodic (raga), rhythmic (tala), and compositional (*bandish*) repertoires with equally elaborated but highly flexible procedures for generating musical structures in performance. Performers must be able to retain and recall all aspects of musical knowledge in order to generate such structures through processes that might be described as quasi-improvisational or oral-compositional. "It's all in the head, like a vast ocean contained in a small cup," explained my guru, Ustad Sabri Khan, one of the greatest and wisest musicians in India today. There is nothing written down and nothing else is needed. There is no separation between music and music maker—the Musician Is the Music. Or, as Shujaat Khan, the illustrious offspring of India's most venerable sitar lineage, responded to Canadian students: "I am Indian culture."

This chapter addresses oral transmission and discipleship in the hereditary community of *sārangī* players who continue to practice family-based teaching, principally because their instrument never became part of the middle-class teaching establishments of Hindustani music. Their voices have been largely left out of the considerable literature generated by formally educated scholars and performers. Many such scholars and performers have themselves benefited from discipleship with hereditary masters and adapted that knowledge to the needs of the national culture establishment and its educated middle-class constituency. Individual discipleship and the hereditary milieu remain the acknowledged source of the Hindustani musical heritage. I know no better validation of this claim than the recent publication of the invaluable book *Musicians of India: Past and Present,* which contains nothing but annotated genealogical tables of musical lineages (Dasasarma 1993).

My exploration of this oral hereditary milieu is grounded in ethnographic documentation of discipleship as I observed and experienced it personally as a longtime disciple of Ustad Sabri Khan and the late Ustad Hamid Husain, both of the Muradabad Rampur *gharānā*. The goal is to bring this exclusively oral process of teaching and learning into focus, not only as a means of transmitting musical content but also as a fundamental process of musical enculturation and socialization that may well account for the unique qualities hereditary musicians have brought to Hindustani music and its performance. Today, in the face of the increasingly global spread of their music, it is particularly important to explore how these musicians have continued to maintain the local intimacy of oral, discipular learning, not only within but also beyond the confines of locality territorially conceived. Could they be teaching us to rethink the local as a space that is orally and relationally constituted?

In the context of the present volume, asking this question amounts to interrogating the substantive confines implied in the very concept of "the local." I believe that such a rethinking of the local as oral and relational can be a potentially significant contribution to Western "theories of the local," if it can take the form of a local theory of Hindustani musical transmission and can be understood to be embodied in the local practice of its hereditary musicians. To access the premises underlying this rethinking, however, would demand a major intellectual shift, not only on the level of concepts but also in categories of thinking. I see it as a shift toward an imaginary where the musical is inherently social, as is the temporal and the local, so that time lines are lineages and localities are a network of family sites. And all learning is interpersonal, that is, located in personal interaction and commitment.[1]

In my experience, such a shift cannot be made by intellectual fiat; it is the stuff of participation and interaction as well as reflection, and of confronting one's own assumptions, as universal as they may seem. To illustrate, I offer my own encounter with such an altered premise in the seemingly small matter of translating the title of this paper. *Sīna ba sīna* is a phrase used universally by hereditary musicians and others who wish to identify the process by which such musicians have gained their knowledge of music. In a generic sense, *sīna ba sīna* signifies "oral transmission from a master to a student." Like many authoritative sayings in Urdu (or Hindi) *sīna ba sīna* is drawn from Persian, the Indo-Muslim elite and court language. *Sīna* literally means chest or breast, but it is as widely used in the extended sense of a person's inner repository of what is most valuable—emotions, knowledge, and memory. The preposition *ba* is a connective signifying: "with," "together with," "to," and also, "from . . . to," as in the oral transmission of knowledge that is enshrined in one breast and transferred to another as an exclusive bestowal that connects the two. *Sīna ba sīna,* in effect, encapsulates the core relationship governing oral transmission, from a master who gives his uniquely personal knowledge to a disciple who receives and internalizes it. It is a foundational concept of everything that discipleship contains, hence my choice as the title of this paper.

There is also a personal reason for this choice: *sīna ba sīna* became a touchstone for my own rethinking of discipleship. As a professional cellist with years of music lessons, I already knew that sequestered domain of oral transmission, having experienced the mystique of "the studio," the will to imbibe the master's wisdom, the penitential discipline of practicing, and the exhilarating moments when the master accepts the student's efforts, then returns to his relentless demand for more and better. I could relate to the notion of the famous Indian metaphor as a version of the same process in India. To me *sīna ba sīna* meant "from the teacher's breast to mine," or simply "from one heart to another." When discussing an adequate translation for my title with a cultural expert, however, his choice completely surprised me. Not from heart-to-heart, but "from father to son" was what he considered the most adequate rendering of the phrase. Clearly, the primary hereditary as well as generational meaning of *sīna ba sīna* and the social embeddedness of oral transmission evoked by the phrase had totally eluded me.[2]

Once I began exploring the meaning of *sīna ba sīna* in this sense it opened up a rich set of very different but interconnected dimensions, all emanating from the primary father-to-son kinship relation. At the center are lineage, heredity, and seniority, pointing above all to the agents and relationship of oral transmission. Implied equally are memory and value of the transmitted content, and, by further implication, the immediacy and intimacy of the situation of transmission. I came to experience these meanings in the context of discipular families and their senses of belonging. Most significantly, this entailed sharing a group intimacy, rather than through the personal intimacy of the Western studio, where the creative individual is cultivated above all.

Discipleship as a Site of Ethnographic Learning

What notions and priorities did this Western disciple bring to the music room of an Indian master, and what was I capable of receiving? And how, in the end, should the disciple, now turned scholar, represent the experience by means of print, to an audience of cultural outsiders?

For ethnomusicologists studying professionalized art music in South Asia, discipleship has been paradigmatic, and it is foundational to many important studies of diverse aspects of Hindustani and Karnatak music (Bor 1986–87; Brown 1965; Kippen 1988; Neuman 1990; Powers 1959; Slawek 2000; Viswanathan 1974; Wolf 1991).

Almost invariably a starting base, if not the primary reason for field research, learning to sing or play has perhaps contributed to the formation of authors as much as their scholarly findings. This becomes evident in the remarkable sense of kinship between those of us who share the Indian discipleship experience. Perhaps most remarkable, the discipular way of learning a music culture marks ethnomusicology as an inclusive cross-cultural practice, because it counterposes the student's submission to the scholar's entitlement to know.

Marked by respectful discipular learning, the resulting studies have made seminal contributions to our understanding of what is taught inside musicians' families. The discipleship process itself, however, has remained generally opaque in both theory and practice. I became interested in discipular ethnography as part of my search, via my own discipleship, for understanding the uniquely oral foundation of Hindustani music. During the early years of my *sārangī* study I found that my Western discipular priorities quite matched the Indian bourgeois version of music lessons provided to amateurs for a monthly fee at their house or in a music school; in Hindi/Urdu the English term "tuition" is used. Teaching consisted of memorizing, with the help of a notebook of *sargam* (solfège) notation, condensed versions of ragas, including brief compositions (*cīz*) and brief insertions of passage work (*tān*). We worked on each raga for about two months or until it was brought to a passable level of playing.

My discipleship with Sabri Khan changed all that. Although he occasionally came to my residence room to teach me, and we did agree on a monthly remuneration, the norm was for me to go to his house and stay there, waiting to be taught or joining his sons in practicing together. Increasingly, I became a learner and a member of the musical family of *shāgird bhāī* (disciple brothers or, in my case, *bahin* or sister). It was this experience that for me came to validate the "father-to-son" perspective on *sīna ba sīna*. Above all, this was a social as much as a musical universe, anchored in the family and its wider network of kinship and community.[3]

From my place of discovery and enculturation into being a disciple, I see the need for a conversation about the process of discipleship that focuses on its relational character and, most important, incorporates the equation of music and musician which is so central to the oral world of musical transmission.

My approach references three complementary perspectives: the master's teaching, the student's learning, and the scholar's representation. The first two perspectives are directly informed by my own experience, principally as a long-time disciple of Ustad Sabri Khan. The master's teaching embodies the central goal of helping to bring the remarkable oral theory and practice of my teachers into focus, both within the realm of Indian music and within a global horizon of musical thinking. The student's learning addresses the relational dimension of discipleship from the only perspective I can own—that of a foreign student who must situate herself and problematize her assumptions accordingly. Finally, the scholar's representation focuses on the textualization of oral transmission and interrogates the process in relation to the authority and agency of the master's oral teaching.

Analytical categories, however, often seem elusive in the holistic milieu of *sīna ba sīna*. My primary goal has been to explore discipleship and the oral milieu itself, and that points directly to family and kinship as the bedrock of music making. In doing so, I draw as much on my uncritical aesthetic experience of music making as on my critical exploration of the same in relation to relevant contexts, including what the researcher brings to the intimate domain of the music room. For if orality means the inseparability of music and musician, of words and their speakers and hearers, then the ethnomusicologist's access to oral musical knowledge is likewise personal and participatory, and she must factor the impact of her presence into the mix and into its representation.

Balancing out the reflexive stance is the set of voices that speak from recordings I made of my discipular encounters, embodying the master's words and actions in their living context. I was fortunate to have my teachers' permission to record on tape and videotape how the *sīna ba sīna* process unfolded in my presence. To provide a modest degree of access to these primary sources here, I include summarized and transcribed excerpts from recordings of the *shāgirdī* (ritual formalizing discipleship) and of teaching sessions. The scenes represent salient aspects of *sīna ba sīna,* each encapsulated within a pithy saying of traditional musicians' wisdom. Together they illustrate the nature of my discipular encounter, both by offering as unmediated an introduction as possible to the *sīna ba sīna* milieu, and by making apparent the privileged, quasi-insider place I occupied in that milieu. Above all I use the transcribed and translated teachings and conversations in order to share some of the multilayered meanings that were revealed to me in the process of the local-oral events in Ustad Sabri Khan's music room.

Although other foreign students had preceded me, most prominently Sabri Khan's long-time disciple Daniel Neuman, I had the privilege of being able to join in the unmediated flow of interaction in Urdu which Sabri Khan used in a pithily idiomatic and richly referenced way to get his teaching points across. Sharing the language also activated a bond of shared meanings that quickly dispelled the inherent awkwardness of a foreign woman planting herself in the all-male music room where women were simply not part of the company.

The Kinship Context

How does the family occupy such an important place in the culture of discipleship? Without dealing with source readings (Neuman 1990; Dasasarma 1993), this brief sketch of the kinship context is intended to convey something of the social-musical nexus that underlies the *sīna ba sīna* / father-to-son paradigm. The master-disciple relationship of musical transmission constitutes a personal bond that has spiritual and musical dimensions as well as social ones, particularly of recruitment and reproduction for the discipular chain. Both Hinduism and Islam offer spiritual validation for discipleship through the paradigm of spiritual guidance, through the Hindu concept of *gurukul*.[4] And the Sufi discipleship ritual of *pīrī-murīdī* invokes a commitment modeled on the "father-to-son" relationship that directly validates kinship, descent, and family as a crucial pivot for all musical interaction.

Among hereditary musicians of northern India, the social network for musical transmission is a kinship-based universe of actual and potential relatives. Collectively that network is called *birādarī,* the "brotherhood" or community of musicians, as they are identified by people of other professional networks or social status. Within this collective identification, what makes hereditary *musical* identity possible for an individual artist? The first answer that my experience has generated is family, both in the immediate sense of household and in the broader sense of kinship. *Birādarī* is, in practice, an extension of kinship.

The immediate and primary sense of family is patrilineal: a hereditary line of musical succession from fathers to sons—including also nephews and grandsons (and perhaps daughters)—that is based on a commitment to invest their musical heritage in their own lineage first and foremost.[5]

In my experience, a core meaning of "from heart to heart" is the generational succession of the master's music. The intermeshing of musical and filial succession is simply a given. As a concept, master-disciple equals father-son, but with the understanding that this relationship includes a variety of equivalences: "father" can include father's brother(s), paternal grandfather, and his brother. Maternal uncle and grandfather can also become "fathers" cum teachers—in other words the notion of family extends to members on both parents' sides. Marrying within the group creates both close-knit families and widely cast networks of relatives who are linked to each other by marriage ties. For Muslims, unlike (north Indian)

Hindus, endogamy includes marrying paternal or maternal cousins; this results in a highly flexible and often bilaterally oriented family structure, where the mother's (male) lineage can be as important as the father's. In terms of managing the musical heritage, marrying within the family permits keeping its immediate musical heritage intact, while the wide marriage universe of the *birādarī* permits accessing the desirable musical heritage of other families through either a son's or a daughter's marriage. Musical expertise is collectively preserved in the family. It is also legitimized by senior master musicians and ancestors. In a formal sense, senior members representing the *birādarī* may be called in to monitor teaching results in a guild-like manner. Assuring the level of expertise is important for disciples who will carry forward the heritage and use it to support the master/father and family in turn. Discipleship in the formal, ritual sense (*shāgirdī*), cements this musical filiation and its mutual obligation between teacher and student.

Masters do not enter this lifelong commitment lightly. This holds for students from within the family and particularly for students who come from outside the *birādarī* and whose long-term commitment is difficult to assess. *Shāgirdī* (discipleship), or more properly, *ustādī-shāgirdī* (mastership-discipleship) is the richly meaningful ceremony in which the ustād (master) formally establishes the lifelong bond of discipleship with his *shāgird* (disciple).

Ustad Sabri Khan's Teachings in the Music Room, 1984

The Shāgirdī (Discipleship) of Nasir Khan: A Teaching Ceremony

I was fortunate to attend and capture on videotape a memorable *shāgirdī* ceremony held by Ustad Sabri Khan in 1984. The first excerpt encapsulates the central portion of the event as it unfolded. My brief interpretive comments point to the "lessons" conveyed by each segment (as I have come to understand them during my own learning period with Ustad Sabri Khan).

THE SETTING In Sabri Khan's music room the floor was covered with a fresh white sheet, with bolsters lining the walls, offering flexible and comfortably informal seating. Already present were his sons and disciples, as well as several senior members of the community (*birādarī*) who had come to witness the *shāgirdī*.

The *shāgird* was a nephew of Ustad Sabri Khan and already living in his house. Also present were Sabri Khan's two older sons, Ghulam Sarvar (an accomplished tabla player) and teenager Jamal, as well as his two younger sons Kamal (who at nine was learning the *sārangī*) and Gulfam (who at seven learned harmonium and tabla). At Sabri Khan's side was his best student and second cousin, Ghulam Sabir (a very fine young professional *sārangī* player), at his right was his elder brother; and several other senior musicians from the *birādarī* gradually appeared, including the *shāgird*'s father (a tabla player). Newly arrived, a young *sārangī* student from Poland was also present with her husband, who played the tabla.

The formal ritual of *shāgirdī* is embedded in musical conversation, both technical and social. Technically, an important part is for students to perform something to show their progress and the teacher's accomplishment. Socially, the central ritual is the ceremony of binding the thread, symbol of the new disciple's permanent tie to the master. After reciting a special prayer requesting God's blessing for this lifelong relationship, the master also feeds the disciple a sweet (*laḍḍu*), symbolic of the nurturing paternal role he is assuming. The senior musicians are there to witness the ritual and ensure appropriate continuity of the *birādarī*'s musical heritage and competence. Noteworthy are the offerings made to seniors, as well as to brother disciples, to obtain their blessings.

THE PROCEEDINGS First the new shāgird was told to play something; he stood up and requested "permission" (*ijāzat*) to play from all senior musicians by putting his raised palms together in the standard Indian gesture of offering respect (*namaskār*). Being a beginner, he started by playing what I had already heard him practicing every day: the scales of evening raga *yaman* and morning raga *bhairav*. Then his father entered the room. Ustad Sabri Khan stopped the playing to tell a story about a time when someone else's student, who had difficulty positioning his left hand on his instrument, came to ask Sabri Khan for advice. Sabri Khan's answer was, "Ask your own ustād whom you have chosen. I cannot help you."

Teaching points: Juniors play, elders permitting. Discipleship is the only access to the teaching of a master. Choosing the right ustād is of crucial importance.

THE CEREMONY Now the ustād began the ceremony by covering his head and silently reciting verses from the Koran as well as a special prayer (*du'a*) for the occasion; then he asked God for blessings (with the standard gesture of upturned palms). The student also covered his head, as did the other men.

Sabri Khan now prepared a special red and yellow raw thread (*gaṇḍā*), which is used by Hindus to symbolize significant spiritual ties. He asked the *shāgird*'s father and the senior musicians touch the thread. Then he tied the thread around Nasir's right wrist and fed him, by hand, a piece of sweet (*laḍḍu*). At my own *shāgirdī,* he had told me: "Now, from this day on, the student stands in the same relationship to me as my offspring (*aulād*). It is the duty of the master to teach the disciple the way one teaches one's child. And likewise, it is the duty of the disciple to learn." Sabri Khan also pointed to the uniqueness of this ceremony: "We have a special *shāgirdī* for the *sārangī*. Singers have a different one. Tabla players have one that is yet different."

Teaching points: Begin everything in the name of God (the student's day starts with a devotional song—in both Hindu and Muslim families). Show respect to God by covering your head.

The raw thread ties the *shāgird* to the ustād forever. The ustād feeds the *shāgird* like his child. He is now is obligated to teach, and the *shāgird* to learn.

OFFERINGS TO USTĀD, MUSICIANS, BROTHER DISCIPLES Nasir now stood up and made a money offering (*nazrāna*) to his ustād, bowing before him, and then to senior musicians, as guided by Sabri Khan's teenage son Jamal. Then Nasir's older brother made an offering to Ustad Sabri Khan in the same way. Nasir also offered money to all senior students, including me. I asked Ustad Sabri Khan why I, a beginning student, should get an offering, and the ustād's brother explained that I am Nasir's (older) sister now, and therefore I also have a right to receive an offering. In turn, it is appropriate for me, he said, to make an offering to my ustād at this time. I rose to do so, bowing down to place the money before Sabri Khan. Sabri Khan then asked me to tell the Polish student about making an offering too, and I explained to the student in English what kind of offering to give.

Teaching points: Offerings are tokens of the giver's respect and submission in return for the ustād's benefaction, and of respect for senior disciples. Every offering reminds the student never to forget the authority of their teachers and all senior artists. Offerings also reinforce sibling bonds between disciples.

FEEDING ALL DISCIPLES Now Sabri Khan asked Nasir to take the tray of sweet *laḍḍus* and distribute them to all members of the musical family, immediate and extended. "This is another customary practice (*dastūr*): to feed all the other students who are present as well" said the ustād.

Teaching points: In giving sweets to all his disciples, the ustād affirms his nurturing role. Sharing *laḍḍus* is also sharing the blessing of the occasion (obligatory feeding and eating of *laḍḍus* is a standard practice at weddings and other auspicious events).

DISCIPLES PERFORM Ustad Sabri Khan now called to me to play for the guest musicians who hadn't heard me yet; he asked the Polish student's husband to play tabla with me. Meanwhile, the ustād and senior guests started smoking cigarettes and talking (juniors maintain respect by not smoking before seniors). I requested permission from everyone and played raga *mārubihāg,* which I had been learning. While I was playing, Sabri Khan told his guests about the success of more senior Western students, like Nicholas (Magriel) or Daniel (Neuman). Next came Ustad Sabri Khan's young son Kamal's turn to play. He too stood up and asked permission from all. He played a scale in raga *yaman,* followed by *palṭe* (sequential patterns) until he got a signal from Sabri Khan to stop. Now it was the turn of Kamal's younger brother Gulfam, who was learning voice and harmonium. Gulfam had to be exhorted to ask permission, then he intoned the early morning raga *bhairav,* but was corrected by his father and moved to raga *yaman* like his brother, singing and playing a famous composition. Asked to go faster, he did so successfully and was praised by all.

Teaching points: Eliciting a hearing from the students is to gain evidence of the master's work and that of his students. Students, even children, do their performing naturally as requested and enjoy the praise, while getting trained to perform for formal audiences.

QUALITY CONTROL Now the newly arrived young brother of a *shāgird* was asked to perform; he sang, choosing a composition in raga *multānī* (an afternoon raga), but his first improvisation caused consternation and criticism because he used a tonal sequence that is unacceptable in *multānī.* Shocked at this breach, the senior musicians deliberated and questioned the boy, then concluded that the mistake came from the boy's teacher in the far-off town where they had resided. Either he had misled the boy, or he did not know the raga correctly himself. Either way, he was to blame, not the student. "Never in life can raga *multānī* have this tonal sequence" said Ustad Sabri Khan. "Did you understand?" he said to me.

Teaching points: In the hands of *birādarī* elders, quality control of teaching is crucial and ongoing. Oral knowledge is controlled and legitimized by oral consensus. The teacher is responsible for the student's progress. Even a mistake will serve as a teaching point.

Ustad Sabri Khan's Teaching Session

The concluding excerpt, of a teaching conversation, is drawn from three sessions in Ustad Sabri Khan's music room; it was chosen to hear the ustād's own words as he directed them to me. The idea is to convey how musical content is transmitted within the oral milieu of *sīna ba sīna,* along with other teaching priorities conveyed by the ustād while also dealing with the derailing questions that only Western students feel entitled to ask. Thematic headings point to the particular content categories discussed. I include a notated music example in raga *mārubihāg* (signature: a raised *ma,* or fourth degree), using Indian *sargam* (as well as number notation for broader access).

In 1984 Ustad Sabri Khan taught me all summer, creating for me an intense and comprehensive learning process. Starting from the competence I had from my earlier study of the *sārangī,* he began by teaching me a raga (*mārubihāg*) and at the same time integrated into this teaching the very basic practice routine that his junior students shared, attending to flaws in my bowing and intonation. At first, Sabri Khan was cautiously assessing my commitment and ability. The teaching sessions excerpted here show in a most remarkable way Sabri Khan's holistic concept of teaching, which addresses a range of *sārangī* players' concerns—from playing the notes in tune to shaping a performance. An essential part of the process is teaching compositions as models of ragas.

The ustād is trying out the *sārangī* he has procured for my use that summer. He uses the occasion to demonstrate what he called, for my benefit, "types" or genres of *sārangī* playing: a *ṭhumrī*, then a *k̲h̲ayāl* in raga *madhuvanti*. Then he plays a pattern of raga *mārubihāg*.

BAṚHĀT ("COMPOSING," LIT., "EXPANSION")

SABRI KHAN It is amazing how a person can shape one thing in so many different ways, not just one. [*He demonstrates ma ga re sa (4 - 3 - 2 - 1) in many ways: ma sa ma ga re sa (4 - 1 - 4 - 3 - 2 - 1), sa ga ga ma ga re sa (1 - 3 - 3 - 4 - 3 - 2 - 1), sa sa ga ga ma ga ga ma ga re (1 - 1 - 3 - 3 - 4 - 3 - 3 - 4 - 3 - 2), and more.*]

You should get at least fifty ideas from this, that will be worth something! But you know, this is very difficult work. I have done "research," I have immersed myself, immersed, meaning that I lost myself in it: What more is there in the music? What more can be drawn from it? I have practiced a great deal. Eventually I became so "expert" that I could handle everything.

Now listen to one "idea," out of it come fifty more ideas. [*He shows me how to create numerous transformations of a typical* mārubihāg *phrase: ni sa dha—ma pa sa (7 - 8 - 6, 4 - 5 - 8), singing the syllables to make the notes clear to me.*]

So what I want to convey to you is that music is an ocean. An ocean. When you are in the middle of it, then you realize that this really is a very huge thing. But this huge ocean can fit into a drinking cup; it can fit into this glass! The entire ocean will fit into this cup of yours here. I mean the little cup that is in your brain. No need to put it in writing. It can all fit in here, in the mind. Our music is not "written" at all. I have stored it all right here in my brain, and that's where it comes from when we play. You ask me to perform and I'll play for three hours, or ten hours, or the whole night.

GAZ GAṬṬHĀ (BOW AND [LEFT] HAND)

SABRI KHAN The way you bow gives jolts or jerks. I can't ever play like that. This is not the way the *sārangī* is played, it never will be; it's completely wrong. [*He demonstrates.*] Here is *sārangī* bowing: You just have to control the bow nothing else! Many musicians used to say: he still hasn't learned how to hold the bow (*gaz pakaṛnā*), and he doesn't know how to DRAW (*calānā*) the bow either! They say this when someone isn't competent.

These things are a difficult challenge: How to hold the bow and how to place the hand. That's the first thing to learn. If the hand is right, then your playing will come out right too. Use the first finger. That's not a small point; it is a very big point. It won't solve itself. If you use a wrong fingering then your *tān* will not come together.

RIYĀẒ ("PRACTICE," LIT., "EXERTION")

SABRI KHAN You should play each *tān* a hundred, or two hundred times, at the very least. Then what will happen? It will turn into "GOLD"! This is the way to practice, according to Mamman Khan Sahib and other great masters of the past.

REGULA That's what they said?

SABRI KHAN Not what they said, what they DID. And I have seen their offspring, they too are dead now. I saw his son, Mammu Khan Sahib, he just kept working away.... All right, you've spent an hour practicing the same *tān* (passage) over and over, for at least one hour. No other *tān!* Once you have practiced the same *tān* in this way for a whole week, what's the result? The *tān* will flow like WATER, it will become liquid. You will be able to toss it in at any point in your performance, and play it as brilliantly as can be.

That's the method. But the task is difficult. Why? Because you feel restless for a "change," any change! To kill your desire is very difficult. Now just repeat your *tān*. THAT's the way!

[*Regula plays the tān over and over, now joined by both fellow students in the house, Sabri Khan's nephew Nasir Khan and his young son Kamal Sarvar. The music room resonates with the bright sound of three sārangīs, when a guest arrives....*

Regula starts playing ālāp in mārubihāg, while Sabri Khan and his visitor discuss something.]

NAQL (METHOD OF LEARNING, LIT., "IMITATION, COPY")

SABRI KHAN [*Suddenly turns to Regula*] Listen, did you memorize this from the tape of my performance that I gave you?

REGULA I did.

SABRI KHAN Very good. Your playing is absolutely right. Now I will put it in a sequence: first you play *ālāp* the way you just started now. YES! Play it JUST this way! It will sound far and wide as if Sabri Khan is playing. Absolutely!

REGULA I have copied you. As the Sufis say: imitation leads to the real thing (*naql se aṣl paidā hotā hai*).

SABRI KHAN That is absolutely correct. I mean, just seeing a Sufi always reciting Allah, Allah, Allah, will turn a person into a Sufi himself. Imitation leads to the real thing, that's a correct saying. Just play the way you were playing. I liked it.

* * *

Strikingly few specifics of musical and technical content are verbalized—teaching is accomplished through the student's imitation, not the teacher's explanation. Transmission takes place through the medium of music itself, as I have tried to convey with notation. Theory in the Western sense of systematic abstraction and elaboration is not extensively verbalized; words are used when musical communication does not succeed, or when it needs to be summarized, as is exemplified by the ocean-in-a-cup metaphor—also of Sufi provenance.[6] Where theory operates more vigorously is in the project of securing the discipular relationship from which musical knowledge flows. *Sīna ba sīna* itself is a theoretical model that is shared by all the hereditary musicians I have known, though today some only talk about it, while having adapted their practice to harmonize with modern bourgeois teaching styles and substance. The theory of imitation, too, is predicated on the discipular relationship, where the disciple copies the master. At the back of *sīna ba sīna* appears to be the experience of learning by growing up in a family of musicians. From the very beginning of a child's life, music is taught and learned at many levels at once, much like a language. Before and while basic units are practiced, named, and reproduced by repeated playing and singing, constant auditory exposure to the family's parental experts gradually imparts larger musical units to the memory of the student. When nonhereditary disciples are inducted into their master's musical family, they acquire the opportunity to enter in this immersion environment, traditionally by living in the master's house and thus being at his musical beck and call to receive training (*ta'līm*), or simply to listen (as well as accompany him on tour and in concerts). This priceless and limitless familial right to partake of the ustād's knowledge is bestowed on the *shāgird* in the *ustādī-shāgirdī* ceremony. The ceremony also binds the disciple to the master, implying filial obligations and devotion. Both are embodied in the *nazrāna,* an offering of money made to the ustād by bowing in a gesture of submission.

Knowing how to be a disciple is therefore a foundational concern for the master, socially as well as musically; hence the prominence given to the act of making material offerings. Teaching discipular devotion addresses the priority of the ustād's survival and the need for his disciples, like his children, to be guided toward sharing the material rewards with their ustād in gratitude for the gift of his knowledge, which has made the *shāgird* what he is. For the disciple, then, lifelong access to the ustād's knowledge means a lifelong obligation to acknowledge its benefice by contributing to the ustād's material well-being, through service and financial gifts. Musically, the foundation is above all receptiveness—keeping one's ear and memory open—and dedicated practice so as to internalize what was heard or taught. Only then will the student be capable of creating his own musical statements. Learning is of course always focused on the music rather than on the instrument per se. A lot of instrumental teaching is done vocally, and corrections are made to the student's playing technique as needed. Instrumental technique is learned, or, rather, absorbed largely by observation and imitation, once the basic hand position and movements have been "set" (*hāth rakhnā*) by the teacher.

All this is the beginning of discipleship. Sabri Khan's later teaching is focused on performance and includes getting launched in the playing field as well as gaining patronage or employment. This also means carrying the name and musical identity of the teacher and his family forward. Even today, in teaching his son Kamal and now his grandson Sarvar, Sabri Khan's method is entirely oral, and so is the knowledge they gain from his teaching. Now Kamal Sabri is prepared not only for India but for the world, and ready for change as well as for transformation of that knowledge.

Twenty-three years after the *shāgirdī* and the teaching sessions presented here, Sabri Khan's family room in Old Delhi is no more. In the family's new Asiad Village home, music is made in a designated furnitureless part of a modern, open-floored house flanked by well-furnished living and dining areas. Birādarī members rarely travel the long bus ride from the Old City, but other privileged musicians and artists visit from surrounding houses in their New Delhi housing complex. The ustād's two youngest boys have become professional musicians, and he now teaches his first grandson *sārangī*. Nasir, whose *shāgirdī* I recorded, is employed as a *sārangī* player at the national dance academy (Kathak Kendra) and married to our ustād's daughter. Ghulam Sabir is now the most senior brother disciple, training his own son on the *sārangī*.

There are antecedents for the family's move: Sabri Kahan himself grew up in Muradabad, a small town northeast of Delhi, where his family was part of a large community of musicians. Today they have generally moved to larger cities, although their playing style or *gharāna* is still identified by this town of origin, or rather, the community that was settled there. Sabri Khan's grandfather told him that the family came originally from Panjab and settled in Muradabad. Later Sabri Khan himself moved to Old Delhi for employment and engagements, especially at All India Radio, and more recently top artists were offered government-sponsored housing in New Delhi, but only for the period of their own life, so that further moves can be anticipated for the family.

Today such moves are extending beyond India, as musicians are attracted by global touring and teaching opportunities that lead to long-term or even permanent settlement abroad. Sabri Khan's eldest son, a fine tabla player, is long settled in England. Young Kamal is touring Europe, and recently Sabri Khan toured with son and grandson as a triple *sārangī* embodiment of *sīna ba sīna*. A new interest in the mystery of hereditary musicians worldwide has generated a number of lineage concert teams, including the world-famous tabla masters Ustad Allah Rakha and his son Zakir Husain along with his brothers, and now Pandit Ram Narayan with daughter Aruna and a grandson, preceded, much earlier, by Nikhil Ghosh with sons Dhruba and Nayan (Qureshi 2007). Interestingly, all four families have children living in the West. From this geographic overlay, musicians' local identities get further blurred, so that a town of origin, long left behind, now serves the need of identification attesting to a recognizable musical past.

Family coherence, on the other side, has become a renewed asset and an identifier with universal resonance. Against this context, *sīna ba sīna* will require new ways of thriving within the family, through translocal adaptations, and possibly even recreations of the local family universe of *sīna ba sīna*. One such adaptation is for transnational disciples to find ways of living and learning in the same musical environment with their teacher. Living with the ustād has already found a new form in the diaspora, where émigré disciples invite their ustād to live with them for a period of time, emulating the same twenty-four-hour immersion environment as the music room of Sabri Khan.

Inside India, too, lineage and family are finding new appreciation in the face of accelerated modernization and participation in globalization. Ustad Sabri Khan only recently performed a three-generation concert for the president of India!

Locating Oral Transmission

Where does all this leave the discourse of the local? Today, the "local" is once again a priority in scholarship focused on India as well as elsewhere, in response to the increasing impact of globalization, and in the face of local change. Now that Indian music has "gone global," its local roots become a matter of renewed interest; the discourse is becoming focused on continuity and preservation, about how this music continues to be learned and lived. Another focus is the quest to gain not only access but recognition for noncanonical or otherwise marginalized cultural practices, so as to open up and teach Westerners new ways of hearing, seeing, and thinking. *Sīna ba sīna* certainly qualifies on all these counts. In the process, however, the culture of discipleship puts into question the very notion of the local, especially in relation to the traditional concept as it has been used in Indian ethnography.

Local studies have been the special purview of anthropologists in India, epitomized by the village studies initiated as early as the 1930s and rooted in a nineteenth-century concept of static, unchanging rural communities. Varying in thematic focus, village anthropology developed a fine-grained, holistic, and interactive model for the study of self-contained social, kin, and occupational groups sharing the bounded terrain of a village. What the studies have in common is an ethnographic approach to social and cultural environments that are orally based, marked by oral knowledge and communication, hence confined to the locality of the village (Eglar 1960; Wadley 1994; Wiser 1963). Robert Redfield's village studies (1955) and Clifford Geertz's concept of local knowledge (1983) reference oral knowledge embedded within local confines or "micro-environments," most famously taking the form of "common sense" or practice theory as observed by Bourdieu in Algerian villages and imported into the literature of high theory (Bourdieu 1977). An important theoretical counterpoint comes from the Subaltern Studies initiative that pioneered a locally centered historiography based on written sources by and about subaltern communities of nonelite groups, mostly in urban environments (Guha 1982–89).

In their scheme to theorize the relationship of local cultures to the urban, cosmopolitan religious and cultural superstructure of scripture-based "Indian civilization," Milton Singer and Robert Redfield further characterized the local and oral as the "Little" Tradition, which they contrasted with the "Great" Tradition of Indian civilization and high culture, built on and disseminated through written texts; they called for an anthropology that would embrace and complement both (Singer 1972, and see Wolf's Introduction to this volume). While the scheme is problematic in its categorical subordination of the local, it represents a landmark in Indian anthropology, a field that traditionally "studied down," leaving the study of high culture or civilization to the humanities. Remarkably, Singer first proposed the inclusion of "civilization" on the basis of his observation of oral practices even in the textualized culture of Hinduism (Singer 1958).

Professional practitioners of the Great Tradition of music—as of other arts—have long shared an exclusively oral culture of knowledge and transmission that has been locally cultivated within their hereditary communities. Yet the art they produce is supralocal and an integral part of Indian high culture as patronized by feudal courts across all of northern India. Now state institutions patronize art music as an icon of national culture. Clearly, these hereditary cultural specialists bridge and thereby invalidate the Great-Little dichotomy. Still, the oral confines of their theory and practice can usefully be situated within the concept of the local, if only to problematize its traditionally geographic basis. These local musical communities have long been nurturing their individual mobility as a means for gaining widely dispersed princely and elite patronage within India.

In the field of Indian music studies, the high-low divide has generally persisted. It has been reinforced by an institutional as well as conceptual separation between art and folk music (Babiracki 1991b), and by the legacy of the early-twentieth-century reform movement to codify (in writing) Hindustani music. The reformers emphasized the structural dimensions of Hindustani music as a normative system transcending local variation, and thereby deemphasized what was transmitted (orally) by hereditary musicians (Misra 1985; Nayar 1989; Qureshi 1991). An important concomitant of this legacy has been the systematic abstraction of the music from its oral source, the hereditary musician, who is perforce locally situated in a familial milieu of practice and transmission that negates any separation between the musician and his orally transmitted music, both in the form of sound and verbal discourse. Including musicians in the scholarly focus on music calls for a scholarship that is socially as well as musically oriented, and that recognizes that musicians are situated as well as mobile, while their music is not reified but in process and variable.

What is situated, and in that sense "local," about the making of this music is its milieu: its relations of production and reproduction, and its musicians, masters, disciples, patrons, listeners, and other musical consumers. All are human agents who can and do historically move beyond the geographic confines of the local, because producers of music, unlike those of silk cloth or art objects, are required to be present in the elite milieus wherever their art is consumed. The history of this translocality is clearly connected with shifting patronage, from local landlord to princely states, to urban bourgeoisie, to global "public culture" and "world music" scenes, including an increasing emphasis on recordings and their ever wider distribution.

Yet to be explored is the effect of these shifts on the discipular core of transmitting the music and reproducing the musician. Historically, communities of musicians were settled in areas adjacent to feudal centers of patronage for immediate access, as can still be seen in the designated quarters near the courts of Lahore, Delhi, Banda, and others. When more distant patronage was enabled by railway travel, musician families and their elders also lived in small towns where discipular training took place. Post-feudal radio, concert, and teaching patronage had musicians, as family units, move to urban centers, from where they could also access international patronage. Teaching continues within the family, as before, and in the major cities (Delhi, Bombay, Calcutta), is easily extended to an increasing number of foreign students like myself.

What then is "the local" here, if not the intimacy of the family and of *sīna ba sīna* within the four walls of the music room, with its continuity of transmission, wherever it may take place? At the same time, supralocal musical trends are bound to be introduced and absorbed, brought home by the practicing and traveling professionals of the family. Ustad Sabri Khan significantly refers to his own quest and learning of new repertoire and methods of improvising. Does this undermine the discipular process, which is firmly rooted in discipular commitment? The community beyond the immediate family, perforce, becomes more remote for families that moved away from their *mohalla*s, the defined neighborhoods that had been assigned to musicians by princes and later also by the British. I saw the effect of such a move happen to my ustād, since he has been living in New Delhi's Asiad Village, an hour's travel from his earlier home in a traditional musicians' *mohalla* in Old Delhi. The musical impact of this move is yet to be assessed, but the musicians themselves are embracing change with the certainty that filling the ocean in their cup through imitation and repetition will equip their children with the competence and flexibility to excel in the new environments in which they find themselves. This is also what I learned from my first teacher Mirza Maqsud Ali in Lucknow, when he quoted the famous musicians' saying that sums up the entire teaching process: *dikhiyā* (apprehend, imbibe), *sikhiyā* (learn, memorize), *parikhiyā* (assess, discern), meaning: first you apprehend (hear the music), then you learn (memorize it), and only then can you assess it (have the discernment to create it yourself).

Representation

Straightforward textualizing of *sīna ba sīna* (as in this chapter) is a start, simply to enable its value to be recognized and thereby to acknowledge its agents not only as musical practitioners in need of higher-status authors of theory, but also, *pace* Bourdieu, as theorists of their own practice. However, textualizing also, malgré soi, amounts to a gesture of converting the oral and particular (read: "Little") into the literate and universal (read: "Great"), thereby reinforcing the "littleness," (read: limited significance) of the *sīna ba sīna* practice. I believe that self-representation can ultimately be the only right answer to this conundrum: Musicians themselves need to tell us about their milieu and about discipleship within it. As scholar-disciples we need to find respectful, collaborative ways to capture and represent this musical milieu to those outside of it, ideally through the actual interactive teaching and conversations of hereditary masters. Their words can contribute to the broader discourse on musical transmission and creativity as the primary source material of their oral milieu. I have been working on this challenge of representation, focusing on appropriate linguistic and cultural translation, as well as on mediation, to render the oral milieu comprehensible to those outside of it (Qureshi 2007). Such a translation is inevitably a written text as well. The next step should be to hear these masters themselves join the Western-dominated conversation on discipleship in their oral world of music, by bringing their mastery to the home ground of their

Western disciples. Thanks to the Western discipular tradition in university music programs, this has been happening already. My ustād, Sabri Khan, was visiting professor at the University of Washington in the early 1980s, while Shujaat Khan has an ongoing teaching appointment at UCLA; both appointments were facilitated by Daniel Neuman, chief Western disciple of Sabri Khan.

Such initiatives will also, in time, address the major postcolonial goal Dipesh Chakrabarty calls "provincializing Europe" (2000). This would potentially reduce a Western intellectual/artistic concept for teaching and learning music (here: discipleship) from what is considered a universally valid tool to a Euro-American particularity. More important, it would acknowledge the presence, in India and elsewhere, of different discipleship concepts that have equal centrality and theoretical power. To start with, Indian discipleship could equally well become a productive ethnographic tool to examine performance training for art music in the West.

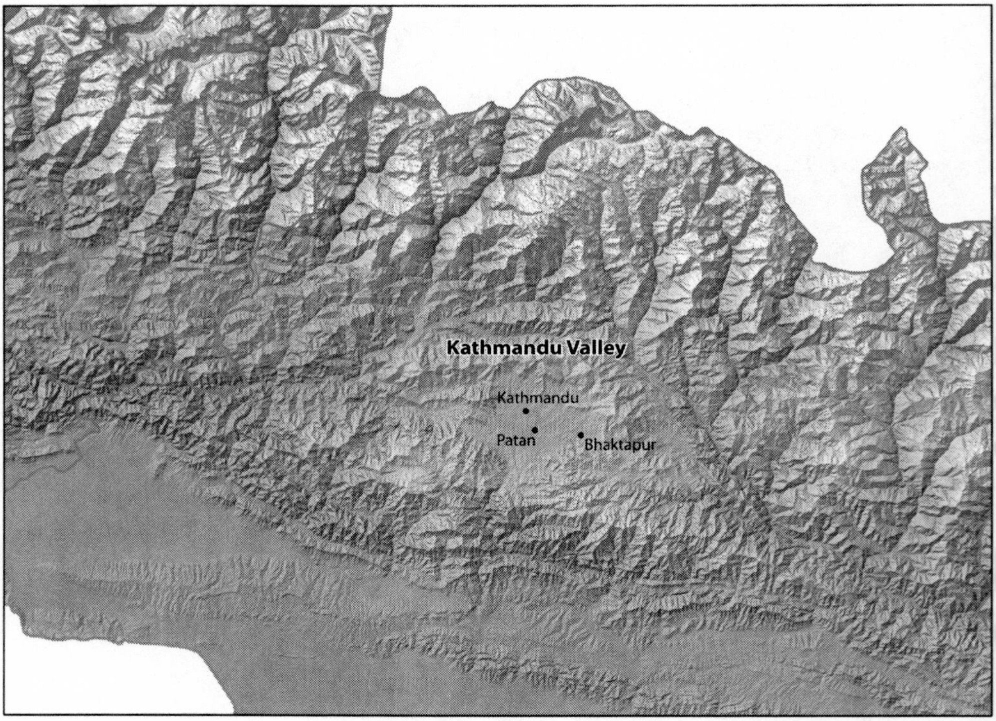

Kathmandu Valley
Kathmandu
Patan
Bhaktapur

CHAPTER 10
Handmade in Nepal

DAVID HENDERSON

Most of what I know about drumming I learned from two remarkable men in 1995. Pandit Shambu Prasad Mishra, then seventy-seven years old and living in a boxy concrete house in a quiet suburb of Kathmandu, taught me tabla.[1] Hari Govinda Ranjitkar, then sixty and living in a narrow old brick home in Bhaktapur, taught me the three barrel drums, *dhā̃, dhimay,* and *pachimā.*[2] Reflecting later on my studies with them, I puzzled over the fact that I could not remember not knowing how to play these drums. I could remember a time when I did not know how to play. I could also remember my feelings of clumsiness in lessons, my impatience with my stupid hands when practicing, my frustrations at not being able to shake free from seemingly ingrained and persistent ineptitudes. But I could not make my body feel as if it did not know how to play. I could sit down at any of these drums and tell my hands to pretend they did not know anything, and make them behave as if they didn't, but this was only a feigned absence of knowledge.

In this chapter, I focus on the acquisition of bodily knowledge, or what is sometimes called procedural knowledge as opposed to declarative knowledge: knowing how to do something rather than knowing something.[3] How did the knowledge of how to drum get into my hands? Where else was that knowledge lodged? The difficulty is in trying to think about how it is that we can think unthinkingly. My hands became more and more able to produce sounds seemingly on their own, without my having to pay attention to what they were doing. But clearly I must have been thinking about them in some way, and this chapter is in part an exploration of what my teachers did to inculcate in me this capacity for thoughtless thought. At the end of this chapter, I also consider how the development and maintenance of bodily knowledge leads toward a particular way of being in the world, a way of being that may be interpreted as well as a critique of other ways of being in the world.[4] In short, what did my teachers do to urge my hands into particular shapes and patterns, and why did they agree to undertake this work?[5]

I consider here two excerpts from my lessons with Shambu Prasad Mishra and Hari Govinda Ranjitkar, episodes that are representative of the larger texture of my studies. In describing these episodes, I emphasize how what seemed like rote repetition was really a complex maze of interactions between my teachers and me, and how language was critical for what we were doing. "Knowing bodies beget other knowing bodies" (Groesbeck, this volume), yet the peculiar osmosis of learning to drum in Nepal is not simply a matter of gradually absorbing knowledge through dedicated observation and practice. A knowing body—and one in the process of becoming a knowing body—sits at the center of a "network of overlapping representations" (Henderson 1997, 82). That is, the knowledge of drumming is inscribed in multiple forms in and beyond the body: in the feel of drumming, in the sound of drumming, in the sound of one's teacher drumming, in the sight of one's teacher drumming, in the memory of all these things, in the collaboration of all these things. And woven through my lessons was language—Nepali phrases, occasional English interjections, more indefinite exclamations, and the words of the drums themselves. All this talk anchored my body as it struggled to repeat, to imitate, to learn, to know.

Alternating with excerpts from my lessons are discussions of three different studies of bodily knowledge: first, Antonio Damasio's neurological work (1994) opens up one way of thinking about how knowledge gets encrypted in the body and the brain; second, David Sudnow's work (1978) is a phenomenological study of the feeling of learning how to play a particular instrument in a particular way; and third, Michael Herzfeld's recent writing on apprenticeship (2004) locates bodily knowledge within larger spheres of knowing and doing. The theoretical direction of this chapter, then, moves from inside to outside, proceeding from a consideration of bodily knowledge from a perspective within the body, biologically speaking, to a consideration of bodily knowledge from a perspective on the body, culturally speaking.[6]

* * *

Antonio Damasio's neurological work on how reason, emotion, and sensation are bound together is useful for thinking about how different ways of representing and learning the knowledge of drumming overlap. *Descartes' Error* (1994) begins with the tale of Phineas Gage, a nineteenth-century railroad worker who was packing down blasting powder with an iron rod when the powder exploded, shooting the rod through portions of both frontal lobes of his brain and out the top of his skull. Gage survived, remaining conscious and seemingly rational even as a doctor in a nearby town examined him and dressed his wounds. Within two months, he appeared to have recovered completely. Yet while both his reasoning and his emotions seemed unimpaired, it became clear over the next few years that there was a severe disruption of the collaboration between reason and emotion. Gage was no longer capable of making sound decisions about his own life, and the remaining thirteen years of his life were wrecked by his own incapacity for living.

In this prelude to his work, Damasio foreshadows the conclusion he draws from his research with brain-damaged patients: emotion and reason are elaborated in neural circuitry that connects the brain with the senses; emotion has its roots in sensation; and reason does not normally operate in the closed theater of our minds but in conjunction with sensate experience. Damasio argues that the body represents the sensate and emotional components of memories in feedback loops that make us feel our memories, or the physical traces of how something felt, rather than just recall content. His "somatic-marker hypothesis" suggests how reasoning must be wrapped up in the fleeting memories of affect that move through the body's neural circuitry (Damasio 1994, 165–201). When experiences are stored in memory, they are marked with basic "dispositional representations" (1994, 94): memory preserves not only what happened, but also the basic neural and chemical effects of what happened—that is, how one felt about what happened. Then, when we recall experiences, these markers are triggered as well. Making decisions typically involves recalling previous decisions and what happened in the wake of them; when we mull over the possibilities, we are weighing our past decision-making experiences at the same time that their emotional heft is weighing on us. Dispositional representations make us cognizant of the possible outcomes of a decision, giving us basic sensate reasons for doing what we choose to do; we know something makes "sense" in part because of how it feels.

While learning appropriate decision making is an important part of learning to drum in Nepal, I want to extend the implications of Damasio's work for the study of musical performance a step further. In discussing how sensation, emotion, and reason are intertwined, Damasio notes that we typically think of perception and action as moving in opposite directions: through perception, things from the outside get in, and through action, things from the inside get out. Yet these are often simultaneous activities. "Perceiving is as much about acting on the environment as it is about receiving signals from it" (1994, 225), and we might conceive of the process of learning to perform as a kind of heightened perception, action and reception bundled together at one's fingertips and linked to one's eyes and ears. In learning where to go in a particular musical style—that is, in learning how to make musically sound decisions—one draws simultaneously on sensation, emotion, and reason, actively perceiving and perceptively acting.

Turning this point another few degrees, the feeling of sound is inseparable from the representation or production of sound. "Contrary to traditional scientific opinion, feelings are just as cognitive as other percepts. They are the result of a most curious physiological arrangement that has turned the brain into the body's captive audience" (1994, xv). In learning to perform, one strives toward a feeling that feels right. The sense of correct or effective performance is a sense that registers at multiple levels—in a muscular sensation, in a feeling of achievement, in the recognition that one has done something right. When something feels right, it feels like the sound one has just made has fallen into place, dropped into alignment with a host of previous sounds made (by oneself, by one's teacher, by one's fellow students) and an array of previous representations (the assorted explanations one has received or concocted for how a sound should sound). It feels good because it fits.

If my use of the word "feel" here seems ambiguous, it is because Damasio as well writes about "feeling" in the dual sense of emotion and sensation, in part to erase the line between them. I have already mentioned particular feelings I experienced in learning how to drum: clumsiness, frustration, ineptitude. These are, quite clearly, feelings in a dual sense, emotions instigated and provoked by sensations of imperfectly rendered drumming strokes and sequences. On the other side of the mistake-riddled process of learning to drum are its often unstated goals: dexterity, satisfaction, competence. These are, too, feelings in this dual sense, emotions inseparable from sensation. I was working toward being a proficient drummer, yes, but I was also striving after this composite feeling of accomplishment.

It was the efforts of my teachers, of course, that got me there: they were the ones who made me recognize, imitate, and elaborate upon their performative habits. Both Shambu Prasad Mishra and Hari Govinda Ranjitkar built models of effective performance for me through their own bodily practice; they also, in the course of drumming, provided verbal instructions for shaping my hands around the strokes and patterns I was working to replicate. Their verbal instructions were of two sorts: they provided directions on how to reproduce their own body movements, and they trained me in the arts of expectation, in knowing where to go next within the course of a performance. My learning was primarily grounded in understanding these two kinds of motion, in the body and in the musical form. Sometimes these were discrete instructions within a lesson, but often language and movement together comprised an elaborate polyphony that drew upon a longer history of learning.

* * *

Twice a week, I went to Shambu Prasad Mishra's house in New Baneshwar for tabla lessons. Early in the morning, I walked up to one of the main intersections of Sanepa, the neighborhood in the city of Patan where I lived, to find a tempo for hire. As I slid onto the back seat, the driver cranked the engine, slicing through the quiet fog. The three-wheeler skittered along the pockmarked streets, and I held on tight, trying at the same time to keep my arms and hands relaxed in anticipation of the work to follow.

When I arrived for my lesson, Shambu's wife usually brought us each a cup of tea. And then, without comment or explanation, Shambu would often begin playing something. One morning, he started playing a kind of short composition called a *bā̃ṭ* (a genre common in the Banaras tabla tradition), set in the sixteen-beat rhythmic cycle, *tīn* tala.[7]

Shambu almost immediately began transforming this initial pattern through a sequence of variations, called *palṭās* (lit., "turns" or "transformations"). Rather

FIGURE 10.1. Shambu Prasad Mishra outside his home in Kathmandu. Photograph by Susan Grant.

quickly, he brought this exposition and development to its expected close with a threefold cadential pattern called a *tihā'ī*.[8] He then began to speak.

Shambu always taught me in Nepali, but his speech was peppered with English words. In the following excerpt, italics indicate that the original language was Nepali; words spoken in English are not italicized.

SPM *Now you should set up a* line. *First what do you play? After that, the* second time *what do you play, the* third time *what do you play, the* fourth time *what do you play, the* fifth time *what do you play? Doing this, you should build a* line. *And in order to speak you should do it* by heart. *If after this you play this, then you should make the words* come out. *Don't you understand?*[9]

DH *I understood.*

SPM *Since you understood, then what do you play first?*

DH *First? What's your meaning?*

SPM *First you start with, begin with the uṭhān [lit., "lifting up," the rhythmic gesture that begins a performance].*

DH *Eh, you should play the uṭhān, hai?*

SPM *Doing the* beginning. *Now in that, the laharā sounds.* Sixteen-beat. [The *laharā* is a simple melodic pattern that serves as a timekeeper for classical tabla or dance performances.]

It was becoming clear that Shambu's initial demonstration was meant to frame the work that followed, providing a performative model of what he wanted to work on that day. He did this often enough. But he never drew my attention to it. It was my

1	2	3	4	5	6	7	8
dhā ge	terekiṭa	dhī	nā	nā	tī	tī	nā
X				2			
9	10	11	12	13	14	15	16
tā ke	terekiṭa	dhī	nā	nā	dhī	dhī	nā
O				3			

FIGURE 10.2. *Bā̃ṭ* played by Shambu Prasad Mishra at the start of lesson on September 18, 1995. The syllables transcribed here represent different drum strokes, or *bols*. This *bā̃ṭ* uses the metric cycle known as *tīn tāl (tala)*, a cycle of sixteen beats (indicated above the *bols*) divided evenly into four sets of four beats (indicated below the *bols*); the vertical lines show the divisions of the cycle. Several *bols* in the space of one beat are articulated evenly: thus, *dhā ge* is two strokes in one beat and *terekiṭa* is four strokes in one beat, with the rest of the first line of the piece matching a single stroke to each beat. The second line of the piece repeats this pattern using slightly different drum strokes. *Tīn tāl* begins on the beat called *sam*, conventionally indicated with an X; it is the strongest beat of the cycle. The weakest beat, called *k̲h̲ālī*, appears at the midpoint of the cycle; it is indicated by an O. The beginning beats of the other two four-beat sections, or *tālī*, are given some emphasis, but not as much as *sam*; they are indicated by the numerals 2 and 3. The two halves of this *bā̃ṭ*, as in many pieces, are rhythmically identical; the difference is in terms of emphasis. The first half begins with primarily strong articulations, followed by weaker strokes. The second half of the piece is the opposite, moving from weak to strong.

duty to become clever enough to grasp the intent of his initial, seemingly offhand, forays into performance.

Shambu, in this lesson, said very little about what precisely I was going to play, but instead described how I should think about what I was going to play. With nothing in front of me but a pair of tabla, it was now my obligation to create a path from one point in time to another. Using the English word, "line," Shambu suggested a direct route—a potential way through a chosen piece, a line known so thoroughly that one can draw it again and again, without stopping, deviating, or backtracking. Although a good tabla player is likely to interrupt a line on occasion, toying with listeners' expectations and taking unexpected paths, this is not something Shambu ever taught me, for I would only be able to do this after I had learned how to establish a sense of where a line was going. At this point in my studies, Shambu was encouraging me to take the knowledge I had collected about kinds of pieces and their kinds of variations and turn it into an elaborate compass, a tool to take me from the known into the unknown and back out again. His imagery of a "line" suggested efficiency: a good performance does not dawdle or meander, but continuously moves forward, both creating and fulfilling listeners' expectations.[10]

After this brief demonstration and explanation of what we were going to do, in which Shambu first played and then spoke, the lesson became more a juxtaposition of playing and speaking, an ongoing sequence of coordination interrupted by my occasional lapses into uncoordinated action. Generally, Shambu spoke the *bols*, and I sometimes spoke them as well. Usually we both played the *bols*. Occasionally Shambu noticed a faulty hand of mine and corrected it on the fly, telling me, above the sound of our tablas, to pay closer attention to what my hand was doing. Sometimes Shambu moved ahead into a new *palṭā*, and I either caught on immediately and followed or dropped out to hear the pattern he was playing better. And sometimes he fell back and let me take the lead. Alternately moving forward and dropping back, showing me a possible way of doing something and letting me find my own way, Shambu effortlessly established the ebb and flow of the lesson.

After explaining that the *uṭhān* was the starting point of a longer sequence, Shambu began singing a wordless *laharā*. While doing this, he accompanied his own voice with a standard pattern played at about a quarter of the speed of the *bā̃ṭ* on which he had been improvising. When I could not quite pick out the simple eight-beat pattern, he spoke it, and let me fumble through it until I mastered it.

At least, I thought I had it. Several times I got it mixed up and Shambu scolded me, saying, "*Don't forget it,*" or "*Remember it.*" While I was playing it, he said, "*Look at the* timing," and counted out the beats, or *mātrā*s, for me on his hand. This is a common practice in South Asia: a musician will count time by touching the thumb of his right hand to different points on the fingers of his right hand. The tala, as I noted earlier, is divided into segments: each segment is mapped to one of the four fingers, and each beat within a segment is mapped to a separate finger joint. Counting out the sixteen-beat *tīn* tala, Shambu began by touching his thumb to the fleshy

9	10	11	12	13	14	15	16
tat	tā	—	ke	ke	tat	tā	terekiṭa
O				3			

FIGURE 10.3. Simple *uṭhān* for leading into a tabla solo. The dash in this example indicates a pause: nothing happens on that beat.

part of the hand just below his little finger, and proceeded to mark the three beats following *sam* by moving up through the three joints of his little finger; he moved to his ring finger for the next four beats, to his middle finger for the third set of four beats, and to his index finger for the final four beats of the cycle. Shambu also used another counting scheme familiar among South Asian musicians, thwacking his palm on his knee for *sam,* giving lighter whacks for the *tālī* beats, and hitting the back of his hand on his knee for the *k͟h͟ālī* beat. Sometimes he combined the two systems as well, showing me on his fingers and with his knee slaps where I was as I played.

As in other lessons, Shambu let me know when my playing was right by interjecting an assenting "*āh*" amid the spoken *bols*. Sometimes, he contracted this "*āh*" into one of the beats of the pattern—a pattern might start with the *bol,* "*dhā,*" which would combine with "*āh*" to become an emphatically spoken, slightly higher-pitched "*dhāh.*" Shambu rarely played the *uṭhān* he gave me exactly as he spoke it, throwing in a few extra strokes here and there. When I looked puzzled, he recited a few of these for me, as well.

After getting the *uṭhān* into my hands, we moved through the *bā̃ṭ* and into a strand of *palṭās*. The template for creating these variations was relatively familiar to me, and we went through four *palṭās* before having to stop and return to our beginning point. *Palṭās* are typically made by repeating segments of the *bā̃ṭ,* by rearranging portions of it, or by doing both at once. One might start with a simple threefold repetition of a fragment of the pattern, then move on to a more complex variation on that variation. From there, one might push on into an even more complex *palṭā,* or drop back down a notch to a simpler *palṭā* and begin building up an extended set of variations again. It is, of course, crucial to keep the line moving. However, along the line, it is possible to push forward, pull back, or create the illusion of equilibrium. One might move into a *palṭā* with greater rhythmic density, giving a sense of pushing forward, or into a *palṭā* of lesser rhythmic density, giving a sense of pulling back; one can also build a sequence of *palṭās* with similar rhythmic densities, providing a momentary sense of stasis.

Starting from the beginning again, Shambu played the *ṭhekā,* the basic pattern of beats used to articulate the tala—the drum strokes, that is, that characterize the rhythmic cycle itself. As he played the *ṭhekā,* he told me to come in with the *uṭhān* at the appropriate place, then do a *ṭukṛā,* a short "piece" based on the *bā̃ṭ* we had been working on. After playing the *ṭukṛā,* I was to play the *bā̃ṭ* itself—"*usko bā̃ṭ,*" said Shambu—its *bā̃ṭ* (meaning the *bā̃ṭ* from which the *ṭukṛā* had been derived) and its *palṭās.* Done explaining what he wanted me to do, he started singing the *laharā,* the basic melodic pattern underlying everything, and continued playing the *ṭhekā.* Since the *uṭhān* was eight beats long, and I was to start the *ṭukṛā* on *sam,* the first beat of the sixteen-beat rhythmic cycle, I gathered that I would have to start on the ninth beat of the cycle. I found my place to come in, and tried to follow his instructions. Whenever I stumbled, he fit the *bols* I was to play into the *laharā* he was singing, fitting my line into his voice, until I was back on track, following the line that he imagined for me.

If what was remarkable about the beginning of the lesson was how little Shambu said about what I was going to play, what was surprising about what followed was how much he said about what I was playing. But it is a strange way of speaking that is shared between teacher and student, a hodgepodge of drumming syllables, technical terms, interjections, occasional phrases uttered on top of or between drumming sequences. In listening to the recording I made of the lesson, talk is the least prominent sound, but it is perhaps the most crucial. Talk sustains and reinforces movement. Without this verbal scaffolding, the lesson would crumble.

A keyword for me was *bigriyo*—"broken" or "ruined." When I first started taking lessons with Shambu in February, he was appalled at how sloppy my hands were. "*Eh, bābu, tyo garne hudaina,*" he said. "*Hāth bigriyo.*" (Hey, *bābu,* you shouldn't do that. The hands were broken.) Although I had studied tabla some before, my hands did not fit his conception of what tabla-playing hands should look like. Shambu filled my first lessons with corrections in my hand positions; I learned, slowly and tediously, the appropriate shapes for accurate performance. This we accomplished through much demonstration on his part, much imitation on my part, and much discussion together about how my hand should feel. Ultimately, though, it was up to me to go home and laboriously turn the words of those discussions into a memory existing in my hands. And my hands have not forgotten since. But once my hands worked right, I was still liable to break things. I would forget what came next, and break the pattern I was playing. Or I would be playing along just fine, but perhaps not concentrating enough, and the timing *bigriyo.* There is little room for error in thinking through and acting on a *bā̃ṭ.* You have to keep the line going; once you start it, you must complete it. I continued to struggle to merge the paths of the hand with the performative structures Shambu was teaching me, striving to keep my hand, and the line, unbroken.

* * *

David Sudnow, in *Ways of the Hand* (1978), gives a detailed phenomenology of his experience of learning to play jazz piano. He describes how his hands began to take on memories of their own as they found their way across the landscape of the piano keyboard: they began to form "constellations," gradually finding "places to go," and eventually taking "tactilely appreciable paths" (Sudnow 1978, 9, 28, 32). Sudnow explores how expertise got into his hands, how he moved toward a literal grasp of how to play, and in his writing he tries to preserve the feeling of finding his way through his own practical mimesis.[11]

Ways of the Hand is particularly useful for thinking about how to write ethnography and phenomenology simultaneously. How does one convey the bodily knowledge one acquires in doing fieldwork? How does one preserve the pragmatic and accumulative sense of learning how to do something? Granted, Sudnow's work is more phenomenology than ethnography: his focus is on his experience, and his teachers are mostly invisible. But it is suggestive. Part of the difficulty with writing about bodily knowledge is that it seems to be an order of knowledge outside of language, a way of knowing that is at once deeply ingrained and frustratingly elusive. Bodily knowledge seems to be knowledge inculcated so thoroughly as to be impossible to extract in the logic of language. Nonetheless, in a growing segment of anthropological and philosophical literature, the reconsideration of the body as a potent and potential location of culture has helped refine our conceptions of agency. Reason is clearly not the only reason we have for doing things. And Sudnow's work is helpful in thinking about how we write about doing things, or about getting ourselves to the point of being able to do things.

In *Ways of the Hand,* Sudnow conveys the experience of being simultaneously lost and found in the process of tracing alien movements through an unfamiliar landscape. His concern is "description and not explanation, a phenomenologically motivated inquiry into the nature of handwork from the standpoint of the performer" (Sudnow 1978, xiii). From the beginning, he writes as if his hands have become strangers, as if he must reacquaint himself with them; he sits at the piano, watching and listening to them try to reproduce memories of sound and work to build memories of feeling. "From the middle of the piano, the beginner gradually acquires an incorporated sense of places and distances, 'incorporated,' for example, in that finding the named, recognizable, visually grasped place-out-there, through looking's theoretic work, becomes unnecessary, and the body's own appreciative structures serve as a means of finding a place to go" (Sudnow 1978, 12–13). Sudnow seeks traces of memory in the first clunking motion of hands looking for the right notes, and then tries to follow the hands as they develop an inter-subjective engagement with the keyboard. The notes take shape, acting as if they were there all along, and the keyboard becomes "a setting of places, with measurable dimensions. The hand is an 'organ' with measurable dimensions. The knowing relationships obtaining between them, the way the hand finds itself correspondingly configurated to fit dimensions of this keyboard, involves a mobile hand engaged in a course of action" (Sudnow 1978, 58). The hand studies the terrain of the keyboard and maps its dimensions, but never from a steady vantage point: it is always on the move.

Sudnow's attribution of agency to his hands shows his struggle to find a language for describing bodily knowledge in the making. "My hand had absolutely nothing to say in this language," he laments at an early stage; later, becoming more comfortable with the piano, he writes, "My hand had ways with the keyboard." Elsewhere, he even seems to refuse to associate with his hands, omitting the possessive pronoun. "The hand was able to get into a good next arena," he writes, and the photographs of disembodied hands moving around piano keyboards throughout the book further reinforce this quality of manual detachment (Sudnow 1978, 18, 47, 50). Commenting on this sense that the hands, and, by extension, the body, seemed to take over, acting independently of the forced will of the brain, Sudnow remarked of his first public jazz piano performance, "I was on a bucking bronco of my own body's doings" (Sudnow 1978, 30).

Indeed, Sudnow's work is valuable precisely because of his eloquent sense of detachment. He locates knowledge less in the brain than in the hand, which for him becomes an intersection of sensation, emotion, and reason. Albeit a very different work from Damasio's *Descartes' Error,* Sudnow's *Ways of the Hand* points in a similar direction. Absent from his account, though, are his teachers: absent, therefore, is a sense of the complex communication that passes between teacher and student, the interplay of language, gesture, and motion that provides the ground for knowing how to play. I do not mean to point this out as a weakness of Sudnow's work; I mean to suggest that ethnomusicological writing about performance could fruitfully combine elements of ethnography and phenomenology, working to understand performance by considering both bodily knowledge and the inculcation of bodily knowledge. This, of course, is my intent in this chapter.

* * *

In me, Shambu Prasad Mishra had a student who had learned some tabla previously. Although he deemed my initial hand position unacceptable, he found me to be a relatively quick student in other respects, as I already had some understanding of how pieces typically unfolded. But Hari Govinda Ranjitkar had to start from scratch when he began to teach me *dhā̃, dhimay,* and *pachimā.* These seemed alien to me at first, felt strange in my hands; their mnemonic syllables, also called *bols,* didn't make sense to me until I had been at it for quite a few weeks.

Twice a week, late in the afternoon, I rode a packed minibus out to Bhaktapur. Usually I arrived for my lessons shortly after Hari Govinda had returned home from work. We relaxed and talked for a few minutes, then began. He was clearly most comfortable speaking in Newari, but I had only studied that language for a few months, and wasn't at all adept in it, so he taught me in Nepali instead.

In the early stages, Hari Govinda mostly demonstrated strokes and short patterns, making me work hard to imitate his movements; I had to stop him frequently to ask him to recite the *bols* slowly so that I could write them down. I was especially bad at mimicking his movements on the *dhā̃,* the first instrument I studied with him: this was the first instrument I had ever played that required the use of a stick. It seemed easy enough, but it took time for my wrist to learn how to relax and let the stick do

FIGURE 10.4. Hari Govinda Ranjitkar at his house in Bhaktapur, 1995. Photograph by the author.

some of the work for me. Hari Govinda was content to let my wrist learn on its own, but sometimes seemed a little concerned that it was not catching on very quickly.

During one lesson, Hari Govinda mimicked my incorrect playing of the *dra* drum stroke. "*Mildaina,*" he said. It didn't go together, it didn't agree with the *bols* around it. What I observed then was a rendition in which the stick didn't bounce off the head quickly enough, giving a dampened sound rather than a clear ringing stroke. It sounded mushy, not quite matched to the prevailing rhythms. I could hear it, but I couldn't yet feel a proper *dra* in my hand.

A week later, I caught on to how Hari Govinda was playing his *dra.* I had started playing through a piece he had taught me earlier that month, and he interrupted. (Words in brackets in this transcription are implied; material in braces indicates nonverbal action.)

> *Like this, you're* [playing] *a little bit at first:* {Here he plays the piece using a closed, damped stick stroke. Then he pauses, and plays a sloppy *dra.*} *This also happened.* {He shows me again.} *A little bit:* {He plays a slower, cleaner version of what I had been trying to do. After listening some, I jump in, but I'm still not getting it, so he stops and speaks the

> *bols* while playing them.} *ghe dra ghe tā ghe, tā tā....* {I join in and try it.} *Yes. Okay.* {I start playing just *dra,* as it still doesn't sound right to me. Hari Govinda draws my attention to his left hand.} *Here it is also.* {He demonstrates.} *Here it comes.* {He shows me again. I work on this for a minute. *Dra* is played as a fast triplet. Holding the drum stick loosely in his right hand, Hari Govinda first hits the drum sharply, then catches the rebound of the stick in the flesh between his thumb and forefinger and sends it immediately back onto the drum head. He then hits the opposite drum head with the open palm of his left hand. I had heard the last part of the sound before, but had never seen what Hari Govinda was doing. I start trying this out.} *Yes, yes.* {We both play some more.} [If] *it goes* [like that], *it becomes good.*

Hari Govinda's speech during our lessons consisted mostly of reciting the drum strokes as we played them. He reserved his use of language to frame or introduce drumming segments: for example, he would say, "*You should play it like this,*" and launch into a played and spoken rendition of a phrase. During a tea break or while having a smoke, though, he sometimes expounded further. Shortly after my hands at last found their way around *dra,* he elaborated on my progress. A crucial word he uses here is *man,* a word used in other South Asian languages as well; it is associated both with emotion (often linked to the heart in English-language contexts) and with thought and memory (usually located in the mind in English-language contexts). "Heart-mind," then, is my somewhat cumbersome translation (cf. Qureshi's discussion of *sīna,* this volume). "*Now this that you've written, put everything here* {pointing at his chest}, *in your heart-mind.* [This is how] *you should play. Wait, and don't write any others. Clean these up, see them* [just as you have written them] *in your heart-mind. Outside* [where performances take place] *you won't be able to see this* {pointing at my notebook}." Hari Govinda's teaching style forced me to participate in sound differently than I had before. When he saw that new patterns and new *bols* were not fitting immediately into my hands, he slowed down his playing so that I could observe and imitate, but he rarely offered verbal metaphors or explanations to help. I heard and watched Hari Govinda's movements repeatedly, and wrote down sequences of *bols* in my notebook. At the end of almost every lesson, Hari Govinda told me to take home what I had learned and "*saphā garnus na*" (please clean it up). Practicing on my own, I could look at my notebook and listen to my recordings of my lessons, and work to smooth out the ungainly movements of my hands and arms. My work between lessons was to make my hands find their way into the grooves that my heart-mind saw, but didn't follow.

Hari Govinda sometimes expressed concern that if I tried to learn too many pieces at once, "*almal huncha*" ("confusion would happen"). Not only was I liable to lose my way through a piece by playing a garbled stroke and throwing myself off; I was also susceptible to getting confused within pieces, starting one and tripping into another. Even though I had only just begun my studies, Hari Govinda was already pushing me toward public performance, and such mistakes would, of course, be unacceptable outside.[12] He later taught me a simple sequence of pieces for use in a particular ritual procession, but the *dhā̃* repertoire that he was teaching me at that time was a flexible set of comparatively complex pieces. What he was giving me was something like a kaleidoscopic jigsaw puzzle, a collection of precisely cut pieces that I could later reassemble in a variety of ways on the streets of Bhaktapur. However, if the pieces weren't accurate in themselves, they wouldn't hold together in performance. The puzzle would fall apart, and the audience would hear a meaningless jumble rather than a coherent whole.

In telling me to put the pieces in my *man*, in my heart-mind, Hari Govinda drew attention to the difference between declarative knowledge and procedural knowledge: writing down something in a notebook correctly, and being able to read it back accurately, is not the same as being able to play it effectively. But, in making this distinction, he referred back to a visual analogy, saying that I should be able to see the pieces in my heart-mind just as I saw them in my notebook. These are clearly different ways of seeing. Sometimes, when I asked Hari Govinda to clarify a part of a piece, he, like most musicians working from memory, could not explain just that part in isolation; instead, he backed up in the piece and drummed forward until he got to the point in question. Occasionally, too, he would recapture a piece by reciting its *bols*, again often by backing up and speaking his way forward. Certainly, then, he did not expect me to read the pieces in my *man* in the same way that I would pick up a book or a written sequence of *bols* and start reading anywhere. Being able to see the pieces was not a skill developed independently of other skills. His hands often helped his *man* remember, and mine gradually became adept at reminding my *man* of things it knew too. And *bols*, the words of the drum, served as a prompt for both hands and *man*. Through my lessons, language became inextricably linked to movement and memory.

Shambu Prasad Mishra and Hari Govinda Ranjitkar were quite different teachers, but they shared some ways of speaking in my lessons. For instance, although I have not transcribed these passages from my lessons here, both used metaphors to describe gestures, to explain musical forms, and to talk about the study of drumming. Both also used *bols*, the syllabic speech of the drums, to recite pieces—sometimes speaking alone, sometimes speaking and playing, sometimes speaking while I played. Shambu's language served as scaffolding for both knowing and doing; Hari Govinda's words, though, typically worked more like cues in an unscripted script. He used speech to interrupt my action, to draw my attention to his action, to preface his action, to assess my action. He kept telling me to clean up the pieces I was learning, nudging me gently toward a sense of competence and further away from the feeling of awkwardness; he urged my hands to take hold of the drumming strokes and implored me to put longer sequences and pieces in my heart-mind.

* * *

How is bodily knowledge, like that I was getting from Shambu and Hari Govinda, situated within larger regimes of value? Michael Herzfeld, in his study of apprenticeship, situates bodily knowledge within concentric circles of meaning, placing it in the context not only of what is significant locally but also in the context of what is significant regionally, nationally, transnationally, and internationally (cf. Reed, this volume). In *The Body Impolitic* (2004), he investigates master-apprenticeship relationships in the Cretan village of Rethemnos that differ significantly from the teacher-student relationships I have enjoyed in the Kathmandu Valley of Nepal; his ethnographic concerns therefore develop in different directions. But the issues he raises regarding how and why artisans and apprentices cultivate particular traditions in response to particular modernities helps me understand drumming in Nepal as knowledge of something markedly traditional in a place that has its sights set on being decidedly modern.

Considering the relevance of the local in the face of processes of globalization, Herzfeld proposes a "search for the global in the heart of the local—for the hidden presence of a logic that has seeped in everywhere but is everywhere disguised as difference, heritage, local tradition" (Herzfeld 2004, 2). He notes the presence, often felt if not easily articulated, of a "global hierarchy of value" (2004, 3), a hierarchy that continues to reproduce notions of centrality and marginality, importance and insignificance. The task Herzfeld sets for himself, then, is to uncover the "hidden presence" that shapes the life and work of artisans and apprentices in Rethemnos, to reveal how a "global hierarchy of value" exists in a place far removed from the center. He asks bluntly, "*Who* is responsible for that hierarchy; who are its agents?" (2004, 4). It is clear that in Rethemnos its agents are not anonymous outside purveyors of an equally anonymous globalization, but are in fact those who subsist on the margins, artisans who both knowingly and unwittingly instill in their apprentices a seemingly paradoxical combination of humble docility and fierce independence in the face of harsh reality.

Herzfeld uses the metaphors of the pedestal and the tethering post throughout his book to highlight a sharp ambiguity apparent in artisan work. The products of Rethemnos artisans are elevated to the status of honored tradition by a nation-state not quite sure of its modernity, but certain of the importance of both its emerging modernity and its distinctive traditions. Simultaneously, Rethemnos artisans are tightly yoked by this hierarchy of value that insists on the importance of tradition and heritage as the foundation of the modern nation-state; they are unable to escape their marginality except by abandoning pride of place altogether.

Musicians like Shambu Prasad Mishra and Hari Govinda Ranjitkar occupy a similarly precarious position in Nepal. Shambu enjoyed the patronage of the king of Nepal for many years, playing and teaching tabla in the royal palace. This is hardly the sort of position enjoyed by artisans in Rethemnos, yet tabla playing in Nepal, like the work of artisans in Greece, has in recent years become more a relic of the past, a reminder of a time when such handiwork was of considerably greater

FIGURE 10.5. Shambu Prasad Mishra performing at his house, 1995. Photograph by the author.

local value. Whether or not there ever was such a time does not really matter: what is important is that Shambu believed that his work was valued in the past, and while people perhaps still considered *śāstriya saṅgīt* (classical music) to be a venerable tradition, nobody wanted to listen to it.

He chafed at the fact that Radio Nepal dedicated less than fifteen minutes of air time to *śāstriya saṅgīt* each week, considering this more an insult than a sign of respect for his work, but he nonetheless did perform on the radio when asked, perpetuating his own marginality. One day, he criticized younger musicians in Nepal, suggesting that they have been responsible for a widespread decline in musical values.

> *They are too proud. After becoming proud . . . they say to themselves,* "Ah, I am very top, man!" *They think they're* top, man, famous! *That's the way it is now. If it's like that, knowledge doesn't come, they can never become good. In this Nepal, there are a few too many like this. It's not like that in India. Before it might have been like that in India, but not now. In this* classical [music], *earlier it was just like it was in* India. *Now, now, this* [music]

> *has already become weak.*... Light song, folk song, pop song—*yeah, here they've become really popular, bābu.*

Here, Shambu implied that the kind of work that he used to do was still of value elsewhere, but of dwindling importance locally. His relegation to the margins in Nepal was mirrored in the declining powers of his aging body. "*Hāt bigriyo, bābu,*" he complained often, when his hands couldn't keep up with what he wanted to play. His hands had become broken—in his case not from too little practice, but from too much. His hands remembered what they used to be capable of doing, but he could not make them do it any longer.

Hari Govinda Ranjitkar, meanwhile, knows a drumming repertoire that is of utmost importance for ritual activities in the city of Bhaktapur, yet he has had few students. Perhaps his most adept student is the ethnomusicologist Gert-Matthias Wegner (see Wegner, 1986; 1987); his work has received less acclaim and attention locally. Hari Govinda has always been stoic about having few heirs for his knowledge, but there is a vexing irony here. The city of Bhaktapur has been venerated in the national and international discourse of heritage as the most traditional of the three cities of the Kathmandu Valley; while Kathmandu and Patan have witnessed widespread urban sprawl and modernization, Bhaktapur, from the 1970s to the 1990s, received significant funding for the restoration and preservation of its architecture. The development

FIGURE 10.6. Hari Govinda Ranjitkar and the author performing during *gāi jātrā* in Bhaktapur. Photograph by Ramesh Ranjit.

of Bhaktapur as a site of cultural heritage, evident especially in how the city looks, has generally bypassed the agents of culture. People like Hari Govinda seem to be of great value, but there is little investment, financial or otherwise, in this value: it seems that the residents of Bhaktapur are considered more a renewable resource, providing an endless display of local color. And what they know is markedly traditional, not modern: it is valuable because difference is a valuable commodity in the tourism industry, formerly (and potentially) a vital sector of the national economy.

While Shambu was more vocal in his critiques of modern musical values, both Shambu and Hari Govinda embodied alternative values in their drumming, and they inculcated these values in me as well in teaching me to drum. If "the body is the site of memories made materially accessible in complex ways" (Herzfeld 2004, 26), the bodily dispositions I acquired through my study of drumming provided partial access to what drumming meant to my teachers. Why did they persist? Why did they persist in teaching me? Both Shambu and Hari Govinda spoke with pride and pleasure about what they knew, even as they recognized the dwindling accord allotted to their work. But the value of drumming is predominantly implicit, evident in the sight, sound, and feel of drumming itself. Its value is evident in manner and posture; it is marked in the precision of the sound, the poise of the hand, the confidence of the presentation. The value of drumming is a nameless value, a critique of modernity inscribed in the body, etched on its dispositions.

* * *

In discussing my lessons with Shambu Prasad Mishra, I focused on a point of modest accomplishment, showing how language was an important component of the elaborate process of learning to build a sequence of musical events. In writing about my lessons with Hari Govinda Ranjitkar, I described instead a point of relative awkwardness, noting how language framed even the rudimentary imitation of bodily movement. The importance of language for shaping the understanding of musical form was more apparent in the former, and its use in shaping the understanding of physical form was more evident in the latter. Striving to grasp a feeling for these two ways of drumming, I became aware of how sensation was becoming linked to emotion and reason, and watched with avid interest as my hands began to think and feel for themselves. Trying to write both phenomenologically and ethnographically, I have depicted my hands struggling to find their way, sometimes impatient with my lagging mind, in the social circumstances (my drumming lessons) in which they were moving. Working to secure a kind of knowledge that would only be audible and visible in my ability to recreate that knowledge in performance, I came to understand my drumming as an expression of value, a vastly rewarding activity of fluctuating worth in a global hierarchy of value. Reflecting now on my study with these two men, I wonder how I could ever not have known these things.

PART IV

THEORIZING SOCIAL ACTION

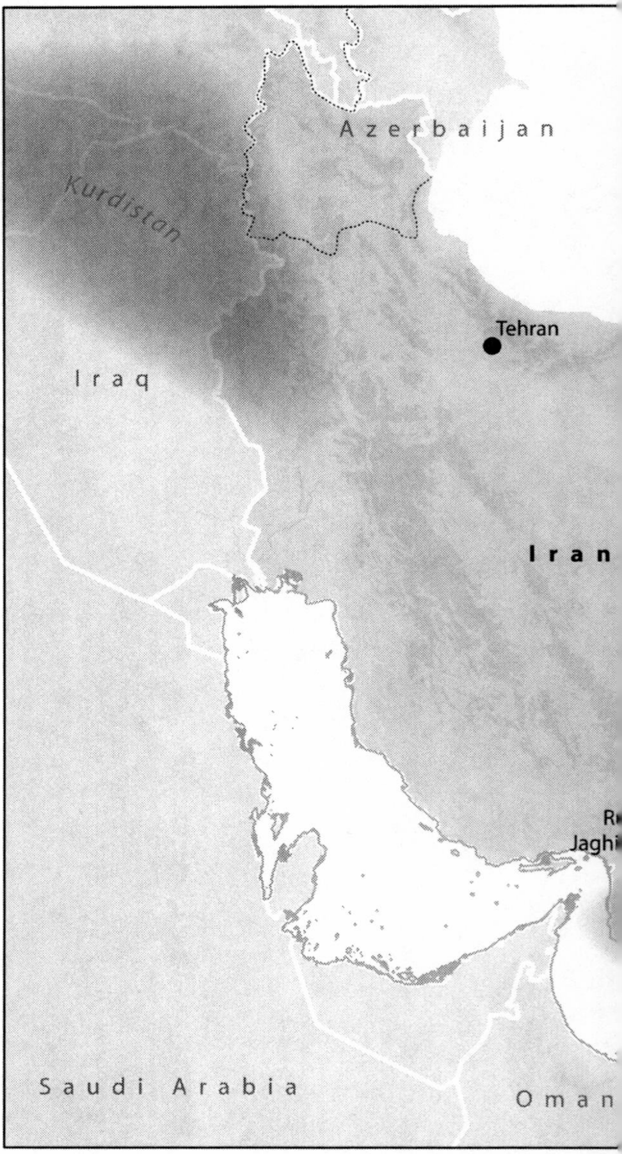
Azerbaijan
Kurdistan
Tehran
Iraq
Iran
Saudi Arabia
Oman

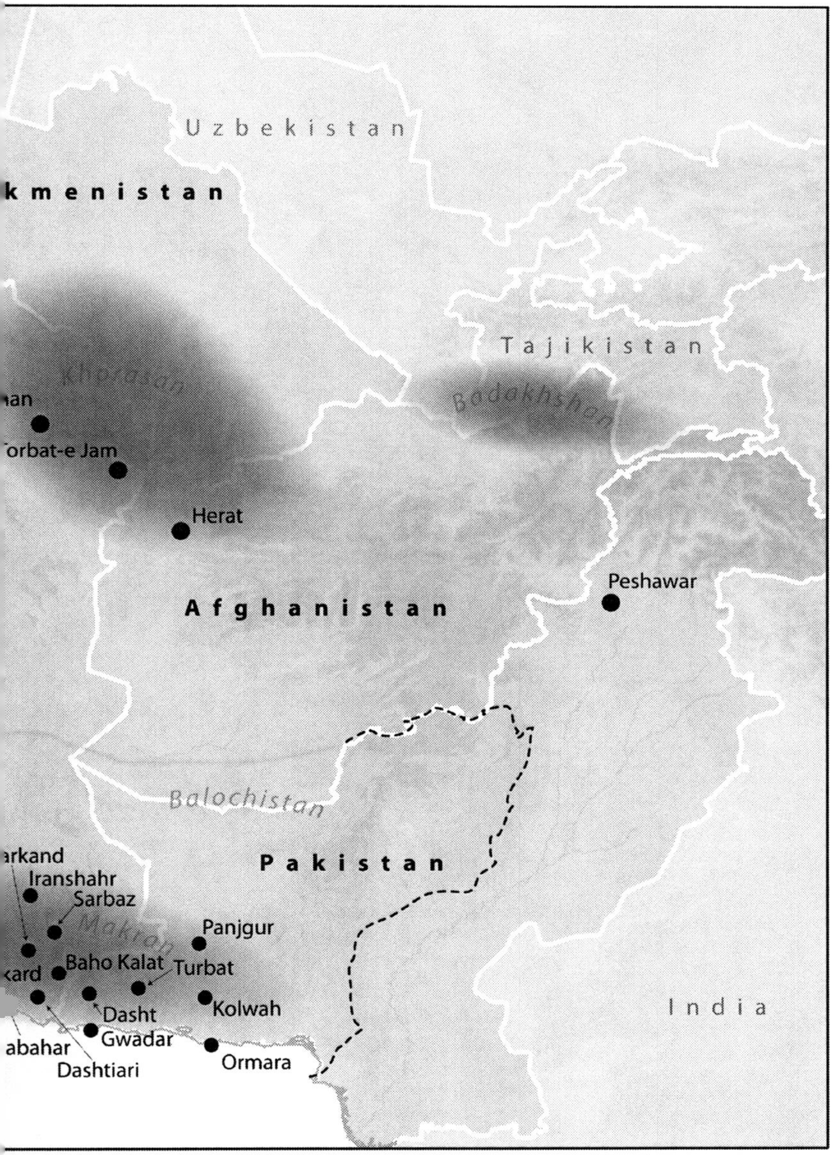
Uzbekistan
kmenistan
Tajikistan
Khorasan
Bodakhshon
ian
Torbat-e Jam
Herat
Peshawar
Afghanistan
Balochistan
Pakistan
arkand
Iranshahr
Sarbaz
Makran
Panjgur
Baho Kalat
Turbat
kard
Dasht
Kolwah
India
Gwadar
abahar
Ormara
Dashtiari

CHAPTER 11

Modes of Theorizing in Iranian Khorasan

STEPHEN BLUM

Knowledgeable Performers

In a great many local practices, musicians present themselves as knowledgeable by adopting appropriate modes of behavior and conventional rhetorical devices. The modes of behavior and the rhetoric are necessarily consistent with shared conceptions of how musicians can become and can remain knowledgeable. This chapter discusses "theorizing" as an activity that prepares and accompanies the acquisition, retention, and expansion or contraction of musical knowledge.

Some performers profess the belief that no one could possibly master *all* the musical knowledge that exists. [**Video example 11.1**] 'Ali Ǧolāmrezā'i (known as 'Ali Āqā), one of the bards who are called *baxši* in Iranian Khorasan, made such a claim with respect to the knowledge he understands as linked to his instrument, the long-necked lute with two strings called *dotār*.[1] "*In dotār 'ilmi and... va in 'ilm-e tār yek 'ilmi bi pāyān. Kasi be pāyān-e 'ilm naxwāhad rasid be joz'.*" (This *dotār* is [an instrument] of knowledge...and this *tār*-knowledge is an infinite [realm of] knowledge. No one will reach the end of this knowledge in full detail.)

When 'Ali Āqā's master, Ostād Mohammad Hoseyn Yegāne, publicly handed over his *dotār*—to his son, not to 'Ali Āqā—at a festival held in Tehran in 1991, a few years before his death, the instrument clearly stood for the knowledge that had been transmitted earlier. In words that were included on the first cassette in the album released to commemorate the *Haft awrang* (Seven Thrones, also Ursa major) festival (Bustān and Darviši 1992), Yegāne charged his son with the responsibility of keeping a certain mode of performance alive as he handed him the instrument he had played for fifty years: "I, your servant [*bande*], am your servant [*čāker*] Mohammad Hoseyn Yegane, a resident of Quchan. It is now fifty years [since] your servant made this *tār,* and [performance practice of] this *tār* was likewise transmitted from one heart to another. In the presence of this assembly, I in turn bestow what was given your servant. I expect the same of him, just as I your servant brought [the performance practice] heart to heart, [in order] that this manner of singing poetry not die out."[2] [**Audio example 11.1**]

Musical knowledge can also be characterized metaphorically, rather than metonymically in its dependence on an instrument and/or authoritative sources. John Baily's film about an Afghan refugee musician in Peshawar, *Amir,* includes a scene in which Bakhtiar Ustaz, a Pakistani master musician, says, "Amir Mohammad, music is like a river, like an ocean. Nobody can exhaust it. Some take pebbles, some boulders from the shore. It's a great science." Other South Asian musicians have described a master's knowledge as "a vast ocean contained in a small cup" (Qureshi, this volume). In Iranian Khorasan, few performers would have occasion to speak of "musical science," metaphorically or otherwise: the inexhaustible knowledge that some performers claim access to is associated either with sung poetry alone or with sung poetry performed to *dotār* accompaniment. It is knowledge of what verses can be performed and of how they can be performed, rather than "musical science" as an identifiable discipline.

Knowledge transmitted from master to pupil and perhaps linked to an instrument can be regarded as "theory": a heterogeneous collection of doctrines and other forms of knowledge, made available to pupils through the demonstrations and the speech or writing of masters. Two central terms with which musicians refer to pertinent doctrines are Sanskrit *śāstra* and Arabic *'ilm* (also used in Persian, Kurdish, Urdu, and Turkic languages), together with the adjectives derived from them; *'ilm* is extended as well to less formalized knowledge. Harold Powers's observation (1980, 72) that "*śāstra* means either a text containing an authoritative exposition of doctrine in a particular field, or the body of doctrine itself" does not fully apply to *'ilm,* which may refer to the subject matter of a text but not to the text itself. More significant is the point that "Hindustani classical musicians from the seventeenth century to the nineteenth were mostly Muslim, largely associated with courts, normally considered fairly low in the caste hierarchy, and concerned less with *śāstra* (doctrine) than with guarding their *sampradāya* (oral traditions)" by emphasizing lines of transmission (1980, 73; see also Neuman 1985, 103). *'Ilm* may designate a highly codified body of knowledge transmitted orally from master to pupil (or presented in a treatise) but, as in 'Ali Āqā's remarks quoted above, it may also refer to all that a musician claims to know or deems knowable, whether or not this lends itself to verbal formulations.[3]

Conceptions of how musical knowledge is organized are implicit in performers' evaluations of themselves and of their competitors. Among the *baxšis* of Khorasan a major concern of such evaluations is the extent to which one knows the verses that best fit particular tunes as well as the tunes that are most appropriate to a given story or poem—an issue that can be addressed by referring to the contents of the notebooks in which *baxšis* have copied verses, but not by appealing to a settled body of doctrine. Where appeals to doctrine are possible, musicians may argue about which doctrine, if any, is most pertinent to a particular genre or practice. In his study of discourse about improvisation in *tāyampaka,* a genre of temple drumming in Kerala, Rolf Groesbeck examines differences in the attitudes toward "ancient laws and structure" (*ciṭṭa*) that drummers articulate in evaluating performances as *śāstriya* or not (i.e., *aśāstriya*). Some drummers respond to criticism that their "idiosyncratic improvisation" fails to respect the norms of *tāyampaka* by maintaining that their playing follows the rules of Karnatak *tala* theory (Groesbeck 1999b, 22–23). Both bodies of knowledge are sufficiently codified to enable identification of specific violations.

Figure 11.1 represents the body of one musician's knowledge at any given time at the top of a triangle, and at the lower left and lower right our two main means of access to portions of this knowledge—our interpretations of the musician's performances and of pedagogical actions (including, but not limited to, verbal formulations). Even the best hearing and analysis of a musician's performances, and even the most lucid reading and analysis of the most articulate musician's pedagogical presentations (and critiques of competitors), should not be mistaken for a fully detailed map or inventory of the musician's knowledge.[4] For musicians to have total control over all the potentially pertinent information stored in their memories is perhaps more an ideal than an everyday reality. Their performances and pedagogical presentations are necessarily shaped by portions of their knowledge, and vice versa, but the relationship between performances and pedagogical presentations can be far more tenuous—hence the dotted line and question mark in figure 11.1.

Scholars have often struggled to reconcile the disparities between their analyses of performances and their analyses of theories and pedagogies, yet the existence of such disparities should not surprise us. Teachers have been known to hold back from their pupils some of the knowledge that informed their own performances. More

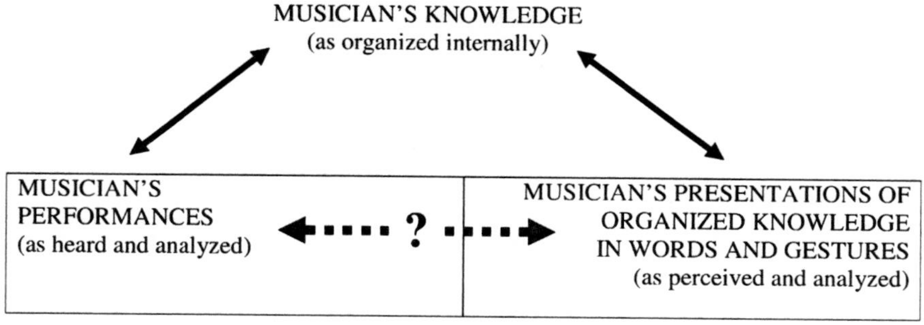

FIGURE 11.1. Two means of access to a musician's knowledge.

generally, we have no reason to suppose that the rather different aims of performances and lessons would be equally well served by structuring the results of both kinds of action in recognizably congruent forms. The pedagogical devices employed by master musicians often include models with different functions, such as the two types that John Baily (1988b, following Caws 1974) terms "representational" and "operational."[5] Models of the latter type are by definition more directly linked to performance.

Differences we observe between what musicians do in performance and their statements about what ought to be done may seem at times to support Charles

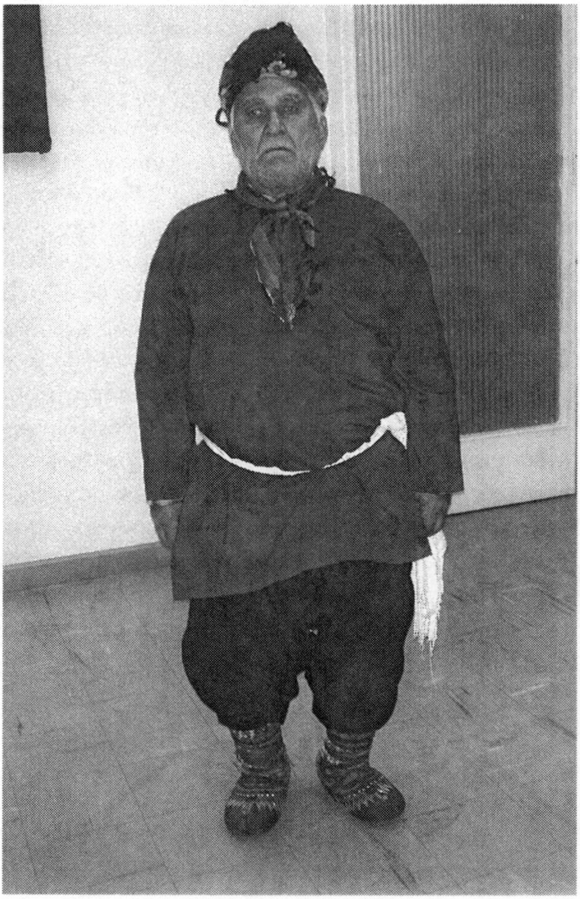

FIGURE 11.2. The *baxši* Sohrāb Mohammadi of Ashkhaneh, dressed in the costume normally worn for festival performances by musicians from northern Khorasan. Photographed by Ameneh Youssefzadeh at the research program of the Fajr Festival, Tehran, January 13, 2006.

Seeger's conception of a radical disjuncture between what he called "music-knowledge of music" and "speech-knowledge of music" (Seeger 1977, 16). I doubt, though, that the knowledge musicians have internalized could be adequately represented in the terms of that dichotomy. Could musicians, in performance, draw on knowledge acquired through prior musical experience, if we organized and stored that knowledge with little or no reliance on verbal categories?

One justification for emphasizing the distance between what musicians know and what can be learned from their actions as performers and teachers is the dissatisfaction musicians register with some of their own performances, and with attempts by themselves and others to find the right words in which to articulate the norms, principles, or procedures that musicians presumably follow in making the right moves. With greater or lesser frequency musicians recognize that their singing or playing falls short of what they know, or think they know, how to do, and many are quick to bemoan the limitations of verbal discourse. No genre of speech or writing could accommodate all that might be said about a musical practice, nor could a single theorist's work in multiple genres take in the perspectives of all that theorist's contemporaries and competitors.

Theorizing: Incentives, Resources, and Outcomes

More work has been done in identifying variables pertinent to the analysis of performances than in identifying those that are pertinent to analysis of how theories are structured, presented, and debated. Box 11.1 lists six of the main areas in which it is possible to identify clear motivations for certain kinds of pedagogical or otherwise theoretical statements. A penetrating analysis of multiple incentives to adopt a new theoretical system is provided by Baily's studies of the uses of musical knowledge (*'ilm-e musiqi*) by professional musicians in Herat, the main city of Afghan Khorasan. For the musicians in a particular network, laying claim to a body of musical knowledge associated with Kabul became "an important part of *honarmand* [artist] status and high rank. It rendered respectable both music and musicians: the very possibility of speech discourse about the structural elements of music changed the status of music in an Islamic society which regarded it with some suspicion" (Baily 1988a, 162; see also Baily 1981, 5–10, 33–37).

More often than not, in responding to these incentives, people appropriate fragments or larger chunks from the theories of others—perhaps by recycling proverbs, rules or norms of behavior, enumerations of familiar categories, or stock explanations. Such recycling inevitably looms large in most local and supralocal practices, and the extent to which fragments are assembled into larger configurations, such as models and doctrines, varies greatly. Whether or not specific outcomes of theorizing qualify as "theories" or "models" by one or another set of criteria, I doubt that there is any musical practice in which musicians do not

BOX 11.1. Six areas in which incentives for theoretical formulations can be identified.

a. Needs of court musicians (as defined by themselves and by patrons)
b. Needs of religious observances and training
c. Needs of bards and storytellers
d. Needs of professional networks and lineages in competition with others
e. Needs of secular educational institutions
f. Inquiries of (and hospitality or resistance toward) ethnographers, journalists, bureaucrats, and so on

reproduce (silently from memory, or articulated with words and gestures) portions of earlier theories while considering alternatives, even if only to reject them. I agree with Lawrence Zbikowski (2002, 114) that "the process of theorizing is both various and omnipresent."

"Theorizing" seems as good a term as any to take in the (momentary or protracted) episodes of generalizing that may occur in most genres of speech or writing and in other modes of communication as well. Goethe ([1810] 1989, 11) justified his claim that "with every attentive glance at the world we are already theorizing" by naming four phases of a coherent sequence: each act of looking (*Ansehen*) becomes contemplating with attention (*Betrachten*), then reflecting (*Sinnen*), then connecting (*Anknüpfen*). He added the qualification that agility (*Gewandtheit*) in theorizing reflexively—with self-knowledge, freedom, and irony—is crucial if the results of the experience are to be useful and are to avoid the dangers of excessive abstraction.[6] Both as ethnographers of local theory and local practice, and as participants in institutionalized scholarship, we deal every day with results of theorizing that cannot be described as useful by Goethe's criteria but that evidently have other uses. Presumably, the connecting of which Goethe spoke involves comparing one's immediate experience with representations of prior and/or anticipated experiences. If the connecting is "theorizing," perhaps the representations—to the extent that they are treated as alternatives—can be called "theories." I regard theories as tools that are used, modified, or produced as people theorize.

In my view, then, theorizing starts as we make connections among our thoughts and perceptions with some awareness of alternatives that we remember or imagine or explore through speech, writing, drawing, gesture, music, or some other medium or combination of media. When we are able to perform with little or no such awareness, we are not actively theorizing; as musicians we depend on habits and procedures we may have acquired from teachers who showed us the right moves without encouraging or even allowing us to consider alternatives. In some circumstances, it may be possible to follow the prescriptions of an existing model or theory without theorizing oneself, that is, without trying to imagine any phase of the process of weighing alternatives that resulted in the model. But sooner or later most musicians become more attentive than that, as they respond to cues given by fellow performers and listener-spectators.

I persist in thinking that "any musical practice... presupposes an underlying theory" (Blum 1975, 218), portions of which are at any given time "implicit" rather than explicit.[7] Yet I do not assume that any two musicians involved in what is commonly regarded as a single practice must necessarily share an implicit theory that is identical in every respect. In his critique of *The Social Theory of Practices: Tradition, Tacit Knowledge, and Presuppositions,* Stephen Turner rightly cautions against making that assumption. He wishes to use the word *practices* "not for some sort of mysterious hidden collective object, but for the individual formations of habit that are the condition for the performances and emulations that make up life" (Turner 1994, 123). I see theorizing as partly responsible for the "individual formations of habit" that take shape as musicians interact with others. Some habits are acquired or strengthened through theorizing and some provide a basis for theorizing that challenges or replaces earlier sets of habits.

FIGURE 11.3. The late *baxši* Haj Qorbān Soleymāni performs for four guests as his son, Ali Rezā, looks on. Photographed by Ameneh Youssefzadeh, January 11, 2006, Aliabad (a village outside Quchan), Khorasan.

Theorizing, in this broad sense, encompasses what Anthony Giddens (1984, 5–6) called "the reflexive monitoring and rationalization of action." Discussions of what I would call tools used in or produced by theorizing include, among many others, Steven Feld's remarks on "interpretive frames" (1984, 12), Alfred Gell's account of "underlying maps [that] indicate all possibilities deemed feasible according to a particular system of temporal belief" (1992, 254), and Zbikowski's consideration of "conceptual models" (2002, passim). The knowledge that pupils acquire from master performers consists not only of tools but also of rules or at least hints on how to use and, if need be, replace the tools.

Qualities, Names, Repertoires

People who theorize cannot avoid using names, gestures, or other varieties of sign to designate some of the qualities, entities, and relationships with which they are concerned. Similarly, when speakers and writers name or otherwise designate objects of their concern, they are involved in theorizing, even if they do little more than repeat bits and pieces of existing theories. Scholars of European musical terminology—notably H. H. Eggebrecht, for many years the editor of the monumental *Handbuch der musikalischen Terminologie*—have distinguished between *terms,* which are defined with specific reference to a discipline like music or mathematics, and *names,* which they presume to be used "unreflectively." Eggebrecht acknowledged (1981, 777) that "within a culture (like the European) in which music is set off as a discipline, there are many sorts of naming between the extremes of theoretically oriented comprehension and that which is unreflective and relates to action and function."[8] This view of a continuum defined by two familiar extremes—detached contemplation and engaged action—does not provide an adequate basis for studying local theories in any part of the world: the fact that musicians in South and West Asia, like those of Europe, theorize in a variety of ways should not inspire us to evaluate approaches to naming according to their distance from an imaginary "unreflective" extreme, even if we recognize that in all societies much is said and written with little if any reflection on the part of the speakers or writers. Even those who are the least inclined to reflection are obliged, sooner or later, to consider alternatives. All humans "represent the world as being *capable of being otherwise* than we believe it to be, actually" (Gell 1992, 217).

In any musical practice, as in other social practices, much is left unspoken—and unnamed—for a variety of reasons (see also Brinner 1995, 36–39, and Gerstin 1998, 143–59). We can attempt to make some implicit assumptions and procedures explicit by addressing the question, "What kinds of names have been applied to what kinds of entities and relations in this practice?" The theoretical implications and associations of various sets of names constitute an area of inquiry with a long history in the musical scholarship of South and West Asia. Sometimes a collection of proper names is unified under a rubric that fully meets Eggebrecht's criteria for technical terms—for example, the names of Hindustani or Karnatak ragas, or the names of Persian *dastgāh*s and their constituent units (*guše*s). Clearly the creation and use of such unifying terms has been, and remains, a fundamental aspect of theorizing in a great many musical practices. While it is common for a repertoire of names to be subsumed under a general term or a group of related terms, it is also possible for musical resources to carry names that have not been ordered within general categories. In Iran, during the past decade the government's cultural policy toward "music of the regions" (*musiqi-ye navāhi*) has favored increased use of the term *maqām* as a general term for musical resources, to the point that *musiqi-ye maqāmi* is now a synonym for "regional music" (Darviši [1380b] 2001b) and is often contrasted with *musiqi-ye dastgāhi,* the music based on the canonical *radīf.*[9] An item that is now a *maqām* might once have been called an *āhang* (tune), one difference between these categories being that a *maqām* has a proper name while an *āhang* may not.[10] In most regional practices, general terms that are loosely synonymous with *maqām* or *āhang* are followed by words that distinguish the more specific varieties within each category (see Faridi-Haftkhâni 2005: 6–10 of Persian section, 2–6 of English section, for a description of the terminology in Talesh, where several types of melody termed *tāleši* are sung).

The discourse about music that I began to study in northern Khorasan during the late 1960s and early 1970s centered on names of performance genres and roles of performers; such general terms as *āhang, tariqe* (way), and *jur* (manner) were far more common than *maqām,* and many performers—even *baxši*s—did not seem much concerned with names of tunes. The *baxši*s with whom Ameneh Youssefzadeh began to work in the mid-1980s made greater use of names and of the term *maqām* (see Youssefzadeh 2002a). The Azerbaijani *aşıq,* a figure comparable in many respects to the Khorasani *baxši,* controls a large repertoire of melody-types (*havalar*) that are named (for Iranian Azerbaijan see the tables in Farr 1976, 83 and 86–88). Names of many important religious figures are included in the set of names assigned to the seventy-two ritual *maqām*s (also called *nazm* or *nağme*) of the Yārsān religion of Iranian Kurdistan (see Moradi 2002); such names have the power to evoke whatever performers or listeners might know about the figures named. Each of the repertories mentioned here includes at least a few items whose names also turn up in the canonical *radīf* (see the table in Ardelān [1375b] 1996b, 6).

Less complex than the large sets of names for modal entities in South and West Asia are the vocabularies in most human languages that enable people to identify distinctive features of sounds and of the movements that produce sounds. This is one of the many topics treated in an original manner by al-Fārābī (d. 339 AH / 950 CE), a native of Khorasan, in his *Great Book on Music.* Fārābī described four types of distinctions (*fusūl*) among sounds, some of them dependent on quantities (*maqādir*)—such as different magnitudes of acuity (*hidda*) and gravity (*ṯiql*)—and some dependent on qualities (*kayfiyāt*). Some distinctive features have their own names (*asmā'*); some have names based on a resemblance (*ašbāh*) to "things perceptible through senses" (*mahsūsāt*) other than hearing, such as vision and touch;[11] some sounds have names that imitate them (*tuhākihā*); and there are also sound qualities that have not received names, which makes it difficult to talk about their meanings (Khashabah and al-Hifnī 1967, 1069; French paraphrase in Erlanger 1935, 57). Fārābī listed seven such qualities, which he evidently thought were not normally discussed: clarity (*safā'*), muddiness (*kudra*), coarseness (*xušūna*), smoothness (*malāsa*), softness (*na'ama*), forcefulness (*šidda*), and hardness (*salāba*). He went on to mention four additional qualities created by different types of vocal production, remarking that some had names and others did not: wetness (*rutūba*), dryness (*yubs*), nasality (*ǧunna*), and humming (*zamm*, "fastening" the lips so that the air passes entirely through the nose).

Fārābī's small repertoire of qualities could be interpreted as an inventory of seven binary choices: clear or muddy, coarse or smooth, soft or forceful, soft or hard, wet or dry, nasal or not, hummed or not. Most of the polarities, however, also allow for comparison of sounds in relation to one or the other extreme: a sound might be clearer, softer, and drier relative to a preceding or following sound. Lists of qualities attributed to sounds, not necessarily articulated as sets of polarities, can be located in other writings on music, and we can assemble more such lists from the speech of musicians.[12] Pertinent attributes of sounds, melodies, rhythms, or textures are often identified in negative judgments of a particular performer or class of performers.

The scope and structure of the vocabularies that enable musicians and others to identify qualities of sounds, discrete motions, rhythms, melodies, textures, phases of a ceremony, and so on, begin to become apparent as we reflect on the formats of the sentences in which names or terms are used. They become more apparent, needless to say, as we gain experience of the manner of performance and the contexts in which sentences in each format are uttered, and as we attempt to analyze that experience.[13] The following discussion is limited to a few formats used by Iranian performers in making theoretical statements. An adequate study of modes of theorizing, in Iran or elsewhere, would require a much more extensive roster of conventional formats, followed by ethnographic study of the circumstances in which statements in each format are made and analysis of the ways in which such statements are joined together.

It is common for *baxšis* to say something to the effect that "We must know melodies with qualities Q1, Q2, Q3 . . . Qn."[14] Lists of qualities of sound or motion in this format may be compared with lists of the names of entities belonging to larger systems, such as the subdivisions of one modal category, the branches of one story, or the available resources for performance of a story or genre:

a. The main [branches / subdivisions] of this [story / modal category] are named N1, N2, N3 . . . .
b. Some [branches / subdivisions] of this [story / modal category] are N1, N2, N3. . . .

c. All the [branches / subdivisions] of this [story / modal category] are N1, N2, N3 . . . Nn.
d. The available resources for performing this [story or genre] are N1, N2 . . . Nn.

An important difference between the names represented by N and the qualities, attributes, or properties represented by Q is that a name generally stands for a bundle of features rather than for a single attribute. Nonetheless, in West and Central Asia words readily pass back and forth between Q statements and N statements. For example, a melody described by *baxšis* with the epithet *suznāk*, "plaintive," uses a tone-system which resembles that of the Turkish *makam* named *Suzinak*. [**Audio example 11.2**]

Other words that evoke one emotion or condition turn up in more than one repertoire, as epithets or names, generally with little or no structural resemblance among the entities sharing a name or epithet. Good examples are the names and epithets derived from three Arabic roots—HZN "to sadden," ZHR "to groan," and HYR "to be at a loss," all of which point to fundamental motivations for music making. *Baxšis* describe some melodies as *hoznāvar*, "sorrowful," and two *dastgāhs* of the Persian *radīf* include units (*gušes*) called *Hazin*. As Badalkhan notes in the following chapter, the Persian adjective *zahiri* is an attribute of the genre *falak* in Afghan Badakhshan, whereas the genre called *zahīrok* in Balochi is regarded as the

FIGURE 11.4. The *baxši* Sohrāb Mohammadi strikes the side of his *dotār* while singing. Photographed by Ameneh Youssefzadeh, January 10, 2006, Ashkhaneh, Khorasan.

very basis of Baloch music. Without necessarily sharing any melodic or rhythmic traits, the *maqām* called *Heyrān* in Gilan, and the vocal genre called *Heyrān* in Kurdistan may well evoke states of wonderment or bewilderment similar to those called forth by the short *guše* of *Mohayyer* in the *dastgāh* of *Māhur* and the important *maqāms* that have borne that name in earlier systems. Mohammad Massoudieh has noted the correspondence between the name of the *guše Muye,* "lamentation" (in the *dastgāhs* of *Segāh* and *Čahārgāh*), and the name of the genre *Āwāmuri,* "vocal lamentation" in Lorestan (Massoudieh 1992, 318–19).

Several other names of *gušes* that evoke emotional states are constructed of a noun plus a verb stem, for example *Ğam-angiz,* "arousing sorrow," *Del-kaš,* "attracting the heart," and *Ruh-afzā,* "soul-enhancing." Still, most *guše* names in the canonical *radīf,* and most *maqām* names in regional practices, do not make explicit reference to an emotion but are drawn from other vocabularies. These include words denoting a gesture, attitude, action, process, or performance technique (*Kerešme,* "glance, wink"; *Nahib,* "wailing"; *Nešib o ferāz,* "descent and ascent," *Zir-afkand,* dropping the string called *zir*), and names of localities, ethnic groups, religions, and prominent figures from history and literature. The vocabularies from which repertoires of names are constituted remain available for use in discussions of performance genres, pieces, rhythmic patterns, and the like. For instance, the reversal of direction denoted by *Nešib o ferāz*—down, then back up—can be perceived in situations with no connection to the Persian *radīf,* such as drumming patterns (see Sharar's remarks, quoted by Wolf 2000, 91).

In regional practices such names commonly denote specific entities belonging to a class with two or more members. According to one Khorasani singer, "there are two *jur* [manners] of singing [the genre] *masnavi:* the *tariqe* [way] of Safi 'Ali Šāh and the *tariqe* of Šāh Ni'matollah Vali." By *masnavi* this singer did not mean a poem matching the conventional definition but any poem composed in the quantitative meter of the famous *Masnavi* of Jalāl al-din Rumi; one meter and two possible melodic frameworks were the attributes with which he defined a vocal genre. In the *radīf* the name *Šāh Xatā'i* denotes a *guše* that is suitable only for verses in that same meter, and in the regional music of Khorasan the same name denotes a few *maqāms* (also called *tariqe*) used exclusively for verses in a longer version of that meter, with fifteen rather than eleven syllables.

Assigning names to modal entities—and to performance genres, pieces, rhythmic patterns, and the like—evidently helps them to acquire associations that extend well beyond whatever meanings the names bear in their nonmusical uses. The name becomes an index for information about the circumstances in which a specific item is normally, or sometimes, or never performed—for example, before or after some other item or activity (box 11.2a); in response to some type of situation or demand (box 11.2b–c); or in order to achieve a particular effect (box 11.2d–f). Some names of Persian *gušes* are in fact names of genres—*Masnavi, Dobeyti, Sāqi-nāme,* to mention three with a rich range of associations, both musical and poetical.

BOX 11.2. Some formats for statements about selection of named items.

a. *Moment M in situation S calls for performance of N1, followed by N2, N3...*
A baxši: "In any gathering (*majles*), when they want to start to sing, first they play one *panjeh-tar* [tuning exercise] and they play [the genre] *Navā'i*. Then they sing other poems about other stories."
b. *Performance of genre G is a response to situation S*
"Some mystical verses were sung [by me] as my condition at that time was a journey on high (*yeki še'r-hā-ye 'erfāni xunde miše ke dar ham un hālam yek seyri bālā bud*)."
c. *When listeners are judged to have quality Q1, it is appropriate to perform genre G*
A *naqqāl:* "For people [in the tea house] who are worthy, I sing some good [religious] poems (*barā-ye kasāni ke qabiliyat dārand, čand-tā aš'ār-e hesābi barā-ye išun mixwunam*)."
d. *Genre G is performed in order to [produce response R or induce state S]*
A *naqqāl:* "In the tea-house I first sing a ghazal to subdue people's desires (*barā-ye jān-āvari-ye havas čand-tā ğazal dar qahve-xāne mixwunam*)."
e. *Performance of genre G continues until effect E becomes evident or response R is made*
A *naqqāl:* "[The genre] *mosibat* must be sung until I kindle a reverberation in your mind (*bāyad gofte bešavad tā mon'akes konam dar nazar-e šomā*)."
f. *Effect E is symptomatic of response R*
A *naqqāl* active in the Xāksār order: "All repeat [the *zekr*] until its workings become apparent right then and there; their agency is manifest, that is to say Mowla 'Ali gives them an answer (*hame tekrār mikonand tā yek 'avāmeli dar haminjā peydā beše; 'avāmel išun zāher miše, ya'ni Mowlā ['Ali] be un-hā javāb dād*)."

From statements in the formats considered we can infer the existence of repertoires (in other words, collections of the entities identified with capital letters) showing stronger or weaker tendencies toward systematization. In a repertoire that has been fully systematized, the meanings of all components are strongly defined by their interrelationships and the entities do not resemble a roomful of individuals with whom one has yet to become acquainted. When someone plays a quality Q2 melody, part of its meaning for informed listeners results from how it differs from the melodies with other qualities that, conceivably, might have been performed in its place. Depending on the repertoire's size and potential for expansion or contraction, each listener is likely to have a different sense of what conceivably might have been substituted. Some systems are more unstable and more easily altered than others; none is so firmly in place that all musicians and listeners will share a common understanding of its possibilities.

Consider, for instance, Amanda Weidman's attention to "the juxtaposition of different types of women's voices in the public sphere and the ways they may have mutually constructed each other" (2003, 224 n6). We can be certain that the different types of women's and of men's voices to be heard in any public sphere at a given time have to some extent "mutually constructed each other" even if we find ourselves (as, often, we should) considering more than one narrative of how that may have happened. Since the voice types are audible in the public sphere, many listeners will recognize some of the meanings created by their differences. Weidman's study provides convincing examples of how changes may come about, and we can easily imagine the possibility of singers working against the existing system to develop new voice types (even if we find it hard to imagine the actual sound of those possible types before hearing them).

A voice type, like the named entities in a modal system, is characterized by a bundle of features—all the respects in which anyone perceives it as resembling or differing from the other available voice types; hence the emergence of a new voice type in the public space may well increase the number of dimensions pertinent to the recognition of contrasting features. The same point holds, of course, for instruments and for roles taken by performers in ensembles, dramas, and narratives. We can list the voice types, instruments, or roles in a repertoire, and as soon as we attempt to outline the respects in which they are experienced as different, we begin to describe a system. Such efforts engage us in finding words and other means of representation that can help in sorting out the multiple strands that are woven together in each voice type, instrument, role, or performance genre.

Systems and Terms

One of the key questions in our consideration of local theories and local practices must be "What is systematized, along what lines, and to what extent?" We can speak of a system whenever we find terms and categories that are mutually constitutive in specific respects within the practices of identifiable groups. Different interests of groups and individuals generate contrasting approaches to systematization and different notions of how far a particular approach should be followed (compare Lévi-Strauss 1962, 285–86). It is not always easy, and at times not particularly fruitful, to distinguish between well-articulated systems, and repertoires or lists of terms and categories that may appear to be less rigorously organized. But as soon as we are informed about, or start to imagine, the projects of those who intend to make use of a list, we are assessing aspects of its organization. For a scholar concerned with "a folklore system in one village," according to A. K. Ramanujan (1986, 4), "each genre is related to others, fitted, dovetailed, contrasted—so that we cannot study any of them alone for long." We can be certain that some meanings of any genre for those who participate in it depend on how it fits or contrasts with others,

FIGURE 11.5. Gol Nabāt, the only woman *baxši* in Iranian Khorasan, with her *dotār*. Photographed by Ameneh Youssefzadeh, January 10, 2006, Bojnurd, Khorasan.

even if we are not able to estimate the extent to which a participant's experience is shaped by one or another version of a genre system. The same can be said for each repertoire of performance roles, ceremonies, instruments, voice types, melody types, rhythmic frameworks, or textures.

Ramanujan's strategy for describing a genre system was to outline "an *akam-puram,* or domestic-public spectrum of folk genres in a Kannada village" (1986, 46), adopting the fundamental dichotomy of classical Tamil poetics, which is commonly glossed as "inner" versus "outer" or "amorous" versus "heroic" (see Ramanujan 1985; also see Parthasarathy 1993, 281–88). The more public a genre, the more props are used, the less restricted the audience, the more specialized the performers, and so on. Other contrasts in the system are binary oppositions, such as performance by women or by men, and absence or presence of names in the verses or narrative. Richard Wolf's analysis of Kota ceremonies likewise describes a system by positing two opposing orientations, which he calls centripetal and centrifugal, for the two main ceremonies, respectively "god" (*devr*) and "death" (*tāv*) (Wolf 2000/2001b, 165). An important corollary of the opposition between the "complementary notions of unity/sameness/equality and difference/disjuncture" is the greater variety of affects experienced during the two funeral ceremonies, with their focus on differentiation (Wolf 2001, 388). Wolf's table of "Kota Genres of Performance and Contexts" is constructed so as to facilitate discussion of "the kinds of dynamism that take place every time a ritual is performed" (Wolf 2001, 393, 414). In his essay in this book he points out that the opposition of two types of ceremony is articulated and signaled by the different warm-up gestures performed by *koḷ* players.

A list of the skills needed by one kind of performer or a list of the constituents of an art or genre can be understood as a system whose components are identified so that they can be coordinated in an appropriate manner. Some such lists became canonical in theoretical writings—the ancient Greek trinity of *harmonia, rhythmos,* and *logos,* its various Arabic derivatives, and its Sanskrit counterparts such as *svara,* tala, and *pada.* Once such rosters have been drawn up, debate on the appropriate relations between the terms or categories listed may well continue for millennia, as did the arguments about harmony in relation to words that are so prominent in Western music history.[15]

A standard roster of requisite skills is often fundamental to a shared conception of a performer's role. The Azerbaijani *aşıq* should master five skills: poetry, singing, playing the long-necked lute called *saz,* dancing, and animating the assembly. No Khorasani *baxši* would include dancing in a list of essential skills; the *baxši*'s necessary attributes are said to be good diction (*bayān*), a good voice (*sedā*), and a good hand (*dast*) for playing the *dotār* (Youssefzadeh 2002a, 58). This mode of theorizing may turn up in the introduction to a performance, for instance in the opening invocation of a Dholā (a type of oral epic sung in western Uttar Pradesh and eastern Rajasthan that combines song, chant, and prose) that Susan Wadley quotes from a performance by Ram Swarup Kachi in western Uttar Pradesh (Wadley 1989, 75): "Oh (Goddess), I have need of four things: beat, throat, voice, and wisdom" (*Cāri cīz mange mile: tāl kanth svar gyān*).

A minimal system might consist of a pair of terms related by the supposition that one or the other obtains in all pertinent instances (though it is usually more convenient to speak of systems made up of more than one such pair). Mark Slobin (1976, 164) quotes a Paštun musician of Faizabad, the main town of the Afghan province of Badakhshan: "Baba Naim... once told me that all music is divided into *raft* ('going') and *āmad* ('coming'), and that the amad is the more stable and important of the two." Baba Naim describes an asymmetrical polarity, in which one term is "the more stable and important." Another way of making much the same point is to give one name to those parts of a performance that function as returns (e.g., Persian *forud,* Balochi *er ārag,* and Turkish *inmek,* all meaning "descent") and to give several names or none at all to the departures. Anyone who speaks of a "return" is acknowledging the possibility or actuality of departures, whether or not a general term for "departure" (such as *raft*) is available.

To the best of my knowledge, the *raft*/*āmad* polarity rarely figures in Persian discourse about music.[16] A far more common pair of terms that articulates a similar set of relationships is *sowāl-javāb,* question and response. Some Azerbaijani musicians use these terms, borrowed from Persian, in describing relationships among phrases and larger units in the Azerbaijani *muğam* (Čelebiev 1989, 141). For the Khorasani *baxši,* the terms refer to several types of interaction. In the conversation that began with the remark quoted earlier, 'Ali Āqā described question-response exchanges that are pertinent to the *baxši*'s training, performances, and repertoire. His remarks about four situations can be summarized as follows:

1. Two *baxšis*, each holding his *dotār,* sit face to face and answer one another's questions until one of them gains the upper hand (*bālā-dast*) when his opponent is unable to respond.
2. A master (*ostād*) gives instruction (*dars ta'lim*) "in phrases of this question-answer [format] (*dar ebārat-e hamun sowāl-e javāb*)" to the pupils who are sitting before him, using poems that illustrate the format well, such as "Twenty-Nine Letters" (*Bist o now huruf,* sung in Khorasani Turkish despite its Persian name); two pupils may sit face to face and exchange questions and answers until one gains the upper hand.
3. In addition to "Twenty-Nine Letters," other poems in the *baxši* repertoire are structured as exchanges of questions and answers—for example, a debate between earth and sky, which is settled when God tells the sky not to claim superiority over the earth.[17]
4. In the Turkic narratives that constitute the heart of the *baxši* repertoire, two lovers who are sitting face to face may exchange questions and responses. "Apart from them, no one else [in the stories] asks such questions." Exchanges of this kind occur in the stories of Karam and Asli, Tāher and Zohre, Ma'sum and Afruzpari, Šāh Bahrām and Banu Hosne Parizād, among others. (Stories that do not provide enough opportunities for such exchanges are unsatisfactory, according to another *baxši.*)

Like the earth and the sky in their debate, the lovers who exchange strophes are doing what a *baxši* has also learned how to do: they sing in response to song, using conventional melody types.[18] The terms *sowāl* and *javāb* are equally pertinent to exchanges in which a *baxši* participates and to exchanges he enacts or represents in performance. For the most part *baxšis* reenact responses presumed to have been made at other times and places—by characters in a narrative, by authors of the verses or melody types they have memorized, or by themselves on earlier occasions. Although exchanges in which two singers compete to gain the upper hand are not now as common or as public in Khorasan as in some regions of Central Asia, the *baxši*'s repertoire and performance idiom bear many traces of the long history of singing contests among Turkic peoples (see, further, Zemtsovsky 1993). Khorasani *baxšis* remember competitions in which the loser would have his head shaved and the winner would take the loser's *dotār* (perhaps returning it later if he were feeling generous).

Questions are not the only kind of stimulus that may elicit or require a musical response. Hence, the term *javāb* has a much broader extension than does *sowāl;*

in other words, musical actions that were not prompted by sung questions may be considered "responses" all the same (see, further, Blum 1996).[19] *Javāb-e āvāz* is an important category of improvised responses, made by instrumentalists to singers during performances of Persian classical music. In earlier performances, each musician will have heard and performed many realizations of a given phrase, none of which is necessarily closer than others to a definitive model. The realizations singers produce on a given occasion are events to which instrumentalists react, not models they are obliged to emulate.

Sung poetry normally has a dual aspect in Khorasan: singers respond to various incentives and challenges in the immediate context of performance while at the same time representing or reenacting responses presumed to have been made at other times and places—by characters in a narrative, by authors of the verses or melodies performed (some of which the performer may wish to claim), or by this performer on earlier occasions. Possibilities for a single performer to bring together multiple voices at the moment of performance have been richly developed in Iran and Central Asia, as is evident from the emphasis laid on memorization in so many practices, and from rhythmic analysis of sung poetry (Blum 2003). Most solo performances by Khorasani *baxšis*, and by many other bards, represent processes of exchange and interaction; those who listen to such representations could hardly avoid interpreting them with reference to remembered and anticipated exchanges they had experienced or could imagine as possible.

Returning to 'Ali Āqā's remark on the *baxši*'s knowledge and to my figure 11.1, it is clearly necessary to read the heading "musician's knowledge (as internally organized)" as denoting a transitory result of the musician's socialization: what musicians know at any given moment is a product of the exchanges or interactions in which they have participated as well as of their past enactments or representations of interactions.

CHAPTER 12

Zahīrok

The Musical Base of Baloch Minstrelsy

SABIR BADALKHAN

Zahīrok is both a genre of song expressing loss or absence (especially of distant loved ones) and a general term for several melody types used in narrative song (*šeyr*) performance.[1] The term derives from the word *zahīr,* meaning "yearning, longing for, homesick, heartsick," and so on, and has come to mean a lament for one's homeland or a song of yearning for one's family (see Elfenbein 1990, 2:164).[2] According to some Baloch, the term *zahīrok* is composed of the words *zahīr* and *rok* ("burning"), which accounts for an additional meaning: a song "coming from the burning heart of a yearning person."

Some believe that *zahīrok* originated from the cuckooing of the wood pigeon (*kapot/kahnī*). The story is that a man from Makran traveled to Sind, a fertile country whose greenery contrasted the barrenness of the Baloch land. There a wood pigeon, perched on a tree, was singing yearning songs in a wailing tone. The man asked why it was wailing in such a land of paradise. The bird missed its homeland, Makran. This is the source of the famous Balochi proverb, "one wails for the homeland even if it is as dry as a piece of dry wood" (*wāe watan u huškẽn dār*). The bird's melody gave rise to the *zahīrok* genre and from that, all types of Balochi songs and music.

In this chapter I investigate the texts, contexts, and performance characteristics associated with the *zahīrok* genre. Because Baloch understand the *zahīrok* to be at the very foundation of their "local"—that is to say, southern Balochistan—musical tradition, it is an ideal point of departure for considering what it means for the Baloch to "theorize" about music and musical experience. Balochistan straddles the modern republics of Pakistan and Iran; it is our bridge for considering traditions that flow across and beyond the borders of South Asia.

FIGURE 12.1. *Pahlawān* Mullah Saleh sings and performs on the *dambūrag*. Photographed by Sabir Badalkhan, Shahi Tump, Turbat, Pakistan, September 2003.

Only Baloch of the Makran region (Pakistan and Iran) and in the city of Karachi know *zahīrok* tunes, although songs such as *līko* expressing similar sentiments and states of mind have also been recorded in neighboring regions.[3] Lorraine Sakata reports on the *falak* song genre, which is popular in the northeastern areas of Badakhshan and Kataghan in Afghanistan. People in Badakhshan describe *falak*s as being sad (*ghamghin*), expressing "a longing for a lover, friends, family, and home." *Falak*s are also melody types of some five identifiable varieties, including one called *zahiri* (sad, melancholy) (Sakata 1983, 53–59; cf. Slobin 1970, 98). Both genres express similar states of mind and have relatively similar singing styles, though the Balochi *zahīrok* is apparently more elaborate and developed. The *gharībī* song genre of Iran also shares subject matter and singing style with the Balochi *zahīrok* and the Afghani and Tajik *falak*. The *gharībī* (< *gharīb*, "a stranger or outsider") in Iran "gives voice to yearning for a home that has been lost or abandoned" (Blum 2002, 829; see also Cejpek [1968, 608] regarding Tajik *gharībī*).[4] The *gharībī* song genre, with similar connotations, is also found in Sistan, northeastern Iran (Weryho 1962, 292) as well as in Kurdistan.[5]

Zahīrok as a Song Genre

Zahīrok songs are strongly melancholic, expressing deep emotions and strong sentiments about separation: feelings of those who are away from home traveling or in search of labor; deep yearnings of women left behind by their sons, husbands, brothers and/or fathers; the sense of suffering women express over performing heavy chores for client families (in the case of maid-servants) or such repetitive tasks as grinding grain with a hand mill or weaving carpets or quilts on a loom.

Zahīrok and *līko* songs were the only company of camel-drivers in their long journeys.[6] In earlier times, Baloch traveled, traded, and transported goods on camelback. People spent weeks, and even months, traveling from one major town to another or from one region to another. As a travel song, *zahīrok* is almost exclusively related to camel drivers; travelers riding other beasts, such as horses or donkeys, do not sing them. Perhaps this is because people say the *zahīrok* (like the *līko* of the northern and northeastern dialect) in melody and rhythm matches the camel's gait and movements.

Another theory is offered by the Baloch scholar Gul Khan Nasir, who believes that *zahīroks* were originally women's compositions.[7] He maintains that women sang *zahīroks* for their menfolk who were away from home and family fighting tribal wars, exchanging commodities, or searching for pastures (1979, 12, 61).

Singing Technique

When solitary workers or cameleers sing *zahīroks*, the poem is usually in couplets with a third line acting as a refrain; it may also have a two-line refrain with a single line added at the end. Refrains usually follow a couplet or line but occasionally precede them. When the refrain comes first, the singer renders it in a melismatic style. Singers sometime take five to eight minutes, repeating lines and letting the *suroz* (bowed stringed instrument) repeat the whole one or more times before joining the *suroz* and singing the last line. The lyrics of a *zahīrok* describe deep nostalgic feelings of longing and yearning in such a strong melancholic style that they penetrate one's inner feelings. Baloch say that the *surozī* (*suroz* player) often makes his instrument cry.

One person sings a couplet, the second joins in the singing of the refrain and then sings another couplet, then the third joins in the refrain and sings another couplet, and so on. It is never sung in chorus. No instruments accompany *zahīrok* when women sing while working, when men sing while riding their camels, or when they plow land or collect dates. But when professional *zahīrok* singers (*pahlawān*) sit and perform for entertainment, they are ideally accompanied by a *suroz*. Less famous or amateur singers may also sing to the accompaniment of a *beynjo* (a keyed zither), *nal* (flute), or *surnā* (shawm). Baluch say that *zahīrok*s were originally sung with the exclusive accompaniment of a *suroz*, or played on a *suroz* alone. [**Audio examples 12.1 and 12.2**] Since *suroz* is the preferred accompaniment instrument for *zahīrok*, all *suroz* players should know some of their melodies. This is the test for any *suroz* player: in the first encounter with a *surozī*, people will ask him to establish his level of command of Balochi art music by playing some *zahīrok*s. Occasionally, singing with the *suroz* is further accompanied by a *dambūrag* (a fretless lute), which the player strums delicately. When a *suroz* player performs without a vocalist, no other instrument accompanies him.

Singers

Singers of *zahīrok* in the working context may come from any social background. The best known nonprofessional female *zahīrok* singers in Makran, however, belong to a low social class called *molid* (maid-servant), traditionally associated with performing housework for a family. These *molid*s had to grind grain for a large family of their masters as well as for their guests (cf. Hashmi 1986, 111). Each day they would start grinding grain at about three or four in the morning (only a few hours after they would finish the work of the day before, such as washing dishes and clothes) with the millstone (*jintir*), whose heavy weight was often compared with that of a hill (*kohen jintir*, lit., "hill-like millstone"), and continued until daybreak, when they had to prepare breakfast, which was usually not less than a normal lunch, for the family of their masters.

These *molid*s were mainly from low social classes, probably descendants of former slaves of African origin; however, such domestic servants also came from other low social groups. Baloch believe that God endowed them with sweet voices, which, under the burden of heavy tasks, allowed them to sing *zahīrok*s expressing the whole picture of their sufferings and hard life. In this context, *zahīrok* was a song of purgation as well as a strong means of catharsis that accompanied their work on the one hand and provided them with a means to express their sufferings on the other. It was also a means to make the people of the neighborhood share their sufferings. They accompanied their work of grinding grain with such melodious and touching melancholic *zahīrok*s that sometimes whole villages would wake up to listen to their singing. Their sweet voices on the one hand, and their life full of suffering and hardship on the other hand, together with the weepy nature of *zahīrok* songs, made the atmosphere so touching that people began to cry (cf. Hashmi 1986, 111). I was told, for example, that the *molid* of the Sardars of Sami (a village some fifty kilometers east of Turbat) had such a sweet voice and such a vast repertoire of *zahīroks* that each morning she would wake up the whole village with her melodies.[8]

Besides the *molids* who worked for the families of their masters, women of other communities too (i.e., not of low class) had to grind grain for their families. As they also had other tasks, either in the house or in the fields (or herding baby goats/sheep if they were nomads), the best time for grinding grain was, again, early in the morning. Usually two women would ease their burdens by singing *zahīroks* and grinding grain together—first of one and then of the other. The melodies of the *zahīroks* were said to follow the movements of the *jintir* (hand-millstone). Women from all walks of life could sing *zahīroks* in Baloch society, which was otherwise strict about women singing loudly or otherwise appearing in public. Most women should sing only on such festive occasions as the birth of a child, circumcisions, and weddings. Even then, they should sing in groups; the only exceptions are lullabies and religious songs, which can be sung in private, provided men are not present. Other kinds of singing and dancing are appropriate only for women of low social classes.

Until the early 1970s, camel drivers routinely sang *zahīroks* in the morning, especially during the summer, when the date and rice harvests in Makran stimulated trade and travel. In the pleasant early-morning weather, the drivers were lively and exuberant, singing as they passed by settlements during the early hours of the day. The cameleers would take turns: the person riding on the lead camel sang the first couplet, then the second one joined him, singing with the last hemistich or the refrain, and then sang another couplet; then the third joined and followed with another, and so on. They followed other patterns as well: the man riding on the lead camel would sing the first couplet; the last cameleer would join in on the refrain and add a couplet, then the second cameleer from the front would sing and then the second one from the back, and so on. Most often there would be tens of camels, and every cameleer would sing in his turn, often improvising the song and adding more couplets, keeping roughly the refrain only. In the pin-drop silence of the early hours of dawn, along with the jingling of bells tied around the necks of camels, the singing of *zahīroks* created such a wonderful atmosphere that sometimes the whole village would wake up to listen to them. I was told that on many occasions some music-loving people followed caravans of camels for miles just to listen to *zahīroks*. Now traders move goods by truck rather than by camel. Rather than the jingling of bells around the necks of camels and the *zahīroks* of cameleers, one hears instead Hindi film songs played loudly from powerful loudspeakers fixed in front of trucks or buses. These songs are heard miles away. The vehicles arrive much later, descending from one hillock and ascending another one, running on dirt roads with huge stones and dry river beds.

A similar atmosphere was also created by farmers working in their fields. During the paddy-growing season (April-May) men start plowing as early as about five in the morning—as soon as there is enough light. Commonly, in the past, one farmer would start singing a *zahīrok* from his field while plowing. and another in a nearby field would respond with another *zahīrok* or would add a couplet. In a short time the whole oasis would echo with farmers joining in to sing from all sides. This type of singing also functioned to soothe the bullocks, who responded more willingly to the heavy burden in the company of singing men. The same was repeated during the date harvest, when one farmer from the top of a date tree started singing a *zahīrok,* soon joined by another one, then by another. All such practices have been discontinued, and we can only speculate why. I believe that, beginning in the 1970s with the economic uplift and weakening of class stratification in Baluchistan, such singing has been on the decline because it is considered low class. In the not-so-distant past even Baloch from upper social backgrounds sang work songs without any reservations; in modern times people from low social classes consider it shameful to sing in public unless they are professional or amateur singers.

*Zahīrok*s are generally made of couplets with irregular rhymes and more or less fixed refrains. In some cases, such as the following, poets have composed *zahīrok*s

FIGURE 12.2. Surozī Ostad Omar accompanies, on *suroz*, the *šeyr*-singing of *pahlawān* Mullah Saleh. They perform *zahīrok* melodies. Ostad Omar is considered one of the greatest living instrumentalists who perform *zahīrok*s. Photographed by Sabir Badalkhan, Shahi Tump, Turbat, Pakistan, September 2003.

to be sung as whole poems, normally in a working context, especially by women grinding on their millstones, doing embroidery, or working on looms. The texts of all Balochi folksongs are subject to improvisation (cf. Badalkhan 2002, 302 n2) and this is also true for *zahīrok*s in couplets. As in the following examples, not all *zahīrok*s talk of travel, homesickness, and yearning. Some develop themes of love. Being basically a melancholic song, singers always sing *zahīrok*s from the very depths of their hearts.

dil khayāle pa gonage kārīt
dil manā bārt u dīr pirrenīt,
dil manā pešī trānagān gejīt,
konṛumā jant čo banden naryānā,
girr bandīt čo gwānzagī tiflā,
čo ṛāčīā danzīt pa watī hirrā,
još kārīt čo roden lohīā. (Nasir 1979, 62)

My heart brings a remembrance to me in a strange way,
My heart takes and throws me far away,
My heart brings to me the memory of past days,
It [becomes so stubborn that it] stampedes like a fastened stallion,
It demands stubbornly [the lover] like a baby in its cradle,
Like she-camels who kick dust [calling] for their baby camels,
It boils like a bronze pot.

Another beautiful *zahīrok* runs as follows:

zahīr manī baššāmī draden hawr ant,
ki dāimā grewān ant manī čammān,
hič manā naylant pa šapī wābā,
šap manī sāl ant, roč manī šaš māh,
šap manī sālen na bant bāmgāh,
roč manī tīrmāhī tap ant trunden. (Nasir 1979, 64)

My *zahīr* are like heavy showers of monsoon rains,
They always pour down from my weeping eyes,
They never allow me to have a night's sleep,
My nights are as long as full years, and my days are as long as half years,
My year-long nights never see a dawn,
My days are like the burning fevers of early summer months.[9]

The following are a few examples from a famous *zahīrok* in Makran, as sung by the renowned *zahīrok* singer Amir Jusakki, from a village near Turbat. It describes a famous event when a ship carrying passengers from Gwadar to Muscat caught fire and was wrecked, resulting in the death of all passengers. This incident probably occurred in the 1950s, when Gwadar was still under the rule of the Sultanate of Oman. (Several other heart-breaking *zahīrok*s and *motk*s [dirges] also recount this event.) A few couplets of this *zahīrok* show how the refrain is used.

bačč manī sargiptag mazārbīmmen,
deme dātag man Maškatā šūmmen,
kādirey nūr manī baččī taī bāhoṭ int.

My son of the wrath of a lion has prepared [for the journey],
He has started [the journey] to the damning Muscat,
O, the light of the Protector, my son is under your protection.

yā hudāwand u kirdagār šāhen,
malkamūt seylānī [bali nīn] šikārā int,
u keyt hamā arwāhey sarā nindīt,
gwānzagī tiplān ča mādarān sindīt,
kādirey nūr manī baččī taī bāhoṭ int.

O God, the King and Creator,
The watchful Angel of Death is out hunting [for victims],
He comes and sits on the spirit [i.e., on lives],
He separates babies in cradles from their mothers (i.e., he is too cruel and merciless),
O, the light of the Protector, my son is under your protection.

Zahīrok as a Term for "Melody Types"

When cameleers or women at work sing *zahīrok* songs, they may use a single melody or several different ones. But *zahīrok* is also a term for the melodies of *zahīrok* songs, and more abstractly, for melody types. Two Baloch musicians from Karachi, Abdul Rahman Surizai (who is a master of *beynjo*) and Karim Bakhsh Nuri (a *suroz* player) led Jean During to represent *zahīrok* as a kind of incipient classical music: "a significant point is that in the same way that knowledge of the *zahirig*-s as modes serves to increase the competence of a singer or instrumentalist at the height of one's mastery, the *zahirigi*-s are considered as the essence of Baluchi music, i.e., its very principle (*asil*), the matrices of all the melodies, tunes or songs" (1997, 41). Likewise, Baloch men with some knowledge of the tradition often argue that *zahīrok* is the basis of all Balochi music and the essence of the melodies used in singing Balochi narrative song (*šeyr*).[10] Janmahmad, a Baloch writer from Dasht in Makran, maintains, moreover, that "the entire Balochi musical structure is based on *zaheerag*. Some of the folk-music appears to be somewhat different from it, but in their formal structure all musical derivatives have their base in *Zaheerag*" (1982, 59–60).

According to Baloch *pahlawāns* (professional *šeyr* singers), narrative songs (*šeyrs*) comprise tunes that derive from different *zahīroks*. Each part of a *šeyr* has a different message. Some sections are to be sung with different *zahīroks*. In this view, there are *zahīrok* tunes to express any sentiment or state of mind. As a rule, only certain parts of a *šeyr* are sung in *zahīroks* while other parts are sung in different styles, such as *gālreč* (rapid singing without melisma), *dapgāl* (singing in a low register without melisma) and others (see Badalkhan 1994, 147–49). *Pahlawāns* often begin a *šeyr* with an appropriate *zahīrok,* and they usually mark shifts of scene with a *čīhāl*—a free-rhythmic vocal section accompanied by *suroz*—which is in a specific *zahīrok*. [**Audio example 12.3**] The *čīhāl* is an important way of capturing the listeners' attention as well as an indication for the scene shift. Audiences highly appreciate virtuosity, and if a *pahlawān* has a smooth tenor voice with a good knowledge of *zahīroks*, and when he lingers for a long time on a melisma, he is showered with "*šābāš*" and "*wāh wāh*" ("bravo"), and some music lovers in the audience express their appreciation with shrieking shouts and yells.[11]

Being the richest body of Balochi music, *zahīrok* is also the most complex. Not all *suroz* players and minstrels are capable of playing or singing many *zahīroks*. *Suroz* players who perform with *pahlawāns* are expected to be able to play most of the well-known *zahīroks*, while those who do not play for *pahlawāns* have less need even to know *zahīroks* by name. *Suroz* players claim that it takes from ten to thirty years of experience before one is able to play the most common *zahīroks* in full without confusing one with another. In fact, few living *suroz* players can play certain *zahīroks* in full; many, however, can name the most common ones without being able to play them correctly.

Every *zahīrok* has a beginning section called a "picking up" (*čist kanag*) and a rising section called a "carrying up" (*burzā barag*). Once the *zahīrok* has reached its "peak" (*burzī*), the *pahlawān* and/or *surozī* must "bring it down" (*er ārag*) in a prescribed manner in order to conclude or "kill" (*kušag*) the *zahīrok*. [**Audio examples 12.1–12.3**]

Every *zahīrok* has certain vocal/instrumental modulations, and the performer/singer is expected to follow them strictly. If a *pahlawān* or *surozī* does not respect the accepted standards people may shout at them or the singer and the performer may rebuke each other for combining *zahīroks* (cf. Badalkhan 1994, 166).[12] The communication process between *pahlawān* and *surozī* creates a need for *zahīroks* to be named.[13] Usually all *pahlawāns* of some fame have their own *surozīs* who understand their style and mood, and famous *pahlawāns* do not perform with the accompaniment of other *surozīs*.

The vocal-instrumental *zahīrok* in performances of *šeyr* differs from the *zahīrok* as a song genre in the following respects. Foremost is the *čīhāl,* which is highly melismatic and expressive, sung either to a line of poetry or on a single vowel or

FIGURE 12.3. Rasul Bakhsh Zangishahi (from Iranian Makran) plays *zahīrok* and sings *šeyr* melodies. He is accompanied by Shahan Bugti (center) from Dera Bugti and Allaidad, son of Rasul Bakhsh Zangishahi. Rasul Baksh Zangishahi is considered one of the greatest living instrumentalists who perform *zahīroks*. Photographed by Sabir Badalkhan, Paris, June 1996.

several vocables. A *zahīrok* always begins with *čīhāl,* which is followed by a small number of lines, some of which are normally repeated. The shift from *čīhāl* to verses is marked by the introduction of a steady beat, which the *pahlawān* keeps by strumming on the *dambūrag* as he sings. *Čīhāl* is always in a high register, and the verses are sung in a lower and narrower register. The *suroz* player begins the *čīhāl* and is joined by the singer. It is as if the *suroz* player takes the singer's hand for climbing a mountain, but the singer takes the lead as soon as he enters, and the *surozī* echoes his phrases. When they have reached the peak of the singer's vocal range, the singer rests a while as the *surozī* continues to ascend. The *surozī* reverses the melodic direction, the singer reenters and takes the lead as they begin the descent. They come down together, and the singer finishes first while the *surozī* continues to descend into the lower register. A *pahlawān* with a good knowledge of *zahīroks* may sing the same lines several times and hang around for up to twenty or more minutes before going on with the *šeyr.* In all these cases the singer is accompanied by the *surozī,* and sometimes this latter repeats the whole *zahīrok* more than once on the *suroz.* It is easier for a *surozī* to accompany a *pahlawān* than to play a purely instrumental *zahīrok,* because in the latter he continues to play in high register rather than subordinating himself to the singer at the melodic climax.[14]

FIGURE 12.4. Ostad Omar Surozī (village Sur, district Gwadar). Photographed by Sabir Badalkhan, Shahi Tump, Turbat, Pakistan, September 2003.

As *zahīrok* is the most important variety of music in southwestern Balochistan, we find different types related to different regions, to different types of work and conditions, taking names of famous singers and musicians, as well as referring to certain states of mind. As the number of expert *zahīrok* players and singers has declined, the actual number of *zahīrok* tunes is difficult to establish. Some put the number at thirty-six;[15] others put it even higher. Someone suggested that there are four main types, related to the four different parts (*pās*) of the night, with tens of other subtypes.[16] Here I list thirty different types that musicians in Balochistan have named over the years. However, this list is far from complete.

All of my *pahlawān* informants agreed that the night is divided into different parts, and each part has its particular *zahīrok*. Basham, one of the most famous *pahlawāns*, inherited the art of minstrelsy from his father, who was a *suroz* player before becoming a *pahlawān* himself. Basham was his father's *surozī* until his father died; then Basham became a *pahlawān*. Basham told me that in the early hours of the night he sings with the melodies of *kurdī, baločī, baškardī,* and other *zahīroks* of low register because these are good to warm the throat as well as the strings of the *suroz;* the *zahīroks* of midnight are *medī, kūkkār,* and others from the same group; while the *zahīroks* sung after three in the morning are *ašrap-i durrā, ṭaṭ,* and others of the high register.

Zahīrok names derive largely from:

1. terms for different parts of the night (*šapey pās*), such as *saršapey* ("of early night"), *nembangāmey* ("of midnight"), *gwarbāmey* ("of early dawn"), or *bāmey* ("of dawn")
2. regional or tribal names[17] with an attributive *ī* suffix, such as *baškardī* ("of Bashkard" in southwestern Iran), *rodbārī* ("of Rudbar"), *jahlāwānī* ("of Jahlawan" in central Balochistan), *sarhaddī* ("of Sarhadd" in Iranian Balochistan),[18] or *baločī* ("of Baloch"),[19] *jadgāley* ("of the Jadgāl" tribe in Makran), *sāsolī* (named after the Sasoli tribe in Pakistani Balochistan), *kurdī* ("of Kurds"; possibly named after the Kurd tribe in Balochistan), *kiblaī* ("western" regions of Balochistan), and *zirkanikkī* ("coastal").
3. the names of singers who introduced new *zahīrok* tunes, for example, *ašrap-i durrā* (named after a famous *zahīrok* singer who came from the Gichki family of Kech, Makran)[20] and *begamī* (after Begam, a nineteenth- to twentieth-century woman *zahīrok* singer from Gwadar).
4. terms for the strings of a *suroz*,[21] for example, *ṭaṭ* (the first string from the upper side, facing the player, also called *ṭīpp*), *myānag* (the middle string, also called *zīll* or *dastgard*), *gor u bām* (*gor* is the gut string and the third in sequence, while *bām* is the fourth and the lowest string); or named after a musical instrument with the possessive *-ey* ("of"), such as *surnā-ey* ("of shawm," which is said to had been invented by a shawm player in response to Ashrap-i Durra) and *gurr-ey* ("of conch/shell instrument").
5. various other aspects, such as context, typical performer, or style, for example, *uštir-ey* ("of camel," sung by cameleers, also called *sārbān-ey*, "of cameleer's"), *jintir-ey* ("of hand-millstone," sung by women while grinding grain), *balluk-ey* ("grand mother's," sung by aged women to show their sufferings under hard working conditions or for their absent sons), *janozām-ey* ("of the widow"), *medī* ("of Med fishermen"), *kūkkār* ("of shouting," which shows the style of the *zahīrok*), *jagarsind* ("heart-rending"), and *salāt-ey* ("of the call to prayers").

Pahlawān and *surozī* informants whom I have interviewed argue that most of these *zahīrok*s have subtypes: *baločī* has *šahr baločī* and *irānī baločī* as subtypes; *kurdī* has *kurdī* and *šahr kurdī* as its subtypes.[22] The legendary *pahlawān* Faiz Mahmad Baloch [**Audio example 12.3**] once said in an interview that there are more than two hundred *zahīrok* tunes (Shad [1998] 2000, 252).[23] Faiz Mahmad was endowed with an hypnotizing tenor voice, ideal for *zahīrok* singing. As a great master of *pahlawān* minstrelsy tradition, he was well aware of the importance of *zahīrok* tunes in Balochi *šeyr* singing, so he would often tell his audience which *zahīrok* he was singing in that particular part of a *šeyr*. As the best time for *zahīrok* singing is in the last hours of the night, Faiz Mahmad would hypnotize his audience with his *zahīrok*s when dawn was approaching. In that part of a night-long performance, a *pahlawān* sings a *šeyr* passing from one *zahīrok* to another. At this stage, the strings of the *suroz* are fully warmed, the audience is selective, and the singing reaches its highest peak.[24] People describe this type of singing as *pahlawānā čīhāl pa čīhāl kutag* (that is, the *pahlawān* is now singing *čīhāl* after *čīhāl,* that is, repeated singing in a virtuoso melismatic style in *zahīroks*).

Zahīrok is one of the most important and well-known song genres as well as the most elaborated music of the Baloch, often described as the "Balochi classical music" by the Baloch themselves. It is also the richest music with respect to its varieties and regional types. At the same time, like the rest of Balochi music and songs, it has not been recorded systematically or studied properly so far.[25]

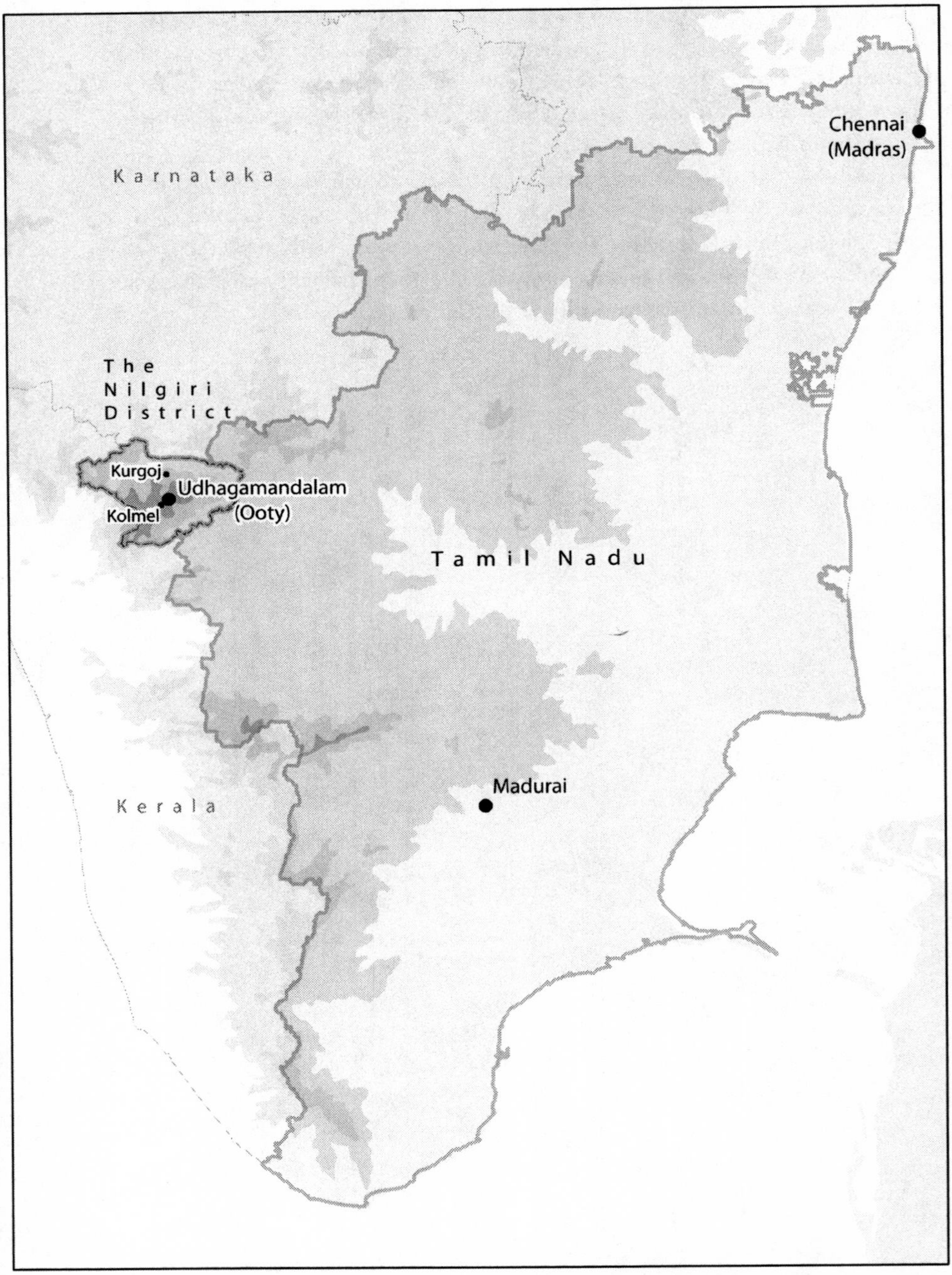
Karnataka
Chennai
(Madras)
The
Nilgiri
District
Kurgoj
Udhagamandalam
(Ooty)
Kolmel
Tamil Nadu
Madurai
Kerala

CHAPTER 13

Varṇams and Vocalizations

The Special Status of Some Musical Beginnings

RICHARD K. WOLF

A beginning in Indian music has no specific locus, no precise moment—it is pure emergence and arises from a continuous and undivided substratum of internal sound. . . . [M]usical beginnings reflect (albeit in a very naive way) the more general concept of beginning held by the parent culture.

—Lewis Rowell (1981, 207, 209)

Here lies the major obstacle to recognizing indigenous theorizing for what it is: we have become hubristially accustomed to recognizing "theory" by a particular and often unattractively pompous kind of language—a special case of the logical error of misplaced concreteness.

—Michael Herzfeld (2002, 189)

Certain kinds of beginnings have the potential to foreshadow, suggest, portend, or otherwise have implications for the future. They may function as something akin to models or theories, they may index models and theories, or they may trigger "assessments" that index indigenous theories (see O'Hanlon 1992). At minimum, beginnings may serve as food for thought, stimulating cogitation and discourse among members of a social group. The problem of musical beginnings is a subset of the larger question of why events happen when they do in a sequence, and relates to the general problem how events acquire meaning by virtue of their syntactical positions.

In this chapter I will follow the lead of a number of authors (Nettl 1987; Rowell 1981; Wong and Lysloff 1991) in asking what is to be learned from certain kinds of musical beginnings.[1] In the epigraph, a few strong statements of Rowell, juxtaposed with an assertion of Michael Herzfeld's on the logocentricity of what gets counted as "theory," are meant to stimulate the following questions: What can musical beginnings tell us about indigenous theorizing? In what ways might local forms of theory be embodied in a musical beginning? What are the cultural implications of musical beginnings and how deep do they run?

I shall approach these questions through three sets of case studies: 1) the well-known south Indian classical genre, the *varṇam;* 2) the contextually varying procedures whereby the south Indian Kota community gets ready to play an instrumental piece; and 3) the prefacing of a piece, or a section thereof, with vocables. The three share their status as gestures of beginning and their special roles in pointing to what comes next, but lack similarity in magnitude, musical sound, immediate function, or cultural context. The following treatment, therefore, is uneven; let this not prevent us from asking questions about these data, even if they seem strangely juxtaposed.

Doing Things with Music: The Varṇam and Other Key Genres

In 1982, when first learning to play the *vīṇā* (a stringed instrument from south India) I asked, "What is a *varṇam*"? My teacher's rather free-spoken daughter, Sashi, consulted her family members about this genre, which she was teaching me at the time, and said: "a *varṇam* gives the performer more ideas for improvising (*rāga ālāpana* and *svara kalpana*) than does a *kriti* [another genre]." Any Karnatak musician might have offered this explanation, which seemed circular to me at the time. A more useful answer, I later thought, would have delineated the structure of a *varṇam* (which usually contains more subsections than do *kritis*) and explained the musical characteristics of each of its sections and subsections.

Both the answer she gave and the one I might have wanted at the time point to the fact that each subsection of a *varṇam* exemplifies a set of different melodic and rhythmic possibilities.[2] Performers explore them, consciously or unconsciously, when they improvise. More parts give the *varṇam* more to "say" about a raga in a given metrical (tala) framework. For south Indian classical musicians, then, the *varṇam* embodies a configuration of relationships which serves as a particularly rich resource for "theorizing" in the sense developed by Blum in this volume.

Since the *varṇam* is a "beginning" in some time sequences and occupies a medial position in others, we should devote some attention to each: the course of musical training, the routine of daily practice, and the performance of a concert.

Elements and Sequences in Musical Training

From a young age, students of Karnatak music study exercises and practice pieces, which they must master before moving on to actual concert repertoire (*sabhā gāna*).[3] South Indians reflect upon their training system in various ways. With regard to length of study, for example, some teachers are criticized for holding students at this practice stage for many years; others are considered irresponsible for not instilling the fundamentals strongly enough. Musical values essential to one individual or school of musical practice (Tamil: *pāṇi*), some maintain, are distilled in these early exercises and pieces.

The first of these fundamentals consist of *saraḷi varicai* ("series of *svaras*"), a set of ascending and descending scales, and permutations of scale segments, of the raga *māyamāḷavagauḷa,* which is composed of seven ascending and descending *svaras*. *Svaras* are scale positions combined with context-sensitive oscillations, called *gamakas*. This raga is suitable for training, in part, because it contains the most common intervals: one half step, whole step, and an augmented second (for further discussion, see Sambamoorthy 1958, 1:56). Students learn the names (shortened forms) of each of the seven *svaras*, *sa ri ga ma pa dha ni sa,* and how to sing or play sequences of these *svaras* while keeping track of the tala (a metrical structure marked by claps and finger counts).

The second set of exercises, *jaṇṭa varicai* ("series of pairs"), consists of permutations of repeated *svaras*. This set of ten or more exercises gives the performer control in articulating musical phrases—on a consonant or a vowel, within a word, or during a melisma. The third set, called *alankāram* (lit., "decoration"), introduces the seven classes of tala, helping the practitioner remain confident in performing rhythmic permutations with respect to different metrical grounds.

The next element in the learning sequence is a type of strophic song, called *gītam,* which gives the student experience in repeating a melody while introducing subtle text-induced variations. Firm control over *gītams* early on may help students when they learn advanced forms of improvisation on lines of text (*niraval*). The first *gītam* contains a kind of structural beginning: it is often addressed to Pillaiyar, the elephant-faced god, son of Śiva, who presides over auspicious beginnings. All the exercises, including the *gītam* songs, are eventually sung/played in three speeds, each twice the speed of the previous one. Performing in multiple speeds solidifies rhythmic control and improves precision.

A good teacher would rarely advance a new student through these exercises in less than a full year. This is not an issue when a student begins young—some before five years of age—but may be an obstacle when experienced performers are made to start from the beginning. In the early 1950s, the late *vīṇā* maestro S. Balachandar (fig. 13.1) was said to have been enraged when he sought additional training from the famed Karaikkudi Sambasiva Iyer, who insisted that he begin with *saraḷi varicai*. Balachandar, insulted, reportedly stomped away in anger. Early exercises are one arena in which an individual or style has the opportunity to make a mark on a student. But this element of control may not be as effective with a student who has already begun training elsewhere.

Following the study of one or more *gītams*, the student advances to the *varṇam,* the pivotal transition point, or as the singer Kamala Ramamurthy put it, "bridge,"

FIGURE 13.1. S. Balachandar performing the *vīṇā* at the Tyāgarāja Utsavam in Tiruvaiyāṟu, Tamil Nadu, February 1983. Photograph by Richard K. Wolf.

between practice pieces and concert repertoire. With a new level of complication, the *varṇam* is rehearsed at an additional tempo, in which three notes of the melody are inserted in the interval of two. The performer is thereby forced to keep track very precisely of the rests (*kārvai*s), or distances between articulations. *Gamaka*s are also integrated more substantially. After learning at least a few *varṇam*s, a student is believed to have acquired the basic skills and knowledge to begin learning *kriti*s, the three-part songs that make up the bulk of the concert repertoire.

Rehearsal Sequences and the Concert Proper

This sense of gradation is replicated in an established tradition of rehearsal routines. Singers assiduously practice *saraḷi varicai, jaṇṭa varicai,* and so on, all the way up to *varṇam* using *svara* names and then vowels (*ākāra cātakam*) for articulation. After running through a *varṇam* in three speeds (tempo 1, 3/2 times tempo 1, and double tempo 1) a musician's morning warm-up is complete. This warm-up can last from one to three hours (very roughly); some musicians focus on particular exercises on alternate days.

Beginnings and endings are particularly important in Karnatak music concerts. One convention going back at least until the first third of the twentieth century has been to begin a concert with a *varṇam*.[4] (Now a concert may also begin with a *kriti* in an auspicious raga dedicated to the god Vināyakar, "remover of obstacles"). This is followed by a sequence of *kritis* contrasting in pitch-content, length, tempo, and tala. About halfway through the concert the performer renders the "main raga," with significant "scope" for improvisation, culminating in a substantial *kriti,* or a *pallavi* (a line of text treated in varying rhythmic and melodic configurations). After about forty-five minutes a drum solo (*tani āvartanam*) follows. The concert gradually concludes with "light" pieces—folk melodies, north Indian ragas, dance pieces, regional language songs, or film songs—the order of which is somewhat flexible. The final piece in the last concert of an evening belongs to a genre called *mangaḷam* (lit., "auspicious").

The *varṇam* integrates warming-up into the concert proper, serving as a concert-opener with its own aesthetic merits, and as a sign of what will to come later. Singers of the early to mid-twentieth century, including Ariyakudi Ramanuja Ayyangar and the Alattur brothers, used not only to embed the *varṇam* in the sequence of contrasts alluded to above but also to preview the raga to be explored in the concert's centerpiece. In this way, the *varṇam* prepared the performer, in mind and body (voice), for improvisation in a particular framework.

Are Varṇams Theorylike?

If a "theory" is "a conception or mental scheme of something to be done, or of the method of doing it; a systematic statement of rules or principles to be followed" (OED online, s.v. theory) and a model is something which "accurately resembles or represents something else, esp. on a small scale" (OED, s.v. model), a *varṇam* would seem to be more model-like than theory-like. In terms of melodic organization, it might be compared with the Venda children's song genre, which, according to John Blacking, contains in simplified form the essential elements of the national dance songs (Blacking 1967, 193 and passim). It could also be compared with the *radīf,* that great inventory of musical ideas in Persian music, though many important differences distinguish them.[5] In terms of performance syntax, the *varṇam* could be likened to the *muqäddimä* ("introduction") in the sequence of pieces making up *muqāms* in the twelve-*muqām* system of the Uighurs. The text to *rāk muqām* in particular is interesting in that it connects epigrammatic expressions of mystic love to times of day, frets on the *satar* (bowed, long-necked lute), and names of all the *muqāms*, of which *rāk* is the first (see text in Light 1998, 422–25).

Despite the presence of a formal resemblance between the structure of a *varṇam* and phrases of improvisation, the *varṇam* is more a means through which musicians internalize organized musical data than it is a model for imitation. *Varṇams* and other compositions are practiced until their commonplace gestures are no longer thought about, but felt; their rearticulation in improvised form becomes an extension of bodily habit (see Bourdieu 1989; Qureshi, this volume; Henderson, this volume). As Kamala Ramamurthy explained it to me, "by practicing [a *varṇam*] over and over 'automatically' that *rāga*'s *svarūpam* [melodic shape] will be gotten into our hearts."

More than that, practicing *varṇams* also gives the performer a sense of a raga's *bhāvam*. Derived from the Sanskrit word *bhāva,* "being, becoming," this term means, roughly, "feeling" or "emotion," and connotes as well the musicality of a raga rendition: its melodic contour and tempo. A performance may be technically correct, but viscerally unmoving if it lacks *bhāva* (Sambamoorthy 1984, s.v. bhava).

According to a widely held view, *varṇams* are put together with great *lakṣaṇa* or knowledge of "theory." Hence, even if a *varṇam* is not exactly a model "for" improvised performance, to use Geertz's (1973) famous phrase, it is often taken as a model "of" musical theory to south Indian musical cognoscenti. This may have practical ramifications. The scholarly vocalist T. M. Tyagarajan (known as T.M.T.) disapproved of the manner in which the "*viribhōṇi*" *varṇam* in the raga *bhairavi* was being performed in the 1980s and set out to correct it, propagating the new version among his disciples and colleagues. [**Audio example 13.1**] Through this strategy he aimed to reform the practice of the raga more generally.[6]

T.M.T. attempted to make his mark on the Karnatak musical world by cleansing the practice of raga rendition at the level of tradition regarded as "fixed." This idea of altering a piece to suit a particular style (*pāṇi*) is not uncommon. Karaikkudi Sambasiva Iyer (who angered Balanchandar in our earlier anecdote) altered that same *varṇam* by adding lines of musical variation, *sangatis*. At that time—and to my knowledge, still—only those who play in the Karaikkudi *vīṇā* style include *sangatis* in certain *varṇams*. By adding *sangatis*, Sambasiva Iyer Karaikkudi-ized it.[7] [**Audio example 13.2**]

If a *varṇam* is not just a piece, a singular item existing only in performance, but a deeply embodied set of structures and procedures, a given *varṇam,* as it exists in the active knowledge-base of any given performer, is also a "theory" of how to perform a raga. In the case of Sambasiva Iyer's rendering of the *varṇam viribhōṇi,* the *varṇam* serves as a strategic encapsulation of some of the *vīṇā* style's important features. It carries some of the configurations of relationships characteristic of *kritis* (*sangatis*) into the *varṇam,* making the *varṇam* more complete, in a sense, as a "map" or "inventory" (see Blum, this volume) of a raga's potential, and it does so in a manner connected with sociomusical identity.

Theory in Karnatak Music

Perhaps we should expect such an embodied form of theory to arise from a tradition that is heavily laden with theories of many kinds, both written and oral, and in which members of the tradition themselves engage in debates over the relative merit of what they call theory and practice. The terms for theory and practice have a long history in Indian thought, bridging Indo-Aryan and Dravidian language families. *Lakṣaṇa,* which we encountered earlier as "theory," is a Sanskrit word meaning "indicating, expressing indirectly." Its derivative in Tamil, *ilakkaṇam,* means, among other things, "grammar." *Lakṣya*, "practice," is, in contrast, a Sanskrit term meaning "to be marked or characterized or defined." Transformed in Tamil, *ilakkiyam* is "the thing defined," or "example from classical writings to illustrate a rule of grammar, or the different meanings of a word or an expression, or to justify the use of a word or an expression." For some musicians, such as Rajeswari Padmanabhan (sister of Sashi, disciple and niece of Sambasiva Iyer) and the late T. Ranganathan, *lakṣya* is a source of authority. Knowledge of what "moves" to make at the right time derives from practical experience (including knowledge of compositions). Laying these moves out in an encompassing and consistent scheme is not seen as important or useful. For others, and T.M.T. is not alone, *lakṣaṇa* is an absolute standard to which all musical action must conform.

Musical performances, to differing degrees, always give voice to theories of one kind or another. Different musical gestures bear the different relationships to the underlying "theories" that might motivate their production. The *varṇam* may technically occupy a medial position in the traditional learning sequence and in daily practice. But it constitutes a "beginning" in the grander sense of a charter, a means of bodily entrainment, and piece through which a performer proclaims a sociomusical identity. In many ways it serves as a point of departure for musicians and musicologists to think about the significance of what they do and how it fits into broader categories of musical thought.

One element left out of this discussion but nevertheless worthy of consideration is the range of activities that precede the first item of repertoire: personal preparations (including bathing), clearing the floor, tuning an instrument, and so forth. In instrumental music performances of the Kotas of south India, such pre-performance activities are implicated critically in basic sociocultural and religious values.

The Kotas: Getting Ready, Beginning, and Warming Up

The Kotas (pop. 1,500–2,000) live in seven villages in the Nilgiri Hills of northwestern Tamil Nadu state, where they interact with other so-called tribal communities as well as with members of a large number of communities and ethnic groups from the surrounding areas, the plains, and other parts of India. Our focus is the outdoor instrumental music men perform on shawms (*koḷ*), cylinder drums (*dobar* and *kiṇvar*), and a frame drum (*tabaṭk*). Pieces are defined by their melodies, also termed *koḷ*.

The critical and general taxonomic distinction Kotas maintain between god- and death-related activities extends to their division of musical repertoires into "god" instrumental tunes (*devr koḷ*), "death" (*tāv*) and "sad" (*dukt*) tunes, and "dance tunes" (*āṭ koḷ*). These critical distinctions bear on musical beginnings. At the commencement of the annual "god ceremony" (*devr*), all the musicians should play a certain dance tune at once and very loudly.[8] [**Video example 13.1**] The term

FIGURE 13.2. Kota mortuary procession, Kurgōj village, Nilgiri District, Tamil Nadu. Procession is led by two double-reed *koḷ* players, two *kob* (curved trumpet) players, and *par* (cylinder drum) players. November 1997. Photograph by Richard K. Wolf.

for this *ōmayṇ*, "one sound," indexes "oneness" as the most important social form in the ceremony (see Wolf 1997b). To emphasize the unity of their community before god, Kotas explicitly refrain from making any sound at all before they issue these initial bursts of sound. Total participation is felt to be more important than the sound-quality of drums or reeds, or precision of pitch. The sound should be loud enough to reach surrounding areas for others to hear. Also, the louder the sound, the more effectively the Kotas can penetrate the heavens with their entreaties. Loudness is a measure of vitality, strength, and power.

The "one sound" ritual is, however, a special case. Normally, Kotas adjust their instruments before or in between playing pieces. Drummers heat their drum heads in front of the fire. Shawm players adjust their reeds and begin to make tentative sounds, which become recognizable melodic phrases as the moment of playing together draws near. One term for the warm-up process, *koḷ ākicd*, has been translated for me as "testing" of the *koḷ*. Musically, it consists of a crooked melodic phrase that descends stepwise. Each musician may render this phrase slightly differently on his own, but as two *koḷ* players become ready to perform they will play in unison. Testing the *koḷ* also involves wetting the reed, adjusting its depth in the thin tube connecting to the *koḷ*, checking the tightness of fit between the two major sections of the *koḷ* (the bell and the tube with finger holes), and blowing out debris, dust, excess spittle, or whatever gets in the way of producing a consistent, clear sound. [**Video example 13.2; audio examples 13.3–13.6**]

In other contexts, *ākicd* means "cleaning, clearing, or preparing" in both physical and symbolic senses. In the *mand ākicd,* "clearing of the [meeting] ground" ritual, for instance, Kotas cast away fecal matter, cut branches, cover muddy patches, cut steps, and otherwise clear the ground in preparation for a secondary mortuary ritual (*varldāv*). This not only makes it more pleasant to carry out the ceremony but also demonstrates respect for the memory of the dead and the associated set of social customs.

As in Karnatak music, then, the beginning of Kota musical performances involves attention to matters of both physical and moral importance. Unlike in the *varṇam,* the actual sounds produced in the Kota case have no bearing on how a musician makes a melody, nor do they relate in musical structure to the repertoire. The manner of deploying the gesture, however, is important, because it intentionally inflects the god-death distinction.

Two slightly different musical gestures are called *koḷ ākicd* in Kolmēl village. One precedes repertoire associated with the gods as well as the most ordinary pieces of dance repertoire, played at festivals or demonstrations for visiting dignitaries. [**Audio examples 13.3–13.4**] The other is performed only during funerals, or when funeral melodies are practiced or demonstrated. [**Audio examples 13.5–13.6; video example 13.3**] The latter version consists of a short phrase, which proceeds by a more straightforward descent than does the *koḷ ākicd* for the god ceremony or for more general music making. The use of a shorter phrase in a lower pitch range to mark a "funerary" musical domain is not surprising, for Kota hierarchical matters are often played out in terms of size, length, and height.

The Kota example is not anomalous in the world of music. Modern Gagaku (a type of Japanese classical music), for example, includes categories of pieces called *netori* ("tuning up") and *choshi* that formally present the mode that follows. Modal preludes and items for tuning up appear in early notations for the *piba* (now called *pipa* in China and *biwa* in Japan) brought from Chang'an (Xian) and elsewhere on the Chinese mainland during the T'ang Dynasty (see Picken et al. 2000; Togi 1971, 71). In the ancient theater of India, as described in the *Nāṭyaśāstra,* performances began with extensive ceremonial beginnings, which included special preliminary music and dance pieces, including nine instrumental items, "each marking a gradual transition from tuning and musical exercises to formally conceived music" (Rowell 2000, 26). These early Indian practices typologically encompass both realms of "beginning" described above, in the Karnatak and Kota cases.

* * *

Another preliminary aspect of Kota instrumental performance is musically more substantial. When the time comes to play a ritually appropriate melody that he has not played for several months or years, a *koḷ* player often requires a moment to remember. He may softly or tentatively whistle the tune, or someone may help him by whistling it into his ear. He may also hum the melody using the set of syllables, *gag gil lil le*. These do not correspond with precise pitches, but they do share some features of what Hughes (2000) calls an "acoustic-iconic mnemonic system" in which phonological properties of the syllables resemble the sounds they represent.[9] A musician's ability to perform this kind of humming is a recognized sign of musicianship, in part because the musician is able to use it to teach. Whether teaching, reminding, or remembering, the hummer uses these syllables to motivate someone to play a version of the same melody on an instrument. These syllables, unlike those of *sargam*, are not normally performed alone or incorporated into songs (*pāṭ*), but they clearly have a generative capacity, playing a role in the memory and transmission of the tradition (cf. Collinson 1971, 35ff.).

When I have compared the hummed performances of melodies to the "same" melodies played by the same musician on the *koḷ*, however, there are often discrepancies, sometimes significant ones—even in performances of well-regarded musicians. The interesting question here, which will require additional research to answer, is how the somewhat ambiguous musical signals are converted into instrumental melodies, and likewise, how ideas or memories of melodies are converted into hummed or whistled representations (see the related problem in Blum's diagram, this volume). The more general issue is how some strings of vocables stand as abstractions, local encapsulations of musical information that function rather like simple musical models. Such vocable strings may not precede the main performance, as they do in the Kota case, but they often appear at the beginning of a piece or section.

Vocables at the Beginning

Interest in the study of vocables in ethnomusicology, anthropology, and folklore dates back to the early days of these disciplines. The most substantial work to date concentrates on Native American music, where vocables serve multiple functions and appear at the beginning of songs as well as in other positions. Charlotte Frisbie lays out five functions, among which the most important for the present purposes is that of "outlin[ing] the song's structure" (1980, 376).

The function of Tamil vocables (called *col,* meaning "word" or "sound") as refrains and as means for maintaining the rhythmic structure of folksongs is well established.[10] One scholar ventured that "folk melodies are conceived, remembered and expressed musically first and verbally only in a secondary manner" on the basis that "different words are sung with slight adjustments to different tunes, only after such [vocable] refrains" (Balakrishnan 1969, 47) Whether or not the capacity of passages with vocables to condense information about a song's structure is evidence of such musical priority, the study of vocable patterns surely fits into our larger concern with the "theoretical" implication of musical beginnings.

Solmization

Solmization syllables are a special case in which vocables correspond with specific pitches, or in the case of *sargam* in Karnatak music and dance, with *svaras*. The type of composed *sargam* passage called a *ciṭṭasvaram* is of interest to us because it provides musical information at two temporal levels, which I will call "synchronic" and "diachronic," for want of better terms. Synchronically, each solmization syllable name points to the musical note or contour with which it is being sung at that moment. Diachronically, the whole *ciṭṭasvaram* passage sets up the expectation for the return of that same passage later in the piece. This convention is manipulated when, for instance, the passage returns as a *svara sāhitya* ("svara lyric"), in which the melody is rendered syllabically with meaningful text.[11]

Synchronic relationships established by the *sargam* system are important in settings of lyrics in Karnatak music generally. Composers will cleverly align some syllables of meaningful text with their corresponding pitches in the solfa system.[12] These alignments may be precise, where, for instance, *pa* in the lyrics corresponds with the fifth scale degree, "Pa"; or they may merely be suggestive, where only the consonant (e.g., the /d/ in *du*) matches that of the *svara* name (e.g., "Dha" the sixth degree [Sambamoorthy 1973, 3:157]). The alignments may also be offset, or overlap (K. S. Subramanian 1993).

Other kinds of connections exist between syllables and what they represent or index. Some may arise from the ways in which members of many cultures (implicitly) recognize iconicity between relative pitch and the phonological properties of syllables.[13] Potentially, any sung textual passage could point to pitch relationships that are conventionally possible, or which are acoustically or phonologically implied. These indexed musical features might lie beyond those actually contained in the tune and rhythm as rendered at a given time. Musicians may actively manipulate such relationships between vocable strings, various meaningful texts, and melodies. Solmization systems are resources for composition and improvisation, and they provide configurations of relationships which listeners may use to gain a deeper understanding of music.

When passages of solmization syllables are incorporated into the structure of a piece, they function in a manner somewhat comparable to that of the *varṇam*. No doubt important differences remain, in scale and complexity, for the *varṇam* has more parts. But both *sargam* passages and *varṇams* index important systematic aspects of Karnatak music.

Meter, Melody, and Flow

A function of memory and transmission reminiscent of our last Kota example is associated with vocables in several genres of Tamil folk song. Vocable strings often outline aspects of a song's metrical structure and melody, for which the general term *cantam,* "musical flow" or "rhythmic movement of verse," is used in Tamil.[14] This term has resonances of folkiness or informality when contrasted with the more formal term for prosody in Tamil, *yāppu* (figuratively, "binding words together"), or *yāppilakkaṇam* (the grammar of binding words together).[15] Notably, vocable strings that outline the *cantam* of a song come to be named after, or identified with, the *cantam* itself. The vocables come to embody musical information, act as musical models, or serve as the basis for the ways in which performers and listeners alike engage in "episodes of generalizing" (see Blum, this volume). My intent in the following examples is to explore some of the complexity with which vocables serve these functions.

In the following *temmānku* Tamil folk song, the initial two lines of vocables set up melodic, rhyme, and metric patterns that are maintained in some parts of the song and varied in others (Ramji 1989; see box 13.1 for full text). I will focus here on rhythmic and textual organization.

tantānti nāttu naṉṉēṉ tintānti nā

tiṉattanti nāttu naṉṉaṉ tintanti nā [**Audio example 13.7**]

Lines of syllables and texts appear in pairs. Most text lines end with some variation of the second half of the vocable string, *tintānti nā.* At first, the vocables appear merely to be conduits for rhythmic ideas. Each line is divided into eight beats, consisting usually of three pulses (sometimes two pulses). The rhythmic choices boil down to how many syllables will be allotted to each beat and where the gap, if any, should be placed. Comparing the rendition of the vocables with the first lines of text shows a significant degree of isomorphism.

As the song progresses, other rhythmic possibilities are explored as well. Indeed, perhaps too strict adherence to the initial pattern would be considered insipid. The text also constrains adherence to the pattern, as the number of syllables accommodated by the first four beats ranges from seven to nine. After each sung unit (sequence of vocables or line of text) the double-reed *nāyaṇam* repeats the melody, matching the articulation of the text quite precisely. Note the contrast: the *cantam* embodied by the initial syllable sequence is prescriptive. The double-reed imitations are descriptive of particular texted iterations of the melody. The *naiyāṇṭi mēḷam* (lit., "teasing ensemble") that often plays *temmānku* and other kinds of folk songs and dances consists of a range of drums as well as the *nāyaṇams* (see figs. 13.4 and 13.5). The antiphonal organization of the performance and the playfulness of the ensemble (reflected in part by the name) highlight the contrast between the male and female characters that is characteristic of the *temmānku* genre.

BOX 13.1. "ātta kuṟukka," Side A, item 2 on Ramji (1989): *Temmānku temmānku.*
Sung by Tēkkampaṭṭi S. Cuntararājaṉ; antiphonal response by *naiyāṇṭi mēḷam* (ensemble consisting of double-reed *nāyaṉams*, cymbals, and several kinds of drums) (see figs. 13.4–3.5).

Text	Translation
tantānti nāttu naṉṉēṉ tintānti nā	(vocables)
tiṉattanti nāttu naṉṉaṉ tintanti nā	(vocables)
ātta kuṟukkaṭaccēṉ tentānti nāṉ	I blocked off the river (+ vocables)
aḻaku campā nāttu viṭṭēṉ tiṉattanti nāṉ	I planted excellent *campā* paddy seedlings (+ vocables)
kuḷatta kuṟukkaṭaccēṉ tentāntu nāṉ (x2)	I blocked off the pond (+ vocables)
[tune changes, register higher]	
kulavāḻai nāttu naṭṭēṉ tiṉattanti nāṉ	I planted *kulavāḻai* paddy seedlings (+ vocables)
caṉtaṉak kalappai veṭṭi kaṇṇaṉ uḻuvāṉ	Having carved a plow of sandalwood, Kaṇṇaṉ will plow
cātilinka nāttu eṭuttu kaṉṉi naṭuvāḷ	Having taken out the "vermillion" paddy seedlings, Kaṉṉi will transplant
vēlān kalappai veṭṭi kaṇṇaṉ uḻuvāṉ (x2)	Having carved a plow of *vēlān* wood Kaṇṇan will plow
viniyāki campā nātteṭuttu kaṉṉi naṭuvāḷ	Having taken out *viniyāki campā* paddy seedlings, Kaṉṉi will transplant
nāttu naṭṭu nāṉ aṟiyēṉ tentānti nāṉ	Planting seedlings, I don't know (+ vocables)
naṭavu naṭṭu nāṉaṟiyēṉ tiṉattanti nāṉ	Transplanting, I don't know (+ vocables)
cettukkuḷḷē iṟankikkiṭṭu tentānti nāṉ	Having gotten into the mud (+ vocables)
cella mukam vāṭuṟaṉē tiṉattanti nāṉ	The face of the one who has never had to work hard is wilting (+ vocables)
cenkuruva nellukutticōṟukaḷ ākki	pounding paddy, preparing rice
cenkuḷattu mīṉ piṭicci āṉamum kāycci	Having grabbed fish from the red pond and brewed liquor
koṇṭaiya kulukki ava eṭuttu vanta cōṟu kaṟi	hairbun shaking, she brings rice and curry
kumpiṭṭu iṟakkiṉēṉōm kōkulak kaṇṇā	Having given thanks I took down (the basket of food from her head), Oh dear (Krishna) of Gokula!

TABLE 13.1. "ātta kuṟukka," rhythmic notation

1	2	3	4	5	6	7	8
tan . tā	n . ti	nāt . tu	naṉ ṉēṉ .	tin . tā	n . ti	nā . .	. . .
ti . ṉa	tan ti .	nā . ttu	naṉ ṉaṉ .	tin . ta	n . ti	nā	
ā . tta	. . ku	ṟu . kka	ṭa ccēṉ .	ten . tā	n . ti	nāṉ	
aḻa ku	cam pā .	nā . ttu	viṭ . ṭēn	ti ṉat	tan ti	nāṉ	
ku ḷat	ta ku	ṟuk ka	ṭac cēṉ	ten . tā	n . tu	nāṉ	
ku la vā	. . ḻai	nāt. tu	naṭ ṭēn .	ti ṉat	tan ti	nāṉ	
can . ta	ṉa ka .	lap . pai	veṭ . ṭi	kaṇ ṇaṉ	u ḻu	vāṉ	
cā . ti	lin ka .	nāt . te	ṭut . tu	kaṉ ṉi	na ṭu	vāḷ	
vē . lān	. ka .	lap pai .	veṭ ṭi .	kaṇ ṇaṉ	u ḻu	vāṉ	. . vi
niyā . ki	cam pā .	nāt . te	ṭut . tu	kaṉ ṉi	na ṭu	vāḷ	
nā . ttu	naṭ ṭu .	nā . ṉa	ṟi yēṉ .	ten . tā	n . ti	nāṉ	
na ṭa vu	naṭ ṭu .	nā . ṉa	ṟi yēṉ .	ti ṉat .	tan ti .	nāṉ	
cet . tuk	kuḷ ḷē .	i ṟan kik	kiṭ ṭu .	ten . tā	n . ti	nāṉ	
cel la .	mu kam .	vā ṭu .	ṟa ṉē .	ti ṉat .	tan ti .	nāṉ	
cen . ku	ru va .	nel . lu	kut ti .	cō . ṟu	kaḷ āk .	ki	
cek . kuḷ	at tu .	mīṉ . pi	ṭic ci .	ā . ṉa	m . kāyc	ci	
koṇ . tai	ya ku .	luk . ki	ya va .	e ṭut tu	van ta .	cō . ṟu	ka ṟi .
kum . piṭ	ṭu . i	ṟak ki .	ṉē ṉōm .	kō . ku	lak . kaṇ	ṇā	

Cells represent beats and are divided into three or two pulses, as indicated by syllable, letter, or period (rest) separations.

1	2	3	4	5	6	7	8
tan . tā	n . ti	nāt . tu	naṉ ṉēṉ.	tin . tā	n . ti	nā . .	. . .
ti . ṉa	tan ti .	nā . ttu	naṉ ṉaṉ	tin . ta	n . ti	nā	

First line of text

ā . tta	. . ku	ṟu . kka	ṭa ccēṉ.	ten . tā	n . ti	nāṉ	
aḻa ku	cam pā .	nā . ttu	viṭ . ṭēn	ti ṉat	tan ti	nāṉ	

FIGURE 13.3. *Cantam* (rendition of tune and rhythm with vocables) and first line of *āttakuṟukka.*

FIGURE 13.4. *Naiyāṇṭi mēḷam*, a kind of instrumental ensemble that performs Tamil folk songs and dances, including *temmānku* (as in Audio example 13.7). Drummers clockwise from left play the following: 1. *pampai*, 2. not visible, 3. *tamukku*, 4. *uṟumi*, 5. *tavul*, 6. *tavul* . See figure 13.5 for the double-reed *nāyaṇams*. Madurai, Tamil Nadu, October 24, 1992. Photograph by Richard K. Wolf.

FIGURE 13.5. *Naiyāṇṭi mēḷam*, with two double-reed *nāyaṇams* and cymbals (*tāḷam*). See figure 13.4 for drums. Madurai, Tamil Nadu, October 14, 1992. Photograph by Richard K. Wolf.

When the lyrics begin, some of the seemingly meaningless vocables take on new life: "*nāttu*" is revealed as a "seedling" of paddy. The agricultural activities, narrated alternately of the man Kaṇṇaṉ, and the woman Kaṉṉi, are sexually metaphoric: Kaṇṇaṉ plows with an implement hewn of sandalwood, and and Kaṉṉi transplants the "vermillion" paddy seedlings.

The choice of names, Kaṉṉi and Kaṇṇaṉ, highlights the more general importance of alliteration in this song. Alliteration is but one of several devices of sound repetition common to literary Tamil poetry and folksong alike. In Tamil poetics, a device called *mōṉai* is the repetition of the line's initial vowel or consonant in some other foot. In line five, the syllables *ku* form one such pair: ***ku**ḷatta **ku**ṟukkaṭaccēṉ tentāntu nāṉ*.

If this were a formal work of poetry, metrical rules (*yāppilakkaṇam*) would dictate the number of feet in a line, the number of lines in a stanza, and on which foot the *mōṉai* should appear. In another repetition type, the second consonant, syllable, or group of syllables will remain constant between two or more lines or among feet of a particular line. Both devices are controlled and used for literary effects, such as creating semantic parallelisms (Peterson 1991, 81 and *passim*).

No such formal rules pertain in most Tamil folksongs, but I mention them because they indicate some of the range of variables recognized in the larger Tamil tradition. Consonant and vowel repetitions are significant independently, not just in combined form as syllables. This was already suggested by our earlier discussion of Karnatak music, in which merely the similarity between the consonants of successive syllables and the first letter of *svara* names is enough to evoke recognitions among connoisseurs.

Here, every pair of lines begins with the same syllable or the same consonant, vowel, or semivowel (note the first syllable of line 10 begins on the final pulse of the notation of line 9). Furthermore, the second syllables on beat four are parallel in almost every pair of lines (except 13–14 and 17–18). Careful examination of the text organized into word clusters (box 13.1), and in a chart showing musical rhythm (table 13.1) will reveal additional examples of vertical and horizontal repetition which, in interest of space, cannot be detailed here.

In our next example, belonging to the Tamil folksong genre called *oyilāṭṭakkummi* (lit., "graceful dancing"), vocables do not appear in the initial position, but as a refrain (fig. 13.6).[16] [**Audio example 13.8**]

In contrast to our previous example, where the syllables roughly paralleled the rhythmic organization of the text, the syllables here provide a precise rhythmic and melodic analog to almost all the lyrical lines. The first line alone allows us to see the

taṉ ṉē . ṉa	nā . ta ṉan	taṉ ṉē . ṉa	nā . ta ṉan
taṉ ṉē . ṉa	nā . ta ṉan	taṉ ṉaṉ nā .	ṉē . . .

FIGURE 13.6. *Cantam* to *oyilāṭṭakkummi* example, *kuṇṭamalai mēl.*

kuṇ ṭa . ma	lai . mē la	koñ ci . vi	ḷai . yā ṭum
pō ṟa . va	ḻi . mē la	van tē . ṉu	ṉka . . .

FIGURE 13.7. First line of *oyilāṭṭakkummi* example, *kuṇṭamalai mēl.*

matching pattern (see fig. 13.7). The pattern is only slightly broken in lines 8 and 10, where a bit of complex duple is introduced and then echoed in the last refrain (see bolded passages in table 13.2).

The *tān nān nē* syllables serve multiple functions in these kinds of songs. They encapsulate the melodic and rhythmic feel of the song and can be remembered independently from any particular lyrics. While two or more singers are performing the song, the syllable refrain gives the main singer time to rest his voice, clear his throat, remember the next line of text, or come up with a new line on a given theme (cf. Frisbie 1980, 376). In the *oyilāṭṭakkummi* example, a song about going on pilgrimage, the singer merely needed to think of appropriate actions or sights along the way and sing them according to the established pattern. Having the refrain sung in between verses, sometimes two or three times, allows the singer to mentally try out

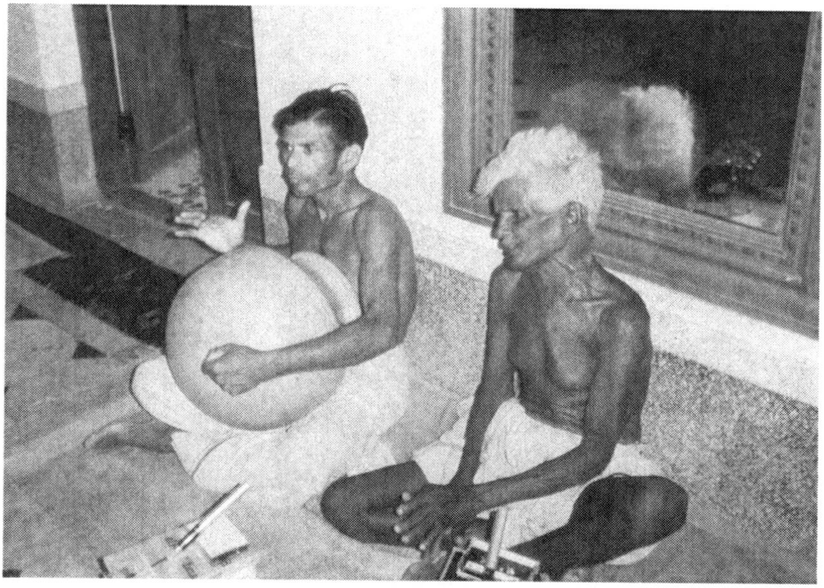

FIGURE 13.8. Kaṇṇiyappaṉ (*oyilāṭṭakkummi* singer, right) and Paḻani (backup singer and *kuṭam* [clay pot] player, left) singing folk songs in a house in Madurai, Tamil Nadu. March 20, 1983. Photograph by Richard K. Wolf.

TABLE 13.2. *Oyilāṭṭakkummi*: "kuṇṭa malai mēl"; text, verse/refrain structure, and rhythmic organization

	1	2	3	4
				... ey
1	kuṇ ṭa . ma	lai . mē la	koñ ci . vi	ḷai . yā ṭum
	pō ṟa . va	ḻi . mē la	van tē . ṉu	ṅka ...
R (1)	taṉ ṉē . ṉa	nā . ta ṉan	taṉ ṉē . ṉa	nā . ta ṉan
	taṉ ṉē . ṉa	nā . ta ṉan	taṉ ṉaṉ ṉā .	ṉē ...
2	aṉ ṉak . ko	ṭi . kaṭ ṭi	cat ti . ra	mum . ta va
	aṉ ṭa . ṉā	rē . ta ku	mē ṉa ta ka	ḷē . [a te]
R (2)	taṉ ṉē . ṉa	nā . naṉ ṉan	taṉ ṉē . ṉa	nā . naṉ ṉan
	taṉ ṉē . ṉa	nā . naṉ ṉan	taṉ ṉaṉ ṉā .	ṉē . [ey] .
(repeat	2 and R)			
3	[vi kē . ṉē]	rā . ka vaṉ	mī ṉāṭ . ci	vā . tat te
	vē ṇā . va	ram . koṇ .	ṭāṉ . ko ṭu	pāṉ ...
R (1)	taṉ ṉē . ṉa	nā . ta ṉan	taṉ ṉē . ṉa	nā . ta ṉan
	taṉ ṉē . ṉa	nā . ta ṉan	taṉ ṉaṉ ṉā .	ṉē ...
4	ma lai . ya	pāk . ka ṟa	vē ṟa . ma	lai . ma lai
	vin tai . yai	pāt . tāṉ .	kum pa . kar	ṇaṉ ...
R (1)	taṉ ṉē . ṉa	nā . ta ṉan	taṉ ṉē . ṉa	nā . ta ṉan
	taṉ ṉē . ṉa	nā . ta ṉan	taṉ ṉaṉ ṉā .	ṉē . [an ta]
5	kum pa . kō	ṉat . tu le	nā ka . ca	ṉat . [ta rum]
	pō yi . ru [k	[ke .] ta ram	mā ya . ḻa	kaṉ ...
R (1)	Then Repeat [5 + R (1)] and R(1) sung again 2 times . [an ta]			
6	man tai . yil	le . vāḻum	nan tak . ka	rup . pai yaṉ
	van tē . ṉuṅ	ka . ko ṭi	tan tē . ṉuṅ	ka ...
R (1)	Then Repeat [6 + R(1)] . . [an ta]			
7	kam māk . ka	rai . vaḻi	kaḷ ḷa . mēṭ	ṭuc . cā mi
	kai ye . ṭut	tu . ti ram	cey tu . coṉ	ṉēṉ ...
R (1)	Then repeat [7 + R (1)] . . [an ta]			
8	mūn . ki na	kar . vaḻ i	**mūñ . ji pa . ṟa**	**ka . rup pai . ya**
	van tē . ṉuṅ	ka . ko ṭi	tan tē . ṉuṅ	ka ...
R(1)				
9	man tai . yil	le . vāḻ um	man ta . mut	tā . ram mā
	van tē . ṉuṅ	ka . ko ṭi	tan tē . ṉuṅ	ka ...
R (1)				. . [an ta]
10	**mā . vi ḷa . ka**	**rā . ja mā . ṇi**	**[ni li ka nīḷ . ka]**	**[e tu ka ḷi . ya]**
	van tē . ṇuṅ	ka . ko ṭi	tan tē . ṉuṅ	ka ...
R (3)	ta ṉa ṉa ṉa	**nā . ṇa ṇaṇ . ṇaṇ**	taṉ ṉē . ṉa	nā . ta ṉan
	taṉ ṉē . ṉa	nā . ta ṉan	taṉ ṉaṉ ṉā .	ṉē . [an ta]
R (1)	10 + R (1) three times and end on "a..."			

Lead singer: Kaṇṇiyappaṉ from Paṭṭūr village. Backup singer (?): M. Rasu. Recorded in 1982 by Richard K. Wolf in Madurai, Tamil Nadu. Tempo: Starts at about 85/min and increases to about 97/min.

a new line while listening to someone else maintain the *cantam*. The instrumental recapitulation of the melody in the *temmānku* example performs a similar function.

Genre-Specific Vocables

Some syllables are common across genres and are used by multiple communities, others are limited to particular genres or communities (Vēnukōpāl 1982; cf. Frisbie 1980, 37 and Hinton 1980 [cited in Mulder 1994, 83]). In south India, lullabies use genre-specific vocables, such as those mimicking the sounds of a mother cajoling a crying baby. Kota *jo jo pāṭ*, or "jo jo songs," for example, use the syllables *jo jo* to soothe the baby. The Tamil word for lullaby, *tālāṭṭu*, means, literally, "tongue rocking." The syllables *tā lē lō* which conclude the lines of some Tamil lullabies, poetically transform those of the genre name, *tālāṭṭu*, into soothing conduits for vocalization.

Our detailed example is one that transcends the folk and classical divide. [**Audio example 13.9**] Although set in a raga, *nīlāmbari*, the lullaby *ārārō ārirarō* is not part of a concert repertoire. A functional lullaby, the song has been passed down for at least three generations from mother to daughter in the village of Tuvariman, outside of Madurai. *Nīlāmbari* is generally associated with lullabies in south India, although the actual use of lullabies in this raga is probably more common among individuals with access to classical music education and members of relatively high castes—in this village, Ayyangar (Vaishnava) Brahmans.

The syllables in this case, *ārārō ārirarō*, and so on, are not vocalizations of sounds spoken to babies to make them stop crying, but rather imitate the way babies cry. This similarity is brought to the fore by the high opening register of the performance. The text and its formal organization with melody is seen in table 13.3 (see complete transliteration and translation in box 13.2).

TABLE 13.3. Outline of melodic structure in relation to text of *tālāṭṭu* (lullaby), "ārārō ārirarō ārirari ārārō ō . . "

Text	Melody
ārārō ārirarō ārirari ārārō ō . .	A
ārirārira rārō . . śrī rāmacantirarō ō . .	B
āṟiranṭum kāvēri ataṉ naṭuvē śrī rankam	C
śrī rankamāṭi // kaṇṇē nī tiruppāṟ kaṭalāṭi	D // B′
māmānkamāṭi nī maturaik kaṭalāṭi	A′
taipūcamāṭi nī tavam ceytu vantaracō	B
pāṭṭi aṭiccāḷō pāl pōṭṭum cankālē	C′
citti aṭiccāḷō // cīrāṭṭum kaiyālē	D // B″
māmi aṭiccāḷō mallikaippū cenṭālē	A′
attai aṭiccāḷo araḷippū cenṭālē	B
yār aṭitta kaṇṇīru āṟāyperukaṟatu	C′
ārāy peruki // āmellām ōṭaṟatu	D // B″

BOX 13.2. Tālāṭṭu (Tamil lullaby): "ārārō ārirarō ārirari ārārō ō..."
Text as sung by Jeyalakshmi Sundar, June 24, 2004 (Queens, New York).

Tamil text	Translation
ārārō ārirarō ārirari ārārō ō ...	Vocables
ārirārira rārō... śrī rāmacantirarō ō ...	vocables. [The name of the god] Sri Ramachandran
āṟiranṭum kāvēri ataṉ naṭuvē śrī rankam	[the place called] Sri Rangam [is located] in between the two [sections of the] river Cauvery
śrī rankamāṭi kaṇṇē nī tiruppāṟ kaṭalāṭi	Sri Rangam, rocking, dear, you are the "The Great Ocean of Milk" (where Vishnu sleeps), rocking
māmānkamāṭi nī maturaik kaṭalāṭi	You are the "Ocean of Madurai" [the river Vaigai] [during] Mamangam, rocking[1]
taipūcamāṭi nī tavam ceytu vantaracō	[During the holiday in honor of the god Murugan, called] Taipucam you came [as a result of my] having performed austerities
pāṭṭi aṭiccāḷō pāl pōṭṭum cankālē	If grandma hits [you], [it will be] with the conch [shaped spoon] with which [she] feeds [you] milk
citti aṭiccāḷō cīrāṭṭum kaiyālē	If [your] citti [maternal aunt or paternal uncle's wife] hits [you], [it will be] with the hand with which [she] demonstrates affection [for you]
māmi aṭiccāḷō mallikaippū ceṇṭālē	If [your] mami [maternal uncle's wife] hits [you], [it will be] with a ball of jasmine flowers
attai aṭiccāḷo araḷippū ceṇṭālē	If [your] attai [paternal aunt] hits [you], [it will be] with a ball of oleander flowers
yār aṭitta kaṇṇīru āṟāyperukaṟatu	The tears from whoever hit you swell like a river
ārāy peruki āmellām ōṭaṟatu	swelling like a river [they] flow throughout the house

1. Māmānkam takes place every twelve years during the full moon in March, when the tides are high in all bodies of water. This overflowing water is considered auspicious.

TABLE 13.4. Outline of thematic structure in relation to melody of *tālāṭṭu* (lullaby), “ārārō āriraro ārirari ārārō ō . . .”

Part	Theme	Melody sections
Introduction	vocables and name of god	A and B
Part I	Mother shows devotion for Vishnu and gets baby (description of famous temple, equation of baby with water body)	C, D // B′, A′, B
Part II	Formulaic: “if such and such relative hits you, it is with flowers or implements of affection”	C′, D // B″, A′, B
Part III	Description of the child’s tears	C″, D // B″

B″ differs from B primarily by omitting an extended, descending melismatic flourish. The relationships between melodic form, textual form, and the details of sound repetition are complex, and suggest that this song was carefully composed by a skillful musician. The subject matter articulates with melody as seen in table 13.4.

None of these formal sections of text correspond with full iterations of the melody (i.e., beginning to end). The introductory vocables present the first half of

TABLE 13.5. Text of *tālāṭṭu* (lullaby), “ārārō āriraro ārirari ārārō ō . . .” Grid provides a reference for textual cells as follows: letter indicating row followed by number indicating column. The column in between the lowercase-letter column and the first numbered column indicates the melodic sectioning (A, B, C, D, B′, and so forth) as described earlier. Each cell is divided into four rhythmic pulses—syllables or dots separated by spaces.

		1	2	3	4	5	6	7
a	A	ā rā . rō	ā . ri ra	rō . . .	ā ri ra ri	ā rā . rō	ō . . .	
b	B	ā ri rā ri	ra rā . rō			. . śrī rā	. ma . can	ti ra rō .
c	C	ā ṟi raṉ ṭum	kā vē . ri	. a tan na	ṭu vē . śrī	ran . kam .		
d	D	śrī ran . kam	ā ṭi . .	. . . .				
e	B′				kaṇ ṇē . nī	ti rup par .	ka ṭa la .	ṭi . . .
f	A′	mā mā . nka	mā . ṭi .	. nī . .	ma tu rai .	ka ṭa lā .	ṭi . . .	
g	B	tai pū . cam	ā . ṭi .	. . . .	. . . .	nī . ta vam	cey tu van ta	ra . co .
h	C	pāṭ . ṭi a	ṭi . cā .	ḷō . . .	pāl . pōṭ .	ṭum . canka	. lē . .	
i	D	cit ti a ṭic	cā . lō .	. . . .				
j	B″				. cīr āṭ .	ṭum ka ya lē	. . . .	
k	A′	mā mi a ṭic	cā . ḷo .	. mal li kai	pū ceṇ ṭā .	lē . . .		
l	B	at tai a ṭic	cā . ḷō	. . . .	. . . .	. . . .	ara ḷī pū .	ceṇ ṭā . lē
m	C′	yār a ṭit ta	kaṇ ṇī . ru	. ā ṟāy .	pe ru ka ṟa	tu . . .		
n	D	ā ṟāy . pe	ru ki . .	. . . .	ā mel lā .	mō ṭa ṟa tu	. . . .	

the melody. The four lines of part I cover the second half of the melody and the first half of the repetition. Part II, which is textually distinctive, follows the melodic pattern of part I. Part III iterates only the last half of the melody.

Other than a general indication of genre, what kind of information does the initial vocable pattern contain here? Obviously it provides melodic information for a bit more than half the song (this is why I note that the final melodic line incorporates a version of B). Like our earlier examples, the syllables provide a basis for word play, alliteration, and here, semantic parallelisms.

For the following discussion, refer to table 13.5. The first row and first column provide location indexes for words and syllables. The second column reiterates the melodic formal scheme. As in our earlier example, each cell is divided into pulses. The song is sung in *viruttam* style (Tamil from the Sanskrit term for syllabic meter), which resembles the "free rhythm" of *ālāpana* in south Indian music.

Alliteration and Sound Repetition

The first cells in the first four lines (a1, b1, c1, d1) seem to grow organically from the initial *ārārō.* When the meaningful text appears, the words are "two rivers," which sets up the brilliant parallel, maintained throughout, between tears, rivers, locations of divinity, and the auspiciousness of overflowing. In d1 the repetition of the name of the temple, Śrī Rankam, which is located in the center of the Kāvēri (Cauvery) River, in the initial position reinforces the set of parallels.[17] The second set of cells (a2, b2, c2, d2) are also strongly parallel in their emphasis on /ā/ and /r + vowel/. In d2, /ṭi/ is a voiced retroflex stop which, on approach, approximates an /r/ sound. The word *āṭi* means "rocking," so not only does the word fit the syllabic rhyme pattern, it also creates another set of links, now between "crying" (*ārārō,* etc.) and "river" (āṟu): the crying baby needs to be rocked and the river rocks.

Thereafter, the parallelisms in the first and second cells are soft pedaled, appearing prominently only when the melody returns. So a1 and f1 share emphasis on the /ā/ and the alliteration internal to each line. In f1 and f2, the alliteration is on /m/ and the "rocking" word, *āṭi,* reappears; /m/ returns alliteratively later in the line (f4). In k1, the next appearance of the A melody, the repeating /m/ sound returns and appears alliteratively in k3. Meanwhile, our rocking word, *āṭi,* has now been transformed, through vowel foreshortening, to the verb *aṭi,* "to hit." The theme of this section is how female family members, if they "hit" the baby (causing tears, of course), they do so using harmless objects of affection or flowers.

As for B section parallels, *tai* (name of month of the holiday during which the baby was born) in g1 is transformed into the *attai* (paternal aunt), in l1 [L-1], who hits the baby with a ball of flowers. The /t/ returns alliteratively only in line g (g5), and subtly as a voiced rather than unvoiced dental. In the C melody, h1 and m1 have loose parallels based on the common /ā/ vowel, and the /ā/ returns alliteratively in m3 and n4. More important sets of parallels, in my view, are those created with the opening three lines. The initial crying syllables, *ārārō* (a1), *ārirāri* (b1), which become two rivers *āṟiraṇṭum* in c1, now become *yāraṭitta* in m1. This is an adjectival form of the question "who hit you?," which is used in m2 to modify "tears" (lit., "eye water"). This "eye water" "grows like a river." "Growing like a river" *āṟāy peruki* is then sung in n1–n2, rhyming with the previous "who hit you" as well as recalling the "two rivers" and the crying syllables of the song's opening.

This discussion does not exhaust all the significant instances of repetition and parallelism in this song, but it should indicate that this is a sophisticated composition indeed, and one in which the composer meditated carefully upon, "theorized" if you will, the implications of the initial vocables. It is also notable that the principal regions of signification were beginnings: the beginning lines of the composition, and in each line, the first few words. Text with strong commentary on the subject of the whole song resumed only in the final two lines.

Ending

Structural endings of many activities, in many cultures, are related in complex ways to beginnings. In *gending lampah* subgenres of Javanese gamelan music, it has been argued, there are no structural beginnings or endings; or, put another way, performers may exercise considerable choice as to which section (*gongan*) to begin or end a performance (Hughes 1988, 26). In other contexts, beginnings and endings are inseparable. Mortuary ceremonies put a cultural "end" to certain aspects of death, while strongly emphasizing symbols of rebirth (Bloch and Parry, 1982). A cycle of Indian tala ends on the first beat, the *samam,* of the next cycle. The Sanskrit root *sama,* meaning "identical" or "homogeneous with," reflects the equation of beginnings and endings at this level of analysis (but let us not err by extending this equation to all levels).

"Episodes of generalizing," then, may follow from—or be embedded in—both beginnings and endings (and, no doubt, many kinds of middles as well), and especially those special endings called "conclusions." Here I would like to simply to reiterate and amplify the ways in which our examples of "beginning" provide insight on the general topics of this book, "theorizing the local," and the "practice" and "experience" of music in South Asia.

1. Some beginnings are "structuring structures" (Bourdieu 1989) which become imprinted on the bodies and minds of performers and facilitate performers' abilities to follow established pathways (Rowell 1981), or make spontaneous departures, while continuing to index one or more dominant frameworks.

2. Beginnings of concerts or pieces do not implant essential structures in the minds of performers or audiences for the first time. They renew a person's familiarity with a set of configurations.
3. Beginnings of some kinds may reiterate, in a manner intended by the performers, essential cultural distinctions that do not pertain to the musical sound alone.
4. Structural beginnings may have pedagogical and heuristic uses in multiple settings.
5. Gestures of beginnings, especially vocables, may be used to actively motivate others (or selves) to sing or play in directly parallel ways.

All such functions may operate at multiple stages of a musical process, so why concern ourselves with beginnings? Perhaps because initial gestures seem to matter more. They demarcate the very onset of a performance. We may reasonably expect social groups to maintain multiple standards whereby one properly "begins." It is not enough, then, to speculate even "in a very naive way" on how beginnings might "reflect . . . the more general concept of beginning held by the parent culture," since we probably cannot come up with a satisfactory "general concept of beginning" with which to work. In the case of the many social formations on the Indian subcontinent, we may also have difficulty justifying the choice of a single "parent culture." Starting with performers, listeners, and/or composers, though, it should be possible to analyze other ways in which musical beginnings embody, or stimulate, particularly *musical* ways of "theorizing" sound and, to a limited extent, other elements of social action that are implicated in music making.

In future studies, it might be fruitful to examine more circumscribed forms of social beginning, such as greetings, which have been described as "formulaic expressions" that "may be adapted to, and at the same time help establish, new contexts."[18] How, then, might greetings relate to music making in cases where music is used for specific types of encounter, such as welcoming guests? More broadly, insights from research (too vast to cite) on analogs between music and speech acts should be germane to the study of "musical beginnings." Improvisatory interactions, in particular, have been analyzed at length by Monson (1996) on the model of a conversation. The double sting of musical-verbal duels in some African interactive contexts (see Chernoff 1979, 81), and the potential for different listeners to receive different verbal messages from a single utterance in an African "drum language," are particularly suggestive of the ways in which agonistic gestures and intentional ambiguities (see Fisher 1976) generate complicated forms of "theorization" on the part of listeners when they contemplate the "real" intentions of manipulative actors. The question for further study, in the musical case, is what kind of "sequencing" (Schegloff 1968) takes place in such musical gambits. What are the various pre-performance acts that may "instigate" (Goodwin 1982) a particular performance?

T.M.T.'s motivation for "correcting" *viribhōṇi* was that he believed (as many do) that a raga should be established firmly and unambiguously in the first few seconds of any performance. But other musicians—in the *ālāpana* context, where they have some freedom—may wish to leave the audience guessing for a few moments before revealing the raga's identity. Such acts index basic inflections of value in south Indian classical music and, obviously, can only be accomplished at structural "beginnings."

GLOSSARY

Key to languages

A.	Arabic	Np.	Nepali	T.	Tamil
B.	Balochi	Nw.	Newari	Te.	Telugu
P.	Persian	H.	Hindi	S.	Sanskrit
M.	Malayalam	U.	Urdu	Si.	Sinhala
Mr.	Marwari				

Language(s) specified in parentheses below refer to specific usages found in this book. In some cases, the specified language is a source language, such as Sanskrit, from which several regional languages draw versions of the same term. In other cases, when the local version of a term is given, the local language is indicated. Cognates of many of these terms appear across languages of South and West Asia. Designations as to Hindi or Urdu are based on etymologies in Sanskrit/Prakrit and Persian, respectively (from *A Dictionary of Urdu, Classical Hindi, and English* by John T. Platts).

Note that ā̃ (and equivalent with other vowels) indicates nasalization in some of the transliterations used in the text. The Library of Congress system, which is largely followed in this volume, indicates nasalization in a way that reflects spellings in Hindi. So for instance, a retroflex nasal appears before a retroflex *t* in the word *bāṇṭ*.

The final *a* in *saṅgīta* and most other Sanskrit words is silent when the word appears in Hindi, Urdu, Nepali, and other related north Indian languages. It is pronounced in south India, where Sanskrit terms continue to be used. In Tamil, that final *a* often becomes *am*—e.g., *saṅgīta* becomes *saṅgītam* (or *caṅkītam,* as it would be transliterated from Tamil). Long vowels (*ā, ī, ū, ē, ō*) are marked with a macron in transliterating Dravidian languages. In Hindi, *o* and *e* are always long and so remain unmarked.

For consistency and convenience, when a term is derived from Sanskrit, and that Sanskrit term continues to be used in South Asia, the Sanskrit version appears as the headword and variations appear afterward separated by slashes. Slashes are used to separate other variations in spelling as well.

āhang	(P.) tune or melody type; *215*
ākāra cātakam	(T.) practicing Karnatak music exercises on the vowel /a/; *242, 287*
alankāram	(T.) lit., "decoration"; third set of exercises in the sequence of Karnatak music training, consisting of patterns in each of seven talas; *241*
ālāpana/ālāp	(T./H.) lit., "conversation, speaking"; free-rhythmic exploration of a rāga in South Asian music; *55, 57, 59, 60, 161, 176–177, 240, 260, 263, 296n2*
ansārī	(U./H.) Muslim caste traditionally associated with weaving, often engaged in professional musicianship as well; *85*
antarā	(H.) second section of a song (usually focusing on the upper tetrachord); *75*
araṅkēṟṟam	(T.) "ascent [to the] stage"; ceremonialized debut dance performance, especially in Bharatanāṭyam dance; *44*
āvāz	(P.) melody; a secondary system in a *dastgāh;* classical singing in which rhythm is based on quantitative poetic meters; *228*
baila	(Si. from Portuguese) popular dance and music form in Sri Lanka; *43*
bajrācarya	(Nw.) Buddhist priests and artisans; *113, 116, 119–122; 127–140, 290*
bandish	(U.) composition in Hindustani music; *165*
baṛhāt	(H.) lit., "expansion"; composing; *9, 175*
bā̃ṭ/bāṇṭ	(H.) a type of short composition common in the Banaras tabla style (*gharānā*); *188, 190, 192–193*
baxši	(P., Turkish, and Kurdish of Khorasan) bard who in Khorasan sings in three languages; *207–211, 213, 215–217, 219, 221, 222–224, 293n14, 17*
Berava	(Si.) drummer caste; *31, 33, 34–37, 38, 42, 46, 280n1, 281n9*
beynjo	(B.) a keyed zither found in Balochistan and other parts of South Asia. In Makran, this instrument may be used to accompany *zahīrok* singing. *228, 232*
Bhaṭi	a Rajput clan. Most members of this clan live in Jaisalmer district. *98, 107, 109*
bhāvam	(T./S.) feeling or emotion associated with a raga in Karnatak music; *244*
Bhomiya	(Mr.) village deities of Rajasthan who are deified due to their sacrifice in protecting village cows; *100*
bhopā	(H./Mr.) priests of rural deities who perform various services at shrines and assist in worship of the deities; *99, 100, 102, 104*
bhuchyāḥ	(Nw.) thin-walled, brass cymbals; *117, 120*
birādarī	(U.) brotherhood; *161, 170, 171, 172, 174, 178, 287n2*
caitya	(Np.) Buddhist monument; *116, 118, 124, 129–137, 286n12*

cantam	(T.) in the context of Tamil folk music, musical and metric flow of a song melody; *21, 250, 252, 254, 257, 298n14*
caṛhāvā	(H.) ritual offerings made to a deity; *99*
carya	(Nw.) Tantric Buddhist songs; *285n1*
cātakam	(T.) practice (*see* sādhakam)
cāti	(Nw.) musical instrument made of bamboo and ram horn; *117*
ceṇṭa	(M.) cylindrical stick drum, used for Kathakaḷi and Kerala instrumental genres; *145–148, 151–154, 156–160, 162*
čīhāl	(B.) in Makran, Balochistan, a free-rhythmic vocal section of a *šeyr* sung by a *pahlawān*. Sung to a line of poetry, a vowel, or several vocables, a *čīhāl* is in a *zahīrok* and accompanied by a *suroz*. *21, 233–234, 237*
ciṭṭasvaram	(T.) syllabic passage of melody in a Karnatak composition; when sung, *sargam* syllables rather than meaningful texts are used. *255*
colliyāṭṭam	(M.) "spoken/dance"; group rehearsal in Kathakaḷi with actor-dancers, singers, drummers; *146, 147, 151–153, 157–160, 288n15*
dabadaba	(Nw.) hourglass drum; *118, 122, 286nn8, 15*
dambūrag	(B.) a fretless, long-necked lute of Balochistan with two to four strings; *226, 228, 234*
dapgāl	(B.) a style of singing in a low register without melisma that forms part of *šeyr* singing in Makran, Balochistan; *233*
dastgāh	(P.) one of the "systems" of Persian or Azerbaijani classical music, whose constituent units are arranged in a more or less prescribed order; *215, 217, 218, 236, 297n5*
dastūr	(U.) customary practice; *173*
deśī	(S.) "[of the] country" or "provincial," a term used to mean the often idiosyncratic cultural practices of the local region as opposed to the systematic and wide-reaching practices of the great "way" (mārga); *13, 14, 279n14*
devr	(Kota) "god"; the Kota god ceremony, with which a special musical repertoire is associated; *221, 245*
dhā̃	(Nw.) a double-headed drum played by several Newar castes with a wooden stick in the right hand and with an alternation of open and closed strokes in the left hand; *117, 120, 122, 125, 127, 138–140, 190, 192, 195, 198, 286n5, 290n2, 291n12*
dhalak	(Nw.) double-headed drum; *117, 122, 138, 139, 286n15*
dhamānī	(U./H.) a Muslim caste of western India, often engaged in professional musicianship; *85, 86*
dhimay	(Nw.) a double-headed drum played with a bamboo stick in the right hand and with an alternation of open and closed strokes in the left hand, used in ritual processions in the Kathmandu Valley; *23, 121, 185, 195, 290n2, 291n12*
dhimaycā	(Nw.) small *dhimay; 122, 139, 286n15*

ḍhol	(H.) a double-headed cylindrical drum, common in most parts of India. In Rajasthan it is played with the hand as accompaniment to singing. *99–101, 102, 104, 106, 110, 285n8*
Ḍholī	(H.) lit., "one who plays the *ḍhol*"; a musician caste of north India; *102, 104, 110, 285nn7, 8, 15*
dobeyti	(P.) a genre of verse composed of couplets; also the name of a *guše* in Persian classical music; *218*
dotār	(P.) a long-necked lute with two strings played in Khorasan and Central Asia; *9, 207, 208, 217, 211, 212, 213, 291n1*
dyaḥlhāygu	(Nw.) musical invocation; *115, 120, 122, 124, 125, 136, 138, 139, 140*
gālreč	(B.) a style of rapid singing without melisma that forms part of *šeyr* singing in Makran, Balochistan; *233*
gamaka/gamakam	(S./T.) context-appropriate slides, oscillations, and forms of attack integral to the performance of a *svara* in a particular raga; *54, 55, 57, 58, 59, 154, 241, 242, 297n6*
gaṇḍā	(H.) thread used to symbolize master-disciple relationship; *172*
gaṭṭhā	(H.) lit., "cupped hand"; left-hand technique on the *sārangī; 175*
gāthā	(Nw.) gardeners and ritual dancers; *134*
gāyakī	(H.) "vocal," referring either to vocal style in general or to specific styles or genres; *58, 62, 76, 284n9*
gaz	(U.) bow; *175, 176*
gharānā	(H.) lit., "of the house"; lineage or chain of discipleship or school, usually associated with a musical style; *95, 166, 178, 290n6*
ghulu	(Nw.) musical instrument made of buffalo horn; *117*
ghūmar	(H.) a traditional dance of Rajasthan. The songs with an identifiable melody are in praise of deities. *110, 285n15*
gītam	(T.) strophic song used in south Indian (Karnatak) music training sequence; *245*
gūlābājā	(Nw.) lit., "music of *gūlā* (month)"; Buddhist processional music; *17, 113–140*
gurukula/gurukul	(S./H.) system of learning whereby the disciple lives in the house of the master for an extended period of time and assists him or her in a variety of activities; *57, 159, 160, 170*
guše	(P.) one of the constituent units of a Persian dastgāh; *215, 217, 218*
gvarāḥ	(Nw.) auspicious instrumental and/or vocal piece with drumming; *140*
Haimādyāḥ	(Nw.) lord of music and dance (the negative aspect); *115, 122*
Hashimī	(U./H.) a Muslim caste, often engaged in professional musicianship; *85*
ijāzat	(U.) permission; a concept embodying aspects of etiquette and respect in the master-student relationship; *172*
ʻilm	(A.) lit., "science"; applied to various bodies of knowledge and technical lore; *207, 208, 211, 291n3*
jāgaran	(H.) all-night performance of religious rituals, often musical. *See* rāti jāga

jajmān	(H.) One who, by virtue of his or her caste, patronizes and receives services from a member of another caste. Such patron-client relationships are common in north India and have been described by some scholars as "the jajmānī system." *97*
jaṇṭa varicai	(T./Te.) second set of exercises in Karnatak music training, consisting of permutations of *svaras*, repeated with emphasis; probable literal meaning: "series [of] pairs"; *241, 242*
javāb-e āvāz	(P.) lit., "response to the *āvāz*," performed by an instrumentalist during and immediately following each phrase sung by a vocalist; *224*
jāru	(H.) slide; *58, 61, 283n11*
Jugi	(Nw.) tailor musician; *116, 121, 122, 127, 286n6*
kala eli mangallaya	(Si.) first public Kandyan dance performance; *44, 45*
kaḷari	(M.) open-air pedagogical arena; *147, 153, 157–161, 287nn11, 15*
kalāśam	(M.) cadential passage in Kathakaḷi; refers both to the dance and the drumming composition that accompanies it; *151–153, 156, 158–160, 287nn10, 11, 288nn14, 19*
kalāyatanaya	(Si) art, dance, or music school; *31*
kalpana svara	(S.) (also svara kalpana) in Karnatak music, improvisation using melodic and rhythmic patterns of svaras. These passages must return to the place in the tala where the line of text, on which the improvisation takes place, begins. Singers use svara names when singing this form; instrumentalists articulate the svaras individually to reproduce the syllabic effect. *55, 144, 161, 240*
kā̃tā̃dabadaba	(Nw.) hourglass drum; *118, 122, 286n8*
Kathakaḷi	(M.) dance-drama of Kerala; *18–19, 35, 145–148, 151, 162, 286–289*
kathakaḷi koṭṭu	(M.) lit., Kathakaḷi "beating"; in practice, the improvisational drumming that accentuates the actors' movements in Kathakaḷi *padams*; *147, 153, 155, 160, 288nn17, 19, 289n24*
kēḷviññāṉam	(T.) lit., "hearing knowledge"; musical knowledge gained through active listening; contrasts with book knowledge; *35*
k̲h̲ālī	(U.) section of tāla understood as void in comparison to the struck (*tālī*) sections. *190, 192*
kohoṃba kankāriya	(Si.) all-night Kandyan village ritual propitiating local deities; *31, 33, 34, 38, 46*
koḷ	(Kota) shawm used by the Kotas of south India; a melody played on any Kota instrument; *245, 248*
koḷ ākicd	(Kota) characteristic melody used for warming up on the *koḷ;* inflected depending on the context (e.g., god ceremony or funeral); *246–247*
kriti/kiruti	(S./T.) most prominent compositional genre in Karnatak music; *35, 59, 61, 240, 242–244*
laharā	(H.) melodic ostinato that serves to outline the metrical cycle (tāla) while drummers and/or dancers improvise; *190, 191, 193*
lakṣaṇa	(S.) in the Karnatak music context, musical theory; *244–245*
lakṣya	(S.) in the context of Karnatak music, practice as opposed to theory; *245*

lāsya — (Si.) soft, gentle, graceful style of dance; *15, 34, 38, 40, 281n8*

līko — (B.) a work and travel song, usually sung by travelers on camelback during long journeys, or by farmers plowing their fields. It replaces the *zahīrok* in the northern areas of Balochistan and is often sung with the accompaniment of a *suroz* when sung out of the context of work or travel. *Līko* couplets concern themes of tender love and are often improvised. *226, 227, 294n3*

maddaḷam — (M.) barrel drum that accompanies Kathakaḷi, also used for Kerala instrumental genres; *145, 147, 153, 154, 158, 162, 287n11*

mālik — (U.) "owner"; in the context of brass band music in north India, owners of a band's name, instruments, uniforms, and shop; *82, 87*

maṇḍala — (S./Nw.) ritual diagram consisting of circles and squares; the outer circle separates a protected area from its surroundings; *17, 114–115, 124, 129, 131, 138*

mă̄ṇḍiya — (Si.) basic, foundational position in Kandyan dance; *31–33, 37*

mangaḷam — (T.) lit., "auspicious"; auspicious piece used to end a Karnatak music concert; *243*

Māngaṇiār — (H./U.) a Muslim hereditary musician caste of western Rajasthan who have Hindu patrons. (In Sindh, Pakistan, the related musical community is called Manganhār.) *5, 17, 23, 24, 97–111, 284–285*

maqām — (A./P.) Arabic term for modal entities and suites; in Khorasan and other regions of Iran, a synonym of *āhang; 19, 215, 218, 292n10*

mārga — (S.) lit. "way" or "path," a term used variously over the centuries to mean a set of musical, literary, or other cultural practices that are widespread, systematic, and hierarchically above those that are "provincial," or *deśī. 13, 14, 297n14*

mas̱navi — (P.) a poetic genre in which the two halves of each line rhyme; also the name of a *guše* in Persian classical music; *218*

mātrā — (S./H.) lit., "measure"; a counting unit. When musicians say "*tīn tāl* [i.e. tala] has sixteen *mātrās*" they mean that it consists of sixteen equal parts. The duration of a *mātrā* varies according to the tempo of a performance. *189, 289n10*

mēḷappadam — (M.) performance in the Kathakaḷi preliminaries that features singing and drumming; *147, 151*

mīṇḍ — (H.) a slide or glissando between notes; *76*

Mīrāsī — (U.) hereditary musician communities of northern India and Pakistan; *97*

Molid — (B.) a low social class in Makran, Balochistan, associated with performing housework for a family; known as some of the best nonprofessional performers of certain kinds of *zahīroks*; *228–229, 294n8*

mudra — (S./M.) mimed hand gesture; *153, 157*

muğam — (Azerbaijani) general term for the classical music of Azerbaijan as well as for several types of modal entity; *227*

muqām	(Uighur) term for compound form consisting of modal entities, songs, poetic forms, and musical metric forms in the classical music of Xinjiang, China; *243*
nāgasvaram/ nākacuvaram	(S./T.) double-reed instrument used in Karnatak music; *60, 282n4*
nāga vannama	(Si.) cobra dance; *42*
naiyāṇṭi mēḷam	(T.) "teasing ensemble"; a Tamil folk ensemble of drums and double reeds; *250, 251, 253*
ṅakha dhalā	(Nw.) collective worship with animal horns; *117, 135*
naqqāl	(P.) a performer who sings verses from the Šāh-nāme of Ferdowsi and narrates the stories in prose; *219*
naql	(U.) imitation; *176, 177*
namaskār	(H.) Hindu demonstration of respect, veneration, or greeting to a respected person or god; *172*
Nāsaḥdyaḥ	(Nw.) lord of music and dance (the source of inspiration); *115, 122, 127, 136, 285n4*
nauhah	(U.) metric dirge recited tunefully by groups of men or women during Muharram; *280n20*
nāyaṇam	(T.) A double reed instrument similar to the *nāgasvaram* (and sometimes called *nāgasvaram*) used in Tamil folk music; *250, 251, 253*
nāykhī	(Nw.) butcher's drum (also played by other castes); *120, 122, 125, 129, 136, 139, 140, 286n15*
nāykhībājā	(Nw.) processional music played by Newar butchers; *129*
nhyāḥ	(Nw.) processional drumming pattern; *138, 139*
nṛtta/nṛttam	(S./M.) pure dance (no mimetic, representational content); *31, 147*
oḷakh	(Mr.) lit., "to know" or "introduce"; songs in praise of goddesses in Rajasthan; *99, 106, 108, 110*
ōmayṇ	(Kota) lit., "one sound"; an important ritual beginning of Kota music at certain moments: all instruments play suddenly and loudly together; *246*
oyilāṭṭakkummi	(T.) a type of Tamil male folk dance and song; *254–256*
pachimā	(Nw.) a double-headed drum used in some ritual performances in the Kathmandu Valley; *117, 122, 136, 139, 185, 195, 286n15, 290n2, 291n12*
padam	(M.) sung verses in Kathakaḷi; in these the actor-dancer mimes the singers' words with hand gestures; *147, 153, 154, 157–159, 288nn14, 16, 17*
pahlawān	(B.) lit., "singer of heroic deeds"; professional *šeyr* singer in Makran, Balochistan. Traditionally *pahlawān*s were hereditary but now anyone with a good voice and knowledge of music can become one. *Pahlawān*s are almost always men and sing exclusively with the accompaniment of stringed instruments of *suroz* and *dambūrag*. No *pahlawān* of any fame would sing short love lyrics or other songs other than narratives (*šeyr*) and with the accompaniment of

	any musical instrument other than *suroz.* *23, 226, 228, 230, 233–237, 295nn12, 13, 15, 296nn23, 24*
palṭā	(H.) (pl. palṭe) lit., "turn"; rhythmic variation; sequential patterns; *173, 188, 190, 191, 192*
paṇḍit	(H.) expert, master; *179, 185*
pāṇi	(T.) stylistic school associated with Karnatak music; *7, 12, 15, 241, 244*
perahăra	(Si.) procession; *31, 45, 46*
piṭi	(T.) lit., "clutch, hold"; term for Karnatak violin left-hand techniques involving use of discrete fingers rather than sliding along the fingerboard: trills, turns, and finger flicks (finger very lightly and quickly touched to the string); *57, 58, 61, 62*
pūjā	(S./Nw.) religious worship/offering; *39, 40, 42, 44*
puṟappāṭu	(M.) preliminary dance in Kathakaḷi, intended for beginners; *145, 147, 151, 153*
pvaṅgā	(Nw.) natural trumpet; *117, 286*
qawwālī/qavvālī	(U.) genre of South Asian sufi music; *5, 6*
radīf	(P.) the canonical repertoire of melody-types and fixed compositions used in the pedagogy of Persian classical music; *215, 217, 218, 243, 297n5*
rāga/rāg/rāgam	(S./H./T.) framework for organizing melody, consisting of characteristic phrases, *svaras*, pitches, and rules for combining them; spelled raga in this volume; *7, 21, 25, 54, 56, 65, 74, 75, 165, 168, 172–175, 215, 240, 243, 244, 293n15, 295n16, 297n6*
Rājput	(H.) a dominant caste in Rajasthan and many other erstwhile princely Indian states; *7, 97–11*
Rāmdev	a fifteenth-century saint of Rajasthan who is widely worshiped in other parts of western India across Hindu and Muslim communities; *101*
rasika	(S.) a connoisseur, one who savors the "sap" (*rasa*) of a performance of music, dance, or drama; *162*
Rāṭhor	a Rajput clan; *98, 100, 101, 111, 112, 285n9*
rāti jāga	(Mr.) all-night singing of devotional songs; *107, 108*
sabhā gāna	(S.) concert repertoire in south Indian (Karnatak) music; *244*
sādhakam	(M.) technical exercises practiced in Kerala; also, in drumming, the technique that one achieves as a result of doing these exercises. The same term appears in other languages, including Tamil (*cātakam*) to refer to extensive practice. *146, 147, 153, 160, 287n9*
sākya	(Nw.) Buddhist artisans (gold- and silversmiths); *112, 115, 119, 121, 125–126, 129*
sam/sama/samam	(H./T.) the first count of a tāla; *190, 192, 193, 261, 290n8*
saṅgati	(Te.) in Karnatak music, a line of text that is repeated with melodic embellishment, usually as part of a fixed composition; *55, 244, 297n7*
sāqi-nāme	(P.) a poetic genre (one variety of *ğazal*) addressed to a cup-bearer; also the name of a *guše* in Persian classical music; *218*

saraḷi varicai	(T./Te.) first set of excercises in Karnatak music, consisting of permutations of seven *svaras* ascending and descending. Possible literal meanings: a contraction of *svara āvali varicai,* or "*svara* sequence row," or possibly "simple row." *241, 242*
sārangī	(H.) bowed musical instrument of South Asia; *19, 144, 166, 168, 171, 176, 178*
sargam	(S.) solfège system in Indian classical music; term derived from the syllables denoting the scale *sa re ga ma pa dha ni sa; 60, 74, 168, 174, 248, 249*
śāstriya saṅgīta/ śāstriya saṅgīt	(S.) music that adheres to *śāstras* (rules or texts in which rules are inscribed); used as a Sanskrit equivalent for "classical music"; *200, 209, 289n1*
satī	(H.) The self-immolation of a widow on the funeral pyre of her husband. The deceased widow is herself called a sati and worshiped like a goddess. In Rajasthan, the sites of these suicides were often consecrated as sati stones. Any self-perpetrated death is also considered sati by those in mourning in parts of western Rajasthan. *17, 98–101, 103–104, 285n16*
Sāymi	(Nw.) oilpressers; *113, 114, 116, 119, 136, 186nn12, 13*
šeyr	(B.) Balochi narrative song; a narrative in verse sung with the accompaniment of stringed instruments of one *suroz* and one or two *dambūrag*. Professional singers of *šeyr* are called *pahlawān. 225, 229, 232, 233, 234, 236, 237, 296n23*
shāgird	(U.) disciple; *171, 172, 173, 177*
shāgird bhāī	(U.) lit., "brother disciple(s)"; disciples of the same master; *168*
shāgirdī	(U.) formal ritual of establishing discipleship; *19, 169, 171, 172, 173, 174, 177, 178*
shubhrāja	(Mr.) panegyric genealogy recited by musicians in western Rajasthan for their patrons; *106, 107*
sichyāḥ	(Nw.) thin-walled, brass cymbals; *117, 120, 129*
sīna ba sīna	(U.) heart to heart, chest to chest, father to son; a principle of oral transmission; *14, 19, 161, 167–170, 174, 177–182, 287n2*
sthāyī	(H.) first section of a song; *75*
stotra	(S.) Buddhist unaccompanied hymns (Nw.: *tutaḥ*); *122*
suroz	(B.) an upright, bowed, waisted lute made of mulberry wood. A goat skin covers its belly; associated strongly with Baloch identity. The instrument's four main playing strings (one gut, three metal) are tuned E-A-E-A (the pitch is not absolute); sympathetic strings give the instrument additional resonance. *25, 227–228, 230, 232–237, 295nn12, 13, 21, 296nn23, 24*
sūvisi vivaraṇa	(Si.) Buddhist temple performance commemorating the Buddha's twenty-four lives; *281n10*
svara	(S.) in south India, a theoretical pitch position combined with context-appropriate slides, oscillations, and forms of attack (*gamaka*); *56, 222, 241, 242, 249, 254, 296n2, 298nn11, 12*

svara kalpana	(S.) *see* kalpana svara
svara sāhitya	(S.) section of Karnatak composition that is sung syllabically using meaningful text; *249, 298n11*
svarūpam	(T.) melodic shape; *243*
tablā	(H.) pair of drums used in a variety of styles and genres throughout much of South Asia; *19, 66, 171, 172, 173, 179, 185, 188–192, 195, 198, 283n17, 293n1, 294n9*
tāḥ	(Nw.) thick-walled brass cymbals; *117, 120, 122*
tāl/tāla/tāḷam	(S./H./T./M.) technical term for metrical framework in South Asia; also used in a more generic and general sense for aspects of rhythm. Spelled "tala" in this volume. *7, 21, 56, 145, 147–151, 153–156, 157, 188, 190–192, 209, 222, 240, 241, 242, 251, 280n7, 287n10*
tālāṭṭu	(T.) lullaby
tālī	(H.) strike at beginning of certain sections of *tāla* (defined in opposition to *k̲h̲ālī,* "void"); *190, 192*
ta'līm	(U.) training; *177, 233*
tāṇḍava	(Si.) forceful, vigorous style of dance; *34–35, 37, 38, 40, 281n8*
tariqe	(A./P.) "way," a specific manner of singing poetry; also a term for a Sufi order; *215, 218*
tāyampaka	(M.) solo *ceṇṭa* genre, performed at Kerala festivals; *147, 151, 153, 161, 162, 209, 287nn3, 7*
temmāṅku	(T.) a type of Tamil folksong often involving a dialog or alternation of characters. Often features refrains with syllables strings such as "tan nān nē," and so forth. *250, 251, 253, 257, 296*
thān	(H./Mr.) a small informal shrine, often without a priest. It is derived from "sthān" meaning place, indicating the presence of a deity. *102, 109, 110, 111*
ṭhekā	(H.) specific sequence of syllables or drum strokes marking out the principle parts of a tāla in Hindustani music; *192, 193*
tihā'ī	(H./U.) rhythmic cadence formed by repeating a figure three times to arrive at the first count of the *tāla* (*sam*); *189, 290n8*
tiranōkku	(M.) lit., "curtain look"; performed by a fearsome character in Kathakaḷi at the beginning of certain scenes. Also, the drum compositions that accompany this dance; *147, 153, 162*
tititālā	(Nw.) musical instrument made of bamboo and goat horn; *117*
ṭukṛā	(H.) (lit., piece or fragment) a short piece; *192–193*
tutaḥ	(Nw.) Buddhist unaccompanied hymns (S. *stotra*); *122, 136*
ustād/ostād	(U./P.) master; *19, 25, 83, 144, 172–175, 177–179, 182, 183*
ustādī-shāgirdī	(U.) lit., "mastership-discipleship"; *171, 177*
uṭhān	(H.) lit., lifting up; a rhythmic gesture that begins a performance; *190–193*
vannama (pl. vannam)	(Si.) stage dances based on movements from the *kohoṃba kankāriya; 33–34, 39, 40–44, 281n7*

varṇam	(T.) a kind of composition in Karnatak music used as an exercise and as a first piece in a concert; viewed as a repository of information on melodic and rhythmic possibilities; *21, 54, 144, 161, 240–245, 247, 249, 297nn5, 6*
vaṭṭam veccu kalāśam	(M.) a type of Kathakaḷi *kalāśam* in which the dancer traces circles on the stage, one circle per cycle of *tāla; 147–151, 287n10*
ves taṭṭuva	(Si.) silver headdress traditionally worn by dancers in the *kohoṃba kankāriya; 31*
vēśam	(M.) lit., "costume"; in practice, "dancer-actor" or "dancing-acting"; also, the role played by the Kathakaḷi actor-dancer; *153*
vīṇā	(S.) south Indian plucked lute; also called *sarasvati vīṇā; 35, 240, 241, 242, 244, 279n19*
yāppilakkaṇam	(T.) Tamil metrical rules; *249, 254*
Yuga Nāṭuma	(Si.) a contemporary Sinhala dance duet; *40*
zahīrok	(B.) a genre of Balochi song from the Makran regions of Pakistan and Iran that expresses loss. *Zahīrok* is also a general term for melody types used in Balochi narrative song performance in Makran. *Zahīroks* are generally made of couplets of irregular rhymes and relatively fixed refrains. The beginning section is called a "picking up" (*čist kanag*), and the rising section is called a "carrying up" (*burzā barag*). Once the *zahīrok* has reached its "peak" (*burzī*), it must be "brought down" (*er ārag*) to "kill" (*kušag*) it. *21, 22, 23, 24, 25, 217, 225–237, 295nn1–2, 294nn6–8, 295nn12–16, 19, 296nn23–24*

NOTES

Chapter 1

1. The "global hierarchy of value... entails a strongly reified... usually implicit and diffuse—notion of culture.... More constant than any particular set of its expressions is the comfortably vague sense—the common sense—that, at any given moment, people know what it is, that they know what the good, the beautiful, and the appropriate are. As in any system of ethics or aesthetics, its constancy lies above all in the assumption of a consensus that papers over differences and changes and declares them irrelevant to the main business at hand" (Herzfeld 2004, 2–3).

See also Stokes (2004, 58–62) on the special status of music in studies of hybridity and of hybridity (what Frith terms the "new authenticity") in world music discourse.

2. Thomas Turino's influential book *Nationalists, Cosmopolitans, and Popular Music in Zimbabwe* (2000) addresses this problem with great subtlety; Turino expresses discomfort with the ways in which some writers "argue alternative cultural spaces into the realm of the imaginary, thereby implying that cosmopolitan spheres define a totalized reality" (Turino 2000, 18–19).

3. It is admittedly problematic to argue for an alternative to something as variegated as the "globalization literature." Participants in the scholarly conversation, however, provide useful typifications. William Mazzarella, for instance, deftly describes some of the "interest in globalization" in anthropology in the early 1990s as providing an ethnographic challenge "to conceptualize and describe the ways in which the construction and experience of locality is frequently a product of struggles by cultural producers (anthropologists and their informants among them) to generate value out of translocal circuits of images, objects, and money." Over the next decade, many anthropologists and marketers, he argues, began to understand "the local" and "the global" as "mutually

constitutive imaginary moments. . . ." (Mazzarella 2003, 16–17). The point to be reiterated here is that much global-local talk continues to be concerned with issues of "generating value" out of things that circulate. Focusing on such processes in music narrows the range of viable ethnographic subjects (possibly favoring the hybrid and spectacular) and creates a hierarchy that has the potential to belittle some of the kinds of musical traditions discussed in this book.

4. Numerous other publications consider more than one tradition. But they do not exploit the variety and scope of musical traditions and approaches to them that characterize contemporary understandings of South Asian music. Nor do they problematize the boundaries of South Asian musical scholarship. None are as wide in scope as the South Asia volume of the *Garland Encyclopedia of World Music* (Arnold 2000); some represent attempts by a single author to cover a range of genres (e.g., Thielemann 1999); others are collected essays by a particular author on a range of topics (e.g., Kuckertz 1999; Ranade 1998).

5. *Karam,* a term derived via local vernaculars from the Sanskrit word *karma,* is the Munda name for the monsoon season repertoire of communal song and dance. Mundas borrowed these songs and dances from Hindu and Muslim outsiders, whom they regard as intruders (Babiracki 1991a).

6. See also Michael Herzfeld's discussion of "social poetics," whereby social actors creatively "deform" dominant cultural structures and reposition themselves within different "concentric" levels of identity (Herzfeld 1997).

7. Simultaneity is also exemplified in longing for two places at once, as when Tibetans in many places think of both Tibet and Dharamsala as legitimate sites of home.

8. This is not to downplay the streams of influence among networks of musicians in India, and the many filters (intermediate persons and recordings) through which musical materials reach and become incorporated into a musician's bag of tricks.

9. On responses to inequalities, for instance, see Lipsitz (1994), who conterposes the emerging "transnational culture" that "speak[s] to shared realities" with local sensibilities of "aggrieved communities." The oppressed offer "cross-cultural resistance" through their music, which travels along global networks (1994, 7, 181). Obviously taken for granted in this popular music study is that the music is "popular" and therefore already translocal. What can be said about the music of aggrieved communities (or those not so aggrieved, but just small) that doesn't travel along global pathways?

10. These issues arose in the period following World War II, during which anthropologists were drawn into projects of "global" proportions—in the sense that Americans were made aware of their connections and responsibilities to others in the world at war. Beginning in the late 1940s and early 1950s, anthropologists in the United States began to consider what an anthropology of a civilization might look like. As the specific concerns of Singer and Redfield began to recede and the terms by which intercultural change were described began to become more refined, little remained in the common language of Indic anthropology from this work other than the terms themselves, "great" and "little," which had, in time, been rendered raw. And these, out of their historical and intellectual contexts, are easy to criticize. "Little" has obvious pejorative connotations now that were certainly unintended.

11. Joan Erdman (1985), for instance, implied an alternate category in the title of her book, *Patrons and Performers in Rajasthan: The Subtle Tradition.*

12. See L. Subramanian (2004; 2006), Bakhle (2005), and Weidman (2003) on linguistic, national, and colonial trends regarding mapping classical music onto larger social entities. See Allen (1998), Groesbeck (1999a), and Wolf (this volume) on some of the obvious problems in deciding what is classical in music.

13. Bakhle, for example, makes sweeping statements about "music" that cannot possibly be substantiated. Even taking into account the limited musical practices she intends to describe in the Deccan, her account is undermined by statements like, "By the last two decades of the nineteenth century, music, however and wherever performed, had been disciplined, cleansed, and regulated"; later on the same page she writes, "Music went from being an unmarked practice in the eighteenth century to being marked as classical music in the twentieth" (2005, 4).

14. In music, the terms *mārga* and *deśī* signal an awareness on the part of theorists of a distinction between system (one aspect of *mārga* in music) and regional, individual, instances of rhythmic patterns, melodies, or songs. *Deśī* forms came from particular regions, were in regional languages other than Sanskrit, and were not easily accommodated by the *mārga* systems. *Deśī* forms of music began to be mentioned in treatises in the second half of the first millennium (Rowell 2000, 20; 1992, 198 and passim).

15. The intent here is not to develop a theory of space. Suffice it to say I use the term with Edward Casey's (1996) critique in mind, namely, that "places" are not made by carving up "space." The logical process is the reverse. Moving from place to space is consistent with our inductive approach more generally.

16. By expansions and contractions of space I am invoking aspects of what anthropologist Nancy Munn (1992) calls spacetime in the sense that she refers to "*extension*... [as] the capacity to develop spatiotemporal relations that go beyond the self, or that expand dimensions of the spatiotemporal control of an actor" (1992, 11). See my own monograph (Wolf 2006) for a similar notion of spacetime discussed in the Kota ritual and musical context. This should not be confused with the very different but oft-cited notion of "space-time compression" developed by David Harvey. This refers specifically to a process in the capitalist world, an example of which began around 1972, whereby "time horizons of both private and public decision-making [shrink]... while satellite communication and declining transport costs... [make] it increasingly possible to spread those decisions immediately over an ever wider and variegated space" (1990, 147).

17. On theories of mental and practical maps, see Gell (1985). One of Booth's points is not that (what Gell terms) non-token-indexical representations of the geography are malleable, but that subjects understand their abilities to practice successfully within a geographic territory to be changeable.

18. Moreover, neither the guitar nor the band cultures have, in the way of classical music, been able to serve as a powerful sign of "South Asia." South Asians have made these instruments their own, but they by and large do not present the mastery of Western art music as an achievement as is the case in Japan, China, or Korea; band music, local rock, and even film music, remain stepchildren of the Indian nation (for example) despite their various kinds of popularity.

19. A simple example is the south Indian *vīṇā,* gendered as female in its association with the female body and the goddess Sarasvatī. It is also gendered female in its association with domesticity and the skills and charms an old-fashioned, perhaps conservative, family of relatively high-ranking caste would desire for their female child to enhance her

attractiveness for an arranged marriage. In the public sphere, the history of great *vīṇā* players is largely a history of great men. In the home, a large proportion of amateurs and teachers is female.

20. Exceptions include new, intentional formations of processions by women, such as in Lucknow during Muharram in 1998 (the women chanted *nauhah*s but did not play musical instruments), and traditional communities of dancer-singer families. The public presence of the latter women, singing and dancing, usually feeds into a general reputation for prostitution.

21. Indeed, they are so strongly gendered that male devotees in some Hindu and Sufi traditions take on the persona of a woman (often in singing or poetry) to adopt the appropriate, loving stance in relation to god.

22. Peirce's definition of these three terms needs to be understood within his broader classification of signs. A short definition of Peirce's "symbol" is "a conventional sign, or one depending upon habit (acquired or inborn)" (Peirce 1955, 113).

23. In Weidman's discussion, the identity of neither Indian nor Western is uniform or preconstituted in these cross cultural engagements. See also Turino (2000, 9), who distinguishes "imitation" from "internalization." The latter, a mark of cosmopolitanism, "allows for internally generated cultural creativity, practices, and identities."

24. Gupta and Ferguson, Appadurai, and other critics have argued against "map[ping] anthropological discourse onto social space" (Werbner 2003, 56).

25. Even though these Tibetans appear hybrid in a formal sense (Diehl 2002, 18), this hybridity is superficial; their engagement with others lacks depth. Tibetans in India react to what they perceive as sinicization in the language and musical styles of Tibet today, but embrace, in a limited way, aspects of rock and roll and Hindi film songs in India to promote what it now means to be Tibetan.

Chapter 2

Field research in Sri Lanka was funded by the Asian Cultural Council, Fulbright-Hays, the National Science Foundation, and the Social Science Research Council; my thanks to these agencies for their support. I am grateful to my fellow participants at the Radcliffe seminar for providing such stimulating company during the course of our time in Cambridge. I would especially like to thank Rustom Bharucha, Michael Herzfeld, and Amanda Weidman for their critical input. Versions of this chapter benefited greatly from the comments and suggestions of Elizabeth Tolbert, Bill Smith, and my brother, Bob Reed. H. L. Seneviratne provided invaluable assistance on numerous matters, large and small. Finally, I am deeply grateful to Richard Wolf for his meticulous reading and thoughtful comments and suggestions on this chapter.

1. In Sri Lanka, the role of embodying and preserving tradition was shared for several decades with Berava males, whose dance and music traditions comprised the core of "traditional Sinhala culture" (Reed 2002).

2. Due to the inherently polysemous quality of dancing bodies, where meaning is often ambiguous, contradiction and paradox seem to be the rule rather than the exception in women's dance. For a review of issues in dance and gender, see Reed (1998, 516–20).

3. This chapter is based primarily on field research conducted in Sri Lanka in 1986–89, 1991–92, and 1997, and with Sri Lankan dancers in the United States in 1994 and 2000.

4. An exception was the dance known as *digge nāṭuma,* a dance performed in major deity shrines by women of a particular subcaste. By the mid-twentieth century, however, only a handful of *digge* dancers remained, and by the 1980s the dance was no longer performed.

5. Male dancers still dominate the sphere of traditional village rituals and they are the featured "star" performers in major religious and state-sponsored festivals and processions.

6. This is also reported by Kapferer for rituals in southern Sri Lanka: "Dance is an extension of music; this is explicit in exorcist theory. It is a visualization of the duration and dynamic rhythm of exorcist drumming" (Kapferer 1983, 192).

7. For details on the *vannam,* see Kotelawala (1998, 61–67).

8. *Tāṇḍava* and *lāsya* are quite complex terms in South Asian dance theory, and they are not used uniformly by practitioners or in dance texts. Kapila Vatsyayan notes, for instance, that the Sanskrit drama and dance treatise, the *Nāṭyaśāstra,* does not make an overt distinction between *tāṇḍava* and *lāsya,* "though it is implied in certain portions of it" (Vatsyayan 1967, 232). The *Nāṭyaśāstra* uses the word *tāṇḍava* as a "generic term for dancing which cannot necessarily be interpreted as denoting violent dancing, or as that performed by men alone, or even a special type of dancing" (Vatsyayan 1967, 232). Mohan Khokar argues that although in many of the ancient dance treatises of India *tāṇḍava* is associated with men and *lāsya* with women, "this does not mean that men alone may dance *tāṇḍava* and women *lāsya.* The two aspects refer simply to the style of rendering the dance, not to who is qualified or privileged to do the rendering" (Khokar 1984, 59).

9. Most Berava dancers regard handsprings and backflips as inappropriate for *ves* dancers, as these movements place the sacred *ves* headdress near the ground, which is considered defiling. Those Berava dancers who do perform these moves typically wear a white cloth turban instead of the *ves* headdress.

10. Ironically, the one exception is the performance of dances at Buddhist temple ceremonies such as *sūvisi vivaraṇa,* in which some girl and women dancers incorporate acrobatic movements.

11. Sexualized images of women dancers are common, however, and can be found in many kinds of visual media, including drawn illustrations in dance textbooks, dance programs, and note cards. One image that has been reproduced consistently since the 1950s depicts women in semitransparent dance costumes.

12. "Fun in the village" folk dances are a staple of state dance troupes worldwide (Shay 2002, 9). See Shay (2002) for further discussion of this ubiquitous genre of folk dance.

13. *Daily News,* February 4, 2002. http://www.dailynews.lk/2002/02/04/fea04.html, accessed March 10, 2008. The online article includes a photo of the five women initiates in the *ves* costume.

14. *Daily News,* February 18, 2003. http://www.dailynews.lk/2003/02/18/new25.html, accessed March 10, 2008.

15. Most of the following information is based on interviews with Mrs. Hemalatha and her students conducted in March and June 2008. I am deeply grateful to H. L. Seneviratne and Sachini Weerawardena for their assistance in conducting these interviews.

16. Sanghamitta, the daughter of the Indian Buddhist King Asoka, came to Lanka in the third century B.C.E. with her brother Mahinda to establish the Buddhist order on the island. The Sanghamitta Perahara commemorates this event.

17. *Daily News,* February 4, 2002. http://www.dailynews.lk/2002/02/04/fea04.html, accessed March 10, 2008.

18. Ibid.

Chapter 3

A version of this chapter appeared as "Gone Native?: Travels of the Violin in South India" in *Singing the Classical, Voicing the Modern: The Postcolonial Politics of Music in South India,* 25–58 (Durham, N.C.: Duke University Press, 2006). All rights reserved. Used by permission of the publisher.

1. For more on the dynamics of this "revival" and its context, see L. Subramanian (2006) and Weidman (2006).

2. *Icai veḷḷāḷar,* literally "cultivator of music," was a name coined in the 1950s for a group of caste communities whose hereditary occupation was music.

3. A type of composition roughly equivalent to an étude.

4. S. K. Ramachandra Rao suggests that, before its use in the concert hall, the violin was first adopted for use in dance music and that many dance teachers were also violinists (1994, 18–19). It was also used in *mēḷa*s (musical processions at temples or weddings usually featuring *nāgasvaram,* a double-reed instrument). The association of the violin with dance music, and thus with the *dēvadāsi* community (hereditary musicians and dancers, often attached to a temple), Ramachandra Rao suggests, produced a certain resistance among Brahmins to taking up the instrument. Such resistance was first overcome in the early twentieth century when the violin began to be used as accompaniment in *kathā kalākṣēpam,* a kind of storytelling (ibid., 21).

5. Compare Daniel Neuman's discussion of melodic accompaniment in Hindustani music (1980, 121–22, 136–40).

6. Sambamoorthy (1901–73) was born in the Tanjavur district to a family that had had musical connections to the Tanjore court under King Serfoji. He studied violin and vocal music in Madras and became a lecturer in music at Queen Mary's College in 1928; in 1931, he went to Munich for five years to study Western music and comparative musicology. Upon returning to Madras, he served as lecturer and head of the Madras University Department of Indian Music from 1937 to 1961 and from 1966 to his death. He wrote numerous books on the history of Karnatak music and musicians and developed teaching curricula for university music departments.

7. The place where the text of a composition starts in the tala cycle, which is not always the same as the first count of the tala.

8. Also see L. Shankar's doctoral dissertation, "The Art of Violin Accompaniment in South Indian Classical Vocal Music" (1979).

9. The best-known violinists of the generation previous to Dwaram's were Tirukkodikkaval Krishnayyar (1857–1913) and "Fiddle" Govindaswamy Pillai (1878–1931). More information about them can be found in P. Sambamoorthy's *Dictionary of South Indian Music and Musicians.*

10. Personal communication, Dwaram Mangathayaru, Madras, June 1998.

11. *Jāru* comes from the Telugu verb *jāra-*, to slide. Such descriptions of Dwaram's playing can be found in writings by the musicologists T. S. Parthasarathy, B.V.K. Sastri, and T. V. Subba Rao.

12. Personal communication, Srimathi Brahmanandam, Madras, February 1998.

13. Barbara Benary (1971) and Gordon Swift (1990) also mention this shift from a fingered technique to a technique more reliant on *jāru*, or sliding.

14. I thank V.A.K. Ranga Rao, record collector of Madras, for sharing recordings of violinists from 1910 on with me.

15. I am grateful to Adrian L'Armand, who was a student of Karnatak violin in Madras in the 1960s, for discussing this division of violin styles with me.

16. Alan Hovhaness (1911–2000) went to Madras in 1959–60 on a Fulbright scholarship. He studied Karnatak music and was one of the first Western musicians invited to participate in the Madras Music Academy's annual music festival. Many of his subsequent compositions were influenced by Karnatak music, including his "Madras Sonata," premiered in 1960 in Madras. More information about Hovhaness can be found at www.hovhaness.com.

17. The original group comprising Shakti was brought together by British guitarist John McLaughlin and included McLaughlin, violinist L. Shankar, tabla player Zakir Hussain, mridangist Ramnad Raghavan, and ghatam player T. H. Vinayakaram. Their first album, "Shakti with John McLaughlin," was produced in 1975.

18. "Fantasy on Vedic Chants" was commissioned by Zubin Mehta, then the conductor of the New York Philharmonic. A description of the piece by Subramaniam himself can be found at www.indianviolin.com/compositions/fantasy.htm.

Chapter 4

Recordings mentioned in this chapter are as follows: Colonial Cousins, *Colonial Cousins,* Magnasound D4GP1573 (CD), 1996; Colonial Cousins, *Aatma,* Sony Music 502307 2 (CD), 2000. Interviews are as follows: Amit Dutta, Kolkata, August 25, 2001; Dominic Fernandes, Mumbai, August 18, 2001 (DF); Dilip Naik, Mumbai, August 18, 2001; Gary Lawyer, Mumbai, August 19, 2001; Hannibal Castro, Mumbai, December 15, 1998; Kennedy Hlychho, New Delhi, January 11, 1999; Leslie Lewis, Mumbai, August 20, 2001 (LL); Tushar Parte, Mumbai, December 15, 1998 (TP).

1. Pyarelal R. Sharma (b.1940) is one of Indian film music's most famous music directors, famous primarily for his work with Laxmikant S. Kudalkar (1937–98).

2. Babla moved to Trinidad, where he has enjoyed a successful career playing chutney with his wife Kanchan (Myers 2000, 592).

3. Bandra is a suburb of Mumbai with a significant Christian population.

4. Mercury (Bulsara) was actually born in Zanzibar, but his parents were Indian Parsis and he went to school in Bombay.

5. In fact one of my informants, Arthur Gracias, emigrated to Australia shortly after our meeting.

6. Political interference was a bigger issue in the period 1998–2001 when I carried out these interviews, due to the anti-Christian and anti-Western rhetoric of Hindu nationalist parties. Such rhetoric was much less in evidence in metropolitan India in 2007.

7. What follows concentrates on a limited sphere and does not address the many musicians who focus on performing Western music.

8. Music directors often work in teams, such as Kalyanji-Anandji or Laxmikant-Pyarelal.

9. Gāyakī indicates "vocal," that is, imitative of a particular vocal style.

Chapter 5

1. See Booth (2005) for a broader overview of the brass band tradition. As processional music, brass band performance is more ritual than concert oriented. Chaudhuri and Wegner (this volume) describe similarly functional music traditions that are, however, less commercialized and less explicitly capitalist.

2. Bikaner and other cities discussed in this section are shown on page 88.

3. This places them in the *ajlāf* (so-called clean occupational castes) category of South Asian Muslim hierarchy (Ahmad 1978).

4. These and other cities discussed in this section are shown on page 89.

5. Mumbai and Ahmedabad are roughly 550 and 1,100 kilometers, respectively, from the central Deccan village where Razak lives.

6. There are personal and even structural exceptions.

Chapter 6

My greatest debt is to Komalda, Komal Kothari, for all that I have learned about Rajasthan and its music. I had the good fortune of discussing this work with him. I am also grateful to Daniel Neuman, with whom I first visited the Rāni Bhaṭiyāṇi shrines and began my research on the musicians of western Rajasthan. I have greatly benefited from our many discussions and from his encouragement and guidance. Manohar Lalas, who was a companion and colleague for my travels to the Rāni Bhaṭiyāṇi shrines, shared generously not only his knowledge and insights but also his meticulous field journals of previous trips. I thank Jyoti Rath for his photographs and for accompanying us on the Rāni Bhaṭiyāṇi trail. Shirley Trembath generously shared her experiences and insights. I was also able to refer to her collection of recordings at ARCE (Archives and Research Centre for Ethnomusicology, American Institute of Indian Studies). I am also indebted to numerous Mānganiār musicians who made this journey possible and opened many doors, especially Multan Khan of Beesoo. Finally, I would like to thank colleagues at the seminar "Local Theory/Local Practice" at the Radcliffe Institute for Advanced Study for their encouragement and valuable comments.

1. In recent years, Mānganiārs have performed on the urban stage, nationally and internationally, which contributes significantly to their financial support. However, the links to the traditional patronage remain unbroken.

2. According to Joseph Campbell, myths are important for "supporting and validating a certain social order" (Campbell 1999). I should clarify that the Rāni Bhaṭiyāṇi tale is not a myth in the sense of a fable. The characters did exist. The recurring famine and drought (among from other misfortunes), which forced the family to move to Balotra, and the move back to Jasol after constructing the shrine to Rāni Bhaṭiyāṇi, are well documented.

3. This version of the story was collected in 1989, as recounted by Manohar Lalas and Komal Kothari. It appeared to be the commonly known version at the time.

4. This was a common practice in Rajasthan, especially among the Rājputs.

5. See Neuman and Chaudhuri with Kothari (2006) for a detailed discussion on shrines and musicians.

6. However, not all satis are worshiped, nor are shrines built for all those who died unnatural deaths.

7. Ḍholīs, like the Mānganiārs, are a caste of hereditary musicians. They are the musician community in the part of Barmer where Jasol is situated.

8. The place of the *ḍhol* is dealt with in detail by Varsha Joshi (1995). The *ḍhol* was used to make royal announcements, and accompany officials in situations such as collecting taxes. The role of the Ḍholī was like that of a herald and carried the resultant prestige. The *ḍhol* thus became a symbol of authority that is related to its communal status.

9. This trust is managed by the Rāṭhors of Jasol.

10. In 1990, the shrine at Jasol had already come under the Rāni Bhaṭiyāṇi trust, run by the family of Rāni Bhaṭiyāṇi's in-laws. This is an increasing trend where, under the Devasthanam Act, religious trusts are formed to control the temples.

11. Offerings of alcohol and *bīḍīs* (a kind of cigarette) as well as incense are typical of shrines where the person who is enshrined has died an untimely death.

12. *Suhāg* are the signs of a *sadhvā*—a married woman as opposed to a *vidhvā*, a widow. Rāni Bhaṭiyāṇi remains a *sadhvā*, as she was a married woman when she died. Some of these changes—banning alcoholic offerings and animal sacrifices—are also due to regulations by the Government of India. These are generally not enforced at small shrines, but perhaps it is due to the current prominence of the Jasol temple that official regulations are now being enforced.

13. Some shrines only have footprints or some other manifestation of the deity.

14. This eyewitness account was provided by Manohar Lalas.

15. The *Ḍholī ghūmar* recorded at the Rāni Bhaṭiyāṇi shrine at Jasol can be downloaded from www.smithsonianglobalsound.org.

16. The collection is available at the Archives and Research Centre for Ethnomusicology, Gurgaon.

Chapter 7

1. I plan to publish the complete drumming repertoire of Bhaktapur with selected musical analyses, an outline of its social and cultural context, and a consideration of the meanings of the music for those who perform it. My earlier publications on Newar drumming (1986 and 1988) include musical transcriptions and ethnography. My studies in Bhaktapur are complemented by Richard Widdess's research in Newar vocal genres *carya* and *dāphā*.

2. I was an apprentice with the oilpressers of Sākvalā/Bhaktapur and, a year later, with gold- and silversmiths from Inācva/Bhaktapur.

3. Some of the evolving information relating to music and locality was processed by Niels Gutschow, who prepared a series of excellent maps based on surveys carried out by my field assistants Ganesh Man Basukala and Buddhalal Manandhar. My research work would have been impossible without the generous support of the German Research Council (DFG), Leverhulme Foundation, and the German Academic Exchange Service (DAAD).

4. Wegner 1992, "Invocations of Nāsaḥdyaḥ."

5. The *Svayaṃbhū Purāṇa,* a medieval treatise about Svayaṃbhūnāth hill west of Kathmandu, mentions processions with musical instruments (*paṭcatāla, dhā̃,* and so forth) that are similar to those of today. The treatise was completed by the mid-fourteenth century and was probably based on an older, orally transmitted compilation. Several handwritten versions are kept in the National Archives in Kathmandu.

6. These tailor musicians are called Jvagi in Kathmandu Newari; in Bhaktapur they are called Jugi.

7. Bajrācaryas call these natural trumpets *pañcatāla;* oilpressers, *pastā;* and all other castes, *pvaṅgā.*

8. The only Bhaktapur player of the hourglass drum *kā̃tā̃dabadaba* who was able to produce more elaborate patterns than just a brief rattle died in 1987. This art is not completely lost yet, however. There is one *dabadaba* player in Banepa and one in Patan.

9. For a detailed description of such an apprenticeship, see Wegner (1986, 12–17)).

10. *carhe:* lit., "fourteenth day" (of the lunar month); *pañjadān:* lit., "giving five kinds of alms"

11. Lokeśvar is Newari for Avalokiteśvar, Bodhisattva of compassion.

12. Bajrācarya and Sākya groups may perform their *gūlā* processions without organizing elaborate *caitya* productions at home, but Sāymi oilpresser groups always combine men's musical processions with women's *caitya* production.

13. For the Sāymi this is on the new moon day. For the Bajrācarya and Sākya this is the day after the new moon.

14. The five Buddhas are: Vairocana, Akṣobya, Ratnasaṃbhava, Amitābhav, and Amoghasiddhi. The priest also invokes the four Tārās: Locanī, Māmakī, Pāṇḍurā, and Aryā; the four Karuṇamayas, Aryāvalokiteśvara, Padmapāṇi Lokeśvara, and two others.

15. *Dhimaycā* plays *calti. Nāykhī* plays *calti. Dhalak* plays *dehra* and *tatali. Pachimā* plays *partal. Dabadaba* plays a piece without name. *Kvakhīcā* plays *calti. Nagara* plays *dehra* and *brahmatal.*

16. This composition is not played anymore.

17. Gutschow (1982, 186).

Chapter 8

I would like to thank the American Institute of Indian Studies for funding my research between 1988 and 1990, and the Kalamandalam for allowing me to study there. I particularly wish to thank V. Kaladharan, my research associate at the Kalamandalam; V. V. Balaraman, my primary *ceṇṭa* teacher; K. Vijaykrishnan, my *colliyāṭṭam ceṇṭa* teacher; and Unnikrishnan, who further assisted me with my *Kathakaḷi ceṇṭa* studies. I am also deeply indebted to Richard Wolf for organizing the ICTM seminar at which I read an earlier version of this paper (Radcliffe Institute for Advanced Study, February-March 2004), and to the participants in the seminar for their enlightening commentary and criticism. I particularly wish to cite Michael Herzfeld, who introduced me to the writings of Jean Lave and the literature on apprenticeship in general. The faults in this paper are mine alone.

1. A number of South Asia scholars have emphasized that, for the disciple, becoming a musician entails becoming a specific type of person; social and musical enculturation are interwoven. "The guru-shishya parampara . . . is the cultural model of the natural

relationship between father and son. The disciple learns not only the craft, but also the trade secrets. He learns how to behave as a member of the artist's community" (Neuman 1990, 58). See also Qureshi (this volume) for similar points.

2. Qureshi's discussion of discipleship in this volume, however, portrays a situation in which peer-group immersion continually reinforces the preceptor's authority, and vice versa. The peers who study with a common preceptor constitute a "brotherhood" (*birādarī*), and the model for the preceptor-disciple relationship is from father to son (implied by the concept of *sīna ba sīna*). The two experiences do not constitute separate stages of pedagogy; both, in the ideal environment, are lifelong. The distinctions between the two localities will be revisited later.

3. Also relevant here is the relationship between *eṇṇam* ("number"; fixed, foundational, learned by rote from the primary teacher) and *manōdharmam* (improvised, advanced, often learned through observation outside of the primary pedagogical arena) within the Kerala solo *ceṇṭa* (drum) genre *tāyampaka*. See Groesbeck (1999b).

4. I know of no instance in which a woman drummer has accompanied Kathakaḷi. Even in one long-standing all-female Kathakaḷi troupe, the drummers are men (Pitkow and Daugherty 1991).

5. Most of the characters (and until recently all of the actors who played them) in Kathakaḷi are men, but female characters are accompanied by the *iṭakka* (a small tension drum) instead of the *ceṇṭa*. For more thorough introductions to Kathakaḷi, see Jones and Jones (1970), and Zarrilli (1984b; 1990; 2000).

6. A Malayali is a speaker of Malayalam, the language of Kerala.

7. Artists tend to train privately for such temple drumming genres as *tāyampaka, mēḷam, pañcavādyam,* and others (see Groesbeck and Palackal 2000).

8. See Groesbeck (1995), chapter 7, for a fuller discussion; Zarrilli (1984b; 2000) for more on the Kalamandalam and other Kathakaḷi institutions; and Neuman (1990) and Ramanathan (2000) for data on the marginality of institutions to pre-professional training in Hindustani and Karnatak music, respectively.

9. See Groesbeck (1995, chapter 7) for an extensive discussion of *ceṇṭa sādhakam*. Also see Wolf, this volume ("*Varṇams* and Vocalizations") for material on Karnatak music introductory technical exercises analogous to *ceṇṭa sādhakam*. Note that one of these is called *ākāra cātakam,* the latter word a transliteration from Tamil of the same word, *sādhakam*.

10. The talas of the *vaṭṭam veccu kalāśams* vary widely in length; I have learned *vaṭṭam veccu kalāśams* in talas ranging from six to fifty-six counts per cycle. A note on the word "count": Kerala drummers use the terms *mātrā, akṣara* ("syllable"), and *akṣarakāla* more or less interchangeably. Each can mean either the tala beat (the duration of one normal stroke played by the tala keeping idiophones), a subdivision of this beat, and/or the duration of the drum stroke. In this chapter I use "count" to mean the tala beat. For a further discussion see Groesbeck (1995, chapter 8, especially 365–70).

11. An interlocking *maddaḷam* drum pattern, which forms part of this *kalāśam* (and all *kalāśams*), is not discussed or transcribed here. *Maddaḷam* and *ceṇṭa* artists learn their *kalāśams* in separate drum *kaḷaris,* from separate teachers; *maddaḷam* players generally do not know how to play the *ceṇṭa,* and vice versa. They only encounter each other's parts in the *colliyāṭṭam kaḷaris*, when each is told to focus primarily on the actor, not on each other.

12. The separation to which I refer is of the same sort that appears in Karnatak music; Nelson (2000) gives copious examples. For instance, Nelson notes a segment of a drum duet in which the drumming flows in repeated "seven-pulse phrases," while the tala (*ādi*) uses eight counts (32 pulses; he uses "pulse" to mean one-fourth of a count) per cycle (2000, 160). He cites another cadential pattern in which consecutive drum phrases consist respectively of sixteen, fourteen, seven, five, three, seven, three, and nine pulses, for a total of sixty-four; meanwhile those who clap the tala will clap two cycles of eight-count *ādi tala* within the same period (ibid., 158). The flow of the drum's rhythms in both cases diverges wholly from that of the tala.

13. When I was in Kalamandalam in 2000, the length of the training program in the drumming classes was usually four years. Acting students (and possibly singing students) studied for longer. When the institution became a university in 2006, and students were required to take courses in subjects like Hindi and Malayalam literature, the time available for arts training decreased, so that the length of the training programs had to expand in compensation. Now the drum training courses last eight years.

14. The main sections of the *padam* are the *pallavi,* the *anupallavi,* and the *caraṇam,* in addition to the cadential *kalāśam*. Zarrilli (2000, 42–43) provides a diagram showing the relationships among these within the *padam* in the structure of a Kathakaḷi scene.

15. During my 2000 trip to the Kalamandalam, the institution had six *ceṇṭa* preceptors. Four—the primary preceptors—taught students in the drum *kaḷaris*, and two others were assigned to the *colliyāṭṭam kaḷaris* to observe the students there. One primary preceptor would instruct the fourth-year students, another the third-year students, and so on.

16. Zarrilli (1984b; 2000) discusses the role of the actor in *padams* in considerable detail.

17. Actually, not all Kathakaḷi *koṭṭu* consists of improvisation underneath the singers' lines in *padams*; it also includes, perhaps more crucially, the drum performances during the actors' *iḷakiyāṭṭams* (interpolations into the story, without singers). Drum accompaniment of the *iḷakiyāṭṭam* is far beyond the scope of this paper.

18. Nelson's data on how the *mridang*ist figures out how to accompany singers and melodic instrumentalists in Karnatak music are analogous; he reports that "drummers are expected to absorb the principles of effective accompaniment by listening: first to the teacher, then to other senior drummers," and that "teachers almost never teach the art of accompaniment formally" (Nelson 2000, 157).

19. *kalāśaṅṅaḷ paṭhikkaṇameṅkil, raṇṭō mūnnō māsam mati; Kathakaḷi koṭṭu paṭhikkaṇameṅkil, raṇṭu varṣam pōrā.*

20. Elsewhere, Lave uses a case study of tailors in West Africa to show how a seemingly informal apprenticeship process embodies elements of structure and curriculum that enable apprentices to learn skills needed for their jobs (Lave 1977; 1982).

21. This was the case at Margi, an institution in Thiruvananthapuram, south Kerala, as of 1988.

22. I would like to thank Regula Qureshi for this insight into the general effects of institutionalization.

23. Relevant here is the literature on the intensity of same-sex peer-group relationships in Kerala; see especially Osella and Osella (2004), on homosociality among young male connoisseurs of film.

24. I discuss this stroke, and its significance in this play, in Groesbeck (2003), 47–48. The sound is played by crushing successive bounces of the right stick against the drum head, and moving the stick from the center of the drum (where the pitch is lower) to the edge. Connoisseurs describe the stroke's effect in this play as eerie and bizarre; it accompanies the snoring of the wild hunter Kattalan. A shortened crushed stroke is also played as part of normal Kathakaḷi *koṭṭu* in other plays, as noted earlier, but when it is played quickly and softly in fast, metric Kathakaḷi *koṭṭu,* it loses these associations and timbral idiosyncrasies.

Chapter 9

1. Of course I acknowledge the fact that fieldwork, and discipleship in particular, have generated such insights in the works of other ethnomusicologists (among them Rolf Groesbeck in this volume). My attempt here is to recognize these insights as instances of difference in fundamental assumptions and to face the challenge of acknowledging and learning from them.

2. Platts's dictionary of Urdu and classical Hindi actually lists a similar definition as one of the meanings of the *sīna ba sīna* phrase; I had simply ignored this as outside my field of vision at the time (thanks to Richard Wolf for pointing this out).

3. Rolf Groesbeck (this volume) discusses fellowship and mutual learning outside a familial setting.

4. The Hindu (and Sufi) use of a raw thread (*kaccā dhāgā*) tied to the wrist of a spiritual disciple attests to this validation.

5. Teaching of women was generally limited to courtesan singers who did not continue the musical lineage, but there have been exceptions.

6. Perhaps the most famous poetic expression of this metaphor is found in the best-known *ghazal* (in Persian) by the thirteenth-century Sufi saint Khwaja Nasiruddin Chiragh-e-Dehli, spiritual successor of Khwaja Nizamuddin Auliya: *īn turfa tamāshā bīn, daryā ba ḥabāb andar* / Behold this miracle, the river inside a bubble.

Chapter 10

My research in Nepal in 1995 was supported by a Fulbright grant from the Institute of International Education. Thanks especially to Carla Krachun, who commented on an earlier draft of this chapter and pointed out places where my work echoed issues in cognitive science. Although drumming lessons were not central to my research on music and social change in the Kathmandu Valley, they provided a space in which to think and talk about issues I was confronting or investigating elsewhere. I am indebted to Shambu Prasad Mishra and Hari Govinda Ranjitkar for agreeing to teach me, and to their families for looking after us. A different take on different aspects of studying with these two men appears in Henderson (1997); this chapter is a revision of chapter six of my doctoral dissertation (1998).

1. The tabla is a pair of tuned hand drums commonly used throughout South Asia in such genres as *bhajan* (devotional song), *ādhunik gīt* (modern song), and *ġhazal* (popular classical song) and in the classical music tradition (*śāstriya saṅgīt*) that extends through the urban areas of northern India, Pakistan, Bangladesh, and Nepal. Tabla players provide rhythmic accompaniment for singers and instrumentalists, and, in classical contexts,

interact more equally with the melodic instrumentalist or vocalist; they also occasionally perform as featured artists.

2. These three barrel drums, while distinctive to the Kathmandu Valley, are similar to other drums in South Asia. All three can either be placed horizontally on the floor in front of the performer or hung around the neck. When playing the *dhā̃* or *dhimay,* drummers wield sticks in their right hands; they play the *pachimā* with their hands alone. These three drums are prominent in Newar musical and religious practices (see Wegner, 1986; 1987; see also Wegner, this volume).

3. Procedural and declarative knowledge may also be subsumed under the larger categories of implicit and explicit knowledge. See Dienes and Perner (1999).

4. Pierre Bourdieu's work in *Outline of a Theory of Practice* (1977) has been extremely important in opening up ways to connect "bodily dispositions" to what he calls *habitus* and to what we might think of as "culture."

5. Of course, I paid both of them for my lessons, and they certainly had economic motivations for teaching me, but as I got to know them, I also got to know more of why they themselves drummed and why they were interested in teaching others to drum.

6. I discussed previous ethnographic literature on bodily knowledge—with reference to Nepali song rather than drumming—in Henderson (1996).

7. Shambu told me earlier in the year that his family had come from Banaras in the nineteenth century, and noted occasionally that his tradition was closely related to the Banaras *gharānā* (stylistic tradition).

8. A *tihā'ī* is a sequence made by taking a segment and playing it three times, with the final stroke of the final repetition landing on the first beat (*sam*) of the next rhythmic cycle. This generates rhythmic momentum toward the conclusion of a set of related musical materials. An even stronger cadence can be created by embedding such a threefold repetition into a longer sequence that itself is stated three times.

9. Shambu's initial statement here contains several linguistic points worth elaborating. First, as in many languages, verb conjugations in Nepali usually index the grammatical subject, so when the word "you" appears, it has often been implied, not spoken. Also, some of the verbs that he uses have a slightly different range of referents in Nepali. *Lāunu,* which I translate as "set up," also means put on, wear, or use; *banāunu,* "build," is a word I heard often in lessons, and implies a sense of craftsmanship. When he talks about making the "words" come out, he is talking about *bol*s, a conventional term for tabla strokes. In the previous sentence, he had used the verb from which the word *bol* is derived in Nepali, *bolnu,* "to speak." So in these two sentences he means making the tabla strokes speak. Finally, it is common in the Nepali language to ask for an affirmation by phrasing the question negatively. So at the end of his description of what to do, Shambu is asking if I understood, not assuming I didn't understand.

10. Shambu's imagery here is not unusual, as musicians in other places use similar words—as well as the word "line" itself—to describe how to get from one point to another in a piece.

11. In the extensive literature on musical improvisation, Sudnow's work is unusual in that he explores both how his hands took on particular shapes as well as how he elaborated larger musical structures. Much of the literature bypasses the more basic knowledge of

how it feels to play and focuses on more cognitive dimensions of performance (e.g., Berliner 1994; Nettl and Russell 1998; Sawyer 1997). Sanyal and Widdess (2004) provide an excellent example of such an approach to a South Asian musical practice.

12. For more extensive descriptions of the performance contexts for the *dhã, dhimay,* and *pachimā,* see, again, Wegner (1986; 1987); see also Wegner, this volume.

Chapter 11

1. As a geographic and cultural region, Khorasan may be said to encompass much of western Afghanistan and southern Turkmenistan in addition to northeastern Iran. The *dotār* played by the Turks, Kurds, and Persians of northern Khorasan in Iran differs from the forms of the instrument played by Turkmen musicians to the north, by Persian musicians in the region of Torbat-e Jam to the east, and by Afghan musicians in and around the city of Herat (see Darviši [1380a] 2001a, 119–84 and Baily 1988a, 31–33).

2. *Bande čāker Mohammad Hoseyn Yegāne hastam / sāken-e Qučān / panjā sāl e in tār rā bande sāxtam / va* **sine be sine** in tār ham in tur āmade / dar hozur-e āqāyān / in bande dāde ba'dan mibaxšam / tavaqo' az in dāram in ham in tur **sine be sine** ke bande avordam / na in jur-e enšād bemire (Youssefzadeh 2002a, 86 transcribes this statement a bit differently). See Qureshi's chapter in this volume for discussion of the phrase *sīna ba sīna* in Urdu.

3. Repertories of several types of performer qualify as *'ilm,* as Katherine Ewing notes in an account of the life of a Sufi pir in Lahore (1997, 135): "In this context ''ilm' means a set of techniques and formulas which, when used properly, draw upon specific spiritual beings or forces and bring them under the control of the practitioner." Sufis and adepts of related practices have developed several conceptions of possible relationships between practitioners, *'ilm,* and spiritual forces. No less important than the idea that some sort of *'ilm* enables practitioners to draw upon spiritual forces is the belief that indispensable knowledge is received through the agency of spiritual forces (see During 1996 for a detailed account of one Persian musician's experience and understanding of this relationship).

4. We can hope to learn more about the internal organization of such knowledge as studies of musical cognition proceed and begin to be linked more effectively with ethnographic research. Work along those lines is likely to require reconsideration of what might be entailed in making "a comprehensive map of a musician's knowledge."

5. Compare Gilbert Ryle's distinction between "knowing that" and "knowing how" (Ryle 1949), and the discussion of "models of" and "models for" in Geertz (1973).

6. "Jedes Ansehen geht über in ein Betrachten, jedes Betrachten in ein Sinnen, jedes Sinnen in ein Verknüpfen, und so kann man sagen, daß wir bei jedem aufmerksamen Blick in die Welt theoretisieren. Dieses aber mit Bewußtsein, mit Selbstkenntnis, mit Freiheit, und um uns eines gewagten Wortes zu bedienen, mit Ironie zu tun und vorzunehmen, eine solche Gewandtheit ist nötig, wenn die Abstraktion, vor der wir uns fürchten, unschädlich, und das Erfahrungsresultat, das wir hoffen, recht lebendig und nützlich werden soll."

7. "Implicit theory" has been an explicit concern of scholars with such different projects as those of Coplan (1985, 242)—"Performers accomplish these things by applying an implicit theory of composition and expression"—and Dahlhaus (1984, 1), who argued that historians of music theory should feel obliged "nicht nur sämtliche sprachlichen

Äußerungen über Musik zu berücksichtigen, sondern außerdem die unausgesprochene, 'implizite' Theorie zu rekonstruieren, die in der Kompositionsgeschichte enthalten ist, in den literarischen Dokumenten aber fehlt (aus Gründen, die dann ihrerseits zu den Themen einer umfassenden Geschichte der Musiktheorie gehören würden)." ["not only to take into consideration whatever has been said about music, but in addition to reconstruct the unspoken, 'implicit' theory integral to the history of composition but lacking in literary documents (for reasons that themselves would be thematized in a comprehensive history of music theory")] Dahlhaus was also much concerned with "the implicit listener" to whom a musical work is addressed and acknowledged his indebtedness to Wolfgang Iser's concept of "the implicit reader" (Iser 1972).

8. "[I]nnerhalb einer Kultur (wie der europäischen), in der die Musik zum 'Fach' distanziert ist, gibt es viele Arten des Benennens zwischen den Extremen des theoretisch orientierten und des unreflektierten, handlungs- und funktionsbezogenen Begreifens." ["Within a culture (like the European) in which music is treated at some remove as 'a discipline,' there are many varieties of naming between the extreme of the theoretically oriented and the unreflective understanding related to usage and function."] Jürg Stenzl's contribution to the round table at which Eggebrecht presented this position paper used the distinction between names and terms as the basis for identifying "cultures without theory" (Stenzl 1981).

9. In the 1960s and '70s, the usual term for "regional music" was *musiqi-ye mahalli.* The substitution of *navāhi* for *mahalli* may have been motivated by a preference for words of Iranian rather than Arabic origin.

10. The booklet issued by the Iran Music Association with three albums of six cassettes each devoted to the music of Khorasan contains two tables listing *maqāms* of Torbat-e Jām and one listing *maqāms* of the Khorasani Turks (Ardelān [1375a] 1996a, 29, 36, 52). Only one of the items transcribed and analyzed in Massoudieh's earlier monograph on the music of Torbat-e Jām ([1359] 1970) is called a *maqām, Maqām-e Jal.* It is also the first item discussed in his essay on "The concept of *maqām* in Persian folk music" (1992), which also contains transcriptions of a *Maqām-e Tal* from Lorestan, the initial *maqām* in the Türkmen set of four, and examples of *faryād* and *sarhaddi* from Khorasan, of *Maqām-e Afşāri* from Azerbaijan, and of the genre *lāwok* from Kurdistan. Massoudieh maintains that among the *aşıqlar* (s. *aşıq,* lit. lover. A kind of bard) of Azerbaijan *maqām* is synonymous with *havā* and *māhne,* whereas in Khorasan "the concept *faryād* [cry] is current alongside *maqām.*" He argues that *faryād* and *sarhaddi* are two names for what is in effect a single *maqām.* In my view, *maqām* is best regarded as a term whose uses vary significantly among the various regions and are probably most prominent in Azerbaijan, Kurdistan, and the Turkmen Plain. The authors of a booklet issued with an album of six cassettes with music from Gilan and Talesh complain about imprecise use of the term and attempt their own definition (Pur-rezā et al. 1374 [1995], 19 n).

11. An obvious example is the Greek opposition between "sharp" (*oxys*) and "heavy" (*barys*) sounds, for which theorists found appropriate Arabic and Persian equivalents.

12. Al-Fārābī's list is reworked in the *Kitāb kamāl adab al-ğinā'* of al-Hasan ibn Ahmad ibn 'Alī al-Kātib (ed. al-Hifnī and Khashabah 1975, 44; French translation by Shiloah 1972, 78). Ibn Khaldun offered a rather different list in his great *Muqaddimah*

(Dāghir 1961, 761; English translation by Rosenthal 1967, 2: 398). Baily (1988a, 37–38) lists seven contrasting pairs of terms used by Persian-speaking musicians in Herat.

13. Lortat-Jacob (1998), by applying techniques of musical analysis to the response of a Sardinian singer to one of Lortat-Jacob's questions, was able to account for what in a conventional transcription of the singer's words would have looked like a contradiction; his analysis revealed that the singer had voiced strong disagreement with the response that others could be expected to make to the same question.

14. Youssefzadeh (2002b, 840) quotes ʿAli Āqā as saying that "the interpreter has hundreds of melodies (*āhang*) at his disposal. According to his audience's mood and the poems selected, he can choose happy (*shād*), moving (*sūznāk*), martial (*razmī*), or melancholy (*hoznāvar*) airs." In another publication (2002a, 198) she attributes this remark to Hāj Qorbān Soleymāni. Every *baxši* is apt to say something of the sort, usually underlining the contrast of joy and sorrow.

15. A remark made by Sandhyavandanam Srinivasa Rao in 1967 at a conference of the Madras Music Academy (quoted by Allen 1998, 28) uses a format that insists on the priority of one component over others: "I appeal to all lovers of art to listen to raga and tala in music primarily and bestow only secondary thought to words while listening to their musical rendering."

16. According to Baily (1981, 9), professional musicians in the city of Herat use *raft* and *āmad* as Persian equivalents of Hindi *ārui* and *amrui*. Lorraine Sakata (1983, 64) remarks that she did not encounter the terms in her interviews of Persian-speaking musicians in Herat and two other regions of Afghanistan.

17. For five lines of a Persian-language dialogue between earth and sky from the Torbat-e Jam region, see Massoudieh ([1359] 1980, 22, 94–95). The much longer poems sung on this topic by Khorasani *baxšis* are in Turkmen or Khorasani Turkish.

18. A classic study of the topic "minstrels singing about minstrels" is Başgöz (1952).

19. The reverse situation is also possible—performance of questions to which no explicit responses are offered. One example is a *nowhe* in which Imam Hoseyn asks several questions of his murderer, Šemr, such as "But aren't you apprehensive of the Day of Judgment?" (*magar az ruz-e qiyāmat to nadāri tašviš?*).

Chapter 12

This chapter is partly based on my fieldwork in Balochistan. Financial help was provided by the Ministero dell'Istruzione, dell'Università e della Ricerca (MIUR) through a national research project directed by Adriano Rossi at University of Naples, "l'Orientale." I thank Professor Rossi for reading an earlier draft of this paper and making valuable comments. My participation at the International Council for Traditional Music (ICTM) Colloquium at Radcliffe was kindly financed by the American Institute of Pakistan Studies (AIPS). Very sincere thanks are due to Brian Spooner, president of AIPS. I also thank Stephen Blum of CUNY, who made valuable comments and suggestions on an earlier draft. However, I am responsible for any possible shortcomings in the information provided here.

1. *Zahīrok* is also pronounced *zahīrīg*, and *zahīronk* in different dialects of Balochi.

2. In one *zahīrok* the poet longs for his or her lover as follows: *taī zahīr pa man draden hawr ant / har šapā kāhant u pa manā gwārant*, "your *zahīr* (yearning thoughts) are like heavy rain-showers for me / they come every night and pour down upon me" (Balochi

text from Sabzal Samigi, interviewed in Turbat, January 25, 1995). Compound verbs express the subtleties of such feelings: *zahīr kanag* ("to be nostalgic, to yearn," etc.) and *zahīrīg būag* ("to be suffering from nostalgic feelings").

3. *Liko* is the major genre of work song in the northern and northwestern areas of Balochistan and among the Baloch of Afghanistan (for details on the musical zones of Balochistan, see Badalkhan 2000; see Elfenbein 1966 for Balochi dialectology; and Coletti 1981 and Aksjonov 1990 for *līko*).

4. Blum adds that, "in addition to complaints about fate, the topics may include complaints about unrequited love or requests for a lover's favors; praise of family members (especially father, mother, and brother); the beauty and destructiveness of nature; complaints of hunger, illness, or lack of work; transgressions of the rules of hospitality; and many others" (Blum 2002, 830).

5. This information was provided by Yelmiz Ershahin (Naples, April 2004), a young Kurdish scholar originally from Turkish Kurdistan now studying Kurdish folklore in Germany. See also Allison (1996), 43.

6. We have no early records of the *zahīrok* or other cameleer songs. However, Nicolas Manucci, the Venetian physician of the eldest son of Aurangzeb (late seventeenth–early eighteenth centuries) wrote of Baloch camel drivers and their singing: "There is also another race called Baloche [Baloch], who dwell on the farther side of the river Rāvī, near the city of Multān, and as far as the confines of Persia. In this territory are many camels, which they bring for sale into the Mogul country. Usually they are expert camel-drivers, and serve everyone in that capacity.... *During the march they sing as they ride their camels*" (Manucci 1907, 2: 454–55; emphasis added).

7. Cf. al-Mas'ūdī, who maintains that the *ḥudā'* (camel driver's song) of the ancient Arabs "developed out of the *bikā'* (lament of the women)" (quoted in Farmer 1965, 1073). With regard to the composition of *zahīroks* by women, it is hard to speak with any accuracy, as such songs usually carry no names of composers, but women do sing many *zahīroks*. In the past, women needed to grind grain every day, and *zahīrok* was the best company in these situations.

8. These women had the ability to improvise their songs so that they never ran out of material. I was also told that once the sister of the khan of Kalat (the khans of Kalat were the ruling family that ruled Balochistan from 1666 to 1948) was staying as a guest of the *sardar* (local ruler) of Sami. Early in the morning, a *molid* named Māhān started grinding grain, singing heart-rending *zahīroks* and remembering her son, Allabaksh, who had died in Dubai. The sister of the khan had also lost a brother not long before. The melancholic tune of the *zahīrok,* coming from a broken heart over the loss of a son in a foreign land, was so penetrating and piercing to the heart and mind that the princess fainted and lost consciousness. People immediately ran to the *molid* asking her to stop singing. That *zahīrok,* still famous in the region, begins, *baččī gam u brātī hayāl, hičč bandagey kismat mabāt* ("sorrows of a son, and the remembrance [of the loss] of a brother, / should not befall in the *kismet* of any human being"). This woman was alive in the early 1990s when I was conducting doctoral fieldwork but was aged and weak and could not sing anymore.

9. The Balochi word *tīrmāh* ("months with shooting arrows") refers to May and June, the most difficult period of the year. In this harshest, hottest period in Makran, there is no

harvest. Preceding the date and rice harvests, farmers usually finish their yearly provisions and wait impatiently for the ripening of dates and rice.

10. Cf. Farmer, who writes that according to the Arab historians "the first song is claimed to have been the *ḥudā'* or caravan song.... It is in the *rajaz* metre, a metre said to correspond with the lifting and lowering of the camel's feet" (Farmer 1967, 14).

11. Cf. Allison (2001, 70) for analogies in the performance of Kurdish narrative songs.

12. One sometimes hears audience members shouting at either the *pahlawān* or his *surozī*, "*na kušey-e, na kušey-e*" ("don't kill it [i.e., the *zahīrok*], don't kill it") if they are convinced that the *zahīrok* has not reached its peak and either of them is going to bring it down. This shows that the listeners have a melodic contour in mind. See the interesting discussion by Amanda Weidman (in this volume) about the relationship between the violinist and the vocalist.

13. During (1997, 46–47) describes notebooks in which two instrumentalists have listed names of *zahīroks*, and he sees this as a process of "classicization." However, names of *zahīroks* have long been used by *pahlawāns* and *surozīs*.

14. During concentrates on the instrumental *zahīrok,* describing several of its distinctive musical traits. He notates fourteen *zahīroks* played by Abdul Rahman Surizai on the keyboard of "a synthesiser connected to a computer through a MIDI system" (1997, 49).

15. This number was suggested to me by *pahlawān* Mazar, one of the hereditary musicians coming from a family where all male members play music. He claims to belong to the Dāūdī branch of the Lūṛīs. *Pahlawān* Mazar gave the same number of *zahīroks* also to Lorraine Sakata of UCLA in 1995 in Gwadar (this information is from her field notes).

16. Janmahmad maintains that *zahīrok* is "the Balochi *sur* or *raags* [i.e. raga]" (using Hindi terms to describe the *zahīrok*), which he categorized under two main heads: *baločī* and *kurdī*. He believes that "all others which may be as many as twenty come under these heads" (Janmahmad 1982, 59).

17. Cf. also Sakata, who records *falaks* from Afghanistan, named after local areas (1983, 54).

18. *Sarhadi* ("of the border") is also the name of a *falak* melody type in Afghanistan "whose popularity is more confined to the Herat area" (Sakata 1983, 53) and the name of a melody type in Khurasan (Blum 1974, 90 ff.).

19. This *zahīrok* is probably named after Baloch nomads, who are usually called *baloch* by the settled Baloch population, while the latter are called *šahrī* (settled) by the former.

20. He is believed to have died in 1938 AD (al-Qādrī 1976, 115).

21. A *suroz* has four main strings, "the 2 first being tuned just like those of the 1st and 2nd strings of a violin (E, A) while the 2 others are one octave lower, that is: E called tip string) / A (zil) // E (bam); A (*gor* or *rud* = gut)." During observes that "in the great majority of the performances, the fundamental (*sa*) is given by the 2nd string, A. In addition to the concept of high and low register..., the strings of the sorud bring more of an accurate insight: the highest register is called *tip-zil* (1st–2nd string) and the middle register (one 5th below) is called *gor bam* (4th et 3d) (*sic*), the fundamental one being the E. The use of the 4th string (one octave below) is said to play *gori*" (During 1997, 42).

22. I interviewed most of the minstrels living in the early 1990s as part of my doctoral work on Baloch minstrelsy.

23. Faiz Mahmad (d. 1979), popularly called Payzuk, was probably the last traditional Baloch minstrel with a vast knowledge of *šeyr* singing techniques and a rich repertoire of *zahīrok*s. He had learned from such great Baloch masters as Pahlawān Rami from Gwadar (d. 1950s), and was accompanied by some of the most famous *surozī*s, like the legendary Nuri. [**See audio example 12.3**]

24. *Pahlawāns* and their *surozī*s say that the best *zahīrok*s are sung at early dawn after a performance that had begun at ten o'clock the night before. Rasul Baksh Zangshahi (fig. 12.3), a great master of Balochi classics, hails from the famous Zangishahi family of minstrels and musicians, once told me that he needed to tune his *suroz* twelve times before it was ready for certain *zahīrok*s. He told me that he retunes the instrument after every half hour of playing.

25. I believe that:

1. there is an urgent need to collect as much material as possible, and from as many musicians and minstrels from as many regions as possible;
2. we can learn how many types of *zahīrok*s exist by categorizing the material under names provided by informants. We can further learn if a certain piece has the same name for different informants or the names change from one musician/singer to another or from one region to another or from one performance to another;
3. it would be desirable to organize a musical festival of *zahīrok* singers/players to encourage them as well as to see whether they all agree on certain tunes and their names or not; as a final stage, one could study any relationship between the Balochi *zahīrok,* Afghani *falak,* and the Khorasani and Kurdish *gharībī.*

Chapter 13

I would like to thank Mr. Ramji S. Balan of Madurai, an important preserver and promoter of Tamil folk music, for allowing me to include the Temmangu example he produced in his studio. I am also grateful to Jeyalakshmi Sundar for allowing me to record the lullaby *ārārō ārirarō* and for all her generosity and assistance over the years as she taught me about the folk music of her village.

1. It would be impractical to review the literature of potential relevance to the study of musical beginnings. In addition to those mentioned, musicological studies relating to the function and order of sections broadly pertain, in that they involve discussion of what motivates a composer to proceed with a composition in a particular manner. A flurry of recent writings on the sonata form are relevant here; see, for example, Hepokoski and Darcy (2006).

2. See also T. Viswanathan's study, where he showed that for some ragas, especially *śankarābharaṇam* as performed by several leading artists of the 1970s, raga *ālāpana* phrases would generally begin on a *svara* different from that which initiates a section of a composition. Viswanathan takes this limited result as an indication of historical change, and does not question the idea that compositions are the "repository of tradition" (Viswanathan 1977, 29).

3. These practice pieces are called *abhyāsa gānam* (Sanskrit: "repeated or permanent exercise, discipline, use, habit, custom" + "song"). The sixteenth-century Kannada-speaking "saint" Purandaradasa is credited with standardizing the set of exercises.

4. The basic sequence of concert performance is attributed to the late vocalist Ariyakudi Ramanuja Iyengar (1890–1967).

5. A particular *radīf* is far more complicated and variable in number of parts than a *varṇam;* the number of *radīfs* that exist and are known is very small; the number of supercategories to which they point, *dastgāhs*, is also relatively small when compared with ragas; and finally, a *radīf* is not performed as a piece in a concert.

6. The issue surrounded the distinction between the raga *bhairavi* and the rāga *kharaharapriya.* In south India, rāgas are often described in terms of their ascent (*ārōhanam*) and descent (*avarōhanam*). Both elements of scale and elements of integral ornament (*gamaka*) are discernable in these raga encapsulations. Taking scale alone for the moment, we can see that *bhairavi* and *kharaharapriya* differ in their "theoretical" reductions in the descent.

bhairavi: c d e♭ f g a b♭ c ; c b♭ a♭ g f e♭ d c
kharaharapriya: c d e♭ f g a b♭ c ; c b♭ a g f e♭ d c

In fact, there is a common phrase in *bhairavi* which involves descending to /a/ and then ascending again; most artists use the /a flat/ only when descending to /g/. T. M. Tyagarajan felt that this /a/ was "foreign" to the raga, and lent the raga the flavor of *kharaharapriya.* He taught his students to rest on /b flat/ when they wish to ascend again, rather than descend to /a/. This /b flat/, called *nī* in the local solmization system, is rendered with a deep oscillation spanning a minor third. The beginning of the *varṇam viribhōṇi,* as rendered by most artists, is as follows:

c . . d b♭ . a . b♭ . c . d

T. M. Tyagarajan altered the beginning to conform to his notion of correctness:

c . . d d c b♭ .b♭ . c . d

and in this way avoided the so called "foreign note" entirely.

7. L. Subramanian (2006, 38–39) quotes an unattributed passage published in 1945 which argues that through the development of *sangatis*, the saint-composer Tyagaraja "transformed the recitative hymn into a piece of art music of high aesthetic merit." I would not argue that Sambasiva Iyer's addition of *sangatis* enhanced the "classical" merit of compositions, since the pieces in question were already established as such; it only enhanced the associations between those compositions and the Karaikkudi style.

8. For a detailed description of the god ceremony, see Wolf (1997a).

9. *Gag* tends to be the lowest, followed by *gil; lil* tends to follow utterances of *gil. Lil* and *le* articulate various kinds of contrasts, including pitch, but they do not consistently correspond to high/low or low/high distinctions. Longer note values are held on the *e* of *le* or the liquid, final *l* of *lil.* David Hughes shows that vowels, ordered by their successive second formant frequencies, tend to correlate, cross-culturally, with the relative pitch of the successive notes that the syllables using these vowels represent (2000, 104).

Although I lack precise data on the second formant frequencies of Kota, it is likely that, as in many languages, the vowel /a/ is lower in second formant frequency than is /i/ or /e/. In this Kota humming system, syllables with the vowel /a/ are always lower in pitch than those with the vowels /i/ or /e/.

10. Neither Tamil vocables nor vocables used outside of Indian classical music traditions have, to my knowledge, been dealt with substantially by ethnomusicologists (but see Greene 2001, 167).

11. The *svara sāhitya* (*svara* text) is said to have been introduced by the composer Syāma Sastri (Sambamoorthy 1958, 142).

12. This is called *svarakṣara*. See Sambamoorthy (1958, 3:152 ff.) for examples.

13. For example, in many solmization systems, the vowel /i/ tends to correspond with a higher pitch than that of /a/, and /a/ tends to be higher than /u/. See Hughes (2000, 93) and above, note 7.

14. (*Tamil Lexicon* [1982] s.v. *cantam*), derived from Sanskrit *chandas* (here, "meter"; see Monier-Williams [1990] s.v. *chandas*). Compare with *chand* in Hindustani rhythmic discourse (Kippen 2000, 113).

15. *Yāppu* + the term for "grammar" or "theory" mentioned earlier, *ilakkaṇam*.

16. I am grateful to the artists and to J. Rajasekaran and Lars Kjaerholm for arranging the performance and allowing me to record this selection in 1982.

17. /ā/ becomes /ś/ and one homoorganic nasal/consonant pair, /ṇṭ/, is replaced by another, /ṅk/.

18. See, for instance, Youssouf et al. (1976), and many references in Duranti (2001). Ethnomusicologists may find that some musical encounters fulfill Alessandro Duranti's six criteria for what should count as a "greeting," and their study may counterbalance "the logocentric tendency of other studies of greetings" (Duranti 2001, 209 ff.).

BIBLIOGRAPHY

Abel, Royston. The Manganiyar seduction. Anmaro Asian Arts. www.anmaro.com/docs/manganiyarseduction.htm (accessed March 27, 2008).

Ahmad, Imtiaz. 1978. Endogamy and status mobility among the Siddiqui Sheikhs of Allahabad, Uttar Pradesh. In *Caste and social stratification among Muslims in India,* ed. Imtiaz Ahmad, 207–24. Delhi: Manohar.

Aksjonov, Sergej. 1990. Liko in the poetical folk art of the Baluch of Turkmenistan. *Newsletter of Baluchistan Studies* 7: 3–13.

al-Hifnī, Muhammad Ahmad and Ghattās 'Abd al-Malik Khashabah, eds. 1975. *Al-Kātib: Kitāb kamāl adab al-ğinā'.* [Al-Kātib: The perfection of musical knowledge]. Cairo: al-Hayat al-Misriyat al-Ammah lil-Kitab.

Al-Qādrī, Kāmil. 1976. *Baločī adab kā mut'ālia* [The study of Balochi literature (in Urdu)]. Quetta: Bolan Book Corporation.

Allen, Matthew. 1998. Tales tunes tell: Deepening the dialogue between "classical" and "non-classical" in the music of India. *Yearbook for Traditional Music* 30: 22–52.

Allison, Christine. 1996. Old and new oral traditions in Badinan. In *Kurdish culture and identity,* ed. Philip Kreyenbroek and Christine Allison, 29–47. London: Zed Books in association with the Centre of Near and Middle Eastern Studies, School of Oriental and African Studies, University of London.

———. 2001. *The Yezidi oral tradition in Iraqi Kurdistan.* Richmond, Surrey: Curzon.

Appadurai, Arjun. 1997. *Modernity at large: Cultural dimensions of globalization.* Delhi: Oxford University Press.

Ardelān, Hamid Rezā. [1375a] 1996a. *Musiqi-ye Xorāsān: Tahqiq va tā'lif* [Music of Khorasan: investigation and compilation]. Booklet of 52p. issued with album of six cassettes, *Musiqi-ye navāhi-ye Irān,* I., *Musiqi-ye Xorāsān* [Music of the regions of Iran, I. Music of Khorasan]. Tehran: Anjoman-e Musiqi-ye Iran.

Ardelān, Hamid Rezā. [1375b] 1996b. *Musiqi-ye Kordestān, 2: tahqiq va ta'lif.* [Music of Kordestan: investigation and compilation]. Booklet of 50 pp. issued with album of six cassettes *Musiqi-ye navāhi-ye Irān,* XII., *Musiqi-ye Kordestān.* [Music of the regions of Iran, XII. Music of Kordestan].Tehran: Anjoman-e Musiqi-ye Iran.

Arnold, Alison, ed. 2000. *The Garland encyclopedia of world music.* Vol. 5, *South Asia: The Indian subcontinent.* New York: Garland.

Babiracki, Carol. 1991a. Musical and cultural interaction in tribal India: The "karam" repertory of the Mundas of Chotanagpur. Ph.D. diss., School of Music, University of Illinois at Urbana-Champaign.

Babiracki, Carol. 1991b. Tribal music in the study of great and little traditions of Indian music. In *Comparative musicology and anthropology of music,* ed. Bruno Nettl and Philip V. Bohlman, 69–90. Chicago: University of Chicago Press.

Badalkhan, Sabir. 1994. Poesia epica e tradizioni orali Balochi: I Menestrelli *Pahlawān* del Makrān. Ph.D. diss., Oriental University of Naples.

——. 2000. Balochistan. In *The Garland encyclopedia of world music.* Vol. 5, *South Asia: The Indian subcontinent,* ed. Alison Arnold, 773–84. New York: Garland.

——. 2002. A study of the roles of composer and performer of a Balochi epic. In *The Kalevala and the world's traditional epics,* ed. Lauri Honko, 301–323. Helsinki: Studia Fennica, Folkloristica, Finnish Literary Society.

Baily, John. 1981. A system of modes used in the urban music of Afghanistan. *Ethnomusicology* 25(1): 1–39.

——. 1988a. *Music of Afghanistan: Professional musicians in the city of Herat.* Cambridge Studies in Ethnomusicology. Cambridge: Cambridge University Press.

——. 1988b. Anthropological and psychological approaches to the study of music theory and musical cognition. *Yearbook for Traditional Music* 20: 114–24.

Bakhle, Janaki. 2005. *Two men and music: Nationalism in the making of an Indian classical tradition.* New York: Oxford University Press.

Balakrishnan, Shyamala. 1969. Folk music of Tamilnad. *Sangeet Natak* 12 (April–June): 40–49.

Başgöz, Ilhan. 1952. Turkish folk stories about the lives of minstrels. *Journal of American Folklore* 65: 331–39.

Benary, Barbara. 1971. The violin in south India. M.A. thesis, Wesleyan University.

Berger, Harris M. 2003. Introduction: The politics and aesthetics of language choice and dialect in popular music. In *Global pop, local language,* ed. H. M. Berger and M. T. Carroll, ix–xxvi. Jackson: University Press of Mississippi.

Berliner, Paul F. 1994. *Thinking in jazz: The infinite art of improvisation.* Chicago: University of Chicago Press.

Bharucha, Rustom. 2003. *Rajasthan: An oral history. Conversations with Komal Kothari.* New Delhi: Penguin Books.

Blacking, John. 1967. *Venda children's songs.* Chicago: University of Chicago Press.

Bloch, Maurice, and Jonathan Parry, eds. 1982. *Death and the regeneration of life.* Cambridge: Cambridge University Press.

Blum, Stephen. 1974. Persian folksong in Meshhed (Iran, 1969). *Yearbook of the International Folk Music Council* 6: 86–114.

——. 1975. Towards a social history of musicological technique. *Ethnomusicology* 19: 207–31.

———. 1996. Musical questions and answers in Iranian Xorāsān. *EM: Annuario degli Archivi di Etnomusicologia dell'Accademia Nazionale di Santa Cecilia* 4: 145–63.

———. 2002. Iran: An introduction. In *The Garland encyclopedia of world music*. Vol. 6, *The Middle East*, ed. V. Danielson, S. Marcus, and D. Reynolds, 823–38. New York: Routledge.

———. 2003. Analyzing the rhythms of musical responses. In *Third international symposium "Music in a society," Sarajevo, October 24–26, 2002*, ed. Ivan Čavlović, 178–85. Sarajevo: Musicological Society of the FBiH and Academy of Music in Sarajevo.

Booth, Gregory D. 1990. Brass bands: Tradition, change, and the mass media in Indian wedding music. *Ethnomusicology* 34(2): 245–62.

———. 2005. *Brass baja: Stories from the world of Indian brass bands*. New Delhi: Oxford University Press.

Bor, Joep. 1986–87. The voice of the *sārangī* : An illustrated history of bowing in India. *National Centre for Performing Arts Quarterly Journal* 15(3), 15(4), and 16(1).

Bourdieu, Pierre. 1977. *Outline of a theory of practice*. Cambridge: Cambridge University Press.

———. 1989. *Outline of a theory of practice*. Tr. Richard Nice. Reprint. Cambridge: Cambridge University Press.

Brinner, Benjamin. 1995. *Knowing music, making music: Javanese gamelan and the theory of musical competence and interaction*. Chicago Studies in Ethnomusicology. Chicago: University of Chicago Press.

Brown, Robert E. 1965. The Mrdanga: A study of drumming in south India. Ph.D. diss., University of California, Los Angeles.

Bustān, Bahman, and M. R. Darviši. 1992. *Haft awrang: moruri bar musiqi-ye sonnati-ye mahalli-ye Irān* [Seven heavens: An investigation of the traditional and regional music of Iran]. Tehran: Howze Honari, Sāzmān-e Tabliğāt-e Eslāmi. Book accompanied by four audiocassettes.

Campbell, Joseph, with Bill Moyers. 1999. *The power of myth*. New York: Anchor Books.

Casey, Edward. 1996. How to get from space to place in a fairly short stretch of time: Phenomenological prolegomena. In *Senses of place*, ed. Steven Feld and Keith H. Basso, 13–52. Santa Fe, N.M.: School of American Research Press.

Caton, Steven C. 1990. *"Peaks of Yemen I summon": Poetry as cultural practice in a north Yemeni tribe*. Berkeley: University of California Press.

Caws, Peter. 1974. Operational, representational, and explanatory models. *American Anthropologist* 76(1): 1–10.

Cejpek, J. 1968. Iranian folk-literature. In *History of Iranian literature*, ed. J. Rypka, 607–709. Dordrecht, Netherlands: Reidel.

Čelebiev, F. I. 1989. O morfologii mugama. [On the morphology of the muğam]. In *Narodnaya muzïka: Istoriya i tipologiya. Pamyati Professora E. V. Gippiusa (1903–1985)* [People's music: history and typology. In memory of Professor E. V. Gippius (1903–1985)], ed. I. I. Zemtsovsky, 135–56. Leningrad: Ministerstvo Kulturï RSFSR.

Chakrabarty, Dipesh. 2000. *Provincializing Europe: Postcolonial thought and historical difference*. Princeton, N.J.: Princeton University Press.

Chernoff, John Miller. 1979. *African rhythm and sensibility: Aesthetics and social action in African musical idioms*. Chicago: University of Chicago Press.

Clayton, Martin. 2001. Rock to raga: The many lives of the Indian guitar. In *Guitar cultures,* ed K. Dawe and A. Bennett, 179–208. Oxford, UK: Berg.

Coletti, Alessandro. 1981. *Baluchi of Mirjave (Iran). Liku couplets.* Rome: Edizione A. C.

Collinson, F. 1971. Scottish folkmusic: An historical survey. *Yearbook of the International Folk Music Council* 3: 34–44.

Coplan, David B. 1985. *In township tonight! South Africa's black city music and theatre.* London: Longman.

Cormack, Josepha. 1992. Swara kalpana: Melodic/rhythmic improvisation in Karnatak music. Ph.D. diss., Wesleyan University.

Dāghir, Y. A., ed. 1961. *Tarikh al-allāmah Ibn Khaldūn.* [Ibn Khaldun's history of the world]. Vol. 1, second edition. Beirut: Dar al-Kitab al-Lubnani.

Dahlhaus, Carl. 1984. *Die Musiktheorie im 18. und 19. Jahrhundert,* I. *Grundzüge einer Systematik.* Geschichte der Musiktheorie 10. Darmstadt, Germany: Wissenschaftliche Buchgesellschaft.

Damasio, Antonio R. 1994. *Descartes' error: Emotion, reason, and the human brain.* New York: G. P. Putnam's Sons.

Dandekar, Hemalata. 1986. *Men to Bombay women at home.* Ann Arbor: Center for South and Southeast Asian Studies, University of Michigan.

Daniel, E. Valentine. 1984. *Fluid signs: Being a person the Tamil way.* Berkeley: University of California Press.

Darviši, Mohammad Rezā. [1380a] 2001a. *Dā'iratolma'āref-e sāz-hā-ye Irān,* I, *Sāz-hā-ye zehi-ye mezrābi va ārše'i navāhi-ye Irān* [Great encyclopedia of the instruments of Iran, 1. Plucked and bowed string instruments of Iran's regions]. Tehran: Māhur.

——. [1380b] 2001b. Mahfum-e maqām dar musiqi-ye navāhi-ye Irān [The concept of maqām in the music of Iran's regions]. *Fasl-nāme-ye Māhur* 13: 29–37.

Das, Gurcharan. 2002. *India unbound.* New York: Anchor Books.

Dasasarma, Amala. 1993. *Musicians of India: Past and present gharānas of Hindustani music and genealogies.* Calcutta: Naya Prokash.

De Alwis, Malathi. 1999. "Respectability," "modernity" and the policing of "culture" in colonial Ceylon. In *Gender, sexuality and colonial modernities,* ed. Antoinette Burton, 177–92. London: Routledge.

De Mel, Neloufer. 1996. Static signifiers: Metaphors of women in Sri Lankan war poetry. In *Embodied violence: Communalising women's sexuality in South Asia,* ed. Kumari Jayawardena and Malathi de Alwis, 168–98. London: Zed Books.

Diehl, Keila. 2002. *Echoes from Dharamsala: Music in the life of a Tibetan refugee community.* Berkeley: University of California Press.

Dienes, Zoltan, and Josef Perner. 1999. A theory of implicit and explicit knowledge. *Behavioral and Brain Sciences* 22: 735–808.

Duranti, Alessandro. 2001. Universal and culture-specific properties of greetings. In *Linguistic anthropology: A reader,* 208–38, ed. Alessandro Duranti. Malden, Mass.: Blackwell.

During, Jean. 1996. La voix des esprits et la face cachée de la musique: Le parcours du maître Hâtam 'Asgari. In *Le voyage initiatique en terre d'Islam: Ascensions célestes et itinéraires spirituels,* ed. Mohammad Ali Amir-Moezzi, 335–73. Louvain, Belgium: Peeters.

——. 1997. The Baluchi *Zahirig* as a modal landscape and the emergence of a classical music. In *The structure and idea of Maqām: Historical approaches. Proceedings of the third conference of the ICTM Maqām study group, Tampere—Virrat, Finland, 2–5 October, 1995*, ed. J. Elsner and R. P. Pennanen, 39–64. Tampere, Finland: Publications of Department of Folk Tradition at the University of Tampere, vol. 24.

Eck, Diana L. 1983. *Banaras: City of light*. Delhi: Penguin Books.

Eggebrecht, Hans Heinrich. 1981. Zur Wissenschaft der auf Musik gerichteten Wörter. In *International Musicological Society, Report of the twelfth congress, Berkeley 1977*, ed. Daniel Heartz and Bonnie C. Wade, 776–78. Kassel, Germany: Bärenreiter.

Eglar, Zekiye Suleyman. 1960. *A Punjabi village in Pakistan*. New York: Columbia University Press.

Elfenbein, Josef. 1966. *The Baluchi language. A dialectology with texts*. London: Royal Asiatic Society of Great Britain and Ireland.

———. 1990. *An anthology of classical and modern Balochi literature*. 2 vols. Wiesbaden, Germany: Otto Harrassowitz.

Erdman, Joan. 1985. *Patrons and performers in Rajasthan: The subtle tradition*. Delhi: Chanakya.

Erlanger, Rodolphe d'. 1935. *La musique arabe*, II, *al-Fārābī: livre III du Kitābu' l-mūsīqī al-kabīr et Avicenne: Kitābu' š-šifā' (mathématiques, chap. xii)*. Paris: Paul Geuthner.

Ewing, Katherine Pratt. 1997. *Arguing sainthood: Modernity, psychoanalysis, and Islam*. Durham, N.C.: Duke University Press.

Faridi-Haftkhâni, Armin. 2005. *Tâleshi Havâ*. Regional Music of Iran, 13. Tehran: Mahoor Institute of Culture and Art. Compact disc with notes, M.CD-189.

Farmer, Henry G. 1965. Ghina. In *Encyclopaedia of Islam*, 1072–75. Leiden, Netherlands: E. J. Brill; London: Luzac.

———. 1967. *A history of Arabian music to the XIIIth century*. First published 1929. London: Luzac.

Farr, Charlotte Fey Albright. 1976. The music of professional musicians of northwest Iran (Azerbaijan). Ph.D. diss., University of Washington.

Farrell, Gerry. 1997. *Indian music and the west*. Oxford: Oxford University Press.

Feld, Steven. 1984. Communication, music, and speech about music. *Yearbook for Traditional Music* 16: 1–18.

Fisher, Lawrence E. 1976. "Dropping remarks" and the Barbadian audience. *American Ethnologist* 3(2): 227–42.

Frisbie, Charlotte J. 1980. Vocables in Navajo ceremonial music. *Ethnomusicology* 24(3): 347–92.

Geertz, Clifford. 1973. *The interpretation of cultures: Selected essays*. New York: Basic Books.

———. 1983. *Local knowledge: Further essays in interpretive anthropology*. New York: Basic Books.

Gell, Alfred. 1985. How to read a map: Remarks on the practical knowledge of navigation. *Man* n.s. 20(2): 271–86.

———. 1992. *The anthropology of time: Cultural constructions of temporal maps and images*. Oxford, UK: Berg.

Gellner, David N. 1992. *Monk, householder, and Tantric priest: Newar Buddhism and its hierarchy of ritual*. Cambridge: Cambridge University Press.

Gerstin, Julian. 1998. Interaction and improvisation between dancers and drummers in Martinican Bèlè. *Black Music Research Journal* 18(1–2): 121–65.

Giddens, Anthony. 1984. *The constitution of society: Outline of the theory of structuration.* Berkeley: University of California Press.

Goethe, Johann Wolfgang. [1810] 1989. *Zur Farbenlehre,* ed. Peter Schmidt. Sämtliche Werke nach Epochen seines Schaffens, Münchner Ausgabe 10. Munich: Carl Hansen.

Golledge, Reginald G., and Robert J. Stimson. 1997. *Spatial behavior: A geographic perspective.* London: Guilford Press.

Goodwin, Marjorie H. 1982. "Instigating": Storytelling as social process. *American Ethnologist* 9(4): 799–819.

Greene, Paul D. 2001. Authoring the folk: The crafting of a rural popular music in south India. *Journal of Intercultural Studies* 22(2): 161–72.

Groesbeck, Rolf. 1995. Pedagogy and performance in *Tayampaka,* a genre of temple instrumental music in Kerala, India. Ph.D. diss., New York University.

——. 1999a. "Classical music," "folk music," and the brahmanical temple in Kerala, India. *Asian Music* 30(2): 87–112.

——. 1999b. Cultural constructions of improvisation in *Tayampaka,* a genre of temple instrumental music in Kerala, India. *Ethnomusicology* 43(1): 1–30.

——. 2003. Dhim, Kam, Cappu, Pottu. *Yearbook for Traditional Music* 35: 39–68.

Groesbeck, Rolf, and Joseph Palackal. 2000. Kerala. In *The Garland encyclopedia of world music.* Vol. 5, *South Asia: The Indian subcontinent,* ed. Alison Arnold, 929–51. New York: Garland.

Guha, Ranajit, ed. 1982–89. *Subaltern studies: Writings on South Asian history and society.* 6 vols. Delhi: Oxford University Press.

Gutschow, Niels. 1982. *Stadtraum und Ritual der newarischen Städte im Kāṭhmāṇḍu-Tal: Eine architekturanthroplogische Unterschung.* Stuttgart, Germany: W. Kohlhammer.

——. 1997. *The Nepalese caitya: 1500 years of Buddhist votive architecture in the Kathmandu valley.* Stuttgart, Germany: Axel Menges.

Gutschow, Niels, and Bernhard Kölver. 1975. *Ordered space concepts and functions in a town of Nepal.* Wiesbaden, Germany: Steiner.

Gutschow, Niels, A. Michaels, C. Ramble, and E. Steinkellner, eds. 2003. *Sacred landscape of the Himalaya.* Vienna: Austrian Academy of Sciences.

Harlan, Lindsey. 1992. *Religion and Rājput women: The ethic of protection in contemporary narratives.* Delhi: Munshiram Manoharlal.

Harvey, David. 1990. *The condition of postmodernity: An enquiry into the origins of cultural change.* Cambridge, Mass.: Blackwell.

Hashmi, Sayad. 1986. *Baločī zabān va adab kī tārīx: ek jā'izā* [The history of Balochi language and literature: a survey]. Karachi: Sayad Hashmi Academy.

Henderson, David. 1996. Emotion and devotion, lingering and longing in some Nepali songs. *Ethnomusicology* 40(3): 440–68.

——. 1997. What the drums had to say—And what we wrote about them. In *Creativity in performance,* ed. R. Keith Sawyer, 67–93. London: Ablex.

——. 1998. Collected voices: Echoes of harmony and discontent in the music of the Kathmandu Valley. Ph.D. diss., University of Texas at Austin.

Hepokoski, James A., and Warren Darcy. 2006. *Elements of sonata theory: Norms, types, and deformations in the late eighteenth century sonata.* New York: Oxford University Press.

Herzfeld, Michael. 1997. *Cultural intimacy: Social poetics in the nation-state.* New York: Routledge.

——. 2002. The social life of reality: A review article. *Comparative Studies in Society and History* 44(1): 186–95.

——. 2004. *The body impolitic: Artisans and artifice in the global hierarchy of value*. Chicago: University of Chicago Press.

Hewamanne, Sandya. 2003. Performing "dis-respectability": New tastes, cultural practices, and identity performances by Sri Lanka's free trade zone garment-factory workers. *Cultural Dynamics* 15(1): 71–101.

Hinton, Leanne. 1980. Vocables in Havasupi music. In *Southwestern Indian ritual drama,* ed. Charlotte Frisbie, 275–305. Albuquerque: University of New Mexico Press. [Cited in Mulder 1994.]

Hughes, David W. 1988. Deep structure and surface structure in Javanese music: A grammar of Gendhing Lampah. *Ethnomusicology* 32(1): 23–74.

——. 2000. No nonsense: The logic and power of acoustic-iconic mnemonic systems. *British Journal of Ethnomusicology* 9(2): 93–120.

Ingold, Tim. 2000. *The perception of the environment: Essays on livelihood, dwelling and skill.* New York: Routledge.

Iser, Wolfgang. 1972. Der implizite Leser: Kommunikationsformen des Romans von Bunyan bis Beckett. Munich: W. Fink.

Janmahmad. 1982. *The Baloch cultural heritage*. Karachi: Royal Book Company.

Jayarama Iyer, T. K. 1985. The violin in Karnatic music. *Indian Music Journal* (Delhi Sangeeta Samaj) 4: 27–28.

Jones, Clifford, and Betty True Jones. 1970. *Kathakali: An introduction to the dance-drama of Kerala*. New York: American Society for Eastern Arts.

Joshi, Varsha. 1995. Drums and drummers. In *Folk, faith and feudalism,* ed. N. K. Singhi and Rajendra Joshi, 112–48. Jaipur: Institute of Rajasthan Studies and Rawat Publications.

Joshi, Varsha, and Rima Hooja. 1999. Vrat and vrat kathas: Ritual, women and patriarchy. In *Religion, ritual and royalty,* ed. N. K. Singhi and Rajendra Joshi, 197–213. Jaipur: Institute of Rajasthan Studies and Rawat Publications.

Kapferer, Bruce. 1983. *A celebration of demons*. Bloomington: Indiana University Press.

Khashabah, Ghattās 'Abd al-Malik, and Muhammad Ahmad al-Hifnī, eds. 1967. *Kitāb al-mūsīqa al-kabīr* [The great book on music]. Cairo: Dār al-Kātib al-'Arabī.

Khokar, Mohan. 1984. *Traditions of Indian classical dance*. Second revised edition. New Delhi: Clarion Books.

King, Leslie J., and Golledge, Reginald G. 1978. *Cities, space, and behavior: The elements of urban geography*. Englewood Cliffs, N.J.: Prentice-Hall.

Kippen, James. 1988. *The tabla of Lucknow: A cultural analysis of a musical tradition*. Cambridge: Cambridge University Press.

——. 2000. Hindustani Tala. In *The garland encyclopedia of world music*. Vol. 5, *South Asia: The Indian subcontinent,* ed. Alison Arnold, 110–37. New York: Garland.

Kotelawala, Sicille P. C. 1998. *Kandyan dance: The classical dance of Sri Lanka*. Colombo: Aitken Spence.

Kothari, Komal. 1994. Musicians for the people: The Manganiyars of western Rajasthan. In *The idea of Rajasthan: Explorations in regional identity*. Vol. 1, *Constructions,* ed. Karine Schomer et al., 205–37. New Delhi: Manohar and American Institute of Indian Studies.

Kothari, Komal. 1995. Patronage and performance. In *Folk, faith and feudalism,* ed. N. K. Singhi and Rajendra Joshi, 55–66. Jaipur: Institute of Rajasthan Studies and Rawat Publications.

Kuckertz, Josef. 1999. *Essays on Indian music,* ed. Selina Thielemann. Mumbai: Indian Musicological Society.

Lakshmi, C. S. 2000. *The singer and the song: Conversations with women musicians.* New Delhi: Kali for Women.

Lave, Jean. 1977. Cognitive consequences of traditional apprenticeship training in West Africa. *Anthropology and Education Quarterly* 8(3): 177–80.

———. 1982. A comparative approach to educational forms and learning processes. *Anthropology and Education Quarterly* 13(2): 181–87.

Lave, Jean, and Etienne Wenger. 1991. *Situated learning: Legitimate peripheral participation.* Cambridge: Cambridge University Press.

Leonard, Karen I. 1978. *Social history of an Indian caste: The Kayasths of Hyderabad.* Berkeley: University of California Press.

Lévi-Strauss, Claude. 1962. *La pensée sauvage.* Paris: Plon.

Levy, Robert I. 1990. *Mesocosm: Hinduism and the organization of a traditional Newar city in Nepal.* Berkeley: University of California Press.

Light, Nathan. 1998. Slippery paths: The performance and canonization of Turkic literature and Uyghur muqam song in Islam and modernity. Ph.D. diss, Department of Folklore, Indiana University.

Lipsitz, George. 1994. *Dangerous crossroads: Popular music, postmodernism, and the poetics of place.* New York: Verso.

Liu, Xinru. 1996. *Silk and religion: An exploration of material life and the thought of people, AD 600–1200.* Delhi: Oxford University Press.

Lortat-Jacob, Bernard. 1998. Prononcer en chantant: Analyse musicale d'un texte parlé (Castelsardo, Sardaigne). *L'Homme* 146: 87–112.

Manucci, Niccolao. 1907. *Storia do Mogor or Mogul India—1653–1708,* by Nicolas Manouchy, Venetian: The first Physician to Shāh ʻĀlam, eldest son of Aurangzeb, translated with introduction and notes by William Irvine. 4 vols. London: John Murray, published for the Government of India.

Manuel, Peter. 1993. *Cassette culture: Popular music and technology in north India.* Chicago: University of Chicago Press.

Marriott, McKim, ed. 1961. *Village India: Studies in the little community.* Bombay: Asia Publishing House.

Mascia-Lees, Fran, and Jeff Himpele. 2006. Reimagining globality. *Anthropology News* 47(5): 9, 11.

Massoudieh, Mohammad Taghi. [1359] 1980. *Musiqi-ye Torbat-e Jām* [The music of Torbat-e Jām]. Tehran: Soruš.

———. 1992. Der Begriff des Maqām in der persischen Volksmusik. In *Von der Vielfalt musikalischer Kultur. Festschrift Josef Kuckertz zum 60. Geburtstag,* ed. Rüdiger Schumacher, 311–34. Anif/Salzburg: Ursula Müller-Speiser.

Mazzarella, William. 2003. *Shoveling smoke: Advertising and globalization in contemporary India.* Durham, N.C.: Duke University Press.

Menon, K.P.S. 1957. *Kathakali rangam* [The Kathakali stage]. Kozhikode (Kerala, India): Mathrubhumi.

Misra, Susheela. 1985. *Music makers of the Bhatkhande College of Hindustani Music.* Calcutta: Sangeet Research Academy.

Monier-Williams, Monier. 1990. *A Sanskrit-English dictionary.* Reprint of 1899 edition, Oxford University Press. Delhi: Motilal Banarsidass.

Monson, Ingrid. 1996. *Saying something: Jazz improvisation and interaction.* Chicago: University of Chicago Press.

Moradi, Ali Akbar. 2002. *Kurdistan iranien: Les maqam rituel des Yarsan.* Paris: Maison des Cultures du Monde. Set of four CDs, Inédit W 260110.

Mulder, Jean. 1994. Structural organization in coast Tsimshian music. *Ethnomusicology* 38(1): 81–125.

Munn, Nancy D. 1990. Constructing regional worlds in experience: Kula exchange, witchcraft and Gawan local events. *Man* n.s. 25(1): 1–17.

———. 1992. *The fame of Gawa: A symbolic study of value transformation in a Massim (Papua New Guinea) society.* Durham, N.C.: Duke University Press.

Myers, Helen. 2000. Trinidad. In *The Garland encyclopaedia of world music.* Vol. 5, *South Asia: The Indian subcontinent,* ed. Alison Arnold, 588–93. New York: Garland.

Nasir, Gul Khan. 1979. *Baločī razmīa šā'irī* [Balochi war poetry]. Quetta: Baluchi Academy.

Nayar, Shobhana. 1989. *Bhatkhande's contribution to music: A historical perspective.* Bombay: Popular Prakashan.

Nelson, David. 2000. Karnatak tala. In *The Garland encyclopedia of world music.* Vol. 5, *South Asia: The Indian subcontinent,* ed. Alison Arnold, 138–61. New York: Garland.

Nettl, Bruno. 1987. *The Radif of Persian music: Studies of structure and cultural context.* Champaign, Ill.: Elephant and Cat.

Nettl, Bruno, with Melinda Russell, eds. 1998. *In the course of performance: Studies in the world of musical improvisation.* Chicago: University of Chicago Press.

Neuman, Daniel M. 1980. *The life of music in north India: The organization of an artistic tradition.* Detroit, Mich.: Wayne State University Press.

———. 1985. Indian music as a cultural system. *Asian Music* 17(1): 98–113.

———. 1990. *The life of music in north India.* Second revised edition. Chicago: University of Chicago Press.

Neuman, Daniel, and Shubha Chaudhuri with Komal Kothari. 2006. *Bards, ballads and boundaries: An ethnographic atlas of music traditions in west Rajasthan.* Calcutta: Seagull Books.

Noble, William, and A. D. Ram Sankhyan. 1994. Signs of the divine: *Sati* memorials and *sati* worship in Rajasthan. In *The idea of Rajasthan.* Vol. 1, *Constructions,* ed. Karine Schomer et al., 343–89. New Delhi: Manohar and American Institute of Indian Studies.

O'Hanlon, M. 1992. Unstable images and second skins: Artefacts, exegesis and assessments in the New Guinea Highlands. *Man* 27(3): 587–608.

Osella, Filippo, and Caroline Osella. 2004. Young Malayali men and their movie heroes. In *South Asian Masculinities,* ed. Radhika Chopra, Caroline Osella, and Filippo Osella, 224–61. New Delhi: Kali for Women.

Pandithar, Abraham. [1917] 1982. *Karunamirtha sagaram: On srutis* [The ocean of mercy]. Reprint. Delhi: Asian Educational Services.

Parasuram, Sriram. 1997. The indigenisation of the violin. *The Hindu Folio,* December.

Parthasarathy, R., trans. 1993. *The Cilappatikāram of Iḷaṅkō Aṭikaḷ, an epic of south India.* New York: Columbia University Press.

Peirce, Charles Sanders. 1955. Logic as semiotic: The theory of signs. In *Philosophical writings of Peirce,* ed. Justus Buchler, 98–119. New York: Dover.

Peterson, Indira V. 1991. *Poems to Śiva: The hymns of the Tamil saints.* Delhi: Motilal Banarsidass. [Originally published by Princeton University Press, 1989.]

Picken, Laurence E. R., and Noël J. Nickson, with Nicholas Gray, Okamoto Miyoko, Robert Walker. 2000. *Music from the Tang court 7: Some ancient connections explored.* Cambridge: Cambridge University Press.

Pitkow, Marlene, and Diane Daugherty. 1991. Who's wearing the skirts in Kathakali? *The Drama Review* 35(2): 138–56.

Pollock, Sheldon. 2002. Cosmopolitan and vernacular in history. In *Cosmopolitanism,* ed. Carol A. Breckenridge, Sheldon Pollock, Homi K. Bhabha, and Dipesh Chakrabarty, 15–53. Durham, N.C., and London: Duke University Press.

——. 2006. *The language of the gods in the world of men: Sanskrit, culture, and power in premodern India.* Berkeley: University of California Press.

Powers, Harold S. 1959. The background of the south Indian raga-system. Ph.D. diss., Princeton University.

——. 1980. India. In *The New Grove dictionary of music and musicians,* ed. Stanley Sadie. London: Macmillan.

Pur-rezā, Fereydun, Jahāngir Naseri Aşrafi, and 'Ali Abdali. [1374] 1995. *Musiqi-ye Gilān va Tāleš* [The music of Gilan and Talesh]. Booklet of 27p. issued with album of six cassettes, *Musiqi-ye Navāhi-ye Irān* [Music of the regions of Iran] VI., *Musiqi-ye Gilān va Tāleš* [The music of Gilan and Talesh]. Tehran: Anjoman-e Musiqi-ye Iran.

Qureshi, Regula Burckhardt. 1991. Whose music? Sources and contexts in Indic musicology. *Comparative musicology and anthropology of music,* ed. Bruno Nettl and Philip V. Bohlman, 152–68. Chicago: University of Chicago Press.

——. 2000. How does music mean? Embodied memories and the politics of affect in the Indian sarangi. *American Ethnologist* 27(4): 805–38.

——. 2004. Sīna ba sīna (from heart to heart): Writing the culture of discipleship. Paper presented at International Council of Traditional Music colloquium, "Local Theory/Local Practice: Musical Culture in South Asia and Beyond," Radcliffe Institute for Advanced Study, Cambridge, Mass.

——. 2007. *Master musicians of India: Hereditary sārangī players speak.* New York: Routledge.

Raghavan,V. 1944. Some musicians and their patrons about 1800 AD in Madras city. *Journal of the Madras Music Academy* 16: 127–36.

Rajagopalan, L. S. 1972. The *suddha maddala* of Kerala. *Journal of the Madras Music Academy* 43: 119–33.

Ramachandra Rao, S. K. 1994. *Mysore T. Chowdiah.* Bangalore: Sree Ramaseva Mandali.

Ramanathan, N. 2000. Institutional music education: Southern area. In *The Garland encyclopedia of world music.* Vol. 5, *South Asia: The Indian subcontinent,* ed. Alison Arnold, 449–56. New York: Garland.

Ramanujan, A. K., trans. 1985. *Poems of love and war: From the eight anthologies and the ten long poems of classical Tamil.* New York: Columbia University Press.

———. 1986. Two realms of Kannada folklore. In *Another harmony: New essays on the folklore of India,* ed. Stuart H. Blackburn and A. K. Ramanujan, 41–75. Berkeley: University of California Press.

Ramji [publisher]. 1989. *Temmānku temmānku: kirāmiya icaiyil amainta pāṭalkaḷ* [Temmanku Temmanku: collected songs of village music]. (*Naiyāṇṭi mēḷam*) [ensemble of reeds and drums]. Single audio cassette. Produced and marketed by Sri Renga Agencies, Madurai, Tamil Nadu.

Ranade, Ashok D. 1998. *Essays in Indian ethnomusicology.* New Delhi: Munshiram Manoharlal.

Redfield, Robert. 1955. *The little community: Viewpoints for the study of a human whole.* Chicago: University of Chicago Press.

Redfield, Robert, and Milton B. Singer. 1954. The cultural role of cities. *Economic Development and Cultural Change* 3(1): 53–73.

Reed, Susan A. 1998. The politics and poetics of dance. *Annual Review of Anthropology* 27: 503–32.

———. 2002. Performing respectability: The beravā, middle-class nationalism, and the classicization of Kandyan dance in Sri Lanka. *Cultural Anthropology* 17(2): 246–77.

Richards, Stewart F. 1972. Geographic mobility of industrial workers in India. In *The city as a centre of change in Asia,* ed. D. J. Dwyer, 72–95. Hong Kong: Hong Kong University Press.

Rosen, Lawrence. 1979. Social identity and points of attachment: Approaches to social organization. In Clifford Geertz, Hildred Geertz, and Lawrence Rosen, *Meaning and order in Moroccan society,* 19–122. Cambridge: Cambridge University Press.

Rosenthal, Franz, trans. 1967. *Ibn Khaldûn: The muqaddimah. An introduction to history.* Princeton, N.J.: Princeton University Press.

Rouget, Gilbert. 1985. *Music and trance: A theory of the relations between music and possession.* Chicago: University of Chicago Press.

Rowell, Lewis. 1981. The creation of audible time. In *The study of time IV,* ed. J. T. Fraser, N. Lawrence, and D. Park, 198–210. New York: Springer-Verlag.

———. 1992. Time. In *Music and musical thought in early India,* 180–224. Chicago: University of Chicago Press.

———. 2000. Theoretical treatises. In *The Garland encyclopedia of world music.* Vol. 5, *South Asia: The Indian subcontinent,* ed. Alison Arnold, 17–41.

Rudner, David West. 1994. *Caste and capitalism in colonial India: The Nattukottai Chettiars.* Berkeley: University of California Press.

Ryle, Gilbert. 1949. *The concept of mind.* London: Hutchinson.

Sakata, Hiromi Lorraine. 1983. *Music in the mind: The concepts of music and musician in Afghanistan.* Kent, Ohio: Kent State University Press.

Sambamoorthy, P. 1958. *South Indian music: Book I.* Sixth edition. Madras: Indian Music Publishing House.

———. 1973. *South Indian music. Book III.* Seventh edition, revised and enlarged. Madras: Indian Music Publishing House.

———. 1984. *A dictionary of south Indian music and musicians.* 3 vols. Second edition. Madras: Indian Music Publishing House.

Sankaramurthy, M. R. 1990. *The European airs of Muthuswamy Dikshitar*. Bangalore: Guru Guha Nilaya.

Sanyal, Ritwik, and Richard Widdess. 2004. *Dhrupad: Tradition and performance in Indian music*. SOAS Musicology Series. Aldershot, UK: Ashgate.

Sarachchandra, E. R. 1966. *The folk drama of Ceylon*. Colombo: Department of Cultural Affairs.

Sastry, B.V.K. 1962. Dwaram Venkataswamy Naidu. *Illustrated Weekly of India* 21 (October): 33–35.

Sawyer, R. Keith. 1997. *Creativity in performance*. London: Ablex.

Schegloff, E. A. 1968. Sequencing in conversational openings. *American Anthropologist* 70(6): 1075–95.

Schomer, Karine, Joan L. Erdman, Deryck O. Lodrick, and Lloyd Rudolph, eds. 1994. *The idea of Rajasthan: Explorations in regional identity*. Vol. 1, *Constructions*. Vol. 2, *Institutions*. New Delhi: Manohar and American Institute of Indian Studies.

Scott, Stanley. 1997. Power and delight: Vocal training in north Indian classical music. Ph.D. diss., Wesleyan University.

Seeger, Charles. 1977. *Studies in musicology, 1935–1975*. Berkeley: University of California Press.

Seetha, S. 1981. *Tanjore as a seat of music*. Madras: Madras University.

Shad, Faqir. [1998] 2000. *Mīrāθ* [Patrimony]. First published by Balochi Adabi Juhdkar, Bahrain; reprinted in Karachi, no publisher.

Shankar, L. 1974. The art of violin accompaniment in south Indian classical vocal music. Ph.D. diss., Wesleyan University.

Shay, Anthony. 2002. *Choreographic politics: State folk dance companies, representation, and power*. Middletown, Conn.: Wesleyan University Press.

Shiloah, Amnon, ed. and trans. 1972. *Al-Hasan b. Ahmad b. 'Ali al-Kātib: La perfection des connaissances musicales / Kitāb kamāl adab al-Ġinā': Traduction et commentaire d'un traité de musique arabe du XIe siècle*. Bibliothèque d'Études Islamiques 5. Paris: Paul Geuthner.

Sila-Khan, Dominique. 1996. The Kamad of Rajasthan: Priests of a forgotten tradition. *Journal of the Royal Asiatic Society* 6(1): 29–56.

Silva, Neluka. 2002. Situating the hybrid "other" in an era of conflict: Representations of the burgher in contemporary writings in English. In *The hybrid island: Culture crossings and the invention of identity in Sri Lanka*, ed. Neluka Silva, 104–26. London: Zed Books.

Singer, Milton. 1958. The great tradition in a metropolitan center: Madras. *Journal of American Folklore* 71 (281, Traditional India: Structure and Change): 347–88.

———. 1972. *When a great tradition modernizes*. New York: Praeger.

Singhi, N. K. and Rajendra Joshi, eds. 1995. *Folk, faith and feudalism*. Jaipur: Institute of Rajasthan Studies and Rawat Publications.

———. 1999. *Religion, ritual and royalty*. Jaipur: Institute of Rajasthan Studies and Rawat Publications.

Slawek, Stephen. 1987. *Sitar techniques in Nibaddh forms*. Delhi: Motilal Banarsidass.

———. 2000. The classical master-disciple tradition. In *The Garland encyclopedia of world music*. Vol. 5, *South Asia: The Indian subcontinent*, ed. Alison Arnold, 457–67. New York: Garland.

Slobin, Mark. 1970. Persian folksong texts from Afghan Badakhshan. *Iranian Studies* 3(2): 91–103.

——. 1976. *Music in the culture of northern Afghanistan.* Viking Fund Publications in Anthropology 54. Tucson: University of Arizona Press.

——. 1992. Micromusics of the West: A comparative approach. *Ethnomusicology* 36(1): 1–87.

Slusser, Mary. S. 1982. *Nepal mandala: A cultural study of the Kathmandu Valley.* Vol. 1. Princeton, N.J.: Princeton University Press.

Smith, David A. 1996. *Third world cities in global perspective: The political economy of uneven urbanization.* Boulder, Colo.: Westview Press.

Spiller, Henry. 2004. *Gamelan: The traditional sounds of Indonesia.* Santa Barbara, Calif.: ABC CLIO.

Stenzl, Jürg. 1981. Musikterminologie und "Theorielose Musikkulturen": zum Verhältnis von musikalischen "Termini" und musikalischen "Benennungen." In *International Musicological Society, Report of the Twelfth Congress, Berkeley 1977,* ed. Daniel Heartz and Bonnie C. Wade, 778–80. Kassel, Germany: Bärenreiter.

Stokes, Martin. 2004. Music and the global order. *Annual Review of Anthropology* 33: 47–72.

Subba Rao, T. V. 1962. *Studies in Indian music.* Bombay: Asia Publishing House.

Subrahmanya Ayyar, C. 1939. *The grammar of south Indian music.* Madras: Author.

Subrahmanyam, V. V. 1980. *Vaiyaliṉ varalāṟu* [History of the violin]. Madurai: no publisher.

Subramanian, Karaikkudi S. 1993. Interrelationships among text, tune, and tone in Karnatak music. In *Text, tone, and tune: Parameters of music in multicultural perspective,* ed. Bonnie Wade, 159–75. New Delhi: American Institute of Indian Studies Archives and Research Center for Ethnomusicology; and Oxford and IBH.

Subramanian, Lakshmi. 2004. Contesting the classical: The Tamil Isai Iyakkam and the politics of custodianship. *Asian Journal of Social Science* 32(1): 66–90.

——. 2006. *From the Tanjore court to the Madras Music Academy: A social history of music in south India.* New Delhi: Oxford University Press.

Sudnow, David. 1978. *Ways of the hand: The organization of improvised conduct.* Cambridge, Mass.: Harvard University Press.

Swift, Gordon. 1990. South Indian gamaka and the violin. *Asian Music* 21(2): 71–89.

Tamil Lexicon. 1982. Madras: University of Madras.

Thielemann, Selina. 1999. *The music of South Asia.* New Delhi: A.P.H. Publishing.

Thompson, Gordon. 1995. What's in a *ḍhāḷ?* Evidence of *rāga*-like approaches in a Gujarati musical tradition. *Ethnomusicology* 39(3): 417–32.

Tobler, Waldo R. 1976. The geometry of mental maps. In *Spatial choice and spatial behavior,* ed. Reginald Golledge and Gerard Rushton, 69–81. Columbus: Ohio State University Press.

Togi, Masataro. 1971. *Gagaku: Court music and dance,* tr. Don Kenny. New York and Tokyo: Walker/Weatherhill.

Trembath, Shirley. 1999. The Rani Bhatiyani songs: New or recycled material? In *Religion, ritual and royalty,* ed. N. K. Singhi and Rajendra Joshi, 214–26. Jaipur: Institute of Rajasthan Studies and Rawat Publications.

Tsing, Anna L. 1994. From the margins. *Cultural Anthropology* 9(3): 279–97.

Tsing, Anna L. 2000a. Inside the economy of appearances. *Public Culture* 12(1): 115–44.

——. 2000b. The global situation. *Cultural Anthropology* 15(3): 327–60.

Turino, Thomas. 2000. *Nationalists, cosmopolitans, and popular music in Zimbabwe*. Chicago: University of Chicago Press.

Turner, Stephen. 1994. *The social theory of practices: Tradition, tacit knowledge, and presuppositions*. Chicago: University of Chicago Press.

Vatsyayan, Kapila. 1967. The theory and technique of classical Indian dancing. *Artibus Asiae* 29 (2/3): 229–38.

Vēnukōpāl, Caracuvati. 1982. *Nāṭṭuppurap pāṭalkaḷ: Camūka oppāyvu*. [Folk songs: A comparative investigation (in Tamil)]. Publication no. 62. Madurai: Madurai Kamaraj University.

Viswanathan, Tanjore. 1974. Rāgā ālāpana in south Indian music. Ph.D. diss., Wesleyan University.

——. 1977. The analysis of *rāgā ālāpana* in south Indian music. *Asian Music* 9(1): 13–71.

Wade, Bonnie C., ed. 1983. *Performing arts in India: Essays on music, dance, and drama*. Berkeley: Center for South and Southeast Asia Studies, University of California; Lanham, Md.: University Press of America.

Wadley, Susan S. 1989. Choosing a path: Performance strategies in a north Indian epic. In *Oral epics in India*, ed. Stuart Blackburn, Peter J. Claus, Joyce B. Flueckiger, and Susan S. Wadley, 75–101. Berkeley: University of California Press.

——. 1994. *Struggling with destiny in Karimpur, 1925–1984*. Berkeley: University of California Press.

Wegner, Gert-Matthias. 1986. *The Dhimaybājā of Bhaktapur—Studies in Newar drumming I*. Stuttgart, Germany: Franz Steiner.

——. 1987. Navadāphā of Bhaktapur—Repertoire and performance of the ten drums. In *Heritage of the Kathmandu Valley: Proceedings of an international conference in Lübeck, June 1985*, ed. Niels Gutschow and Axel Michaels, 469–88. Sankt Augustin: VGH Wissenschaftsverlag.

——. 1988. *The nāykhībājā of the Newar butchers—Studies in Newar drumming II*. Stuttgart, Germany: Franz Steiner.

——. 1992. Invocations of Nāsaḥdyaḥ. In *Aspects of Nepalese traditions*, ed. Bernhard Kölver, 125–34. Stuttgart, Germany: Franz Steiner.

Weidman, Amanda. 2003. Gender and the politics of voice: Colonial modernity and classical music in south India. *Cultural Anthropology* 18(2): 194–232.

——. 2006. *Singing the classical, voicing the modern: The postcolonial politics of music in south India*. Durham, N.C.: Duke University Press.

Werbner, Pnina. 2003. *Pilgrims of love: The anthropology of a global sufi cult*. Bloomington: Indiana University Press.

——. 2006. Understanding vernacular cosmopolitanism. *Anthropology News* 47(5): 7, 11.

Weryho, Jan W. 1962. Sīstānī-Persian folklore. *Indo-Iranian Journal* 5: 276–307.

Widdess, Richard. 2004. *Caryā* and *cacā:* Change and continuity in Newar Buddhist ritual song. *Asian Music* 35(2): 7–41.

Wiser, William, and Charlotte Wiser. 1963. *Behind mud walls 1930–1930*. Berkeley: University of California Press.

Wolf, Richard K. 1991. Style and tradition in Karaikkudi *vina* playing. *Asian Theatre Journal* 8(2): 118–41.

———. 1997a. Of god and death: Music in ritual and everyday life. A musical ethnography of the Kotas of south India. Ph.D. diss., School of Music, University of Illinois at Urbana-Champaign.

———. 1997b. Rain, god, and unity among the Kotas. In *Blue mountains revisited: Cultural studies on the Nilgiri hills,* ed. Paul Hockings, 231–92. Delhi: Oxford University Press.

———. 2000. Embodiment and ambivalence: Emotion in South Asian Muharram drumming. *Yearbook for Traditional Music* 32: 81–116.

———. 2000/2001a. Three perspectives on music and the idea of tribe in India. *Asian Music* 32(1): 5–34.

———. 2000/2001b. Mourning songs and human pasts among the Kotas of south India. *Asian Music* 32(1): 141–83.

———. 2001. Emotional dimensions of ritual music among the Kotas, a south Indian tribe. *Ethnomusicology* 45(3): 379–422.

———. 2006. *The black cow's footprint: Time, space and music in the lives of the Kotas of south India*. Urbana: University of Illinois Press.

Wong, Deborah, and René T. A. Lysloff. 1991. Threshold to the sacred: The overture in Thai and Javanese ritual performance. *Ethnomusicology* 35(5): 315–48.

Youssefzadeh, Ameneh. 2002a. *Les bardes du Khorassan iranienne: le bakhshi et son répertoire.* Travaux et Mémoires de l'Institut d'Études Iraniennes 6. Leuven, Belgium: Peeters.

———. 2002b. Snapshot: 'Alī Āqā Almājoqī: The life of a Khorasani Bakhshi. In *The Garland encyclopedia of world music.* Vol. 6, *The Middle East,* ed. V. Danielson, S. Marcus, and D. Reynolds, 839–41. New York: Routledge.

Youssouf, I. A., A. D. Grimshaw, et al. 1976. Greetings in the desert. *American Ethnologist* 3(4): 797–824.

Zarrilli, Phillip. 1984a. Doing the exercise: The in-body transmission of performance knowledge in a traditional martial art. *Asian Theatre Journal* 1(2): 191–206.

———. 1984b. *The Kathakali complex: Actor, performance, structure.* New Delhi: Abhinav.

———. 1990. Kathakali. In *Indian theater: Traditions of performance,* ed. Phillip Zarrilli, Farley Richmond, and Darius Swann, 315–57. Honolulu: University of Hawai'i Press.

———. 2000. *Kathakali dance-drama: When gods and demons come to play.* London: Routledge.

Zbikowski, Lawrence. 2002. *Conceptualizing music.* New York: Oxford University Press.

Zemtsovsky, Izaly. 1993. Dialogie musicale. *Cahiers de musiques traditionnelles* 6: 23–27.

NAME INDEX

al-Fārābī, 215, 216, 292n12
'Ali Āqā. *See* Ǧolāmrezā'i, 'Ali (a.k.a. 'Ali Āqā)
Allen, Matthew, 25, 279n12, 293n15
Appadurai, Arjun, 9, 280n24

Babiracki, Carol, 9, 181, 278n5
Badalkhan, Sabir, 10, 21, 22, 23, 25, 217, 294n3
Baily, John, 208, 210, 211, 291n1, 292–293n12, 293n16
Bakhle, Janaki, 13, 279n12, 279n13
Balachandar, S., 241, 242
Baloch, Faiz Mahmad, 236, 296n23
Blum, Stephen, 9, 10, 14, 15, 20, 25, 77, 213, 224, 227, 240, 244, 248, 250, 294n4, 295n18
Booth, Greg, 16–17, 22, 23, 76, 279n17
Bourdieu, Pierre, 94, 180, 182, 243, 261, 290n4

Caton, Stephen, 6
Chaudhuri, Shubha, 5, 10, 17, 23, 82, 284n5:1, 284n6:5
Clayton, Martin, 10, 11, 15, 16, 17, 22, 23, 25, 66

Damasio, Antonio, 186–188, 195
Daniel, E. Valentine, 25
Darviši, Mohammad Rezā, 207, 215, 291n1
De Alwis, Malathi, 30, 43
Diehl, Keila, 25, 280n25
Dikshitar, Baluswamy (south Indian violinist), 52, 53
Dikshitar, Muthuswamy (south Indian composer), 52, 53, 54
During, Jean, 232, 291n3, 295n13, 295n14, 295n21
Dutta, Amit, 66, 70, 73

Eggebrecht, Hans Heinrich, 214, 292n8

Farrell, Gerry, 49–50
Frisbie, Charlotte, 248, 255, 257

Geertz, 180, 244, 291n5
Gell, Alfred, 214, 279n17
Goethe, Johann Wolfgang, 212, 291n6
Ǧolāmrezā'i, 'Ali (a.k.a. 'Ali Āqā), 207, 208, 223, 224, 293n14
Gopalakrishnan, M. S., 58
Groesbeck, Rolf, 11, 18, 35, 37, 163, 186, 209, 279n12
Gutschow, Niels, 113, 114, 116, 119, 138, 285n3

Henderson, David, 11, 19, 20, 22, 161, 186, 243, 289
Herzfeld, Michael, 9, 186, 199, 202, 239, 240, 277n1, 278n6
Hewamanne, Sandya, 30, 43
Hlyccho, Kennedy, 66, 71
Hughes, David, 248, 261, 297–298n9, 298n13

Ingold, Tim, 7, 18

Jayaraman, Lalgudi, 57
Jayasinghe, Esmee, 30, 38

Khan, Sabri, 144, 161, 166–183 passim
Khan, Shujaat, 166, 183
Kippen, James, 168, 298n14
Kitto, Carlton, 66
Kölver, Bernhard, 113, 116, 119
Kothari, Komal, 102, 284n3, 284n5

Lave, Jean, 146, 158–159, 288n20
Lawyer, Gary, 66, 69, 70, 71, 72, 73
Lewis, Leslie, 66, 71, 72, 73, 76

Manuel, Peter, 76
Menuhin, Yehudi, 57, 61
Mishra, Shambu Prasad, 161, 185–195, 198, 199, 202
Munn, Nancy, 8, 10, 18, 279n16

Naik, Dilip, 66, 68, 69, 70, 71, 72, 75
Nelson, David, 161, 288n12, 288n18
Nettl, Bruno, 239, 290–291n11
Neuman, Daniel, 7, 82, 168, 169, 170, 173, 183, 208, 282n5, 284n5, 286–287n1, 287n8

Parte, Tushar, 66, 68, 70, 71, 76
Peirce, Charles Sanders, 24, 280n22
Pollock, Sheldon, 13
Powers, Harold, 168, 208

Qureshi, Regula, 9, 11, 14, 19, 22, 50, 62, 144, 161, 179, 208, 243, 286–287n1, 287n2

Ramachandra Rao, S. K., 54, 282n4
Ramamurthy, Kamala, 241–242, 243
Ramanuja Ayyangar/Iyengar, Ariyakudi, 243, 297n4
Ramanujan, A. K., 220–221
Rāni Bhaṭiyāni, 17, 23, 24, 97–111, 284n6:2, 285n10, 285n12, 285n15
Ranjitkar, Hari Govinda, 185, 186, 188, 195, 196–199, 201–202
Redfield, Robert, 12, 180, 278n10
Reed, Susan, 9, 15, 21, 23, 32, 199, 280n1, 280n2
Rowell, Lewis, 239, 240, 247, 261, 279n14
Rudner, David, 83, 94

Sakata, Hiromi Lorraine, 226, 293n16, 295n15, 295n17, 295n18
Sambamoorthy, P., 52, 55, 241, 244, 249, 282n6, 282n9, 298n11, 298n12
Sambasiva Iyer, Karaikkudi, 241, 244, 245, 297n7
Sastri, Syama (south Indian composer), 52, 283n11, 298n11
Seetha, S., 52, 53
Serfoji, Maharaja, 53, 282n6
Singer, Milton, 7, 12, 13, 180, 278n10
Slawek, Stephen, 143, 168
Slobin, Mark, 9, 222, 226
Spiller, Henry, 19
Subba Rao, T. V, 51, 283n11
Subrahmanya Ayyar, C. 59, 62
Subramanian, Lakshmi, 13, 279n12, 282n1, 297n7
Sudnow, David, 186, 193–195, 290–291n11
Surasena, Peter, 36, 37, 44

Thompson, Gordon, 25
Thyagaraja/Tyagaraja (south Indian composer), 52, 53, 54, 57, 59, 297n7
Trembath, Shirley, 100, 101, 110
Tsing, Anna, 7, 8, 9
Tyagarajan, T. M., 244, 245, 263, 297n6

Venkataswamy Naidu, Dwaram, 56–59, 283n11
Viswanathan, Tanjore, 144, 168, 296n2

Wade, Bonnie, 6
Wadley, Susan, 180, 222
Wegner, Gert-Matthias, 10, 17, 23, 25, 81, 82, 134, 201, 284n1
Weidman, Amanda, 13, 15, 21, 22, 51, 67, 76, 82, 220, 279n12, 280n23, 282n1, 295n12

Werbner, Pnina, 18, 25, 280n24
Wolf, Richard K., 9, 25, 35, 144, 168, 221, 222, 246, 279n16

Yegāne, Mohammad Hoseyn, 207, 208, 291n2
Youssefzadeh, Ameneh, 210, 213, 215, 217, 221, 222, 293n14

Zarrilli, Phillip, 35, 143, 159, 287n5, 287n8, 288n14, 288n16
Zbikowski, Lawrence, 212, 214

SUBJECT INDEX

Academia
  focus on local, 179–180
  hierarchy of concerns in, 8–9, 14, 182
  intellectual shift needed, 166–167
  key terms in South Asian studies, 12, 180
  stakes in, 6
Aesthetic(s)
  appreciation, 20, 69, 76, 169, 243
  dancing, 31
  Institute for, Studies, 30, 36, 39
  Karnatak music, of, 51
  shared, presumed, 6
  theory, 29
  transformation of, 15, 58
  Western, 54
Affect. *See* Emotion, affect
Agency
  body in conception of, 194
  musicians', 14
  spiritual forces, of, 219, 291n3
  teacher, of, 169
  women's, representations of, 23, 29, 41
  zekr, of, 219
Aphorisms, 182, 225
  See also Metaphors (and comparisons)
Apprenticeship, 10, 114, 115, 120, 122, 158, 186, 199, 285n2, 286n9, 288n20
  See also Transmission; *gurukula*
  discipleship as a site of ethnographic learning, 168–170
Āśān (preceptor), 146, 153, 143–163 passim
  See also Transmission
"Ātta kuṟukka," 250–254
Authenticity, 49, 51, 277n1
  See also Indianness

Baluchistan, 10, 11, 21, 23, 26, 230
Bangalore, 67, 68, 91
Beginnings, 21, 146–147, 178, 190, 193, 233, 239–263
Body, 11, 14–16, 19, 20, 29
  dancer's, 25, 37, 44–46
  fitness, 44–45
  frailty, 201
  Impolitic, The, 199 (*see also* Herzfeld, Michael)
  instrument as representation of, 279n19
  location of culture, 194
  musician's, movements, 188
  preparation of, for performance, 151, 243
  sexuality, 43
  site of memory, 198
Bombay. *See* Mumbai (Bombay)

Brass Band, 16, 23, 76, 81–96, 284n5
  bandsmen, 16–17, 23, 81–95, 270
  English, 52
  "Ladies," 23
Buddhist(ism), 17, 25, 29, 113–140
  womanhood, 29–47 passim

Calcutta. *See* Kolkata (Calcutta)
Caste. *See* Community(ies)
Ceremonies. *See under individual names*
Chennai (Madras), 7, 12, 13, 51–63 passim, 66–68, 91, 282n6
  Music Academy, 51, 293n15
Circulation, cultural, 6
Cīz. *See* Composition
Class, socioeconomic, 36, 230
  identity, 38
  low, 84, 228, 229, 230
  middle, 30, 38, 50, 61, 165, 166
  upper, 30, 37, 38, 44
  working, 30
Classical, 49–63 passim
  dance, in Sri Lanka, 33
  focus on, in scholarship, 9–10, 62–63
  great tradition, problems with mapping to, 13
  Hindu icon, making more, 103
  modernity of, 13–14
  notion of the, 5, 33, 50
  śāstriya saṅgīta, 200, 209, 289n1
  social organization of, musicians, 7
Colonial Cousins, 66, 72, 73, 74, 76
Colonialism, 8, 14, 15, 22, 49–63 passim, 81, 82, 87–88
Community(ies)
  See also proper names
  Anglo-Indian, 10, 16, 23, 66, 68, 70
  Buddhist priests (Bajrācarya), 17, 116, 119–121, 135
    repertoire, 139–140
  Christian, in India, 10, 16, 53, 66, 68, 69, 70, 71, 74, 77, 283n3, 283n6
  control of labor market by particular, 84–85
  control over performance, 102
  dēvadāsi, 22, 282n4
  Ḍholi, 99, 102, 104, 110, 285nn7–8, 15
  goldsmiths (Sākya), 17, 119–121
    repertoire, 139–140
  interchange, socioeconomic, among, 65, 82–83, 94, 97, 116, 177
  Māngaṇiār, 5, 17, 23, 24, 97–111, 284–285
  musician, 85, 99, 165, 170, 178–179, 181–182 (*see also* Musician(s))
  oilpressers, 17, 114, 115, 116–119, 121–122, 125, 127, 128, 135, 138
    repertoire, 138–139
    women, 124, 136
  Parsis, 69, 70, 71, 72, 74, 283n4
  practice, of, 158, 159
  tailor, 105
  tawā'if, 22, 289n5
Comparison
  bases for, 11, 25
  kinds of beginning, 247, 262–263
  methodological value of, 6
  unlike entities, of, 240
Competition(s), 14, 39, 55, 67, 81, 84–86, 88, 93, 95, 208, 209, 211, 212, 223
Composition. *See also* Improvisation
  act of, 19, 175–176
  cīz, 168
  types of (*see under individual entries*)
Concert, sequence of pieces in, 242–243
  See also Performance, times of day for
Consumption, musical. *See* Reception/response, music
Context, transcendability of, 6
Cultural performance, 7, 12

Dance, 29–47
  See also Genres, dance
  development of, in Sri Lanka, 15
  gender and, 15
  Kandyan, 15
Dastgah. *See* Melody-type(s)
Delhi, 68, 69, 83–88, 90, 91, 93, 94, 178–179, 181–182
Dēvadāsi. *See* Community(ies)
Diaspora, 6, 78, 179
Discipleship
  See Transmission; Apprenticeship
  ritual of (*shāgirdī*), 19, 169, 171, 172, 173, 174, 177, 178
Drumming. *See* Instruments, drums

Economy
  capital in world, 6, 11

capitalist, 83–84, 91, 279n16, 284n1
caste relations as capital, 94
impact from elaborate processions, 120
inter-community exchange, 82, 94
national, 202
Embodiment. *See* Body; Experience
Emotion(s)
affect, 50, 62, 187, 221
expression of, through music, 227, 228, 244, 257–260 passim
bhāvam, 244
gender associations of, 23–24
location of, 167, 197, 198
sīna ba sīna, 14, 19, 161, 167–170, 174, 177–182, 287n2, 289n2
neurology of, 186–188
singing, of, 110
states of, 218
words that evoke, 217
Epitomizations. *See* Stereotype(s)(ing)
Errors
dance, 36
god of, in music, 115, 122
musical, 174, 188, 191–193, 198
aśāstriya, 209
bigriyo (broken, ruined), 193, 201
Ethnomusicology, use of terms, 13
Ettayapuram, 52, 53
Experience
See also Hearing; Knowledge/musical Knowledge
bodily, 16, 19, 20, 185–188, 194–195, 290n6, 290–291n11
connectedness, of, 8
correctness, of, 187
learning, shared, 168
sensation and emotion, relationship of, 187, 188

Film
Indian, 10, 73, 74, 76
industry, 68
music, 66, 74–76, 81
stereotyping in, 5
Fusion. *See* Hybridity

Gender, 12, 22–24
bilateral kinship organization, 170
contrast between male and female characters in *temmāṅku*, 250
dance and, 29–47
male versus female singers, 228–237 passim
movement, and, 15
transmission of music in male line, 19, 22, 165, 167, 168, 170, 235, 286–287n1, 287n2
roles, 29
Genres, dance
See also Dance
baila, 43
Kandyan, 15, 31–34
kathakaḷi, 18–19, 35, 145–148, 151, 162, 286–289
Sri Lankan village forms, 33
vannama, 33–24, 39, 40–44, 281n7
Genres, folk
dhola (oral epic), 222
interrelationships of, 220
Genres, musical, 218
See also Melody-type(s)
basis, as, for local theorization, 225–237, 239–245
bāṭ/bāṇṭ, 188, 189, 192–193
eṇṇam, 161
falak, 217, 226, 227, 295n17, 295n18, 296n25
gagaku, 247
gharībī, 226–227, 296n25
ghūmar, 110, 285n15
gītam, 245
hymns, Buddhist (*tutaḥ*), 122, 136
jo jo pāṭ, 257
kallali, 110
k̲h̲ayāl, 175
Khorasan, in, 215
koḷ (*tāv, dukt, devr,* and *āṭ*), 245, 248
kriti, 35, 59, 61, 240, 243, 244
līko, 226, 227, 294n3
lullaby (*tālāṭṭu*), 257
mangaḷam, 243
muqäddimä, 243
"Note," English or Western, 54, 57
oḷakh, 99, 106, 108, 110
oyilāṭṭakkummi, 254–256
padam, 147, 153, 154, 157–159, 288nn14, 16, 17
šeyr, 225, 232, 234, 236, 237, 296n23
shubhrāj, 106, 107

Genres, musical (*continued*)
tāyampaka, 147, 151, 153, 161, 162, 209, 287nn3, 7
temmāṅku, 250, 251, 253, 257
ṭukṛā, 192–193
ṭhumri, 175
transitional between practice and concert, 241–242
varṇam, 21, 54, 144, 161, 240–245, 247, 249, 297nn5, 6
warm-up/tune-up, significance of, 247
zahīrok, 21, 22, 23, 24, 25, 217, 225–237, 295nn1–2, 294nn6–8, 295nn12–16, 19, 296nn23–24
"Global hierarchy of value," 5, 20, 199, 202, 277n1
Globalization, 65–78 passim
See also Local
adaptation of teaching methods to cope with, 179
engagement with others and, 18
hereditary musicians' participation in, 165, 179
literature on, 6, 8–9, 25, 277n3
musician networks and, 94
Great-little tradition, dichotomy, 12–14
Guitar, 10, 11, 15–16, 23, 25, 26, 61, 65–78, 279n18, 283n17
See also Instruments, lutes, plucked
technique, 66
Gūlā, 113–140 passim
gūlābājā, 17, 113–140
Guru. *See* Transmission; *gurukula*
Gurukula, 57, 159, 160, 170

Habit(s), roles in teachings and learning, 35, 62, 188, 212–213, 243, 280n22, 290n4, 297n3
Harmony, issue of in relation to south Asian music, 59, 75, 76
Hearing
See also Experience
knowledge based on, 35, 158, 161
kēḷviñāṉam, 35
new ways of, to Westerners, 180
Hindi, 67, 68, 69, 73, 74, 77, 167, 168, 229, 280n25
Hinduism, 12
mixed with Buddhism, 113–140 passim
weddings, 83–84
Hindustani music, 10, 19, 22, 57, 58, 95, 144, 165–183, 188–193, 208, 215
See also Classical
Hybridity, 25, 277n1, 280n25, 282n3
fusions, 49–50, 53–54, 59–61, 75

'Ilm. *See* Knowledge/musical Knowledge, 'ilm
Imitation and mimesis, 20, 24, 25, 35, 62, 186, 194, 215–216, 280n23
accompanist, by, 50, 55, 56–58, 61, 250, 284n9
creativity through, 144, 182
dance, 33, 36, 41
naql, 176
lullabies, in, 257
student, of, by another student, 153, 160
student, of, by teacher, 196
teacher, of, by student, 19, 36, 143, 146, 160, 177–179, 188, 195
verbalization, in relation to, 197, 202 (*see also* Language, issues of)
Improvisation, 229, 269, 290–291n11
ālāpana, 55, 57, 59, 60, 161, 240, 260, 263, 296n2
coordinating music and movement, 147, 153, 157
cross-cultural, 59
dancing, 39
discourse about, 209
framework for, 19, 25, 243
incorrect, 174
kalpana svara, 55, 144, 161, 240
niraval (in Karnatak music), 241
preparation for, 19, 146, 241
quasi-compositional, 165
resources for, 243
scope of, 243
style of, 146
teaching, 143
texts, of, 231
Indianness, idea of, 15, 50–51, 66, 67, 76
Induction, 8, 24, 279n15
Institutions, 212
See also Kalamandalam
dance, 45
institutionalization, 159–160
musical, 18, 71, 87–90, 145, 146, 159, 180, 287n8, 288n13, 288n21

Instruments
See also under individual entries
brass (*see* Brass band)
clarinets, 82, 121, 125
cymbals, 102, 117, 120, 122, 145, 147, 151, 154, 156, 251, 253
bhuchyāḥ, 117, 120, 121
sichyāḥ, 117, 120, 131
drums, 113–140, 143–163
ceṇṭa, 145–148, 151–154, 156–160, 162
ḍhol; 99–101, 102, 104, 106, 110, 285n8
ḍholak, 104
dobar, 245
drumming, 5, 18–19, 22, 99, 113–140
găṭa bera (Kandyan drum), 33, 41
kiṇvar, 245
machine, 102
maddaḷam, 145, 147, 153, 154, 157, 162, 287n11
naiyāṇṭi mēḷam, of, 250, 253
Nepali, 19–20, 23, 113–140 passim, 185,195–198
pastā, 117, 122, 138
patterns, 9, 17, 129, 138–140, 146, 147–151, 153–159, 160, 188, 189–193, 195, 197, 218, 287n11, 288n12
pedagogy, 145–163
Sri Lanka, 31, 33–35, 38, 41, 46
tabaṭk, 245
tabla, 188–193
tavil, 60
gong, 145, 147, 151, 154, 156
harmonium, 66, 104, 106, 171, 173
idiophones, stone or wood block, 145, 151–152, 153, 154
kuṭam (clay pot), 255
lutes, bowed (*see also* Violin)
sārangī, 19, 144, 166, 168, 171, 176, 178
satar, 243
suroz, 25, 227–228, 230, 232–237, 295nn12–13, 21, 296nn23–24
lutes, plucked (*see also* Guitar)
dambūrag, 226, 228, 234
dotār, 9, 207, 208, 217, 211,212, 213, 291n1
saz, 222
sitar, 5, 49, 66, 166
vīṇā, 35, 240, 241, 242, 244, 279n19
piano, 49, 53, 59, 71, 75, 193–195
shawms, 21, 116, 117, 122, 138, 228, 236, 245, 246
koḷ, 245, 248
nāgasvaram, 60, 284n4
nāyaṇam, 250, 251, 253
significance of, 100, 104
sites of culture and discourse, 14–16
trumpets/horns, 129
cāti,117
ghulu, 117
pvaṅga, 116, 117, 286
tititālā, 117
zithers, 228
Interconnection(s)
creating spatial configurations, 16
experience of, 8
of knowledge across regions, 11
limitations in recognizing, 13
study of, 6, 9, 13
Iran
Baluchistan (*see* Baluchistan)
Khorasan, 10, 20, 26, 207–224, 291n1, 292n10, 293n17, 296n25

Kalamandalam, 18–19, 145–147, 149, 151–161, 287n8, 288n13, 288n15
Kaḷarippayaṯṯu, 143
Kandyan dance. *See* Genres, dance
Karnatak music, 10, 15, 21, 25, 49–62, 144, 161, 168, 209, 215, 240–245
See also Classical
Kerala, 18–19, 58, 143–163, 209, 267, 269, 270, 272, 274, 287n3, 287n10
Khorasan, 20, 26, 207–224
musical terminology, 215
Kinship and family, place of, in musical learning, 68, 70, 83, 86, 96, 170–171, 177
Knowledge/musical Knowledge
accessing, 20, 165, 169, 191
acquisition of, 11, 50, 167, 185, 186, 291n3
adaptation of, 166, 191, 245
associated with musical instrument, 9
in body (*see* Experience, bodily)
conveyed through ritual, 138
conveying of bodily, 194
form of, 19, 232, 244
gender and, 22
"hearing knowledge," 35

Knowledge/musical Knowledge (*continued*)
'ilm, 207, 208, 211, 291n3
implicit, 8, 85, 208, 249, 277n1, 290n3 (*see also* Theory, implicit)
individual versus group, 143ff
limitations of, 87, 153
local, 11–12, 77, 180
oral, 174, 178, 180
procedural versus declarative, 185, 198, 290n3
representations of, 20
rights concerning, 177
system-level, 24
theorizing and, 207–224, 244, 291n4
transmission of, 18, 22, 35, 143–202
value of, 199, 202
Kolkata (Calcutta), 67, 68, 70, 93, 181
"Kuṇṭamalai mēl," 254–256

Language(s). *See under individual languages*
Language, issues of, 67, 73–74, 186, 194, 197, 202, 239, 280n25
alliteration, 254, 260
field method, 169
lack of verbalization in teaching, 177, 193 (*see also* Transmission)
music like a, 165
translation, 167
verbal instruction, kinds of, 188, 189, 196–198
"Lavanasura Vadham" (Kathakaḷi play), 153–157
Listeners. *See* Reception/response, music
Listening. *See* Hearing
Little tradition. *See* Great-little tradition, dichotomy
Local
concept of, 6, 7–8, 11, 14, 166, 180
localization, 65–66, 94
oral and relational, as, 166
situated, as, 181
in South Asian context, 12–14
status of, in relation to global, 8, 12, 65, 179–180, 199
Locality. *See* Place

Madras. *See* Chennai
Makran. *See* Baluchistan
Malaya (Sri Lankan healer-King), 31
Man (heart/mind). *See* Emotion(s), location of
Map(s). *See* Space
Marginality, 9–10, 18, 51, 62, 69, 82, 101–111, 179–180, 199, 200
Mass-Media, 10, 16, 66, 101
Meaning. *See also* Semiotics
horizons of, 8, 10, 18, 169
syntax and, 2393–263 passim
Melody(ies)
appropriateness of, to text, 209
meter and flow, 250–260
rapid passages (*tān*) in Hindustani music, 169, 176
shape of, 243
Melody-type(s)
ascent and descent theorized in, 293n16, 297n6
aśrap-i-durrā, 235
baločī, 235
baškardī, 235
dastgah,
ḍhāḷ, 25
ghūmar, 110, 285n15
guše, 215, 217, 218
havalar, 215
hazin, 217
kūkkār, 235
kurdī, 235
maqām, 243
medī, 235
muqām, 19, 215, 218, 292n10
rāga, 7, 21, 25, 54, 56, 74, 165, 168, 172–175, 215, 240, 243, 244, 293n15, 295n16, 297n6
rāk, 243
subdivisions of named, 236
suznāk, 217
ṭaṭ, 235
varṇameṭṭu, 25
zahīrok names, derivation of, 236
Metaphors (and comparisons), 62, 199
See also Aphorisms
musical, 9, 20, 175, 176, 177, 191, 194, 208
Metonymy, 15, 17, 207–208
See also Nation and nationalism, metonymy associated with
Migrants, 81–95
Mimesis. *See* Imitation and mimesis
Mizoram, 69
Models, 210–214, 239, 243, 291n5
beginnings as, 239

compositions as, 174, 244
cosmic order, of, 114
dance, 36, 44
ethnomusicological, 20, 144–145, 151, 160, 262
father-to-son, 170, 177, 287n2
guru-śiṣya, 35, 143, 161, 162, 286n1
hierarchical, 18
modernity, of, 87
musical, 21, 25, 188, 190, 224, 248, 250
sīna ba sīna, 14, 19, 161, 167–170, 174, 177–182, 287n2
representational and operational, 210
village-based, 180

Modern(ity)
bands as models of colonial, 87–88
Kandyan dance, sexualization of, and, 42–45
of musical classicism, 13
nirmāṇa, 33, 43

Mumbai (Bombay), 58, 66–73, 86, 87, 89, 90–91, 94–95, 181
film, 70

Musee Musical, 66

"Music," in Indian English, 74

Music director(s), 59, 74–76, 283n1, 284n8

Music industry. *See* Recording(s), industry

Musician(s)
See also Community(ies)
bards, 14, 20, 25, 207, 212, 224, 228, 266, 292n10 (*see also* Singers and singing)
Ḍholi, 102, 104, 110, 285nn7–8, 15
hereditary, 13, 14, 17, 19, 97, 165–167, 170, 177, 179, 181, 182, 282n2, 282n4, 285n7, 295n15
Mīrāsī, 97
presentations of knowledge of, 207–224 passim
types of, 227 (*see also* Migrants)

Name(s) and naming, 20, 21, 23, 54, 59, 72, 83, 92, 110, 177, 212, 214–223, 233, 235–236, 241, 243, 249, 250, 254, 292n8, 295n13, 296n24
See also Theory; Theorization

Nation and nationalism
constructions of tribe, 9
cultural establishment, 166
dance songs, Venda, 243
discourse on music, 49, 67, 215, 279n12, 279n18
heritage and, 201
historical forces associated with, 13–14
interaction, 82
metonymy associated with, 9, 22, 29, 180, 199
music industry, 67
politics, 283n6
Sri Lankan dance and, 15, 29–47

Nature/naturalness/naturalization, 22, 23–24, 34, 54, 60–63
authentic Indian, 15, 51
guru-śiṣya relationship as, 286–287n1
unnatural death as basis for deification, 99, 108
vocal sound of violin, 56, 60–63, 76
West in relation to guitarists, 67, 70

Nepal, Bhaktapur, 10, 17, 19, 113–140, 185, 195, 196, 198, 201, 202, 285nn1–2, 286nn6, 8

Networks
See also Space, migratory networks
birādarī (brotherhood),160, 170, 171, 172, 174, 178, 287n2
family, 166, 168, 170
global, 65–78, 278n9
media, 16
musicians', 11, 14, 16–17, 22, 65–78, 170, 211, 212, 278n8
of representations, 186
shrine, 17

Newar (people), 17, 19, 113–140, 195

Nirmāṇa. *See* Modern(ity)

Offerings
dhalāpa, 136–138
musical, 102, 104, 105–106, 108, 113–140 passim
nazrāna, 173, 177
pūjā, 39–40, 138

Ornamentation, 233–234, 242–243
See also under
gamaka, 54, 55, 57, 58, 59, 154, 241, 242, 297n6
palṭā, 173, 188, 190, 191, 192
portamento, 76
saṅgati, 55, 244, 297n7

Pakistan, Baluchistan. *See* Baluchistan

Patronage, 5, 6, 16, 17, 23, 25, 82, 83, 93, 94, 95, 97–111, 157, 165, 178, 180, 181, 199, 212, 269, 273

Perception(s)
action, relationship to, 20, 187, 212
connecting, 77, 212
Performance
relationship with knowledge and pedagogical presentations, 209–210
times of day for, 236–237, 243 (*see also* Concert, sequence of pieces in)
Place
See also Space
deśī and, 13
mapping identities onto, 25
musical meaning related to, 113–140
power of, 17, 115
transcendence of, 5, 25
Popular music, 65–78, 278n9
Possession, 17, 99–100, 104, 107–108
cues for, 110
Practice. *See also* Rehearsal and practice
lakṣya, 245
Practice theory. *See* Theory
Processions, 16, 17, 19, 23, 24, 25, 29, 31, 45, 81–95, 113–140, 198, 246, 280n20, 281n5, 282n4, 284n5:1, 286n5, 286n12

Qualities of sounds or motions, lists of, 216–217
Quchan, 208, 213

Radio, 181
All India, 56, 59, 179
Nepal, 200
Ragas, 7, 21, 25, 54–57, 74–76, 165, 168, 172–175, 215, 240, 243, 244, 253, 257, 293n15, 295n16, 296n2, 297n6
ābheri, 59
bhairav, 172
bhairavi, 75, 244, 297n6
kharaharapriya, 297n6
mārubihāg, 173–176
multānī, 174
nīlāmbari, 257
śaṅkarābharaṇam, 54, 296n2
yaman, 172, 173
Rajasthan, 5, 222, 267, 268, 271, 272
Bandsmen in, 82, 85, 86, 87, 87–88, 93
Mānganiārs of, 5, 17, 23, 24, 97–111, 284–285
Western, 17, 24, 99–111, 273

Reception/response, 219
See also Error
assessment/discernment (*parikhiyā*), 182
consumption, 73
correctness, acknowledgment of, 192
criticism of classical music in Nepal versus India, local, 200–201
dance, to, 39
departures and returns (*raft–āmad*), 222
music, 5, 10, 58, 66, 76, 237
performers' evaluations of one another, 208–209
question-answer (*sowāl-javāb*), 222, 223
Recording(s), 59–60, 72, 76
collections, private, 283n14
effects of, 57, 58, 71, 75, 77
field, 169, 193, 197, 284, 285n15
industry, 6, 73, 74, 101, 102, 104, 181
list of, 283
public playing of, 106
Reflexivity, 165–202 passim, 212, 214
Rehearsal and practice, 25, 143, 146, 147, 160–161, 185, 242–243, 266, 267, 273
See also Riyāẓ
benefits of, 175, 176, 244
dance, 36, 37
discipline of, 167, 176, 243
exercises, 241–242
gītam, 245
group, 19, 146, 153, 158, 159–160, 161
limitations of, 186, 201
pieces, 301n3
preparation for, 158, 247
routine, 172, 174, 240, 241
varṇam, 21, 54, 144, 161, 240–245, 247, 249, 297nn5–6
warming up, 246–247
Repetition, as means of instilling knowledge, 19, 35, 55, 143, 144, 146, 151, 159, 160–161, 176, 177, 181, 186, 192, 219, 241
See also Imitation and mimesis; Transmission
Response. *See* Reception/response
Rhythm
See also Instruments, drums, patterns
cadential pattern, 189
camel-gait, 227
cantam, 21, 250, 252, 254, 257, 298n14

control of, 241
density, 192
flow of, 250, 251
"free-rhythm," 21, 233, 260, 266, 267
permutations of, 21, 147, 160, 240, 241, 250, 269, 272
poetic, 224
pushing and pulling, creating sense of, 192
reckoning on hand, 191–192
rhythmos, 222
tension with tala, 147, 151, 156
tāl/tāla/tāḷam, 7, 21, 56, 145, 147–151, 153–156, 157, 188, 190–192, 209, 222, 240, 241, 242, 461, 280n7, 287n10
tīhā'ī, 189, 290n8
tīn tāl, tabla patterns in, 190, 192
vocable strings embodying structure of, 248
Ritual, 15, 18, 19, 21, 24, 25, 31, 45–50, 97, 100, 113–140, 169, 171–178, 198, 222, 246–247
jātrā, 138
Riyāẓ, 19, 175–176
See also Rehearsal and practice
Rock music, 10, 16, 66, 67, 69, 70, 72, 162, 279n18, 280n25
Rules, 17, 24, 76, 209, 211, 214, 233, 245
See also Theory; Theorization
metrical, 254
in relation to theory, 243

Sampradāya, 30, 208
See also Tradition
Śāstra, 208, 209
śāstriya saṅgīta, 200, 209, 289n1
Scale, concepts of [size, not music], 7–10, 15, 16, 20, 22, 26, 82, 90, 115, 243
See also Local
-making, 9, 17–18
Semiotics, 24, 60–61, 187, 214, 248, 280n22
See also Meaning
iconicity, 58, 248, 249
indexicality, 17, 24, 120, 218, 239, 246, 249, 261, 279n17
symbolism, 24, 30, 31, 87–88, 94, 172, 247, 261, 280n22, 285n8
Sexuality, 15, 23, 30, 42–46, 254, 281n11
Shrine(s), 113–140 passim
relationship of musicians to, 99–114 passim
Singers and singing, 18, 21, 25, 53, 71, 72, 99, 103, 110, 147, 173, 217, 222, 225–237
See also Voice(s); Violin, voice and; Musician(s), bards
assessment, 211
contests, 223
discipleship ritual, 172
English, in, 73
forbidding of, 102
gestures, interspersing, 153
hymns, Buddhist, 122
interview, musical analysis of, with, 293n13
knowledge acquisition through, 50, 168, 242
metric cycle, to maintain, 145, 147, 156–157, 191, 193
multiple languages, in, 73
nightlong sessions (*rāti jāgā*), 107, 108
offering, as, 102, 105, 108
pahlawān, 23, 226, 228, 230, 233–237, 295nn12–13, 15, 296nn23–24
Parsi, 69
poetry, 208, 222, 224, 230–231, 233
procedure, 219, 255
responses, 223, 224
right to sing, 98–99
styles of, 218
"Sukhamō Dēvī" (*padam* transcription), 154–157
syllables, 175
techniques, 227–228, 233–234
women, 23, 24
zahīrok texts, 231–232
Site. *See* Place
Skill(s), 11, 18
See also Body; Experience
accompaniment, 55
acquisition of new, 72, 158–159, 242
as criterion for higher training, 45
demonstration of, 34, 43
as distinct from social identity of performer, 66
instilling, 151
interconnection of bodily, 198
migration of musician with, 91
set of, constituting an organized system, 222
status of disciple on basis of, versus style, 146
Solmization, 168, 249
sargam, 60, 74, 168, 174, 248, 249

Space
  See also Place; Time
  alternative, as imaginary, 277n2
  creation of, through movement, 10, 11, 16–18
  creation of, through volume, 81, 246
  map as musical score, 115, 138
  mappings of, 16, 17, 25, 67, 81, 280n24
  "mesocosm," 114
  migratory networks, 16, 81–95 (*see also* Networks)
  processions and concepts of, 113–140
  relationships in, 279n16
  "sacred," 113
  social, 280n24
  spatial behavior, 90
  spatial representations, 9
  theory of, 279n15, 279n16
Stereotype(s)(ing) 5–6, 7, 15, 23
  gender, 26, 29, 30
Story/charter/dominant narrative, 5, 17, 23, 24–25, 49–50, 245
  See also Theory
  bandsman's, 83–85
  guitar in India, 67
  Rāni Bhaṭiyani, 98–99
  storytellers, 14
  violin in India, 52–54
Style or school, 12, 57–58, 241, 244
  continuity, 143
  gharānā, 95, 166, 178, 290n7
  dance, 34–35
  lāsya, 15, 34, 38, 40, 281n8
  Muradabad Rampur *gharānā*, 166, 178
  pāṇi, 7, 12, 15, 241, 244
  tāṇḍava, 34–35, 37, 38, 40, 381n8
South Asia
  conceptualizing, in world scale, 8
  music of, broadly considered, 6–7
Sufism, 5–6
  ritual of discipleship, 170
  metaphors, 176, 177, 289n6
Surnā (shawm), 228, 236
  See also Instruments, shawms
Systematization, 8, 24, 26, 61, 74, 177, 181, 211, 219–224. *See also* Classical; Theorization; Theory

Tamil
  folk genres, 21, 250, 253, 254, 257
  grammatical terms, 244–245, 250
  influence, 33
  musical terminology, 57, 58, 241
  oyilāṭṭakkummi, 254–256
  poetics, 22, 221, 254
  song language, 67, 73, 248–256, 258
  tālāṭṭu, 257
  temmānku, 250, 251, 253, 257, 296
  vocables, 248, 250
Tamil Nadu, 35, 242, 245, 246, 253, 255
Tanjavur, 52, 53, 282n6
Taste. *See* Aesthetic(s), appreciation
Tawā'if. See Community(ies)
Techniques, dance, 29–47 passim
Techniques, musical
  See also Singers and singing, techniques
  drum, 158, 161–162
    crushed stroke on, 153, 154, 289n24
    dra stroke on, 196
  guitar, Indian, 66
  Indian, for violin, 52, 57, 58, 61
  sārangī, 175, 177
  "setting" the hand, 178
  tān (*see* Melody, rapid passages (*tān*) in Hindustani music)
  Western, for violin, 53, 57
Theorization, 207–224, 241
  See also Rules
  basis for, in this volume, 10–11
  formats, theoretical, 20, 216–217, 219, 223, 293n15
  Goethe on, 212
  incentives to theorize, 14, 211–212, 224
  kinds of, 8
  performing with and without, 212–213
  sites of, 8
  Western genres by Indian musicians, of, 16
Theory, 7–10, 24, 74, 77, 161, 166, 177, 208, 239, 243
  See also Story/charter/dominant narrative
  aesthetic, 29
  agents of, 182, 213
  akam/puṟam, 22, 221
  appropriating from others, 211
  beginnings as, 239–263
  branches/subdivisions in, 216–217, 236
  dance, 281n6
  globalization (*see* Globalization)
  implicit, 15, 17, 161, 208, 213–214, 291–292n7 (*see also* Knowledge, implicit)

inductivity, 8, 11, 12, 24, 279n15
lakṣaṇa, 244–245
local terms for, 14, 244
logocentrism and, 239, 240
mārga/deśī, 13, 14, 297n14
music, in India, 14
naming practices in relation to (*see* Name(s) and naming)
oral, 169, 177, 180
Practice theory, 7, 180, 290n4
tala, 209
Western, 177
Thread, ritual use of, 138, 172–173, 268, 289n4
Time
See also Space
relationship with space, 10
"sacred," 113, 114–115
Tradition
See also Sampradāya
adherence to, 18, 34, 36–38, 103
notion of, 33, 189
Transmission, 7, 11, 14, 18–20, 22, 34–42, 143–202, 208, 248, 250, 273
instilling fundamentals, 241
interpersonality of, 166
withholding knowledge, 209, 241
Tribe(s)
See also Community(ies)
Kota, 9, 21, 26, 221–222, 240, 245–248, 250, 279n16, 297–298n9
Munda, 9, 26, 278n5
Turkic languages and practices, 208, 217, 222, 223, 243, 292n10, 293n17, 294n5

Urbanization, 12
Urdu, 170

Violin, 15, 49–63
See also Instruments, lutes, bowed
colonialism of, 22, 59, 82
experiments with, 59–61
fiddle versus, 51
history of, in India, 51–54
pre-concert-hall use, in India, 282n4
styles of, playing, 56–59, 62, 76
voice and, 15, 25, 51, 54–59, 60–63, 282n8, 295n12
"Viribhōṇi," 244, 263, 297n6
Vocables, 240, 248–261
col, 248
Voice(s), 220–221
changing aesthetics of, 51
drawing together multiple, 224
instrument, relationship with, 25, 50, 54–59, 61–63, 191, 193, 228
modern south Indian, 15, 50, 51, 62
musicians' agency, 14, 166, 169
politics of, 13
preparation of, for performance, 243, 255
qualities of, 23, 222, 228, 229, 233, 236
sedā, 222
teaching instrumental music using the, 178
translation with, 60
types of, 220–221
vocal nature of Indian music, 50–51, 76
women's, 23, 220
vows, dhalā, 119

Wedding band. *See* Brass band
"West," the, 8, 10, 15, 25, 26, 49, 50, 66–78, 280n23
classical music of, 51, 52, 53, 279n18
Indian study of music from, 282n6
instruments, 121 (*see also* Violin; Guitar)
listeners from, 58
localness of, 65
music of, 10, 15, 16, 23, 51, 53, 59–63, 65
scales of, 54
studio of, 167
techniques of, 57
terminology from music of, 75
theory in, 177, 222
musicians, Western, 54, 146, 168, 173, 174, 182–183, 283n16
Western "Notes" (*see* Genres)
"Westernization," 49
Work, music and, 225–237 passim
World Music, 5–6

Zahīrok, 21, 22, 23, 24, 25, 217, 225–237, 293nn1–2, 294nn6–8, 295nn16, 19, 296nn23–24

CPSIA information can be obtained at www.ICGtesting.com
Printed in the USA
LVOW12s1616231013

358274LV00004B/998/P

9 780195 331387